Religion in Gender-Based Violence, Immigration, and Human Rights

This book builds on work that examines the interactions between immigration and gender-based violence to explore how both the justification and condemnation of violence in the name of religion further complicates societal relationships. Violence has been described as a universal challenge that is rooted in the social formation process. As humans seek to exert power on the other, conflict occurs. Gender-based violence, immigration, and religious values have often intersected where patriarchy-based power is exerted.

An international panel of contributors takes a multidisciplinary approach to investigating three central themes. Firstly, the intersection between religion, immigration, domestic violence, and human rights. Secondly, the possibility of collaboration between various social units for the protection of immigrants' human rights. Finally, the need to integrate faith-based initiatives and religious leaders into efforts to transform attitude formation and general social behavior.

This is a wide-ranging and multi-layered examination of the role of religion in gender-based violence and immigration. As such, it will be of keen interest to academics working in religious studies, gender studies, politics, and ethics.

Mary Nyangweso is Associate Professor and J. Woolard and Helen Peel Distinguished Chair in Religious Studies at East Carolina University, Greenville, North Carolina, USA. She is the author of *Female Genital Cutting: Mutilation or Cultural Right?* (2014) and *Female Circumcision: The Interplay Between Religion, Gender, and Culture in Kenya* (2007).

Jacob K. Olupona is Professor of African Religious Traditions, Harvard Divinity School, and Professor of African and African American Studies in the Faculty of Arts and Sciences at Harvard University, USA. He is the author of several books, including *City of 201 Gods: Ilé-Ifè in Time, Space, and the Imagination* (2011).

Routledge Studies in Religion

Religion in Gender-Based Violence, Immigration, and Human Rights

Edited by Mary Nyangweso
and Jacob K. Olupona

LONDON AND NEW YORK

First published 2020
by Routledge
2 Park Square, Milton Park, Abingdon, Oxon OX14 4RN

and by Routledge
605 Third Avenue, New York, NY 10017

First issued in paperback 2021

Routledge is an imprint of the Taylor & Francis Group, an informa business

British Library Cataloguing-in-Publication Data
A catalogue record for this book is available from the British Library

Library of Congress Cataloging-in-Publication Data
A catalog record for this book has been requested

ISBN 13: 978-0-367-78585-7 (pbk)
ISBN 13: 978-1-138-59698-6 (hbk)

Typeset in Sabon
by Apex CoVantage, LLC

Contents

Contributors

Tolu Adegbola Adefi is a doctoral candidate in the Department of Religious Studies at Obafemi Awolowo University, Nigeria. He obtained a BA in Religious Studies from the University of Ado-Ekiti in 2006. He won the award of the best graduating student in the Faculty of Humanities in the 2006 graduating class. He completed an MA in Religious Studies from the same university in 2014 before proceeding to Claremont Lincoln University, California, to obtain another MA in Interfaith Action in 2016.

Elizabeth Ayoola Adeyemi-Adejolu teaches religious education in one of the leading high schools in Ado-Ekiti and plans to enroll for her PhD this next academic session in Obafemi Awolowo University, Ile-Ife. A paper she co-wrote with another author has been accepted for publication by the Faculty of Arts, Obafemi Awolowo University, Ile-Ife. She has just submitted another abstract titled: "An Analysis of Gender Relations and Ritual Practices in the Christ Apostolic Church (CAC) in Ekiti West Local Government" to the AASR Conference organizing committee to be considered for presentation this July in Ghana.

Sloane Burke Winkelman is Professor of Public Health in the Health Sciences Department at California State University, Northridge, a suburb of Los Angeles, California. A Certified Health Education Specialist (CHES) and Public Health Fellow from the University of North Carolina's Gillings School of Global Public Health, Dr. Burke's publications center on women's health; Latino health disparities, including migrant farmworker health; and programs for at-risk populations. Dr. Burke has received over $2 million in federal grants in support of Latinx student success and professional preparation. Her career experience includes close to 20 years of teaching in cultural health and close to ten years in the nonprofit field. Dr. Burke has received global health grants for scholarly initiatives in China, Cuba, Japan, and Peru. She is the primary writer for the California Department of Education's *Health Education Curriculum Framework for California Public Schools, Transitional Kindergarten Through Grade Twelve.*

Jody O. Early is an associate professor in the School of Nursing and Health Studies at the University of Washington Bothell near Seattle, Washington. A social scientist and a Master Certified Health Education Specialist (MCHES), Dr. Early's research, teaching, and praxis largely explore social–ecological factors that impact population health, health inequities, and health literacy. She often applies principles of community-based participatory research (CBPR) to collaborate with communities to design and evaluate culturally tailored health promotion programs and campaigns on a wide array of health issues, with a particular focus on the health of women, college students, and Latinx communities. Jody's most recent scholarly projects include exploring the lived experiences and critical consciousness of Promotores de Salud in Washington State; creating tailored mHealth applications; and collaborating with farmworker women, growers, nonprofits, and other stakeholders to develop a multi-level, English/Spanish worksite training to prevent sexual harassment and sexual violence in the agricultural sector. Dr. Early coauthored the text *The Process of Community Health Education & Promotion* (Waveland Press; 2019; 2019) and has published her research widely in cross-disciplinary, peer-reviewed journals relating to community and public health, global health, and education. She was also a founding editorial board member for the journal *Pedagogy of Health Promotion: The Scholarship of Teaching and Learning*.

Rosinah Mmannana Gabaitse is currently at the University of Botswana in Botswana. She is a Humboldt Postdoctoral Fellow for the year 2017–2018. She is also a lecturer in biblical studies at the University of Botswana. Her research is in biblical theology, bible sciences, and biblical studies.

Enoch Olujide Gbadegesin received his PhD in Religion from Rice University. He teaches religion in the Department of Religious Studies at Obafemi Awolowo University and specializes in anthropology of religion, philosophy of religion, and methods and theories in the study of religion. His academic focus includes gift and reciprocity, interreligious dialogue, religion and ecology, and Pentecostalism. He has published articles in both local and international journals and books. Some of his articles have also been considered for publication in *Encyclopedia of the Yorùbá*, edited by Toyin Fálolá, and Encyclopedia of World Religious Figures edited by Scott Hendrix and Uchenna Okeia.

Petra Klug has received a master's in sociology and cultural studies as well as a master's in the study of religion from the University of Leipzig, Germany. In 2018, she finished her doctorate at the University of Bremen, Germany, with a dissertation on *Anti-Atheism in the United States*. Currently, she is working on a postdoc project on early and forced marriages in religious communities in Germany and the United States. She has published a monograph on the discourse on Islam in Germany (*Feindbild Islam?*) as well as several articles on religion, nonreligion, gender, racism, human rights, and cultural relativism.

Simangaliso Raymond Kumalo is the president of Seth Mokitimi Methodist Seminary in South Africa and a professor of practical theology.

Justice Richard Kwabena Owusu Kyei holds a PhD in Sociology from the Institute of Philosophy and Sociology of the Polish Academy of Sciences. He is a lecturer in the Department of Sociology and Social Work in Kwame Nkrumah University of Science and Technology (KNUST), Kumasi-Ghana. His research interests are: gender, social theory, migration, political sociology, and African studies. He is an adjunct fellow in the Centre for Cultural and African Studies, KNUST.

Precious Nihorowa is a Malawian by nationality. He holds a Bachelor of Arts in Philosophy from the Catholic University of Malawi with a major in Moral Philosophy. He is a student of theology at Holy Trinity College, Faculty of Theology at the Catholic University of Zimbabwe. At the moment, he is doing pastoral work in Arusha, Tanzania. He has been the deputy editor of the Holy Trinity College's *Dare* theology journal as well as the chief editor of the College's magazine and newsletter. He has written a number of scholarly articles for academic journals; recent ones include "The Phenomenon of Childlessness in African Christian Marriages: Some Prospects for Pastoral Action" (*Hekima Review* 2016); "The Fire in These Ashes: Consecrated Life Today" (*Dare* 2016); "Reviewing the Aims and Content of Education in Africa: Retrieving John Dewey's Thoughts on Education" (*Chiedza* 2017); and "Is the Belief in Spirits an Obstacle to Developments and Economic Organisation in Africa?" (*Chiedza* 2017). He has also written several articles for magazines and newspapers.

Sychellus Wabomba Njibwakale is a PhD student with an emphasis in New Testament in the Biblical Studies Department at Piedmont International University, Winston-Salem, North Carolina. His research interest is in examining the sociology of Jesus Christ and how this impacted the early church, as well as its implication today in relation to evangelism and social justice. Wabomba received an MDiv from Emmanuel Christian Seminary, Johnson City, Tennessee, in 2014. He also obtained a BMin from Far Eastern Bible College, Singapore in 2007. Prior to that, he also was awarded an Advanced Diploma in Theology from Bible College of East Africa, Nairobi, Kenya, in 2005. He wrote articles and presented in professional meetings while in graduate school. He has served as pastor for the Friends Church (Quakers) for over 20 years in both Kenya and the USA.

Genevieve Nrenzah (PhD) is a scholar of African Traditional Religion and their diaspora extensions. She also works on women and religion.

Currently, she is a research fellow at the Institute of African Studies–University of Ghana, Legion.

Mary Nyangweso is Associate Professor and J. Woolard and Helen Peel Distinguished Chair in Religious Studies at East Carolina University, Greenville, North Carolina. Her area of specialization is religion, human rights, and gender. She received her Bachelor of Education (B.Ed.) from Kenyatta University (Nairobi, Kenya), Master of Philosophy in Religion (M.Phil.) from Moi University (Eldoret, Kenya), Master of Theology (Th.M.) from Candler School of Theology, Emory University (Atlanta, Georgia), and Master and Doctorate of Philosophy in the Sociology of Religion (PhD) at Drew University. She has published extensively on matters related to gender-based violence. She is the author of *Female Genital Cutting: Mutilation or Cultural Right?* (Praeger, 2014) and *Female Circumcision: The Interplay Between Religion, Gender, and Culture in Kenya* (Orbis, New York: 2007) in addition to several journal articles and chapters on religion and gender in Africa.

Danoye Oguntola-Laguda, PhD, is a scholar of religion specializing in philosophy of religion. He works in the Department of Religions and Peace Studies, Lagos State University (www.lasu.edu.ng), Lagos, Nigeria. He lectures and does research into the social values of religions, especially those dominant in Nigerian religious space. His areas of interest include but are not limited to the teaching and study of religion, philosophy of religion, and religion and social institutions. He is a member of the American Academy of Religion (AAR) and African Association for the Study of Religions (AASR). He has published in several journals of international repute, including *Journal of Religion in Africa* and *Journal of Oriental and African Studies*.

Jacob K. Olupona is Professor of African Religious Traditions, Harvard Divinity School, and Professor of African and African American Studies in the Faculty of Arts and Sciences at Harvard University. Dr. Olupona has written extensively on religion, immigration, and gender. His current research focuses on the religious practices of the estimated 1 million Africans who have emigrated to the United States over the last 40 years, examining in particular several populations that remain relatively invisible in the American religious landscape: "reverse missionaries" who have come to the US to establish churches, African Pentecostals in American congregations, American branches of independent African churches, and indigenous African religious communities in the US. His earlier research ranged across African spirituality and ritual practices, spirit possession, Pentecostalism, Yoruba festivals, animal symbolism, icons, phenomenology, and religious pluralism in Africa and the Americas. In his book *City of 201 Gods: Ilé-Ifè in Time, Space, and the Imagination*, he examines the modern urban mixing of ritual, royalty, gender, class, and power, and how the structure, content, and meaning of religious beliefs and practices permeate daily life. He has authored or edited several other books, including *Òrìsà Devotion as World Religion: The Globalization of Yorùbá Religious Culture*, co-edited with Terry Rey. His *Kingship, Religion, and Rituals in a Nigerian Community: A Phenomenological Study of Ondo Yoruba Festivals* has become a model for ethnographic research among Yoruba-speaking communities.

Susan C. Pearce is Associate Professor of Sociology at East Carolina University, in North Carolina. Her research areas include sociology of culture, migration, gender, race, and social movements. She is a coauthor of the monograph *Immigration and Women: Understanding the American Experience* (2011) with Elizabeth Clifford and Reena Tandon. She is co-editor of the book *Istanbul: Living with Difference in a Global City* (2018) with Nora Fisher-Onar and Fuat Keyman. She has published journal articles, books, and book chapters on the collective memory of the 1989 transitions in Central and Eastern Europe, intimate partner violence and immigrant women, culture in social movements, and the New York African Burial Ground, among others. She earned her PhD in Sociology from the New School for Social Research in New York. She has also served on the sociology faculties of Gettysburg College, West Virginia University, University of Gdańsk (Poland), and Central European University (Poland).

Sonu Shiva is a lecturer in English at Govt Dungar College, Bikaner (India).

Mansi Trivedi is an MD graduate student at Brody School of Medicine at East Carolina University.

Acknowledgements

When we conceived the idea of doing a volume on the intersection of religion, gender-based violence, immigration, and human rights, we did not anticipate that issues of concern in the volume would be magnified in contemporary reality by current events. As concerns about immigration and gender-based events have dominated ongoing discourse in the world, there is the recognition of how the geographic movement of migrants intertwines with the movement of faith and practices as people seek to adapt themselves to living in their host societies. The fundamental question centers around the relation between religion, gender-based violence, and migration and how behavior is informed by this intersection. Throughout this volume, contributors highlight the challenges that religion and gender-based violence present in social dynamics, especially as relates to human movements and contemporary values, and draw on the fact that many religious founders have also been migrants who have experienced significant challenges. As is illustrated in different chapters in this volume, all societies confront gender-based violence in various ways. Recognizing that this behavior is a concern in our societies is significant in efforts to change mindsets and for the flourishment of humans in the global society. We hope that the reader will be inspired by the work of all the contributors to this volume. Our utmost gratitude is to their willingness to share their knowledge on this subject. We are grateful to each other – Dr. Olupona and Dr. Nyangweso – for sharing ideas in the production of this volume. We are grateful to Routledge for accepting our manuscript and for working with us to ensure the production of this volume. We are appreciative of the platform given to us to voice our ideas and to give voice to the experiences of survivors of gender-based violence. Specific thanks go to Jack Boothroyd, Brindha Thirumoorthy and team whose patience and guidance we have greatly appreciated. Of course, the volume would not have been realized without the contributors – Dr. Danoye Oguntola-Laguda, Dr. Sloane Burke Winkelman, Dr. Jody O. Early, Dr. Justice Richard Kwabena Owusu Kyei, Dr. Petra Klug, Dr. Susan C. Pearce, Ms. Mansi Trivedi, Dr. Enoch Olujide Gbadegesin, Dr. Elizabeth Ayoola Adeyemi-Adejolu, Dr. Sychellus Wabomba Njibwakale, Dr. Precious Nihorowa, Dr. Genevieve Nrenzah, Dr. Rosinah Mmannana Gabaitse, Dr. Simangaliso

Raymond Kumalo, Dr. Sonu Shiva, and Dr. Tolu Adegbola Adefi. Your excellent contributions and your patience with the production process is heartily appreciated. Your insights not only give this volume an interdisciplinary outlook, but the various experiences referenced in your work also help to magnify the problem of gender-based violence across the globe. Strategies offered in your work add to existing efforts towards initiating needed discourse on this issue. Not to be forgotten are families and relations to all our contributors who often sacrifice in various ways by allowing time to be carved from their family time towards the completion of this manuscript. It is always great to see how quality collaborative work can be inspiring.

1 Introduction

Mary Nyangweso and Jacob K. Olupona

Introduction

On February 12, 2009, the world awoke to the brutal murder of 37-year-old Aasiya Zubair Hassan, whose body was found beheaded and decapitated at the Bridges Network Inc. Television station, the American–Muslim TV venture located in the village of Orchard Park. She had been killed in an apparent "honor killing" at the station she owned with her estranged husband, only six days after she had filed for divorce on February 6, 2009. Aasiya had obtained an order of protection barring her husband, Muzzammil Hassan, from their Orchard Park home, according to her lawyer, Corey Hogan. The couple had launched their station in 2004 in an effort to counter images of Muslims as violent and extremist. According to the report, the Hassan family had been struggling with Muzzammil's abuse long before the alleged murder took place. Muzzammil would coerce Aasiya into their bedroom, push her down on the bed, sit on her chest, and pin her arms and legs down. These violent acts had been reported by Aasiya in 2007 along with other, previous incidences of gender-based violence, but the couple reconciled afterward. This time, Muzzammil was arrested, convicted of murder, and sentenced to 25 years to life in prison, leaving their four children without parents (Normani, 2009; Sheridan, 2011). In another incident, a 33-year-old American woman, Mariya Taher, recalls how she was forced to undergo of gender based violence, female genital cutting at the age of 7 during a holiday visit with her parents to Mumbai, India. She described how she was taken to an "old looking building," where her dress was lifted and her private parts were cut (Bryant, 2016). These two accounts demonstrate how vulnerable immigrants are to gender-based violence.

Violence is not only a perennial problem, it is also a universal challenge the world over. Studies indicate that modern society is the most violent in all of human history. The twentieth century in particular is considered to be the most violent, with an estimated 191 million people losing their lives directly or indirectly as a result of conflict (World Health Organization (WHO), 2002b). According to the WHO (2002a), violence causes more than 1.6 million deaths worldwide every year and is the leading cause of death for people ages 15–44, with women being the most seriously affected (Krug, Dahlberg,

Mercy, Zwi, and Lozano, 2002; WHO, 2002a). The roots of violence are found not only in the socialization process but also in humans' tendencies towards desire to exert power over one another. Violence can be simply defined as:

> "the intentional use of physical force or power, threatened or actual, against oneself, another person or a group or community, that either results in or has a high likelihood of resulting in injury, death, psychological harm, mal-development or deprivation."
>
> (WHO, 2002a)

Violence is a serious concern in modern society. As a general problem, violence is individual and collective. It is experienced in acts of wars; negligence; interpersonal acts such as sex, street, and hate crimes; abuse of children, the elderly, and the disabled persons. Intimate partner violence, otherwise known as domestic violence is the most prevalent. Even violence includes acts of coercion. It is indiscriminative as it transcends gender, age, individual, family, community, culture, ethnicity, country, region, and even religion – and it sometimes finds legitimacy in culture and religion. It is the main concern of this book to highlight how prevalent gender-based violence is as well as how this violence intersects with immigration, religion, and human rights. The objective is to argue for a more comprehensive interrogation of gender-based violence in the social matrices that inform it and as these relate to social structures of power.

To grasp gender-based violence fully, the complex and interrelated social factors that design violent attitudes and behavior must be interrogated. Not only is viciousness of violence in our society enabled by the inadequate approach to this problem, but the legitimization of violence by cultural and especially religious values also makes it more difficult to challenge attitudes and behavior that promote it. As modern society emphasizes values of democracy and human rights and moves to recognize multiculturalism and group rights, the complex social dynamics that inform violence must be underscored. Effective analysis and resolution of social violence must begin with a recognition of the reality that informs socially constructed behavior. The complex discourse surrounding gender-based violence reflect the difficulty of ignoring values such as human rights and multiculturalism, as these have significant consequences for real life experiences. The implication of the intersection of social realities is a legitimate and long-standing area of academic inquiry and dialogue to which this book makes a contribution. As the matrices and the web that serve as enablers and triggers of violence are identified and addressed, the root causes of violence are clarified. This book draws on the expertise of scholars from various disciplines, including religious studies, sociology, social work, and English, to highlight the intersection of not only gender-based violence but also multidisciplinary approaches to engaging social issues such as gender-based violence. It is argued that, while discourses in human rights, immigration, and social conflict, often based on the approach of a single discipline, have been rich in examining social issues, on their own they offer an inadequate approach and solutions are needed to understand and respond to social concerns such as violence that immigration. Instead of drawing on one of these frameworks in its entirety, this book describes the possibilities and limitations of utilizing interdisciplinary and intersectional frameworks to analyze religion, immigration, gender-based violence, and human rights.

To understand the intersection between violence, immigration, religious values, and human rights, it is argued, theoretical approaches must demonstrate the complex social situations that inform cultural occurrences. Recognizing the complex reality of social phenomenon is vital for adequate social analysis and policy development and enactment. In the book, we draw specifically on theories about immigration, gender, sexuality, religion, and human rights. Most works draw on intersectionality as an approach in the recognition of the complex reality that informs social behavior. Intersectionality as an approach is premised on the understanding that people's lives are defined by multiple layered identities which derive from social relations, histories, cultures, and other operations of structures of power. Intersectionality has been described as an indispensable methodology for the development and promotion of human rights. As an analytical tool, intersectionality helps one to understand and to respond to the way in which social issues intersect with other identities, and how such intersections contribute to unique experiences of oppression and privilege (AWID, 2004). It aims at revealing multiple identities to expose the different types of discrimination and disadvantages that occur as a consequence of the combination of identities. In this way, it addresses the manner in which racism, patriarchy, classism, and other social systems of discrimination operate to create social inequalities. Its breadth lies in the fact that it takes into account historical, social, and political contexts to demonstrate how some individuals or religious communities are pushed to the margins or discriminated against as a result of the multiple identities they possess.

Thinkers such as Kimberlé Crenshaw have articulated how intersectionality works. A legal scholar who specializes in understanding intersections between social factors such as race and gender in the legal system, Crenshaw is known for coining the term intersectionality in her attempt to challenge the use of identity categories without locating them in contextual realities that inform them (1989: 139–167). She argues for intersectional analysis as a tool that recognizes how the complexities of identity produce competing political alliances and allegiances. She explains:

> Recognizing that identity politics takes place at the site where categories intersect thus seems more fruitful than challenging the possibility of talking about categories at all. Through an awareness of intersectionality, we can better acknowledge and ground the differences among us and

negotiate the means by which these differences will find expression in constructing group politics.

(Crenshaw, 1991: 1299)

To Crenshaw, any legal reform that does not incorporate intersectional feminist analysis fails to ensure the unique needs of diverse minority community members that are centered in any discourse. Similarly, Alison Kafer has argued for an intersectional approach that highlights how terms such as "defective," "deviant," and "sick" have been used to justify discrimination against people whose bodies, minds, desires, and practices differ from the norm (Kafer, 2013: 17).

As a theoretical paradigm, intersectionality enables one to understand how oppression, privilege, and human rights intersect locally and globally. By using intersectionality, one is required to think differently about identity, equality, and power. By acknowledging the complex dynamic processes and social structures that define human relations, an intersectional approach deconstructs how thought processes such as identity and power and opportunities are accessed. As members of more than one community at the same time, people can simultaneously experience both oppression and privilege. For instance, a woman may be a respected medical professional yet suffer domestic violence at home. Intersectionality is therefore not just a tool for analysis; it is also an advocacy tool that helps one to understand how different sets of identities impact access to human rights and opportunities. Drawing on interdisciplinary and intersectionality as a framework of analysis, this book explores broader cultural sensibilities reflected in and perpetuated by experiences of immigration, religion, gender-based violence, and values embedded in human rights. The interdisciplinary and intersectionality methods offer a political commitment to equality. The sharing of this political commitment in a book such as this is not only an acknowledgement of the reality of interconnectedness, interrelatedness, and interdependency of social experience and behavior, but also of academic disciplines such as the humanities and social sciences. It is also a rejection of a single straight-jacketed approach that barely addresses issues of violence and immigration. Other theories under consideration in the book include social theories of immigration such as the "melting pot" theory, the salad bowl theory (pluralism), and assimilation theories that highlight the challenges of social integration. Human rights theories such as moral universalism and cultural relativism have also been considered to highlight questions of agency and respect for diverse cultures. These have been engaged with as various aspects of the discourse are articulated in relation to other aspects.

Gender-based violence

Gender-based violence refers to repeated or habitual patterns of behavior resulting in the infliction of physical injury by one family or household member on another. According to available statistics, 35% of women world-wide have experienced violence in their lifetime, an equivalent of one in every three women (WHO, 2017). Some national studies show that up to 70% of women have experienced physical or sexual violence in an intimate relationship (UN Women, n.d.; UN Women Palestine, n.d.). Statistics also indicate that of all the women killed in 2012, almost half were killed by intimate partners or family members (Domonoske, 2017; UNDOC, 2018). Globally, as many as 38% of murders of women are committed by inti-mate male partners (WHO, 2017). A study based on interviews with 42,000 women across the 28-member states of the European Union revealed that only 14% of women reported their most serious incident of violence to the police (European Union Agency for Fundamental Rights, 2014). According to the UN, in the majority of cases, less than 40% of women who experi-enced violence sought help of any sort (UN the World's Women, 2015). In the United States, approximately 1.5 million women are raped and/or physi-cally assaulted by intimate partners annually (Tjaden and Thoennes, 2000). While the prevalence in Europe and the United States is slightly lower due to higher standards of living among women in these countries, the preva-lence rate in developing countries in Africa, the Mediterranean region, and Southeast Asia region is significant, ranging between 37% and 38% (WHO, 2017). Often, this violence is physical, sexual, or both. One in every ten girls under the age of 18 has been forced to have sex (UN Report, 2015). The United Nations acknowledges that women across the world are subjected to physical, sexual, psychological, and economic violence. In 2006, ex-Secre-tary-General of the United Nations Kofi Annan acknowledged that violence against women and girls was "a problem of pandemic proportions" (UN News, 2006; UNIFEM, 2006: 9). In 2010, the Bureau of Justice reported that 25% of women had experienced domestic violence and that 6 million children witness domestic violence annually. This fact is affirmed by studies that show that 20% to over 30% of women experience intimate violence in their lifetime (WHO, 2017).

In the United States, the cost of violence has been estimated at about $300 billion per year. The cost to victims is estimated at more than $500 billion per year. Combined, the cost is nearly 10% of the country's Gross Domestic Product (WHO, 2004). In 1996, the World Health Assembly declared that "violence is a leading world public health problem" (World Health Assem-bly, 1996: 20–25). Gender Based Violence can lead to long-term physical, mental, and emotional health problems such as hemorrhage, infertility, com-plications during childbirth, and the risk of sexually transmitted infections like HIV, with death being reported in the most extreme cases. According to the WHO, women exposed to intimate partner violence are likely to suf-fer from mental health issues, sexual and reproductive issues, and serious injury that can lead to death. These women are twice as likely to experience depression and to have alcohol use disorders, 16% more likely to have a low birth-weight baby, and one and half times more likely to acquire sexually transmitted diseases like HIV, syphilis, chlamydia, or gonorrhea. Forty-two percent of these women have experienced injuries as a result and 38% of them have ended up dead (WHO, 2017). Intimate and culturally legitimate violence can be the most fatal and difficult to contain because, more often than not, cases of violence go unreported.

Immigration

Human migration is a historical reality dating back to the movement of *homo erectus* out of Africa across Eurasia about 1.75 million years ago. An ancient and natural human response to survival, migration is a response to hunger, deprivation, persecution, war, or natural disaster. About 3% of the world's population has migrated across international borders, with over 258 million people worldwide migrating for protection and employment (UN DESAS, 2017). About 65 million of these migrants are refugees who have been forced from their homes due to war, persecution, hunger, crime, and natural disasters. At this moment in time, many more people are expected to leave their homelands, a reality that is very current in the news media. This movement by people from one place to another with the intention of settling temporarily or permanently in the new location is known as immigration and can be voluntary or involuntary. As indicated above, immigration is triggered by many factors ranging from climate change, landscape, and food supply, as for early humans, to labor, refugee status, and urbanization of the modern industrialized world (Manning, 2004). Migration is a natural response to hunger, deprivation, persecution, war, or natural disaster. A migrant is any person who lives temporarily or permanently in a country where he or she was not born. Migrants often leave their countries in search of a decent living for various reasons. Often, they move in search of jobs, opportunities, education, and quality of life. In modern society, the reality of the world's increasing interconnectedness has made international migration easy as transport and thus moving around the globe has become cheaper, faster, and easier.

While globalization has encouraged the free movement of goods, services, and capital, thus intensifying immigration processes, it should be remembered that this is a natural process that has changed with time. While in some instances, migration may enhance individual autonomy, power, and personal growth by providing access to new norms and opportunities, personal growth is inhibited for others, especially where norms and opportunities are suppressed. Most migrants seek a better life in industrialized countries because these countries are associated with modern progress and values that encourage opportunities for autonomy and personal growth. Unfortunately, not all immigrants are fortunate enough to live the dream life they seek. Often, there is a gap between the rights that immigrants enjoy and the difficulties they experience in the countries in which they live, work, or travel. As minority communities, they face challenges related to discrimination, racism, sexism, and economic disadvantage. As immigrants, they face challenges that range from not being citizens in the country in which they live; unfamiliarity with the national language, laws, and practices; and even human rights and not knowing how to assert these. They often face discrimination and may be subjected to unequal treatment and unequal opportunities at work and in their daily lives. Marginalization and exclusion may take the form of racial violence or limited access to citizenship or the administration of justice. Unequal access to economic, social, and cultural rights may mean that migrants, including children, are excluded from education and denied health services. Illegal immigrants are vulnerable to abuse and exploitation – especially extortion. As Stefanie Grant explains, the gap between principles, policies, and lived reality underscores the vulnerability of migrants (Grant, 2005).

Among immigrants, even in developed countries, the prevalence rate of gender-based violence is even higher (UNDP, 2009; UN, 2017; UN DESAS, 2017). While some immigrant women fare well, most find themselves vulnerable due to social and personal barriers such as legal status, illiteracy, language difficulties, deprivation, discrimination, hardship, culture, or religion. Immigrant women are at a higher risk of suffering domestic violence than their counterparts due to their status as both women and immigrants. According to statistics, gender is a significant factor in international immigration. According to the Pew Research Center, women around the world have been migrating more in recent decades due to broad challenges to their social and economic status. Worldwide, the share of female migrants increased from 47.5% in 1980 to 49.6% in 2005 (Fry and Rosentiel, 2006). In Europe, 8.7% of the population are immigrants, with 52.4% of these being women (United Nations Development Programme, 2009). Statistics indicate that gender-based violence among immigrants accounts for 51% of intimate partner homicide, with 60% of immigrant women reporting they have experienced physical and sexual abuse. Sixty percent of Korean women have been battered by their husbands (Orloff and Little, 2004). The risk of violence is even higher on social networking sites (European Union Agency for Fundamental Rights, 2014). Immigrant women are especially vulnerable in these groups.

A recent study in New York found that 51% of intimate partner homicide victims were foreign-born (Femicide in NY City, 2004). Married immigrant women experience higher levels (60%) of physical and sexual abuse than unmarried immigrant women (Dutton, Orloff and Hass, 2000). According to a separate study, violence against women is one of the most common victimizations experienced by immigrants (Raj and Silverman, 2002). Immigrant women often suffer higher rates of battering than locals because they may come from cultures that accept domestic violence as the norm or because they have less access to legal and social services than native citizens.

In such cases, abusers often use their partner's immigration status as a tool of control. As Orloff (1995) explains, it is common for a batterer to exert control over his partner's immigration status in order to force her to remain in the relationship (Orloff, 1995: 313; Orloff and Kaguyutan, 2002: 95–183). Some immigrant women fail to report their situation for fear of deportation or abandonment by their spouses. Others have expressed concern that the perpetrator may withhold important personal documents such as passports to prevent them from seeking or accessing necessary legal services and support services. As women, most face discrimination due to their dependency on relationships with a citizen or a "primary migrant," without which their agency is undefined. Some have limited access to education and consequently lack the employment opportunities of their male counterparts. Women are more vulnerable to sexual exploitation and domestic violence.

As immigrants migrate to other countries, they bring with them their cultural and traditional values. Often, some of these values conflict with those existing in the new country. Sometimes, a conflict in these values including law and policies may lead to a dilemma for the immigrants. Gender-based cultural values reported in local and immigrant communities often include intimate partner violence (IPV), often known as domestic violence (DV), honor killings (HK), child marriage (CM), and female genital cutting (FGC), sometimes known as female circumcision (FC) or female genital mutilation (FGM), just to mention a few. These cultural practices are often justified by certain cultures or religions in communities that embrace them as legitimate values across the globe. Female genital cutting involves excision of the clitoris and/ or the removal of part or all of the tissues around a woman's reproductive organs. It sometimes includes infibulation, the stitching together of the vulva in order to narrow the vaginal opening. Although it was traditionally performed on young girls and women as a rite of passage at puberty, it is now common in younger, unsuspecting children mostly to evade the law against it. The practice is a concern in immigrant communities because it persists in countries such as the US and European countries. In the US, for instance, it is estimated that more than 228,000 live with the risk of genital cutting, a 35% increase (African Women's Health Center, 2012). In the UK, it is estimated that over 279,500 women have been exposed to female genital cutting, with an additional 33,000 living with the risk of having their genitals cut (Leye, 2004, 23–24). In England and Wales alone, *Equality Now* reports, 66,000 women have been subjected to female genital cutting and another 23,000 are at risk (Equality Now, 2012; Nyangweso, 2014).

Religion

Religion is as significant a factor in gender-based violence and immigration as it is in general behavior. The intersection of culture and religion is complex, as religious texts and traditions both perpetuate and destabilize social behavior. Religious diversity is often a consequence of immigration. Of the world's population that has migrated across international borders, Christians comprise about 49% (106 million), Muslims 27% (60 million), Buddhists 3% (7 million), and Jews 2% (6 million). Eleven million (5%) are of a Hindu background. Religious values are closely linked to immigration and social behavior (Demographic Study, 2012; Pew Research Center, 2012).

Religious ideologies have been invoked to justify certain forms of violence. This influence often involves abuse or misuse intended to excuse or condone gender-based violence. Gina Messina-Dysert explains how some androcentric religious texts help to perpetuate sexual violence (Messina-Dysert, 2014). In Judaism and Christianity, for instance, stories of Dinah (Genesis 34), Tamar (2 Samuel 13), the Levite's concubine (Judges 19), Jephthah's daughter (Judges 11), Vashti (Esther 1), Suzannah (Daniel 13), and the persistent widow (Luke 18) can be interpreted as condoning violence (Fortune and Enger, 2005). Other verses, such as Ephesians 5:22–24 and 5:20 and Malachi 2:13–16, communicate female subjugation, perseverance even in an abusive relationship, and prohibition of divorce. Ironically, the same scripture speaks about the liberation of the victim in John 10:10 and the release of captives in Luke 4:18 (also 1 Isaiah 61), while the equality of all before God is emphasized in Genesis 1:22. In Islam, *Sura* 4, *ayah* 34 is the most cited as condoning violence against women. Ironically, *Sura* 30:21 and *Sura* 9:71 also mandate mutual kindness and mercy towards each other in a relationship. As Sharifa Al-Khateeb argues, according to the Islamic foundation of marriage and family, no human being has authority over women (Al-Khateeb, 1999: 55; Al-Khateeb, Ellis and Fortune, 2003: 7–8).

As a personal and institutional reality, religion is significant in addressing many dimensions of social experience. While there are scriptural texts and ideologies that perpetuate violence, scriptural texts and ideologies that condemn violence tend to affirm human rights and social justice in general. The challenge lies in how these scriptures and ideologies are utilized by enablers and social activists to perpetuate or inhibit gender-based violence in their societies. As Rev. Marie Fortune and Rabbi Cindy Enger observe, religion provides texts, traditions, teachings, and doctrines from which religious communities and institutions draw to convey values and a belief system to their members. Religious texts and teachings also serve as resources to assist those who have experienced violence. In addition, community members often seek direct support or counseling, guidance and instruction from religious leaders, since these are the closest models of support and protection in their communities (Fortune and Enger, 2005). In order to respond appropriately to religious teachings that condone gender-based violence, there is a need for articulation of the faith that will provide women with resources for strength rather than for endurance. As Bussert argues, an approach that focuses on a theology of empowerment rather than a theology of passive endurance can be used to critique (or deconstruct) roadblocks that perpetuate patriarchal interpretations of religious teaching (Bussert, 1986). Empowering victims and survivors of gender-based violence should be the goal of religious communities. She argues, a religion that serves as a challenge to dominant patriarchal norms goes a long way to promote social justice. Interpretations of texts and events that lack hermeneutical ethics tend to employ patriarchal assumptions that affirm a tradition of chastity where women's honor and shame are adapted to religious views to fuel societal notions that women who are raped have lost integrity and sullied their relationship with God (Messina-Dysert, 2014).

Many scholars have reflected on the ambiguity of religious traditions including Christianity, Islam, Hinduism, Confucianism, Taoism, Buddhism, and Judaism with regard to gender-based violence and gender roles. For instance, Sa'Diyya Shaikh's work describes the complexity of religious traditions, as they have both perpetuated violence against women and offered resources for healing. She explains how believing men and women draw from these texts to provide friendship and mutual protection for one another. They collectively reflect the Islamic ideal of gender relations that many committed Muslims believe (Shaikh, 2007: 67). Regardless of religious affiliation, studies indicate that the majority of women find religious beliefs and teachings to be either a resource or a roadblock (Fortune, 1987; Fortune and Enger, 2005). This reality presents religious and secular leadership with specific responsibilities: to recognize (1) that religious beliefs, texts, and teachings can serve both as roadblocks and resources for survivors of gender-based violence and (2) the need for a deep examination of religious texts and teachings in order to explore new interpretations that minimize roadblocks while maximizing resources for women. When anyone is forced to choose between safety and their religious community or tradition, the role of religion in behavior formation should be taken seriously. Recognizing that all religions, whether Judaism, Christianity, Islam, Hinduism, Buddhism, Confucianism, Daoism, or indigenous religions, incorporate values and beliefs that greatly impact women who live with gender-based violence is central to addressing the root cause and persistence of gender-based violence in various immigrant communities.

Assumptions that religion is something personal and private fail to see the benefits of integrating religious ideas into secular norms, thus making it difficult to talk explicitly about religion outside of the most intimate contexts (Moslener, 2015). Religion remains a powerful phenomenon, the authority of which continues to police behavior. The influence of religion is both overt and covert, as it is evident in the public, history, modern politics, immigration, gender violence, and human rights. The significant role of religion in perpetuating or challenging social behavior affirms the intersection paradigm that is necessary for understanding social behavior. Thus, the presence or absence of religion as a dimension in discourses about immigration, violence, and human rights is likely to redirect the conversation away from fundamental issues and decisions. As Sarah Moslener and others have argued, understanding the role of religious ideologies helps to determine when and how different religious traditions are made culpable. As long as some in our society continue to pursue what Jessica Valenti describes as "purity culture," religious assumptions about immigration, gendered violence, and social behavior will continue to influence perceptions and general behavior (Moslener, 2015; Valenti, 2009).

Human rights

Gender-based violence, immigration, and religious expression have dominated human rights discourse in modern society. Gender-based violence is recognized as a human rights issue, a public concern, and a barrier to development, because any form of violence has been identified as a violation of articles of the Universal Declaration of Human Rights (United Nations, 1993). Article 3 clearly stipulates that everyone has the right to life, liberty, and security; article 5 states that "no one shall be subjected to torture or to cruel, inhuman and degrading treatment or punishment." Gender-based violence is specifically condemned in the Convention on the Elimination of Discrimination against Women (CEDAW), which was adopted by the United Nations General Assembly. Domestic violence against immigrant women is a violation of human rights per CEDAW General Recommendations No. 19. All country members of the UN are obligated to ensure the protection and support of all women, including immigrant women. Hence, practices in the category of gender-based violence, including domestic or intimate partner violence, sexual assault, child marriage, honor killings, and female genital cutting, are a violation of human rights.

Exposure to violence leads to health consequences for survivors. For instance, female genital cutting is declared a violation of the rights of children because of moral and especially possible health concerns, including severe pain, hemorrhage, urinary tract infection, fractures or dislocation, sexual dysfunction, complications in pregnancy and childbirth, and psychological damage, which is often exhibited as fear, the suppression of feeling, anxiety, flashbacks, phobia, and depression. In some cases, it has led to death. Moral concerns of gender-based violence are viewed broadly as emerging in a culture of gender inequality and discrimination – a culture that is rooted in patriarchal social structures and the claims of which are based on the assumption that the female gender is inferior and therefore ought to be controlled. Health concerns associated with gender-based violence violate article 25, which states:

> Everyone has the right to a standard of living adequate for the health and well-being of himself and of his family, including food, clothing, housing, medical care and necessary social services and the right to security in the event of unemployment, sickness, disability, widowhood, old age or other lack of livelihood in circumstances beyond his control.

It is also a violation of human rights to discriminate against immigrants. Other consequences of violence include the impact such violence has on the quality of life of all, access to education, work, and social integration. Violence can disrupt economic resources and even lead to social exclusion. A study carried out on children revealed that children exposed to domestic violence reported low IQs (8 points lower than average). Another study of women victims revealed that half of the survivors are significantly affected. According to the UDHR and two of its subsequent documents – the International Covenant on Civil and Political Rights and the International Covenant on Economic, Social, and Cultural Rights – the basic rights of all human beings are established regardless of citizenship or immigration status. These rights are not conditional on citizenship. International treaties recognize that noncitizens face exposure to human rights abuses because they are often removed from their communities and support networks. They are often denied access to health care and education, subjected to human trafficking, detained, and deported; immigrants such as refugees and those who have sought asylum are the most vulnerable. In the United States, the Constitution grants certain freedoms and protections under US laws, regardless of whether one is a citizen or noncitizen, documented or undocumented. A year after the Universal Declaration of Human Rights, a Jewish philosopher argued as follows regarding immigrants. The alien, he explained, "was to be protected, not because he was a member of one's family, clan, or religious community; but because he was a human being" (Freedman, 1949). In 1990, all country members of the United Nations agreed to abide by the International Convention on the Protection of the Rights of All Migrants Workers and Members of Their Families, adopted by the General Assembly. This convention reaffirms basic human rights norms and seeks to ensure that the vulnerable and unprotected, such as migrant workers and members of their family, legal or illegal, are protected.

The freedom to move anywhere in the world is enshrined in human rights documents, including the Declaration of Human Rights (1948). The discourse on human rights is rooted in efforts to prevent acts of discrimination and violence. This is because the history of civil rights and human rights in industrialized countries is an attraction for most immigrants. In the 1940s, the world agreed on fundamental rights that all humans should have by establishing the Universal Declaration of Human Rights (UDHR). These were instituted in order to protect humans from atrocities that violated their humanity, including protection from violence. Human rights principles advocate basic rights inherent to all human beings regardless of their nationality, race, gender, and origin. Political theorist Jack Donnelly (2007) has characterized human rights as moral principles that set out certain standards of human behavior. These principles are regularly protected as legal rights in national and international law, and to resist them on any basis, he argues, is to overlook simple moral facts, since all societies have cross-culturally and historically manifested conceptions of human rights and have interpreted these in their own contexts (Donnelly, 2007: 284–290).

Similarly, discrimination of anyone on the basis of religion is a violation of human rights. The United Nations' declaration about religious tolerance was part of the resolution adopted by the 36th session of the General Assembly on November 25, 1981, and in 1993, December 20, a second resolution was adopted by the 48th session. While 1981 called for the elimination of all forms of intolerance and of discrimination based on religion or belief, the 1993 resolution was a reaffirmation of the elimination of all forms of religious intolerance. Member states of the United Nations pledged to promote and encourage universal respect for and observance of human rights and fundamental freedoms of all, without distinction as to race, sex, language or religion by proclaiming the principle of nondiscrimination and equality before the law and the rights to freedom of thought, conscience, religion, and belief.

Article 1 of the declaration reads:

> Everyone shall have the right to freedom of thought, conscience, and religion. This right shall include freedom to have a religion or whatever belief of his choice, and freedom . . . to manifest his religion or belief in worship, observance, practice, and teaching.

Article 2 states:

> No one shall be subject to discrimination by any state, institution, group of persons, or person on grounds of religion or other beliefs . . . the expression "intolerance, and discrimination based on religion, or belief" means any distinction, exclusion, restriction or preference based on religion or belief and having as its purpose or as its effect nullification or impairment of the recognition, enjoyment or exercise of human rights and fundamental freedoms on an equal basis.

Both Articles 2 and 3 clearly states that discrimination of anyone on the ground of religion or belief constitutes an affront to human dignity and should be condemned as a violation of the human rights and fundamental freedoms proclaimed in the Universal Declaration of Human Rights

The human rights approach has, however, been countered by group rights positions, which advocate cultural diversity or multiculturalism by emphasizing the preservation of group identity. They recognize the reality of difference as expressed in a variety of social groups and experiences, such as gender, culture, race, religion, ethnicity, language, tradition, and morality, and argue that morality differs throughout the world because the cultural values that inform it differ (Steiner and Alston, 1996: 192–193). Moral questions raised by activists include the following:

- On what basis should a cultural group be denied the right to engage in its long-held cultural traditions?
- Who grants anyone the right to do this?

In the early 1970s, violence against women was first recognized as a serious social problem, due to the embrace by the women's movement of the human rights rationale and efforts to protect the rights of women by condemning social behavior and practices that undermine this dignity. The Convention on the Elimination of All Domestic Violence Against Women (CEDAW) adopted by the United Nations General Assembly in 1979 is often described as an international bill of rights for women. The issue of "conventions," or international treaties, regarding women's human rights for United Nations member countries to sign, and the Declaration on the Elimination of Violence Against Women affirmed this position (United Nations, 1993).

Feminist theorists tend to view domestic violence as a problem for all women. Feminist approaches draw from theoretical frameworks that advocate for human rights (Billet, 2007). In *Transforming a Rape Culture*, edited by Emilie Buchwald, Pamela Fletcher, and Martha Roth, contributors draw from feminist theorization to challenge sexual violence by contextualizing the problem of violence within general assumptions about gender and gender expectations. Peggy Miller and Nancy Biele, for instance, argue that responding to sexual violence requires changing social assumptions about gender (Miller and Biele, 1995: 52). They critique categorizations of women as a monolithic category, arguing that any analytical framework that ignores the diversity present within women, such as color, disability, gender, poverty, and religious affiliation, is insufficient for addressing social problems such as domestic violence.

Chapter summary

In an attempt to understand the intersections of religion, gender-based violence, immigration, and human rights, this book draws on interdisciplinary theoretical analysis with intersectionality as a tool of analysis. Each chapter highlights specific case studies and datasets, not just to demonstrate the significance of intersectionality as an approach in the examination of the relationships between gender-based violence and other social variables but also to show how social reality is interdependent and interconnected. Chapters are organized in so far as they speak to the individualized theoretical framework and as this relates to intersectionality and holistic views.

In Chapter 2, Danoye Oguntola-Laguda appraises homosexual rights in Nigeria against the backdrop of violence against sexual minorities like gays, lesbians, transgender individuals, etc. He argues that the LGBTQI community in Nigeria has lived with harassment, intimidation, rape, and violence in many forms due to cultural and religious values. The promulgation of the same-sex marriage prohibition acts of 2013 and the glee that greeted the law were based on the notion that homosexuality is alien to Nigerian cultures and therefore should not be allowed to thrive in the country. Using critical analysis as a tool of engagement, Oguntola-Laguda argues that in spite of allegations that serious homosexual advocacy in the media is sponsored from the West, sexual rights as part of human rights should be protected by the government of Nigeria.

In Chapter 3, Sloane Burke and Jody O. Early argue that despite the fact that one-third of all women are expected to experience intimate partner violence during adulthood and that public awareness has increased, there is limited research that explores the incidence and prevalence of this critical issue among immigrant populations. In their chapter, they argue that although Latinos are now the largest and the fastest growing minority group in the United States, there is limited research on intimate partner violence and immigrants or foreign-born Latina women. For this qualitative research study, 15 Latina women above the age of 18, who were survivors of intimate partner violence by self-report, were recruited via community organizations and gatekeepers serving the Latina immigrant population, including social service agencies, health care services, women's shelters, intimate partner and sexual assault services, churches, and universities. In-depth, semi-structured interviews were conducted in Spanish and English. Through the researchers' use of grounded theory methodology, themes emerged from analysis of the interview transcripts. Based on these themes, a substantive theory of the process of immigrant Latina intimate partner abuse was developed. This abuse process includes four phases: *The Pursuit, The Abuse Begins, The Abuse Continues or Escalates*, and *End of the Abuse or Escape to a New Life*. Unique aspects of the Latina woman's experience as an immigrant include fear of deportation, fear of never seeing one's family in their home country again, a concern that children will be taken away, worry over access to finances, and the experience of severe violence, including gun violence and locked confinement. The findings from this grounded theory study, and the abuse process identified from the themes that emerged, provide useful information for the provision of culturally appropriate programs and services aimed at violence prevention and intervention for immigrant Latina women, as well as relevant support services for the victims of intimate partner violence in this population.

Justice Richard Kwabena Owusu Kyei in Chapter 4 contributes to the empirical literature on the intersectionality of gender, religion, and immigration. He addresses the following questions: are second-generation female Ghanaian migrants in Ghanaian churches in Amsterdam oppressed in their access to religious citizenship? How gendered is the sanction on pregnancy out of wedlock within Ghanaian Christian churches in Amsterdam? To what extent does the agency of second-generation female Ghanaian migrants intervene in the gendered right to religious citizenship in Ghanaian churches in Amsterdam? The chapter begins by defining the problem and proceeds with the definition of key concepts. A brief description of Ghanaian immigration in the Netherlands as well as the origin of Ghanaian churches in Amsterdam is provided, followed by the presentation of the data and methods and, finally, a thematic discussion of the empirical findings leads to conclusions and recommendations.

In Chapter 5, Petra Klug draws on the intersectionality approach to highlight the plights of immigrants in Germany. She reveals the voices of immigrant women, queers, and critics that have been muted in Germany's immigration debate, even among German intellectuals who consider themselves feminist, anti-racist, queer, and critical. She argues for the need to criticize harmful cultural or religious practices without stigmatizing adherents. She also draws on human rights and an integrated approach to comment on the ongoing immigration process to argue for human-based guidelines for future policies.

In Chapter 6, Susan C. Pearce presents research on the current country conditions regarding gender-based violence in three Southeast European countries that are not yet members of the European Union, and that had a shared experience as Soviet states before independence in 1991. She examines how Georgia, Azerbaijan, and Armenia as a region remain on the outside edges of the European Union, representing a cultural "otherness" to the West amid uncertainties over democratic governance, internal ethnic and religious tensions, and challenges in economic development. Within this constantly emerging story is the reemergence of nationalistic and religious loyalties in post-Cold War Europe, which play out in pro-natalist positions and result in restrictions on women's and LGBTQI rights. The story is also one of new entanglements between private and public concerns, including intersections between religion, sexuality, and politics. Contributing to the situation is the continued political and cultural dominance of Russia, which has cracked down on LGBTQI rights and activism in recent years. The chapter surveys (1) the cultural contexts of GBV for LGBTQI people in these countries; (2) country conditions regarding these societies' efforts to address the problems; and (3) how migration policy, such as gender-based asylum, is a growing player in cross-border relationships regarding these issues.

In Chapter 7, Mary Nyangweso and Mansi Trivedi examine the intersection between religion, gender-based violence and policy development in Kenya. They argue that religious values have informed gender-based behavior in Kenya. Utilizing intersectionality as an approach, they focus on the need to recognize how intersected behavior and cultural/religious values are in order to develop an adequate policy toward protecting the rights of women. It is therefore important that recognizing the significance of religious values in gender roles and general welfare can potentially help improve gender development in a country like Kenya. Citing examples from gender-based violence, particularly female genital cutting, they recommend that religious literacy should be recognized as an important component of civic education curriculum since religion is a significant variable in attitude formation and general behavior.

In Chapter 8, Enoch Olujide Gbadegesin and Elizabeth Ayoola Adeyemi-Adejolu adopt a socio-anthropological method to argue that religion and culture need to be transformed to purge teachings about violence before the family and society at large can transform violent behavior. As agents of socialization, religion and culture have always shaped the way people interpret and organize their families and the world in general. Among the Yoruba, they argue, instances of religions sanctioning and even abetting domestic violence are numerous, and social justice activists have called for the need to liberate society from the burden of religion. They recommend ways that domestic violence could be reduced or totally eradicated through a reexamination of religious and cultural values among the Yorùbá of Southwestern Nigeria.

In Chapter 9, Sychellus Wabomba Njibwakale examines the role of religion in domestic violent behavior among the Babukusu of Kenya. He highlights the causes, effects, and existing prevention measures against domestic violence. In examining the position taken by the religious groups, he highlights the extent and serious consequences of wife-battery in this millennial community. He argues that men's brutality against women, including wife battery, rape, and femicide, is a natural consequence of women's "feeble" position vis-à-vis male patriarchal and sexist values. It is hard, he argues, to eradicate gender-based violence without reforming social structures that promote social inequality and power in gender relations.

In Chapter 10, Precious Nihorowa explores the influence of religion on reproductive health, particularly on the issue of abortion. He describes the reasons behind this dynamic role of religion as a social phenomenon. Is it a result of modernity and enough awareness of issues of reproductive health? Is it a reaction to the approach that the church uses in imparting its teaching? Or has Christian ethics become so outdated that it needs to be updated and adapt to the changing times? This chapter tries to answer such questions. It acknowledges that African societies have undergone a lot of change. However, it establishes that while Christian ethics on reproductive health has not outlived its usefulness, what is needed is a new approach that suits the current times. This chapter, therefore, proposes the theory of intersectionality as a solution to this phenomenon.

In Chapter 11, Genevieve Nrenzah discusses how the todɔlɛ (vagina) was traditionally venerated as a sacred part of the female body among the Akan Nzema of Western Ghana. She argues that in indigenous religious thinking, the Nzemas perceived the vagina as the entrance to a mother's womb, which is where humanity originates and the gateway to this world, or "*ewiase*." The sacredness associated with the vagina demanded that females should always conceal it from public view. It also imputed a sense of sacredness to the female body. However, in modern Nzema society, she notes, the vagina has lost the sense of sacredness and has become the target of forms of verbal abuse, especially from males. She proposes that the decline in the respect associated with the vagina and its polished violence in modern Nzema society parallels the decline in the viability of indigenous religious ideas about women's spirituality and the consequent loss of the sense of sacredness associated with women in modern Akan Nzema societies. Using empirical data as well as qualitative content analysis, the study identifies ideological and structural shifts such as colonialism, Christianization, Islamization, and the emergence of the modern state as contexts within which the shift in under-standings of the power of women has taken shape.

In Chapter 12, Rosinah Mmannana Gabaitse and Simangaliso Ray-mond Kumalo discuss the implications, claims, and relevance of practicing *botho/ubuntu* as well as applying Mt 25:35–36 in the context of global migration and HIV. With a focus on Botswana, a Christian country that also practices and embodies the values of *botho/ubuntu*, they describe how Botswana's efforts to curb HIV/AIDS have led to the decline of HIV rates. In spite of this, they argue, the country has failed in the global fight against HIV because Botswana's health policy denies cross-border migrants access to HIV services and treatment. They argue that the migrants affected by this policy are the undocumented ones already exposed to different sorts of vulnerabilities because of their illegal status. Although there is no active hostility towards cross-border migrants in Botswana, and Botswana has a good and progressive refugee policy, the health policy is repressive towards migrants as it is designed to exclude and discriminate against them. Drawing on the Botswana *botho/ubuntu* values and their ethic of care of the stranger, alluded to in Mt 25:35–36, the authors argue for the need to utilize these val-ues as a resource for persuading and convincing the Botswana and African governments to offer antiretrovirals to cross-border migrants.

In Chapter 13, Sonu Shiva investigates the link between community, caste, gender, and violence at the time of partition in Indian society. She describes women's unspeakable and horrifying experiences, their painful truth, and their silence as part of the process of healing and forgetting. She argues that while the history of partition is presented by historians as a constitu-tional or political arrangement that has not affected the contours of Indian society, from the survivors' perspective this history is about violence. It is about trauma, painful memories, and the moments of violence women immi-grants faced from strangers as well as from their dear ones. History's failure to address the issue of dislocation, and especially the relationship between community, caste, and gender violence, undermines the processes of healing and forgetting.

In Chapter 14, Nyangweso examines gender-based violence among immi-grants in the West and efforts towards reclaiming immigrant rights. She argues that Africans immigrants to the United States, like immigrants any-where in the world, often import their values, including those gender-based values that promote gender-based violence such as female genital cutting. This practice, which has been described as a human rights violation because of its harmful health consequences to the basic rights of girls, is illegal in the United States. She explains how most immigrants to the United States are drawn to democratic values that promote civil and human rights and pro-tect freedoms such as self-realization, freedom of choice, and protection of basic rights and safety from demeaning and harmful cultural practices and norms. She argues that the dilemma of negotiating these values in a world that embraces cultural diversity is challenging for immigrants. Nyangweso specifically highlights how religion has played a significant role in the persistence of gender-based violence. She argues for the need to protect the rights of immigrants.

In Chapter 15, Gbadegesin and Tolu Adegbola Adefi examine how cultural factors condition the lifestyles of the majority of Nigerian immigrants in American society. In spite of the fact that popular nuances in scholarship often show immigrants to suffer from alienation and marginalization from the dominant culture of the country to which they have emigrated, they argue that the immigrants are themselves negatively affected by some of their African cultural heritage, leading to family violence and alarming rates of divorce in the United States. They argue that exported cultural norms and values from Africa inadvertently lead some Nigerian families to continue to have ugly family experiences, such as broken homes, domestic violence, juvenile delinquencies, and/or maladaptive family structures. They frame their discourse within phenomenological and anthropological approaches to highlight how immigrants turn to religion as a source of relief and a solution to their problems. They conclude with recommendations for immigrants to play down those cultural values to which they have been enculturated, as these could continue to serve as sources of family problems and disintegration.

In Chapter 16, the role of religious leaders as agents of social transformation is examined by Nyangweso. She describes the religious leader as the authority in her community and how this authority can be utilized to transform attitudes and general behavior in the community. Drawing specifically on experiences associated with female genital cutting, she explains the process of religious justification of cultural practices and how this process embeds irrefutable authority in a practice like female genital cutting. She argues that the persistence of a practice such as female genital cutting can be attributed to the continuous citation of scriptures that enable it. To combat this practice, therefore, religious leaders must draw on the same scriptures in order to demystify them. Because religious leaders command trust in their communities, their word is often viewed as sacrosanct. Drawing on this authority, Nyangweso argues that leaders are placed in a special role to form and deconstruct attitudes and behavior. As agents of change, therefore, religious leaders need training in skills that can transform their communities towards social justice.

The book concludes with an emphasis on intersectionality and a holistic integrative approach that frames how gender-based violence intersects with religion, immigration, and human rights as significant dimensions of gender-based violence in society. It is argued that gender-based violence in immigrant communities should be interrogated within the context of value and social formation processes. It is the book's recommendation that attitude formation in the globalizing world not only confront the interconnected social reality but also acknowledge the role of religion in social definitions of behavior as significant. Religious leaders as agents of social change have a significant role in shaping behavior to positive social experience. This fact should not be underestimated.

References

Al-Khateeb, Sharifa. 1999. "Ending Domestic Violence in Muslim Families." *Journal of Religion and Abuse,* 1, 49–59.

Al-Khateeb, Sharifa, Ellis Sharon and Fortune Marie. 2003. "Domestic Violence: The Responses of Christian and Muslim Communities." *Journal of Religion and Abuse,* 2, 3–24.

AWHC. 2012. "African Women's Health Center, Brigham and Women's Hospital: A Teaching Affiliate of Harvard Medical School," accessed at www.brighamandwomens.org on February 26.

AWID. 2004. "Intersectionality: A Tool for Gender and Economic Justice." *Women Rights and Economic Change* No. 9, August, accessed at https:www.awid.org

Billet, L. Bret. 2007. *Cultural Relativism in the Face of the West: The Plight of Women and Female Children,* New York: Palgrave Macmillan.

Bryant, Miranda. 2016. "My Dress Was Lifted Then Something Sharp Cut Me: American Woman Who Was Forced to Undergo Female Genital Mutilation at Age Seven Details the Horrific Ordeal." *Daily Mail,* accessed at www.dailymail.co.uk. On June 22.

Bussert, Joy M. K. 1986. *Battered Women: From a Theology of Suffering to an Ethic of Empowerment,* New York: Lutheran Church in America.

CEDAW (Convention on the Elimination of All Forms of Discrimination against Women). 1992. "General Recommendation No. 19," accessed at www.un.org/womenwatch/daw/cedaw/recommewndations/recom.htm on April 16, 2014.

Crenshaw, Kimberlé W. 1989. "Demarginalizing the Intersection of Race and Sex: A Black Feminist Critique of Antidiscrimination Doctrine, Feminist Theory and Antiracist Politics." *The University of Chicago Legal Forum* (140): 139–167.

Crenshaw, Kimberlé W. 1991. "Mapping the Margins: Intersectionality, Identity Politics, and Violence Against Women of Color." *Stanford Law Review*: 1241–1299.

Demographic Study. 2012. "Faith on the Move – the Religious Affiliation of International Migrants." *Pew Research Center,* accessed at www.pewforum.org/2012/03/08/religious-migration-exec/ on March 8, 2012.

Domonoske, Camila. 2017. "CDC: Half of All Female Homicide Victims Are Killed by Intimate Partners." *NPR,* accessed at www.npr.org, on June 15, 2018.

Donnelly, Jack. 2007. "The Relative Universality of Human Rights." *Human Rights Quarterly,* 2(9): 281–306.

Dutton, Mary, Leslye Orloff, and Giselle Aguilar Hass. 2000. "Characteristics of Help-Seeking Behaviors, Resources, and Services Needs of Battered Immigrant Latinas: Legal and Policy Implications," *Georgetown Journal on Poverty Law and Policy,* 7(2).

Equality Now. 2012. "Celebrating Twenty Years of Advocacy and Action," accessed at www.equalitynow.org on May 10, 2014.

European Union Agency for Fundamental Rights. 2014. "Violence against Women: An EU-Wide Survey: Main Results," accessed on https://fra.europa.eu/sites/default/files/fra_uploads/fra-2014-vaw-survey-main-results-apr14_en.pdf, on May 10, 2017.

Femicide in New York City: 1995–2002. 2004. "New York City Department of Health and Mental Hygiene," accessed at www.ci.nyc.ny.us/html/doh/html/public/press04/pr145-1022.html on October, 2016

Fortune, Mary. 1987. *Keeping the Faith: Questions and Answers for the Abused Woman*, San Francisco, Harper and Row.

Fortune, Marie and Rabbi Cindy G. Enger. 2005. "*Violence Against Women and the Role of Religion*," VAWNET, Applied Research Forum: National Online Resource Center on Violence Against Women, accessed at www.vawnet.org, on April 22, 2018, 1–7.

Freedman, Rabbi Harry. 1970. *Jeremiah, Hebrew Text and English Translation with an Introduction and Commentary*, Vol. 52, Abraham Cohen ed. The Soncino Press.

Fry, Richard and Tom Rosentiel. 2006. "Gender and Migration," *Pew Hispanic Center*, accessed at https://www.incedes.org.gt/Master/myhffryrichard.pdf on March 2017.

Grant, Stefanie. 2005. "International Migration and Human Rights Global Commission on International Migration," accessed at www.gcim.org on May 2016.

Hania, Zlotnik. 2003. "The Global Dimensions of Female Migrations." *The Migration Information Source*, accessed at www.migrationinformation.org on March 2015

Kafer, Alison. 2013. *Feminist Queer*, Crip, Bloomington, IN: Indiana University Press.

Krug, Etienne, Linda L. Dahlberg, James A. Mercy, Anthony B. Zwi, and Rafael Lozano, eds. 2002. "World Report on Violence and Health," *World Health Organization*, Geneva.

Leye, Els and Jessika Deblonde. 2004. "A Comparative Analysis of the Different Legal Approaches toward Female Genital Mutilation in the 15th EU Member States, and the Respective Judicial Outcomes in Belgium, France, Spain, Sweden, and the United Kingdom." *International Centre for Reproductive Health (ICRH)*, Publications No.8, Ghent, *The Consolatory*, April 23–24.

Manning, Patrick. 2004. *Migration in World History*, New York and London: Routledge.

Messina-Dysert, Gina. 2014. *Rape Culture and Spiritual Violence: Religion, Testimony, and Visions of Healing*, Abingdon, Oxon: Routledge.

Miller, Peggy and Nancy Biele. 1995. "Twenty Years Later: The Unfinished Revolution." *Transforming a Rape Culture*, ed. Emilie Buchwald, Pamela Fletcher, and Martha Roth, 2nd edition, Minneapolis, MN: Milkweed Editions.

Moslener, Sarah. 2015. *Virgin Nation: Sexual Purity and American Adolescence*, New York, NY: Oxford University Press.

Normani, Asra. 2009. "The Night of Beheading." *The Daily Beast*, accessed at www.thedailybeast.com/articles/2009/02/28/the-night-of-the-murder.html on May 2016.

Nyangweso, Mary. 2014. *Female Genital Cutting in Industrialized Countries: Mutilation or Cultural Tradition?* Santa Barbara, CA: ABC Clio/Praeger.

Orloff, Leslye and Rachael Little. 1999. *Somewhere to Turn: Making Domestic Violence Services Available to Battered Immigrant Women*, Harrisburg, PA: National Resources Center on Domestic Violence.

Orloff, Leslye and Janice V. Kaguyutan. 2002. "Offering a Helping Hand: Legal Protections for Battered Immigrant Women: A History of Legislative Responses." *American University Journal of Gender, Social Policy and the Law*, 10(1): 95–183.

Orloff, Leslye, et al. 1995. "With No Place to Turn: Improving Advocacy for Battered Immigrant Women." *Family Law Quarterly*, 29(2): 313.

Raj, Anita and Jay Silverman. 2002. "Violence against Immigrant Women: The Roles of Culture, Context, and Legal Immigrant Status on Intimate Partner Violence." *Violence against Women*, 8(3): 367–398.

Shaikh, Sa'Diyya. 2007. "A Tafsir of Praxis: Gender, Marital Violence, and Resistance in a South African Muslim Community." *Violence against Women in Contemporary*

World Religions: Roots and Cures, ed. Daniel Maguire and Sa'Diyya Shaikh, Cleveland, OH: Pilgrim Press.

Sheridan, Michael. 2011. "Muzzammil Hassan Gets 25 to Life for Beheading Wife, Aasiya Hassan." *Daily News*, accessed at www.nydailynews.com/news/national/muzzammil-hassan-25-life-beheading-wife-aasiya-hassan-article-1.120570 on February 2016.

Steiner, Henry J. and Philip Alston. 1996. *International Human Rights in Context: Law, Politics, Morals*, Oxford: Clarendon Press.

Tjaden, Patricia and Nancy Thoennes. 2000. "Extent, Nature and Consequences of Intimate Partner Violence," accessed at https://www.ncjrs.gov/pdffiles1/nij/181867.pdf on January 2016.

United Nations. 1993. "Declaration on the Elimination of Violence against Women," General Assembly, A/RES/48/104, accessed at https://www.un.org/documents/ga/res/48/a48r104.htm, July 2017.

UN DESAS. 2017. "The International Migration Report 2017 (Highlights)," accessed at https://www.un.org/development/desa/publications/international-migration-report-2017.html on March 2017.

UN. 2017. "International Migration Report 2017: Highlights," accessed at https://www.un.org/en/development/desa/population/migration/publications/migrationreport/docs/MigrationReport2017_Highlights.pdf on June 2016.

UNDP (United Nations Development Programme). 2009. "Measuring Key Disparities in Human Development: The Gender Inequality Index." *Human Development Research Paper 2010/46*, accessed at New York UNDP http://hdr.undp.org/en/reports/global/hdr2010/papers/HDRP201046.pdf on April 27, 2014.

UNIFEM. 2006. In-Depth Study on All Forms of Violence Against Women: Report of the Secretary General, A/61/122/Add.1.:42.United Nations, New York.

UNIFEM. 2010. "The Facts: Violence against Women and the Millennium Development Goals," accessed at www.unifem.org/attachments/products/EVAWkit02VAW andMDGsen.pdf on April 2, 2014.

UNDOC. 2018. "Global Study on Homicide: Gender-related Killings of Women and Girls," accessed at https://www.unodc.org/documents/data-and-analysis/GSH2018/GSH18_Gender-related_killing_of_women_and_girls.pdf.

UN Human Rights. 1993. "Declaration on the Elimination of Violence against Women," accessed at https://www.ohchr.org/EN/ProfessionalInterest/Pages/ViolenceAgainst Women.aspx.

UN News. 2006. "Annan Calls for More Political Will to Combat Scourge of Violence Against Women," accessed at https://news.un.org/en/story/2006/10/195532-annan-calls-more-political-will-combat-scourge-violence-against-women.

UN the World's Women. 2015. "Violence against Women," accessed at https://unstats.un.org/unsd/gender/chapter6/chapter6.html.

UN Women. n.d. "Facts and Figures: Ending Violence against Women," accessed at http://www.unwomen.org/en/what-we-do/ending-violence-against-women/facts-and-figures.

UN Women Palestine. n.d. "Facts and Figures: Ending Violence against Women," accessed at http://palestine.unwomen.org/en/what-we-do/ending-violence-against-women/facts-and-figures.

Valenti, Jessica. 2009. *The Purity Myth: How America's Obsession with Virginity Is Hurting Young Women*, Berkeley, CA: Seal Press.

WHO. 2017. "Violence Against Women," *World Health Organization*, November 29, accessed on www.who.int/news-room/fact-sheets/detail/violence-against-women.

WHO. 1996a. "World Health Organization Global Consultation on Violence and Health." *Violence: A Public Health Priority*. WHO Global Consultation on Violence and Health, Geneva, December 2–3, 1996.

WHO. 1996b. also quoted in Morris Stephen C. "The Causes of Violence and the Effects if Violence on Community and Individual Health." *Global Health Education Consortium*, accessed at www.cugh.org/.

WHO. 2002a. *World Report on Violence and Health: Summary*, accessed at www.who.int/violence_injury_prevention/violence on January 2016

WHO. 2002b. *First Ever Global Report in Violence and Health Released*, Geneva, accessed at www.who.int/mediacentre/news/releases/pr73/en/.

WHO. 2004. "The Economic Dimensions of Interpersonal Violence," accessed at http://apps.who.int/iris/bitstream/10665/42944/1/9241591609.pdf.

World Health Assembly. 1996. WHA 49.25 Resolution: Prevention of Violence: A Public Health Priority, 49th World Health Assembly, Geneva, Switzerland, May 20–25.

2 Their rights, our rights

A critical response to homosexuality and violence in Nigeria

Danoye Oguntola-Laguda

Introduction

The social, economic, and political rights of homosexuals have come under severe attack and criticism in some African countries, including Nigeria. Many people with sexualities beyond heterosexuality have been subjected to violent attacks and abuse. These antagonists are of the opinion that such sexual identities are alien to African culture and as such should not be allowed on the continent. Consequently, the mere suspicion that someone is gay or lesbian is a "call" for physical and emotional attacks from society. The situation is more dangerous in Nigeria's urban areas, where many have been molested, raped, beaten, and made to undergo severe punishments due to their sexuality. Questions therefore arise: can sexuality determine the rights of a category of human beings? Are homosexuality and heterosexuality socially constructed? Are homosexuals in Nigeria protected under human rights charters? Is it true that homosexuality is alien to Africa or was imported to the continent by colonial masters?

Historically, homosexuality has come to be seen as the coitus interaction(s) between people of the same sex – male and male, or female and female. The meaning is relative and subjective to societal experiences and cultural determinism. If we remove all the subjective constraints, we can define homosexuality as an expression of sexuality that involves intercourse and interaction between people of the same sex. However, in modern times, the term has been used to describe persons with sexual orientation(s) that cannot be accommodated within heterosexuality. These categories of people include those who identify as gay, lesbian, bisexual, transgender, and even queer. In other words, when a boy has sexual feelings for boys or a girl is sexually attracted to other girls, they are considered homosexuals. From the above, we can argue that homosexuality is a sexual concept/orientation that points to the innate and physical expression of sexuality between people of the same sex. This sexual expression has created serious academic engagement(s) for sociologists, anthropologists, historians, and theologians.

In Nigeria today, there seems to be an unusual ecumenical condemnation of homosexuality. Many religions (especially Islam, Christianity, and African

Traditional Religion) posit homosexuality is a sin. It is also a disease and can be cured just like any other disease. Paris (2011: 3) writes that

> Christian theology about homosexuality borrows from sexual identity category from American culture and then interprets and evaluates it with scripture (which was written in various cultural contexts) and with Christian theology from various places and time.

Adetona (2013), a Muslim cleric and scholar of Islamic religion, has also claimed that sexuality in Islam is based on Islamic scriptures that legislate that male and female should interact (sexually) for the purpose of procreation. This suggests that 'gayism,' lesbianism, and bisexualism, among other modern sexual identities, are not recognized in Islam. In Nigeria, the homosexual debate has in recent times dominated the Nigerian polity. All strata of the populace have engaged in this conversation. The main issue concerns the legality or illegality of homosexual practices and identity. It was a subject of debate in the Nigerian Senate and House of Representatives – the lawmakers. Religious leaders have also lent their voices to the conversation. The crux of the matter is that the Nigerian populace was informed that the Western powers – the United States of America, the United Kingdom, and Germany, etc.– are asking for the legal recognition of homosexual rights in Nigeria; otherwise, they may withdraw their social, economic, and political interventions in the country. At the beginning of 2014, all non-heterosexual sexual orientations were criminalized with the introduction of the Same-Sex Marriage Act (Bolanle, 2013; SSMA, 2013). It was agreed that homosexuality is an alien culture that will only destroy Nigerian cultural values. Homosexual identities, therefore, become moral, legal, and human rights issue in the country.

In this chapter, we seek to determine if homosexual practices are indigenous to popular and minority culture(s), including religions in Nigeria. It is also our intention to engage in the debate and evaluate the submission(s) of the protagonists and the antagonists of the homosexual rights debate in Nigeria. Furthermore, we seek to determine the importance of homosexual rights as a tool of political and economic negotiation(s) within the context of international politics. Historical, analytical, and sociological methods are adopted in pursuance of the thesis that the criminalization of homosexuality is a violation of the fundamental human rights of homosexuals in Nigeria as it denies them their right to social, cultural, and political identification(s).

Sexuality and the homosexual question in Nigeria

Dauda (pseudonym) claimed he had been into "gay prostitution" for more than a decade. His vocation and sexuality had seen him ply his trade in Jigawa, Gboko, and Lagos. He attested to the fact that he had been arrested and once prosecuted for being a gay in Jigawa. In his current location (Lagos), he has had many "customers" who are outright gay or bisexual. Dauda often dressed as a female, with wares including female cosmetics kits, wigs (various types), and dresses. He claimed that he also used female underwear to the "taste of his customers." He makes an average of between 30,000 and 40,000 nairas a night (around 160–200 USD). Dauda would not reveal the identities of his "customers," but he said they cut across all strata of society. During my interview with Dauda, he received some phone calls that he said were from his patrons. He normally "entertained" his customers in his two-room apartment. Some make "reservations" in advance, while others just stroll in for sex. On the "danger" attached to his sexuality, Dauda said he has been harassed many times by security agents in Lagos but has not been prosecuted since the Jigawa's experience. He further claimed that there has been no attempt by government and security agents to protect them (homosexuals) from the assault, intimidation, and harassment that accompany his sexual orientation. He also said he visits the hospital once in two months to consult his doctor, who knows about his sexual identity and vocation.[1]

In August 2013, a man in Ota, a major town in Ogun State (one of the 36 federating states), Southwest Nigeria, was beaten to a state of unconsciousness by members of the "public" for allegedly being gay.[2] This was after Nigeria's House of Representatives (the lower legislative chamber) had passed a bill into law on May 30, 2013 that criminalized homosexual engagements and advocacy. In 2011, the Senate of Nigeria (upper legislative chamber) passed the same bill on homosexual activities into law. The law sets prison sentences of 14 years for offenders and violators of the bill (law). The bill was signed into law in January 2014.

Adeyemi (2015), a gay in Lagos Island (a cosmopolitan environment), was harassed by a group of residents in the same neighborhood at Agarawu Street (April 16, 2015). He was accused of homosexual engagement with one of his neighbor's children. Although Adeyemi denied the incident, my investigation(s) revealed that he had been gay for more than a decade, even though he was only 28 years old as of2015. I called Adeyemi on the phone (having secured his number from a neighbor) and expressed my interest in "male-to-male" sex. He asked for my name and agreed to meet me at a discreet spot, from which he would go with me to my house. We agreed on a price of 25,000 naira (around 130 USD at the going official rate of 197.50 naira to 1 USD). To my surprise, Adeyemi showed up at the agreed-upon spot, unaware that I was the person who had negotiated with him earlier. I approached him and repeated my earlier question about his sexual identity and orientation, and he once again denied his gay status. I confronted him with his phone number on my phone to show that he had just agreed to have sex with me. At that point, he broke down in tears and claimed that he had never been sexually attracted to the opposite sex and had been gay for over a decade. He recounted how, on three different occasions, he was beaten by guys in Lagos who had rejected his sexuality and called him derogatory names such as "dog," "pig," and "whore." This explained his earlier decision not to identify himself as gay. Following our initial contact and conversation, Adeyemi became my resource person on the activities of the gay community in the Lagos Island local government area.

The three stories above present contradictions that deserve academic analysis and critical engagement. In the first instance, homosexuality thrives in our society, but people pretend as if they don't know about such sexual expressions. People with such sexual identities are often mobbed and called names. The point remains that any person with minority sexual orientations, like LGBT individuals in Nigeria, runs the risk of been molested or killed in a violent situation (Discriminatory Laws and Practices and Acts of Violence against Individuals based on Their Sexual Orientation and Gender Identity, A/HRC/19/41). The argument of the antagonists is that such sexual orientations are alien to our culture. Therefore, I raise the question of sexual rights. Can LGBT individuals' rights to sexual identity be denied by the majority heterosexual culture and orientation that dominate the Nigerian nation? How far have the legal instruments put in place to regulate sexuality and sexual engagements and identities responded to the "rights" of minorities with LGBT orientations?

Literature review

The political and economic dimensions of the homosexual debate in Nigeria has often been linked to the claim by David Cameron (former British Prime Minister) that future financial aid to developing countries would be tied to whether or not those countries accept gay rights as human rights. This acceptance of gay rights as a political priority for economic aids has tended to give the impression that gay rights should compete with or supersede other human rights such as the rights to housing, education, economic empowerment, and good governance that other, non-gay people must enjoy (Khan, 2013:35).

Since 2010, studies on homosexuality in Nigeria, as in other African countries, have remained at a trickle. Most of these studies have been dominated by scholars with a religious academic background and religious clerics, thereby giving the impression that issues of homosexuality could only be studied or discussed from moral and ethical perspectives. This, in Khan's opinion, is absurd because "humanity even from the same community hardly agree on point for point to what is moral and ethical in matters of culture that can easily be manipulated to achieve personal interest" (Khan, 2013:36). Such interests may include domination of the minority culture(s) in Nigeria to which homosexuality belongs.

At present, there are few scholarly works on (homo)sexuality in Nigeria that can be regarded as authoritative. Works such as those by Igboin (2010), Samuel (2013), and Oyekan (2013) have presented rigorous analyses but shy away from making a categorical pronouncement as to whether sexual rights should carry the same value as issues of human rights and corruption in the polity. In the homosexual debates in Nigeria, sexual engagements and sexuality (as orientation) are not often clarified. However, those that have condemned homosexuality relied on scriptures such as the Bible (Gen. 19:20 and 23) to reach their conclusions. Consequently, traditional discourses have conceived sexuality as natural and biological constructions that are ethically adjudicated by religion. Therefore, homosexuality could not be an aspect of human rights.

Politicians and religious leaders in Nigeria have reduced the debate on homosexuality to a question of a lack of shame on the part of gays and lesbians. In Morgan (2010: 308) opinion:

> Imposition of a sense of shame on homosexuals suggests that they have failed to be what they ought to be (heterosexual) and therefore are deficient and diminished in the face of those who consider themselves as straight. It is believed that this failure by homosexuals to be ashamed disgraces and embarrasses the community from which they hail.

However, Van Klinken argues that the ruling elites "frequently address, and publicly disapprove of homosexuality and yet use it to serve political purposes within their communities" (Van Klinken, 2011:128).

Igboin (2010), working on trans-sexualism, posits the biological or chromosomal makeup of humanity that determines sex characteristics as fixed and therefore unalterable. This suggests that human sexuality is fixed (determined) by nature or agents beyond the control of man. Although Igboin was not discussing homosexuality, his position supported "anti-homosexuality" claim in Nigeria that human sexuality is a natural, biological, and religious construct that cannot be altered by human will and wishes.

Samuel (2013:170) submits inter alia

> that traditional sexual ethics lay more emphasis on the function of sex . . . incest, rape are discouraged . . . , civilization, education, and science have altered African ethical bases for sex . . . , rape, abortion, incest, homosexuality and infertility are discouraged in Africa.

Oyekan (2013), writing on bestiality, argues that while homosexuality seems to be getting some reprieve (in term of its global acceptance and debates), the same cannot be said of incest or bestiality . . . homosexuality is slowly but surely making progress in terms of social acceptance; with time, homosexuals are winning the battle for recognition in some part of the globe (Oyekan, 2013:234).

From the above, it is clear that scholarship on homosexuality in Nigeria is still few and far between. The many contributions from religious leaders and politicians are often limited to newspaper reports and analyses, much of which forms the basis of this discourse. It should be noted, however, that some of these media reports are part of the homosexual advocacy allegedly funded by funds from Western countries.

In Nigeria, even before the SSMA (2013) that criminalized homosexuality, the mere rumor that a person was gay, lesbian, or bisexual could lead to violence. Persons with homosexual identities cannot flaunt their sexuality for fear of being "mobbed" or killed. This suggests that those individuals who are lesbian, gay, bisexual, and transgender, as well as people with non-heterosexual sexualities, face homophobic situations in Nigeria. Prior to 2014, homosexuals in Nigeria did publicly display their sexuality in a few spots across the country. However, with recent agitation stirred up due to advocacy for the recognition of "gay rights" as part of human rights in Nigeria, homosexuals in Nigerian space have been the subject of harassment and mob attacks. Efforts by Western countries like the United States of America and Britain to align political and economic aid to Nigeria with recognition of "gay rights" has infuriated the Nigerian populace. It has generated great debates in Nigerian media, leading to serious sexual rights activism. The focus of such agitations has been that gay rights are human rights. www.naijanews.com, accessed January 1, 2014.

Lesbian, gay, bisexual, and transgender (LGBT) rights in Nigeria

In Nigeria, lesbian, gay, bisexual, transgender, and queer persons are not often free to express their sexuality in public spaces, often out of fear of intimidation and harassment from the public. Many have been beaten, harassed, and stripped naked by mobs who think that these categories of persons are a disgrace to Nigerian cultures. Consequently, people that with these sexual orientations and sexualities are not very open about their identities and activities (as the three stories earlier in this showed). According to the 2007 Pew Global Attitudes Project, 97% of Nigerian residents believe that homosexuality should not be accepted in Nigerian society. This was the second highest rate of non-acceptance in the 45 countries surveyed (Pew Global Attitudes Project, 2007).

The United Nations (UN), just like the many Western superpowers who provide major aid donors to Africa, has condemned Nigeria for failing to uphold and even violating the rights of LGBT people resident in the country. In 2008, the House of Rainbow Metropolitan Community Church, an LGBT-friendly church in Lagos (Southwest) Nigeria, was attacked by people (Nigerians) who felt their activities and sexualities were a flagrant disregard of the heterosexual orientation of Nigerian cultures. Members of the church, including its leaders, were beaten, and some women were raped to impress upon them the norm of heterosexual intercourse. This singular act and many other "media wars" mounted against the church have forced the church to move from their location. The leader – Rev. Macaulay – now uses social media to provide spiritual services to its members www.revrowlandjidemacaulay.blogspot.com, accessed July 1, 2014.

Homosexuality and legislations in Nigeria

In Nigeria today, homosexual activities are criminal acts. Same-sex marriage is illegal. It is necessary to state here that there are two sets of legal instruments that govern the country: the federal penal code and Shariah law. The former is prevalent in the southeast and southwest of Nigeria, while the latter is dominant in Northern states, where it has been adopted as criminal and penal laws. In the Northern states, sexual identities and expressions that go beyond heterosexuality are illegal and considered sodomy. The federal criminal codes make sexual acts between men illegal and carry a maximum penalty of 14 years. Sex between women is not mentioned, but it could be argued that the gender-neutral term "person" used in section 214 includes women. Chapter 21 of that code provides as follows:

Any person who:

- Has carnal knowledge of any person against the order of nature [order of nature here refers to heterosexual intercourse]
- Or permits a male person to have carnal knowledge of him or her against the order of nature is guilty of a felony and is liable to imprisonment for 14 years.

Section 217 of same code states:

Any male person who whether in public or private commits any act of gross indecency with another male person or attempts to procure the commission of any such act by any male person with himself or with another male person, whether in public or private is guilty of a felony and is liable to imprisonment for 3 years.[3]

From the above, we can see that homosexuality is a felony in the federal criminal code and attracts imprisonment. In Shariah law, gayism, lesbianism, and bisexualism attract death by stoning. This law applies to all Muslims and to those who have voluntarily consented to its application. However, there is a federal penal code specifically for the Northern states of Nigeria's federation. It states that

whoever has carnal intercourse against the order of Nature with any man or woman shall be punished with imprisonment for a term which may extend to 14 years and shall also be liable to fine or both.[4]

Section 405 provides that a male person who dresses or is attired in the fashion of a woman in a public place or who practices "sodomy" as a means of livelihood or as a profession is a vagabond. Under section 407, the punishment is a maximum of a one-year imprisonment or a fine or both.

Twelve Northern states have adopted some form of Shariah law into their criminal status since 1999. These states include Bauchi, Borno, Gombe,

Jigawa, Kaduna, Kano, Katsina, Kebbi, Niger, Sokoto, Yobe, and Zamfara. These states have different interpretations of homosexuality. For example:

- In Kaduna and Yobe, "sodomy" (homosexuality) is committed by whoever has anal coitus interaction with any man.
- In Bauchi, Gombe, Jigawa, Sokoto, and Zamfara, sodomy is committed by whoever has carnal intercourse against the order of nature with any man or woman.

The punishment also varies:

- In Gombe, Jigawa, and Zamfara, a person who commits the offence of sodomy shall be (1) punished with caning of one hundred lashes if unmarried and (2) also liable to imprisonment for the term of one year or, if married, with stoning to death (Federal Penal Code for Northern Nigeria).
- In Bauchi, sodomy shall be punished with stoning to death or by any other means decided by the state. In Sokoto State, sodomy is punished with (1) stoning to death; or (2) if the act is committed by a minor on an adult person, the adult person shall be punished by way of *ta'azir* (discretionary punishment for offenses while punishment is not specified), which may extend to 100 lashes, and the minor with correctional punishment.

In the states of Bauchi, Gombe, Jigawa, Kaduna, Kano, Katsina, Kebbi, Sokoto, Yobe, and Zamfara, lesbianism is committed by

> whoever, being a woman, engages another woman in carnal intercourse through her sexual organ or by means of stimulation or sexual excitement of one another.
>
> (Federal Criminal Code for Northern Nigeria)[5]

It is further explained that "the offense is committed by the unnatural fusion of the female sexual organs and/or by the use of natural or artificial means to stimulate or attain sexual satisfaction or excitement. Lesbianism is often punished by caning, which may extend to 50 lashes, and in addition, a sentence to a term of imprisonment of up to six months. In Bauchi, the prison term could be up to five years.

The laws (federal penal codes and Shariah law) have been the basic instruments used in Nigeria to reprimand those found guilty of homosexual activities. However, of around 20 cases brought before the Shariah Court in Bauchi State between 2000 and 2007, only two have so far been decided, in which gays were given lashes of the cane for indecent dressing and solicitation. Eighteen men were arrested for homosexual activity offenses in the state in 2007. They were charged with "sodomy" (homosexuality), but later the charge changed to vagrancy. As of 2011, no final judgment has been given on any of the cases and all men involved have all been released on bail.

The bill passed by the Nigerian Senate and House of Representatives in 2011 and 2013 respectively was signed into law by the President in 2014. The law, popularly known as the anti-gay law, upholds the provisions of the federal penal codes on homosexuality but added a penalty for homosexual advocacy and concealment.

The homosexuality "rights" and advocacy in Nigeria

Prior to the passing of the anti-gay bill by Nigeria's two houses of parliament, there was a fierce and serious debate over the reality of homosexual practices and identity in Nigeria. The crux of the matter was that homosexuality is un-African and, by extension, alien to Nigeria. There was also the issue of the religiosity or otherwise of homosexuality. The third issue concerned the intervention of Western nations in the debate, especially as it concerns the political economy of the nation.

On his 70th birthday – January 17, 2014 – the Catholic Archbishop of Abuja, Cardinal John Onaiyekan, commended President Goodluck Jonathan's signing of the anti-gay law. In Onaiyekan's opinion, Nigeria should stand firm in its culture, tradition, and morals:

> The Church accepts people as they are, we condemn homosexuality, Nigeria is an independent country and we do not beg for food. . . . We have every right to order our social life in any way we think it should go. Our social life should not be organized on the basis of what other thinks . . . the major religions in the country and even African Traditional religion forbade homosexuality.
>
> (*Daily Trust*, January 18, 2014)

Onaiyekan did not refer to any particular text in the Bible, instead basing his response to the homosexual debate on known Nigerian cultures, traditions, and morality. He alludes to the lobby by international communities to prevent the ban on homosexual activities; for him, the issue should not be about what others think but rather what Nigerians want in their country. Further, the archbishop pointed out that the other two dominant religions in the country are against homosexuality.

Sheikh Dahiru Bauchi, an Islamic scholar and leader of the *Tijaniyah* sect in Africa, commended the National Assembly and the President for the passage and endorsement of the bill banning same-sex marriage in Nigeria. He described same-sex marriage as inhuman: "Even in the animal kingdom, such cannot be tolerated. . . . Has anybody ever seen a monkey marrying its male counterpart, cocks, oxen or even hens, it is abominable"(*Daily Trust*, January 21, 2014). Dahiru's submission is about the human interpretation of homosexuality, which to my mind is subjective. What is human or inhuman should be given a social and environmental interpretation. What is inhuman to Nigerians may be human to some others in Africa and even the world as a whole. So, homosexuality may be an abomination to some Nigerian cultures, but it is normal and acceptable in some cultures, even in Africa.

Rev. Musa Asake, General Secretary of the Christian Association of Nigeria (CAN), was reported to have said:

> We don't have to drift into a situation where we don't have moral values because someone is giving us money.
>
> (*Washington Post*, January 16, 2014)

Monsignor Gabriel Osu, Director of Social Communication, Lagos Catholic Archdiocese, commented on same-sex liaisons as follows:

> It is a result of wrong values, people have lost touch with God, therefore, they do not believe in God any longer. . . . As you already know these set of people [homosexuals] were condemned in the Bible, therefore why should anybody in his right senses indulge or encourage such an unholy act.
>
> (*Washington Post*, January 16, 2014)

Musa Asake and Gabriel Osu's arguments suggest that homosexuality is immoral and those that engage in its practices are appropriating wrong values; in addition, Osu thinks that homosexuals have lost touch with God and, as such, their acts are condemnable and should be considered as unholy, while Asake talks of the political and economic dimensions of the international community lobby to make homosexuality a subject of human rights in Nigeria. Nigerians cannot afford to sacrifice morality on the altar of the economic and political development of the nation.

The National Missioner of the Ansar-Ud-Deen Islamic Society of Nigeria, Abdul Rahman Ahmad suggests that homosexuality is criminal and immoral:

> My position is very clear; homosexuality is condemned in Islam as very unnatural and it also remains a crime under the law of this country. Sodomy is a crime under Nigeria's laws [referring to Shariah law] and the gay lobby will not succeed in stampeding the sane community. . . . As far as I am concerned the gays have freedom of association, they can hold a vigil and they can even decide on perpetual fasting if they so choose. They are entitled to all that so long as they do not attempt to impose upon us their depravity. . . . In fact, they will have faith communities such as Muslims and Christians . . . to contend with.
>
> (*Nairaland Forum*, August 12, 2008)

Although Rahman Ahmad recognized the right of Nigerian homosexuals to freedom of association and religion, in so far as they do not seek to convert or impose their sexuality on the people, he was quick to point out that homosexuality is not allowed in Islam. He also noted that such acts are considered sodomy in the Shariah law operating in most parts of Northern Nigeria. Ahmad also points to the tension that the imposition of homosexuality on Nigerian Christians and Muslims could cause the country in terms of conflict.

The Lagos coordinator of the Conference of Islamic Organizations (CIO), Abdullahi Shuaib, claimed that

> this culture (homosexuality) is alien to us in Nigeria whether as Muslims or Christians or as traditionalists. We have a culture of modesty . . . humility because this act of homosexuality is something unpopular among the populace. It is regarded as a taboo because it is against the nature of man himself. And anything against nature is unholy.
>
> (*Nairaland Forum*, August 12, 2008)

Abdullahi Shuaib based his contribution to the debate on the culture and law of nature. For him, homosexuality is unpopular in the country.

Some Nigerian politicians (Christians and Muslims), just like some Africans in Uganda, Liberia, Mozambique, and Zimbabwe, among others (with the exception of South Africa), claimed that homosexuality is unnatural and un-African. Cornelius Ojelabi (former member of the Nigerian House of Representatives, a church leader, and, currently, Commissioner for Rural Development in Lagos state) posits that homosexuality as a culture was imported into Nigeria from United States of America and Britain. Although he recognized the rights of LGBTs to express their sexuality, he argued that it should not be brought into public spaces, as this would impinge on the morality and sexuality of Nigerian youth (Ojelabi, 2013). Olawunmi Edet (a member of the Lagos State House of Assembly and wife of a church leader) voiced the opinion that homosexuality is not part of known Nigerian culture. She did not deny the existence of homosexuality in Nigeria but instead submitted that the role(s) played by Western countries in Nigeria's homosexual debates was unfortunate. For her, homosexuals are not better than "dogs" (Edet, 2013). This position demonstrates clear ignorance of the content of popular Nigerian cultures. We agree that homosexuality may not be popular, but to deny its existence in Nigerian cultures is begging the issue.

In his article "Homosexuality and its Enemies," Anele (2013) submits that

> those standing against homosexuality in Nigeria are nothing but blind hypocrites who are incapable of informed reasoning . . . merely indulge in lazy reference to ancient superstitious beliefs contained in various religious texts.

This suggests that those who advocated for the criminalization of homosexuality in Nigeria relied on religion to solidify their argument. Joshua Ojo (2013), in his response to Anele's article, argued:

The major point raised by Anele is a lengthy argument which attempts to debunk the existence of two discrete genders – male and female, postulating rather a continuum at which ends stand the male and female gender. In between supposedly; are myriads of people whose hormonal compositions and desires could be that despite their outward gender identifications as either male or female might be naturally drawn to burn with sexual passion for members of the same gender they are identified with.

Ojo's submission represents a wild representation of the anti-homosexuality in Nigeria. Such offensives against LGBTs are legion in Nigeria. Some have even denied the reality of bisexuality in nature. As observed by Ojo (2013):

> Advocates for homosexuality apparently aware of the reality that such myriads of intermediate states [bisexual or hermaphrodites] are simply not stable enough to exist in nature . . . if such state ever finds biological expression at all, they could only be transient phenomena.

Abdul Lateef Adetona, Deputy Imam of the Lagos State University Muslim Community, claimed that sexuality in Islam is based on Islamic scriptures that legislate that male and female should interact (sexually) for the purpose of procreation. This suggests that homosexuality and other modern sexual identities are not recognized in Islam. He suggests that,

> based on experience, there is no bisexual that has not, at the point of maturity found one sexual organ more active than the other and the other has to be jettisoned. The level of functionality determines which sexual identity should be adopted by the person involved. There is no bisexual that has both organs working at maturity.
>
> (Adetona, 2013)

Mustapha Ade Bello, Secretary to the Mission Board of NASFAT (one of the many Muslim "Pentecostals" in Nigeria) submits on bisexuality as follows:

> For every rule there would be an exception. In the Shariah these exceptions are real. If there are cases of bisexuality, inferences should be drawn, and science can also intervene to determine the correct sexuality of such persons. In Yemen, when such a case arose, in the past, the dominant hormone, as determined by medical science was allowed to determine such sexuality. Therefore, *Ijma* (consultation) in Shariah allows for scientific intervention to determine sexuality.
>
> (Bello, 2013)

Kehinde Babarinde, a Baptist priest, suggests that homosexuality is not permissible in any guise in Christianity. He referred to the story of Lot, Sodom, and Gomorra (Gen.19) among other examples in the Bible to support his

submission. LGBTs are created by the social environment where such people grow up. Although more prevalent among Nigerian youth in single-sex
schools and tertiary institutions, it is restricted to the "private engagements"
of such people (Babarinde, 2013).

Anele conjectured that LGBTs are socially constructed. According to him:

> For a male child in which masculine tendencies are not very pronounced
> would encourage such a child to tend toward feminine characteristics
> whilst a particularly masculine family ambiance tends to encourage young
> female children to behave in a more or less masculine manner.
>
> (Anele, 2013)

Although Nigerian clerics are not in agreement with the view of Anele, sexuality is to them spiritually (religiously) constructed by God. Adetona submits:

> Sexuality is a function of biology and by extension nature. For example,
> you are talking of human right, nobody determines his/her sexuality,
> and it is nature that imposes it on humanity. You can also influence the
> sexual identity of a person that is, male or female. So, it is biological.
> It is also spiritual since religion (Islam) determines the way you express
> sexual desires.
>
> (Adetona, 2013)

Mustapha Ade Bello provides an interesting dimension to the construction
of sexual identity. He suggests that

> sexual identity has multiple constructions. Spiritually God controls human
> sexuality by the creation of male and female and how sexuality should
> be used. Biologically, persons like bisexuals are medically reconstructed
> through surgery to regulate and determine their gender. Socially the envi-
> ronment determines, to a limited extent, how we deploy our sexuality.
> Thus, human sexuality is 20% socially constructed, 60% spiritually deter-
> mined by Allah and 20% due to biological situations.
>
> (Bello, 2013)

Rev. Adefoluke of the Anglican Communion in Nigeria believes that human
sexuality is determined by God. It is fixed and cannot be changed by human
beings (Adefoluke, 2013).

In the public space, the anti-homosexual campaign is rife in Nigeria. There
are many cases of harassment and mob action initiated on mere suspicion of
LGBT identities. Based on a survey questionnaire carried out at a motor park
in Lagos, Southwest Nigeria, homosexuality to some people is a sin against
God and society. Over 60% of our sample group (randomly selected based
on age; 25–45 years old) is convinced that there are persons with LGBT
identities in Nigeria. The question, therefore, is how do we respond to LGBTs

in Nigeria? This question became apposite when we consider the fact that these are "real" people who are Nigerians and some foreigners resident in the country. According to Adetona, as Muslims, we should respond to individuals who identify as LGBT by showing love and care. He further claimed that

> LGBTs are products of influences [cultures] other than Islam, thus, if Muslims want to abide by Islamic principles, they should not be influenced by any culture other than Islam which is a way of life. They [Muslims] should show love to LGBTs to attract them to the proper way(s) of Islam. They also need to be educated on the "diseases" that are associated with these perverted sexual acts. They also need rehabilitation through separation from people of homosexual orientations. By all means they should not be rejected.
>
> (Adetona, 2013)

Mustapha Ade Bello, for his part, posits that,

> from the Islamic point of view, LGBT is a sin. This is because Muslims' life is regulated by laws and not by will or wishes of persons or groups. Heterosexuality is the only form of sexuality recognized in Islam. We therefore need to interact with LGBTs in the society to determine what led to their sexual orientation and also put in place programs of action to cure them of their diseases and for them to seek forgiveness from their sexual sins. Since LGBTs could be Muslims (so long as they subscribe to the *Khalimat Shahadah*) they should not be rejected by the Muslim communities but accepted as persons in distress that need spiritual, medical and psychological rehabilitation.
>
> (Bello, 2013)

Niyi Adenuga, a Christian teacher, argues that LGBT individuals are people in distress that need the urgent attention of the government, traditional leadership, and the family. The government should not criminalize their identities. They should be "cured" of the sexual "addiction" that they have brought on themselves. There should be conscious and consistent efforts to rehabilitate homosexual individuals to conform to the cultural norms of sex and sexuality in Nigerian culture. The family (parents) needs to monitor their children as they go into adulthood and educate them on the right/correct and acceptable sexuality in Nigerian cultures (Adenuga, 2013) From the submissions of Adenuga, Adetona, and Bello, it is obvious that the anti-gay laws criminalizing LGBTs in Nigeria need to be revisited to include a program of rehabilitation.

Ojo (2013) offers his opinion on the subject, saying,

> personally, as a Christian, I have a commitment and responsibility to show love and understanding to the increasing number of people being

caught in the web of this deadly disease. The question is what to do about it? Should we as been advocated by homosexual advocates, embrace self-proclaimed homosexuals and give them the podium to continue their campaign to infest the minds of our youths in particular in their bid to attain their desired "critical mass" that will turn them into an unstoppable movement that would engulf the rest of us[6].

Can we go ahead with the new anti-gay law of the federal government that bans the practice and advocacy of this lifestyle? The answer, for me, is that while the issue of sex is very much the right of individuals, to do with as they please in their closets, the right of majority is to a decent and sane society, and since LGBTs are still in the minority in Nigeria today, their right to sex determination and expression is subjective. However, it is expected that in sexuality rights; majority right (heterosexual) need to protect minority right (homosexual) in a pluralistic society like Nigeria. I agree that LGBTQs are the minority sexual culture(s) in Nigeria, but they need to be protected, not criminalized. The implication of these questions is that if homosexuality is limited and restricted to the private practice of individuals and groups, it will not create any problems of identity for those involved in its practice and advocacy. However, when people are mobbed due to them ere suspicion or allegation of homosexuality, this creates homophobia that needs to be addressed by Nigerians, especially the country's leaders. As observed in the comments of religious leaders cited above (both Christians and Muslims), homosexuals deserve compassion, care, and love. There is a need to differentiate between homosexual identities and the militant advocacy for homosexuality sponsored by funds from Western countries, who see homosexual advocacy as a job that must be done. It is this advocacy that dominated the media leading to the enactment of the 2013SSMA.

Concluding remarks

Our discussion so far has revealed that homosexuality is real in Nigeria. Although its cultural origin remains a subject for further critical research, its practice in pre-colonial Nigeria cannot be overemphasized. Nigerians during this period engaged in homosexuality to gain "power," and this power could be spiritual, political, or economical. The spiritual power could be for the benefit of the society, especially during wartime. Such power could also be for material gain. In Yoruba land, Southwest Nigeria, those who engage in homosexuality to make money are known as *Oso* (money ritualists). The concept of *Dandaodu* among the Hausa/Fulani herdsmen of Nigeria is also very instructive in this regard. These tribes are known for their itinerant lifestyle. They can be in the "bush" for months, and when the sexual urge comes during their bush sojourn, it is their fellow herdsmen they turn to. Homosexuality has also generated a very fierce debate in the Nigerian polity, and public religions (Islam and Christianity) have been active participants.

The responses of the clerics, as well as of adherents of these religious traditions cited above, demonstrate an obvious lack of unanimity in the reasons adduced for the condemnation of homosexuality and its practices. While some refer to the scriptures as the basis for condemnation, others point to moral, cultural, and traditional values of Nigerian popular cultures. It is interesting to note that some have even agreed to the idea that homosexuals have the right to freedom of association and religious assembly, as Ahmad Rahman expressed above. However, he was quick to point out that homosexuals will still have to contend with Christians and Muslims in the country.

The Nigerian political elites are more interested in the moral and cultural values of homosexuality in the Nigerian polity and not the issue of rights to sexual identity. Although many allude to their religion (Christianity and Islam) as a basis for the new legal instrument banning homosexual activities in the country, some are involved in the debate to satisfy the political interests of their constituencies. Since many Nigerians are saying no to homosexuality, for politicians to be popular they must support "their" people's position. That was the position of the President of the Senate, David Mark, and the speaker of the House of Representatives, Aminu Tambuwal. It is interesting to note that a reasonable number of the political elites are normative religious adherents who only engage with religion during electoral processes.

Although the new legal instrument that criminalizes homosexual engagement and identity in Nigeria has been signed into law, its content did not really set out to curtail homosexuality (LGBT) per se, but rather sought to respond to militant and vociferous advocacy for the legalization of homosexuality in Nigeria that generated a fierce debate over the legality, reality, and practice of homosexual activities. What is new is the ban on homosexual advocacy, concealment of the act, and same-sex marriage. This supports our position that although homosexuality is not a popular culture in Nigeria, it is not alien to the traditional cultures of the people. Many of those interviewed in the course of this study who are anti-homosexual did not address the question of its traditional origin or practice in Nigeria as they either lack data to back up their claims or are not sure. They are, however, quick to point out that it is inhuman, an act of immorality, atheistic in nature and conception, and against the principles of the country's known cultures and traditions. They also point to its foreign origin. This perhaps was based on the interest of Western countries like the USA and Britain in the legalization of gay rights in Nigeria as part of the global human rights agenda.

In sum, we can argue, based on our observation, that even though homosexuality is a criminal act in Nigeria that attracts jail time, its practice has been on the rise, especially among youths in major cities and tertiary institutions in Nigeria. It is interesting to note the position of the House of Rainbow Church, which seeks to respond to the spiritual needs of marginalized homosexuals in Nigeria. This group is seen as anti-Christian and has faced a series of persecutions from the public and clerics of public religions. This is a clear demonstration of the reality of religious homosexuals in the country.

Notes

1 Dauda, Commercial sex worker, 32, Agege, Lagos.
2 www.nigeriaeye.com/2013/08/nigeria-gay-arrested-in-ogun-state.
3 Federal Criminal Code in all southern states of Nigeria. www.en.wikipedia.org/wiki/LGBT-right in Nigeria.
4 Ibid.
5 Federal Criminal Code in all northern States of Nigeria: *Wikipedia*, 2013. www.en.wikipedia.org/wiki/LGBT-right in Nigeria.
6 www.churcharise.org/9 and www.macfound.org/site/c

References

The American Journal of International Law. 1994. Vol. 88, No. 4 (A Journal Publication of American Society of International Law). www.jstor.org/i312276

Bolanle, Omisore. 2013. "African Connection: Nigeria Legislates against Gay Marriage, Advocacy," *Ebony News*.

DailyTrust Newspapers, Abuja, Nigeria January 18, 2014; January 21, 2014. www.dailytrust.com.ng

Discriminatory Laws and Practices and Acts of Violence against Individuals based on Their Sexual Orientation and Gender Identity, A/HRC/19/41.

Douglas, Anele. 2013. "Homosexual and Its Enemies," *Vanguard Newsletter*, January 29, p. 23.

Federal Criminal Code in all Northern States of Nigeria: Wikipedia. 2013. www.en.wikipedia.org/wiki/LGBT-right, in Nigeria.

Igboin, Benson. 2010. "Trans-Sexualism: A Theological Philosophical Study" an Unpublished PhD Thesis, Ambrose Alli University, Ekpoma, Nigeria, 30–31.

Khan, Khatian. 2013. "Homosexual Debate in Zimbabwe's Print Media" in Oguntola-Laguda (ed.), *Sex and Sexuality in Africa and African Diaspora: A Social and Ethical Engagement*, Zimbabwe: African Institute for Culture, Peace Dialogue and Tolerance Studies, p. 37.

Morgan, Michael L. 2010. "Shame, the Holocaust and Dark Times" in Roth, J.K. (ed.), *Genocide and Human Rights: A Philosophical Guide*, New York, Palgrave Macmillan, pp. 304–325.

Ojo, Joshua. 2013. "Homosexual Advocacy in Nigeria: Response to Dr. Anele," *ARISE: Christian Bi-Monthly Newsletter*. www.churcharise.org

Oyekan, Adeolu. 2013. "The Case Against Bestiality: Some Philosophical Comments" in Oguntola-Laguda (ed.), *Sex and Sexuality in Africa and Africa Diaspora: A Social and Ethical Engagement*, Harare, Zimbabwe: African Institute for Culture, Peace Dialogue and Tolerance Studies, pp. 178–191.

Paris, Janell Williams. 2011. *The End of Sexual Identity: Why Sex Is Too Important to Define Who We Are*, Downers Grove, IL, IVP Books.

Samuel, Olusegun Steven. 2013. "Re-Echoing the Dawn of Cultural Revolution in Africa: The Case of Sex and Sexuality in Social Ethics" in Oguntola-Laguda (ed.), *Sex and Sexuality in Africa and Africa Diaspora: A Social and Ethical Engagement*, Harare, Zimbabwe: African Institute for Culture, Peace Dialogue and Tolerance Studies, pp. 102–114.

Same Sex Marriage (Prohibition) Act. 2013. *Explanatory Memorandum 2014*.

Van Klinken. 2011. "The Homosexual as the Antithesis of Biblical Manhood? Heteronormativity and Masculinity Politics in Zambian Pentecostal sermons," *Journal of Gender and Religion in Africa*, December, Vol. 17, No. 2, 126–142.

The Washington Post, "Nigerian's Religious Leaders Welcome Controversial Anti-Gay Law," January 16, 2014. www.washingtonpost.com
www.africannewspost.com/2013/03

Ojo, Joshua. 2013. "Homosexual Advocacy in Nigeria: Response to Dr. Anele" in *Arise – Christian Bi-Monthly Newsletter.* www.churcharise.org

"Two lesbians in Anambra sentenced to 14years in Prison." www.jointarena.com, accessed December 14, 2014.

"Nigerian President Sign Anti-Gay Bill Into Law." www.naijanews.com, accessed January 14, 2014.
www.Naijaurban.com

"Nigerian Gay Arrested in Ogun State." www.nigeriaeye.com/2013/08/nigeria-gay-arrested-in-ogun-state

"Agonies, Love of a Gay Pastor's doting dad." www.revrowlandjidemacaulay.blogspot.com/01/07/2014

Appendix

Oral interviews

S/N	Name	Occupation	AGE	Interview Location
1	Ojelabi, C.	Politician	50+	Ojo, Lagos
2	Edet, O.	Politician	48+	Alausa, Lagos
3	Adetona, L.M.	Imam-Cleric	46+	Ojo, Lagos
4	Bello, M.A.	Sec. NASFAT, Mission Board	47+	Agege, Lagos
5	Babarinde, K.	Priest, Baptist Church, Lagos Conference	46+	Badagry, Lagos
6	Adenuga, N.	Educationist	51+	Iba, Lagos
7	Adefoluke, G.O.	Priest	62+	Ojo, Lagos
8	Dauda (pseudonym)	Commercial sex worker	32	Agege, Lagos
9	Adeyemi, N.O	Hair Dresser	28+	Lagos Island

3 Intimate partner violence among immigrant Latina women

Sloane Burke Winkelman
and Jody O. Early

Introduction

Approximately one in four women will experience intimate partner violence in their lifetime. When psychological aggression, including name-calling, insults, humiliation, monitoring, controlling, and threatening a partner, is included, the rate increases to 47% in one's lifetime (United States Department of Justice (USDJ), 2016). It is estimated that 34% of Latina women experience intimate partner violence (IPV) (Breiding et al., 2014; Bureau of Justice Statistics, 2016). Although Latina women do not experience higher rates of intimate partner abuse (IPA), they do report higher rates of homicide related to IPA, extreme violence, isolation, poor physical health, and psychological stress than non-Latina populations (Alvarez & Fedock, 2018; Alvarez et al., 2016; Bonomi et al., 2009; Burke & Oomen, 2009; Cuevas et al., 2010; Swatt, 2013). Latina women who are immigrants experience further vulnerabilities, including lack of knowledge and access to health and social assistance programs (Alvarez & Fedock, 2018; Burke & Oomen, 2009; Sherry et al., 2006). Only 37% of Latina immigrants who are survivors of sexual assault seek medical assistance, with even fewer seeking police, legal, or social service assistance (Pitts, 2014). On the individual level, fear of deportation, concern for children's safety, language barriers, shame, and level of acculturation may impact an individual's ability to seek services or leave an abusive environment. From a cultural perspective, additional barriers for Latina immigrants may include attributes such as *marianismo*, which includes machismo, where the husband makes the majority of decisions in relationships; *simpatia*, maintaining harmony in family; and *familismo*, valuing family loyalty (Alvarez & Fedock, 2018; Amerson, Whittington, & Duggan, 2014; Bauer et al., 2000; Burke & Oomen, 2009; Faulkner & Mansfield, 2002; Reina et al., 2014; Vidales, 2010). Latina women who are undocumented have similar rates of IPV to Latina women who are permanent residents; however, undocumented Latina immigrants tend to seek services less frequently (Page et al., 2017; Zadnik, Sabina, & Cuevas, 2016).

However, although Latinos are the largest cultural group in the country (U.S. Census Bureau, 2018), there continues to be a paucity of ethnic studies on IPV and Latina women who are immigrants. Furthermore, it is difficult to find rates on IPV among Latina subpopulations such as Mexican, Puerto Rican, Spanish, Cuban, Dominican, etc., as ethnicity in most national data has commonly been listed as simply Latina/o. Many of the studies that have focused on the Latina population have utilized data collection instruments designed primarily for Euro-American populations and have simply applied them to Latinas and other ethnic groups. Furthermore, statistics regarding domestic violence in Latino communities are problematic due to inconsistent data collection methods, immigration issues, and under-reporting of inci-dences (Klevens, 2007; Perilla, 1999; USDJ, 2016). Marital rape in Latino marriages appears to be disturbingly high, at rates of up to 80–90% for Latina women currently in abusive relationships (Perilla, 1999). One study indicated that 92% of Latino male batterers and 85% of Latina women inti-mate partner support group attendees reported witnessing their father abuse their mother when these individuals were growing up (Erez, Adelman, & Gregory, 2009). In addition to physical abuse, the incidence of psychological abuse is also very high among Latinas. Over 80% report experiencing this type of aggression, and they tend to experience greater trauma-related symp-toms from the abuse than non-Latinas, including depression and lower self-esteem (Edelson, Hokoda, & Ramos-Lira, 2007). Latina survivors of IPV may also experience comorbidities and risk for HIV, substance abuse, and mental health issues (Gonzalez-Guarda et al., 2011). Alvarez and Fedock (2018) confirm the need for more applied, evidence-based, culturally appro-priate interventions and programs for Latina women to increase access to safety and reduce repeat victimization for improved psychosocial and health outcomes.

The purpose of this grounded theory research study was to contribute to the understanding of intimate partner abuse from the perspective of Latina victims and survivors of that abuse, using in-depth interviews with 15 Latina survivors of intimate partner abuse in North Texas. Grounded theory was used in conducting and analyzing these interviews to identify themes and patterns regarding the nature and process of intimate partner abuse among these women.

Methodology

Grounded theory

For this study, the researchers used a grounded theory methodology. Grounded theory is a qualitative research approach used to generate a theory from data that are systematically gathered and analyzed throughout the research pro-cess (Glaser, 1992, 2001; Strauss & Corbin, 1998). Unlike deductive meth-ods in which the researcher starts with hypotheses or research questions, in grounded theory the researcher instead applies an inductive approach, starting with a well-defined research problem based on a phenomenon that is not adequately explained by current theories. Grounded theory methodology is often used in case studies for the investigation of new concepts and formulation of new theories.

Grounded theory assumes that people living with a similar experience share a specific social–psychological problem or issue that is often unarticulated (Hutchinson, 1993). The theory is particularly useful for areas in which existing theory is weak or does not seem applicable to practice. In this study, the researcher utilized grounded theory methodology because of its unique attributes for studying the issue of intimate partner abuse in a population for which limited culturally appropriate research was available.

In the grounded theory research process, themes and patterns are identified from the analysis of the data as they are collected. This process sheds light on additional questions that need to be asked and additional data that need to be examined. Diagrams are used to demonstrate the relationships between the phenomena documented in the data. In the diagram, matrices are used to identify themes emerging from the study and to show the process(es) that appear to be related to the phenomenon (Strauss & Corbin, 1998).

The goal of grounded theory is to determine the representativeness of concepts and how those concepts differ, and then to develop a theory that explains a behavior pattern in terms of its relevance for the population and the problem being studied (Glaser, 1992, 2001; Strauss & Corbin, 1998). To accomplish this goal, the researcher must be able to accurately perceive and present the world of those being studied (Hutchinson, 1993) as well as maintain an objective stance and an openness to listen to different viewpoints (Strauss & Corbin, 1998). One way to accomplish this is through multiple interviews. Because intimate partner abuse is a sensitive and highly charged issue, this approach for ensuring objectivity was followed for this study.

Recruitment of study participants

Study participants for the interviews were recruited from the greater Dallas/ Fort Worth are using a bilingual (Spanish/English) flyer that described the research project and asked those who were interested in participating in the study to contact the researcher via phone or email. Eligibility for the study was restricted to Latina women over the age of 18 who were self-reported survivors of intimate partner abuse. A $20 gift certificate to a national retail outlet store was offered to those who participated in the study. The minimum number of participants to be interviewed for the study was 15 women.

Copies of the flyer were distributed by email, mail, or in person to community organizations, key leaders, and gatekeepers serving the Latina population and IPV in the Dallas/Fort Worth area, including social service and immigrant assistance agencies, health care services, women's shelters, IPA and IPV services, churches, and universities. They were asked to disseminate the study information to immigrant Latinas in their organizations and refer potential participants as appropriate. A bilingual copy of the flyer was also published in a local Latino newspaper. This snowball sample recruitment method was designed to solicit a varied sample representing immigrant Latina women from different socioeconomic levels, ages, and current and/or past status of abuse.

A total of 15 women contacted the researcher by phone to participate in the study. All of these individuals met the study criteria, and an interview was scheduled for each of them at a location that was determined to be safe, private, and convenient. When preferred by the participant, the interview was scheduled to be conducted via phone at a time when confidentiality could be ensured by both parties. Eleven of the interviews were conducted in person, with seven of the participants interviewed in their homes, two in relatively private areas in restaurants, and two in a social service agency meeting room. The other four interviews were conducted via phone, scheduled at a time and/or location that was considered safe by the participants and the researcher. Prior to the interviews, in-person participants submitted their signed informed consent forms (bilingual versions were provided) to the researcher; phone participants submitted theirs via mail. Participants were made aware of local counseling services and a licensed counselor who they could see should participation trigger negative emotions or memories. The participants also were informed that they could stop participating in the study at any time.

The participants ranged in age from 26 to 56 years, with a median age of 39 years. The majority of the women self-identified as Mexican. One woman was Puerto Rican and one woman was Argentinean. Six were married, seven were divorced, one was separated, and one was widowed. Their formal education backgrounds ranged from eighth grade to some college. Four were employed as administrative assistants, three as part-time teachers' aides, three as homemakers, two as clerical staff, two as computer support specialists, and one as a cleaner of homes and businesses. Their annual household incomes ranged from $10,000 to $40,000.

The interviews

The in-depth interviews were conducted on an ongoing basis as participants were recruited. Applying the grounded theory methodology, the participants guided the interview process.

Interview questions became more detailed and specific to the responses of the participants as the themes emerged. The seven core questions, available in both Spanish and English, were:

1   Define abuse.
2   Have you, or someone close to you, experienced intimate partner abuse by a spouse, boyfriend, or loved one?
3   When did this abuse begin?
4   How often did you or someone close to you experience the abuse?
5   What feelings and emotions did you experience as a result of the abuse?

6   How do you feel intimate partner abuse is viewed among people in your culture?
7   What resources such as support services, housing, etc. do you have available to you?

All 15 interviews were recorded with the permission of the participants and were transcribed within one week of each interview. Eleven of the participants were bilingual in Spanish and English, three of whom spoke English as their primary language. For the four participants who spoke Spanish only, two bilingual translators assisted the researcher with the interviews and transcription of the recordings. Both translators were gatekeepers in the Latino community who were familiar to the participants and with whom they felt comfortable discussing their intimate partner abuse experiences. The researcher also took notes on the English-speaking participants' comments, and the bilingual translators took notes on the interviews conducted in Spanish.

While no restriction was placed on the maximum length for each interview, most of them lasted about 60 to 75 minutes. One interview was four hours long. The participants reported experiencing a range of intimate partner abuse, including physical, verbal, emotional, sexual, financial, and property abuse. Despite asking in the interview questions if the participant or someone close to the participant had experienced intimate partner abuse in the past, all women interviewed were currently in, or had been in, an abusive relationship themselves. At the time of the interviews, some of the women were living with their abusive spouse or partner; others were currently remarried to a different spouse; one participant was a surviving widow; and one participant was in a transitional housing (shelter) arrangement. At the conclusion of the interview, each participant was provided with the gift certificate and a referral list of local IPV resources.

Analyzing the data

Once initial interview data were collected, the researcher began analyzing the data using the grounded theory method. Each interview was analyzed line-by-line for emerging themes and patterns. This process involved dividing the data into concepts, identifying categories of concepts, assigning properties to the categories, organizing categories into themes, and developing a theoretical construct from the common themes. Diagrams were used by the researcher to verify a relationship between the researcher's memos, field notes, and the theory. Matrices were then used to categorize the data and further demonstrate the emerging themes.

Results

A number of repeated themes emerged from the interview data. Participants' fear, sadness, immobilization, lack of resources, and self-blame were often cited as reasons the women continued to stay in their abusive relationships.

The Latin American value and expectations of marianismo surfaced as a key cultural influence. Marianismo is a counterpart to machismo, and a traditional gender-role expectation that the Latina woman is self-sacrificing, faithful, family-oriented, and submissive to her partner. Because the women wanted what was best for their families and usually had limited financial and social resources as well as a great deal of fear, they stayed in the abusive cycle. In addition, the women were afraid that if they left, they would not be able to provide for their children, that the abusive partner would kill them, that they would lose custody of their children, or that they would be deported to their home country. By sacrificing their own happiness and needs in the relationship in an effort to uphold their cultural values and norms, the women were able to redefine their situation as livable, tolerable, understandable, reasonable, and survivable.

From the themes and concepts that emerged from the analysis of the inter-view data, the intimate partner abuse process experienced by these Latina women in its various forms included multiple phases, with the final phase involving either continuation of the abuse or escape from it. The phases that emerged from the data include (1) The Pursuit, (2) The Abuse Begins, (3) The Abuse Continues or Escalates, and (4) End of the Abuse or Escape to a New Life. This four-phase process, and the emergent themes, risk factors, and cultural considerations related to those phases, are presented in Figure 3.1.

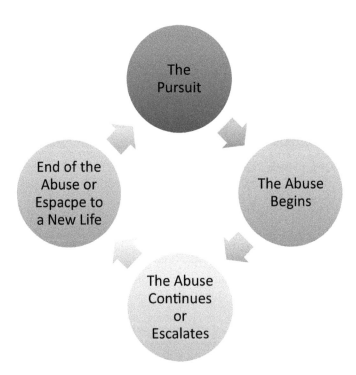

Figure 3.1

Phase 1 – The Pursuit

The first phase identified through the interview data was The Pursuit, which involved meeting the abuser and the courtship process. Themes that emerged were the young age of the woman when she met her partner, the strong intensity of the abuser's pursuit, the initial kind and loving nature of the relationship, and the dependency created by pregnancy.

Twelve of the 15 participants interviewed were either 19 years old or younger when they first met their partner. Some of the women reported that the abuser strongly pursued them and repeatedly asked them for dates. Most of them viewed the treatment of their abusive partners as very sweet and attentive in the beginning, describing their relationship as filled with romance and kindness. Through the interviews, some of the women expressed sadness and nostalgia as they reminisced about happier days. One participant shared her memory of the first encounter as a romantic experience but also had a sense of being stalked by her pursuer:

> I was young and had someone approach me at a bus stop on my way to school. But he approached me in a very peering form. We just talked. But I would see him every morning at the bus stop. We grew to know each other.

Another common theme of this first phase was that many participants said they had gotten pregnant early in the courtship, thereby becoming seriously involved with the partner after only knowing him a short period of time. As pregnant young women without economic resources, they felt very dependent on their partners. It seemed to them that the most logical decision was to marry or move in with their boyfriend, which they did within a few months or less. Due to a lack of money, many of them had to live with the parents of their abusive partner, which added to the stress in their relationship. One woman said that she wished she had stayed with her best girlfriend and not even told her boyfriend (who later became her abusive spouse) about the pregnancy.

Phase 2 – The Abuse Begins

In creating the themes that provided the pattern of behavior identified as the second phase of the abuse process, The Abuse Begins, the women discussed how the abuse started for them. The women characterized the first incident of abuse, the type and frequency of the early incidences of abuse, the unpredictability of how and when it would happen, and the fact that the abuse sometimes occurred in front of the children and other people.

The participants described the type of abuse as emotional, physical, verbal, or mental. In most cases, the women described the first incident of physical abuse as usually starting with a slap, push, or shove, and then later escalating to levels more violent and shocking such as hits to the face, asphyxiation, kicking while they were asleep, marital rape, or use of such force that one woman was bleeding from her ear. Of the 15 women interviewed, six had been the victims of marital rape. One woman said that she had a hard time classifying the abuse she experienced as being physical abuse, since she was not maimed.

Many of the participants reported the abuse as occurring fairly frequently, often daily, sometimes as verbal incidents or forced isolation, with the physical violence being more intermittent. Others shared that the abuse was less frequent, occurring once or twice a month or every couple of months. Although the frequency of abuse varied from person to person, its randomness, incongruence, and unpredictability were constant themes. One participant described her abuse as beginning relatively early in the relationship, and that she never knew what was going to incite her abuser:

> *I would say the abuse started about four or five months into the relationship. It started real light. It started with a slap. And then all of a sudden you are in over your head and it is happening all day long.*

The interviews showed that the abuse sometimes occurred in front of other people, with the most painful recollections being when the abuse would occur in front of the children. One woman spoke of the time when her husband was abusing her while her three children hid under a table, covering their ears, crying hysterically. Another woman shared that she hated how she appeared in her children's eyes when she was being abused. She wanted them to be proud of her and to respect her. However, due to the traditional cultural belief of marianismo that Latina women should value their children and their family as the most important aspects of their lives and demonstrate loyalty and sacrifice for their family, they are apt to tolerate and endure the abuse (Bart and Moran, 1993).

Phase 3 – The Abuse Continues or Escalates

In the third phase of the abuse process identified through the interviews, The Abuse Continues or Escalates, the data collected from the participants shows a pattern where the abuse persists, and in most cases moves to a higher intensity, with the abusers utilizing various techniques to further manipulate the women into staying in the relationship. The themes that emerged for this phase were excessive violence, the threat of taking the children, alienation, and issues of control (social, financial, appearance, driving, working, and other).

Participants provided accounts of their experiences with excessive violence, which included kidnapping and confinement, marital rape, being threatened or attacked with a lethal weapon, and abuse while the woman was pregnant or delivering the baby. In this study, four of the 15 participants reported that they were assaulted with lethal weapons, including guns and knives, and over half of the women reported receiving extreme abuse during their pregnancy such that they had to receive medical attention for their injuries. In one of the interviews, the participant provided an emotional account of her near-deadly abuse:

> *We were living in a garage, where they fix cars, a body shop. We were all living in one room in the garage – all four of us were living in this one room. We would take a bath with a water hose. We had a tiny refrigerator and a little stove-top burner. We lived in a bad neighborhood. His [the abuser's] idea of going out was walking across the street to this bar. At that point in time, it was really bad; it was one time where he really abused me bad. When he was done with me I looked like one of those posters at the shelter. He had totally disfigured my face. I thought I was going to stay that way. He actually put a gun to my head and pulled the trigger. I thought I was going to die, but the gun wasn't loaded. He said, See I can kill you any time I want.*

Repeatedly, the women said that they feared leaving because of the possibility of losing their children. This seemed to be more common among the women who had immigrated from Mexico. One woman shared that her children were number one and that only God could separate them. All of these women had at least two children to provide and care for as they struggled through their abusive situations.

The women shared how their partners would attempt to alienate them from the outside world and used various ways to prevent them from gaining autonomy or independence. A few of the women had moved to the US from Mexico in search of a better life and had limited resources once they arrived as well as language barriers. They described how their abusive partner would control how they could dress, what they could wear, and the money they could spend on clothes, shoes, and make-up. The abusers would also prohibit some of the women from driving, getting rides, or having access to the car.

While these were extremely traumatic and painful experiences for these women, for a few of them the escalating abuse became the turning point for their decision to leave, or at least to question why they were in the abusive relationship.

Phase 4 – End of the Abuse or Escape to a New Life

The fourth and final phase of the abuse process identified through the interviews, End of the Abuse or Escape to a New Life, offers two alternative outcomes: either the abuse stops or the woman leaves the relationship permanently and begins a new life free of the abuse. The themes that emerged for this phase included questioning of why they were staying in the relationship, temporary cessation of abuse, leave/return re-cycling, stalking, assistance from friends/family, use of community support services, feelings of grief and depression, and finding the strength and courage to leave for good.

All 15 of the participants said that they questioned why they were continuing to stay in an abusive relationship in which they were beaten down physically, emotionally, and spiritually. Unfortunately, for these women, the abuse only subsided in frequency or intensity; it did not end permanently. Most of the participants reported going through a repetitive leave/return process during this phase, in which they would leave the relationship when the abuse had reached an unbearable level and then return (often as a result of the abusive partner finding them and convincing them to come back), then leave again when the abuse started again or escalated and then go back, in many cases re-cycling through this process several times. Of the 15 participants in the study, 11 of them eventually left the abusive relationship permanently; the other four reported that the abuse had subsided, at least for the present, and remained with their partners.

To help them escape from the abuse, the women sought the assistance of friends, family, or community support services such as law enforcement agencies and shelters. When they left, some women (n = 6) were stalked and terrorized by their former partners, sometimes across state or US borders, with two of the participants filing restraining orders to help ensure their safety. Some women had considered calling the police to help them, but were afraid that it would make things worse for them or perceived the police as unsupportive. Those who did involve the police said they found them to be very helpful and even pivotal in their escape from their abusive partner.

Community shelters played a role in the women's efforts to escape to a new life. Many of the participants expressed feelings of skepticism in seeking these services, and some of them were unaware that these resources were available to them. Upon referral by the police department, four of the women utilized these shelters. Two of them perceived their experience at the shelters as negative due to issues such as lack of privacy, sleeping on cots, not feeling welcomed, a lack of Spanish-speaking coordinators, feelings of shame, discomfort with relying on governmental resources, or having to share space with homeless people that were dirty men, and decided to return back to their abusive environment.

Most of the women experienced intense grief, depression, and sadness from the loss of the abusive spouse, loss of the memories, loss of a father for their children, loss of what could have been. Two of the women reported that after leaving, they came very close to committing suicide. One woman shared that despite the abuse, she missed her husband, who had died in a car crash, because, believe it or not, there had been some good times.

Despite their sadness, the women who left their abusive partners also described their renewed view of life, free from abuse. As one of the survivors who had escaped expressed her feelings:

> *There is a way, it is not easy. It is never easy. But I look at my life now.*
> *I am a mother of four beautiful children. My oldest is going to the*

Marines. My other ones are graduating from high school. My daughter wants to be a nurse. We have goals. I am an administrative assistant at the elementary school. I am buying my own home. There is a way out. You are either a survivor or not. There is a light down there. You don't see it at first, but eventually you do.

By finding the strength and courage to leave the abusive relationship for good, these women attempted to redirect their lives and begin a new life, free from abuse. They were able to seek a safe place for themselves and, more importantly from their perspective, their children. With the support of friends, family, law enforcement, and shelters, these women were able to begin a new chapter in their lives.

For those that continued in the abuse and remained in Phase 3, one can only hope that they too will ultimately escape from the relationship if the abuse does not stop. If not, the last phase for them could unfortunately be serious debilitating injury or even death.

Risk factors and cultural considerations

Throughout all of these phases, a number of risk factors and cultural considerations emerged from the interview data as important factors that impacted the abuse process. Self-identified risk factors related to the abusive relationships included drugs and alcohol, infidelity, and history of parents having been abused. The themes related to cultural considerations unique to this population that emerged also included the definition of abuse as perceived by Latinas, fear of deportation, non-disclosure of the abuse, marianismo, and religiosity.

Thirteen of the 15 participants reported that drugs and/or alcohol played a large part in the abusive relationship, with the abuse escalating when their partner was drinking or using drugs. A third of the women said that they were afraid for Friday to come due to their partner's alcohol consumption and the subsequent increase in the incidence and intensity of abuse.

Over half of the participants voiced frustration concerning their partner's unfaithfulness. One woman explained that the reason she received the abuse was because she had confronted her husband about his affairs. Another woman shared that her abusive partner would leave for days at a time while she cooked, cleaned, and took care of their two children, and then come home with "hickies on his neck and lipstick on his clothing."

Many of the women (n = 11) reported that their own parents were the victims of abuse. Several said their mother was their role model, and because they witnessed their mother's abuse, they felt it was either an acceptable or normal part of marriage or a reason why they themselves were in an abusive relationship. As one participant recounted:

My mother was in that situation. I remember my mom telling me her hair was in a braid and one night while she was sleeping, my dad cut her braid off. My mom doesn't talk with me about it really and I don't need her too. She doesn't want to think about it anymore.

Another woman reported that her father probably felt that he was unable to offer her advice as she left her abusive spouse because he had been abusive to his family himself.

Many of the immigrant women reported that their abusive partners would threaten them with deportation, making them fear that they would have to go back to Mexico without their children.

One of the strongest cultural-related themes that emerged was the notion of silence to hide the abuse from others. Again, they expressed that they wanted to be a good wife and not make the husband look bad to outsiders or appear to be complaining about their "lot in life; to shut up and take it," as one participant described it.

A theme of religiosity also surfaced in the interviews. Belief in God and faith in the Catholic Church were considered a solace for some, while others considered religion to be an unsupportive entity for them. Most of the participants felt that it was God's intention for them to marry their loved one, but not to endure the tremendous abuse. As some of the women began finding the courage to leave, they also began to question God's intentions. One woman shared that she no longer feels an intimate spiritual relationship with God, as an omnipotent male figure, and feels more comfortable seeking solace with the Virgin Mary. Two of the women interviewed also mentioned the practice of *bruharia*, a Mexican tradition of witchcraft, in trying to deal with and ameliorate their abusive situations.

Discussion

Through this qualitative study, using in-depth interviews and grounded theory methodology, a theory regarding the process of intimate partner abuse among Latina women was developed. From the themes and patterns that emerged from the interview data, the researcher determined that the abuse process for these Latinas involved four phases: The Pursuit, The Abuse Begins, The Abuse Continues or Escalates, and End of the Abuse or Escape to a New Life. In addition to the identification of these four phases of the abuse process, risk factors and cultural aspects that appeared to affect the process also surfaced through analysis of the interview data.

Factors affecting the ability to leave

The study data revealed that for the Latina survivors of intimate partner abuse who are immigrants, finding the courage to leave was a great challenge filled with many hardships, struggles, fears, and painful emotions. Their abusive partners' use of measures to impose control (such as confinement, violence, and withholding money), their tendency toward self-sacrifice, their value of the sanctity of marriage, their feelings of love toward their abuser, and, most importantly, the fear of losing their children or control over how they would be raised kept many of the women in their abusive relationships.

Fear of deportation is also a very powerful tool used by abusers to prevent battered immigrant women from seeking help and to keep them in violent relationships (Page et al., 2017; Shetty & Kaguyutan, 2002). In this research, the fear of being reported to immigration authorities or deportation was found as an emergent theme since almost half of the participants in this study had immigrated to the US.

As in other studies, language was also identified in this study as a barrier to their leaving. For many Latinos, Spanish is their primary or only spoken language, and if they do not feel comfortable or able to communicate with resource agencies due to a lack of Spanish-speaking staff and volunteers, this presents a huge barrier to their willingness to access resources (Amerson et al., 2014; Cuevas et al., 2014; Erez et al., 2009; Sherry et al., 2006). Research has confirmed that due to language barriers, some Latina women are not aware of protective orders or of resources available to them from state and local agencies; several studies have indicated that Latinas are hesitant to use safe living resources such as shelters or to seek assistance from police or other formal sources (Amerson et al., 2014; Cuevas et al., 2014; Ingram, 2007; Shetty & Kaguyutan, 2002), which is consistent with findings among the Latina women interviewed in this study who are immigrants.

The tendency identified in these interviews toward non-disclosure of the abuse has also been reported in the literature as a main theme for all survivors of intimate partner violence, regardless of race or ethnicity. However, this characteristic appears to be more pronounced in the Latino culture, which emphasizes trust, loyalty, pride, marriage, a strong maternal role (marianismo), and commitment, and where women are taught from childhood to be tolerant of the abuse and to be a loyal and accepting wife (Faulkner & Mansfield, 2002; Rodriguez, 1999; Vidales, 2010). The Latino family has been characterized as a sealed container, impenetrable by anyone from the outside (Perilla, 1999).

This study also revealed that while these women sometimes gain the courage to leave, when faced with a lack of resources they may find themselves back with their abusive partner. But when some among them experienced an accumulation of hurt, pain, and disappointment that finally outweighed the hope of improvement or of gaining a positive home life for their children, they were able to break free of their abusive relationships. Eleven of the 15 women interviewed were able to find the resources, both internally and externally, to leave their abuser permanently for a better life free from abuse.

Identifying abuse

The results of this study support many of the findings of other relevant research on this issue and underscore the notion that previous research has been inconsistent regarding what constitutes abuse (Campbell et al., 2003; Edelson, Hokoda, & Ramos-Lira, 2007; Klevens, 2007; Perilla, 1999; Rodriguez, 1999). The study emphasizes the importance of understanding how abuse is perceived or defined by those who experience the abuse. It also reinforces that some aspects of the Latino culture, including religious beliefs and family values, can affect those perceptions and definitions, as well as the woman's decision to stay in or leave the relationship.

Limitations of the study

While this exploratory, grounded theory study provided many important insights regarding the abuse process experienced by Latina women, several limitations regarding this study should be mentioned. A primary limitation was the small sample size (n = 15), with participants recruited via the snowball effect technique. Second, the sample was limited to Latina women living in the Dallas/Fort Worth area and was not very diverse in terms of the participants' Latino heritage, with most self-identifying as Mexican. Therefore, the findings of this study, although they are useful in demonstrating common patterns in the cycle of abuse, should not be inferred to represent experiences of all Mexican women or experiences of women from other Latino subcultures.

It is assumed that respondents answered honestly and to the best of their knowledge with the information presented. However, because many of the abuse incidences occurred in the past, the information collected was based on the participant's ability to recall or recount specific situations as they remembered them, potentially compromising the accuracy of the content.

Implications

The findings from this study provide many implications for intimate partner violence prevention and assistance programs for Latina women. Survivors of intimate partner abuse experience a wide range of emotions, including shame, fear, guilt, pain, anger, isolation, hopelessness, and alienation. The issue of violence is multi-faceted, involving many social, psychological, cultural, and systems aspects. Violence, coupled with the cultural issue of being a Latina immigrant, makes this issue an even more complex and challenging one.

Most of the women in this study gained the courage to leave their abusive partner because they felt they had no more to give. The pain of the abuse outweighed the exchange of security. These women need early prevention strategies and evidence-based and culturally relevant services to assist them before they are broken down and find themselves without resources.

Community outreach and social support offer tremendous potential for helping Latina women. Outreach through trained community gatekeepers, or *promotores*, can provide women with a safe person with whom they can speak confidentially and from whom they can seek assistance. More resources and navigators need to be available for Latina women in shelters, safe houses, and other community centers that provide culturally appropriate relationship abuse information and services in Spanish. In this study, the women's dissatisfaction with the facilities in which they stayed may have been due to the fact that they were general shelters, not specific to survivors of intimate partner violence, and that they lacked privacy, security, and had only minimal domestic abuse counseling or assistance. To increase the likelihood that the women will elect to stay in these safe-haven facilities rather than returning to the abusive situation, it is important that referrals are made to the appropriate culturally enhanced services. Funding agencies must provide financial support for these shelters and ensure that ample room is available for these women and their children. Immigrant service providers can serve as an important gatekeeper to navigate those in need to IPA services.

Our schools are one of the most effective mechanisms for prevention and intervention. Starting at the elementary level, healthy relationships, respectful boundaries, and anti-toxic masculinity education programs should be included as key components in the curriculum, including for English language learners. Educational strategies that include family-approaches and supportive resources are warranted. Prevention strategies, including the recognition of warning signs of control and power abuse, should be developed for the school-aged population. Teaching egalitarian concepts to Latino children would also serve as a key component in educational approaches to decreasing family violence. Instructing children that women have just as much decision-making power and importance in their role in the family as men is critical. Early evidence-based education programs for students that address relationship violence as early as fifth grade in schools may have a positive impact on young individuals before violence occurs. Nonprofit agencies whose mission is relationship violence prevention can play an important role in implementing culturally relevant programs among middle and high schools and with college populations in their local communities and counties (CDC, 2017; WEAVE, 2019).

Because the Catholic Church may play a role within this culture, it is a key entity for the provision of education and resources for victims of IPV and IPA. This study revealed that many of the women found solace in the Catholic Church during their recovery. Others abandoned the church because of the perception that their intimate partner abuse issues were dismissed by the church's representatives. By providing culturally appropriate resource materials and counselors focused on the intimate partner abuse issue in the Latino population, the Catholic Church could be a very effective leader in the prevention of this problem.

Language and transportation problems are issues Latina immigrant women experience and will require additional funding and culturally competent bilingual staffing to be addressed by social service agencies. Police departments, especially in small rural or agricultural areas that may have a high percentage of Latina migrant and seasonal farmworkers (MSFW), should employ at least one bilingual staff person that is fluent in Spanish, comfortable with the Latino population, and aware of the community resources that are available to those experiencing relationship violence.

It is important that Latina women who are immigrants be educated on deportation laws and rights. It is critical to dispel the myth that children can be taken away from mothers when they report being abused by their partner. Information on available resources should be displayed prominently in areas such as markets and local women's clinics that immigrant Latina women frequent.

Since drugs and alcohol were again identified as a risk factor for the abuse, more culturally appropriate intervention programs should be provided by community organizations, nonprofits, service agencies, and gatekeepers that include consideration of cultural factors and an emphasis on coping strategies for the abuser. The public health problem of intimate partner abuse is a complex condition that will be most effectively impacted with a series of integrated, evidence-based approaches.

For the women in this study, pregnancy was identified as one of the main indicators for beginning a committed relationship or marriage with their future abusive partners. A cultural barrier for Latinas may be the Catholic Church's position on birth control. Programs that effectively and openly discuss contraception management and pregnancy prevention are crucial for middle and high school students to prevent teen or unwanted pregnancy. Community gatekeepers of this population with specialization in family planning and contraception management can be an effective outreach resource to educate this population on intimate partner violence.

Employment options and income stability may be a challenge for immigrant women. As such, workforce development and economic empowerment programs may be critical to the well-being of female survivors of IPV and their children (Gilroy, Symes, & McFarlane, 2015; Page et al., 2017). The CDC (2017) recommends strengthening household financial security and engaging influential adults and peers through family-based programs.

Mass media that target the Latino community should be used to increase awareness of intimate partner violence as well as what resources are available to the domestic abuse victims. Novellas, Latino TV networks and talk shows, Spanish online and social media outlets, and other Latino media outlets are key health communication mechanisms that can be utilized for public service announcements and dramatizations showing women overcoming intimate partner abuse.

Lastly, collaborative projects, symposia, and conferences on the topic of relationship violence among Latina women would be useful in sharing research and intervention applications among health and social service professionals.

Future research

Additional studies including both quantitative research as well as qualitative research using a larger sample of immigrant Latina women is warranted in order to gain a rich, reflective, and accurate view of the intimate partner abuse that Latina women who are immigrants experience, and to identify effective intervention and prevention strategies. Further exploration of Latina women's efforts to leave the abusive relationship and the resources they use to help them escape is needed. Extreme violence and stalking were issues that this sample encountered. Further research in these areas could provide insight into any cultural considerations that may be associated with these behaviors. Comparisons between Latina women's experiences and women from other groups, including nonimmigrant Latinas, would be helpful in further defining the abuse processes, and any characteristics unique to those groups would aid in designing more culturally appropriate and effective intervention, prevention, and education programs.

An acknowledgment to the study participants

The women in this study all met their partners with the vision of having a life of love, comfort, and happiness, to be a good wife and mother. Instead, they soon found themselves living in an environment of control, oppression, isolation, fear, pain, and a struggle to survive. By overcoming barriers and cultural challenges associated with intimate partner abuse, most of these women gained the courage and strength to leave and begin a new life. For the four women who are still with their abusive partners, they had the courage to take a risk and speak out by participating in these interviews. They spoke out on behalf of Latina women everywhere who are being abused, so that those women will realize they do not need to suffer in silence; and for that alone, they are courageous.

References

Alvarez, C., Davidson, P. M., Fleming, C., & Glass, N. 2016. Elements of effective intervention for addressing intimate partner violence in Latina women: A systematic review. *PLoS One*, 11(8), e0160518.

Alvarez, C., & Fedock, G. 2018. Addressing intimate partner violence with Latina women: A call for research. *Trauma, Violence, & Abuse*, 19(4), 488–493.

Amerson, R., Whittington, R., & Duggan, L. 2014. Intimate partner violence affecting Latina women and their children. *Journal of Emergency Nursing*, 40, 531–536.

Bauer, H. M., Rodriguez, M. A., Quiroga, S. S., & Flores-Ortiz, Y. G. 2000. Barriers to health care for abused Latina and Asian immigrant women. *Journal of Health Care for the Poor and Underserved*, 11, 33–44.

Bonomi, A. E., Anderson, M. L., Cannon, E. A., Slesnick, N., & Rodriguez, M. A. 2009. Intimate partner violence in Latina and non-Latina women. *American Journal of Preventive Medicine*, 36, 43–48. e41.

Breiding, M. J., Chen, J., & Black, M. C. 2014. *Intimate partner violence in the United States-2010*. Atlanta, GA: Centers for Disease Control and Prevention, National Center for Injury Prevention and Control.

Bureau of Justice Statistics. 2018. *Intimate partner violence. 1995–2015*. Washington, DC: Bureau of Justice Statistics.

Burke, S., & Early, J. O. 2009. Latina women's experiences with intimate partner abuse: A grounded theory approach. *Family Violence Prevention & Health Practice*, 2(9), online.

Campbell, J. C., Webster, D., Koziol-McLain, J., Block, C., Campbell, D., Curry, M. A., Gary, F., Glass, N., McFarlane, J., Sachs, C., Sharps, P., Ulrich, Y., Wilt, S. A., Manganello, J., Xu, X., Schollenburger, J., Frye, V., & Laughon, K. 2003. Risk factors for femicide in abusive relationships: Results from a multisite case control study. *American Journal of Public Health*, 93, 1089–1097.

Centers for Disease Control and Prevention. 2017. Preventing intimate partner violence across the lifespan: A technical package of programs, policies, and practices. Retrieved October 28, 2018, from www.cdc.gov/violenceprevention/pdf/ipv-tech nicalpackages.pdf.

Cuevas, C. A., Bell, K. A., & Sabina, C. 2014. Victimization, psychological distress, and help-seeking: Disentangling the relationship for Latina victims. *Psychology of Violence*, 4, 196–209.

Cuevas, C. A., Sabina, C., & Picard, E. 2010. Interpersonal victimization patterns and psychopathology among Latino women: Results from the SALAS study. *Psychological Trauma: Theory, Research, Practice, and Policy*, 2, 296–306.

Edelson, M. G., Hokoda, A., & Ramos-Lira, L. 2007. Differences in effects of domestic violence between Latina and non-Latina women. *Journal of Family Violence*, 22(1), 1–10.

Erez, E., Adelman, M., & Gregory, C. 2009. Intersections of immigration and domestic violence: Voices of battered immigrant women. *Feminist Criminology*, 4, 32–56.

Faulkner, S. L., & Mansfield, P. K. 2002. Reconciling messages: The process of sexual talk for Latinas. *Qualitative Health Research*, 12, 310–328.

Gilroy, H., Symes, L., & McFarlane, J. 2015. Economic solvency in the context of violence against women: A concept analysis. *Health and Social Care in the Community*, 23(2), 97–106.

Glaser, B. G. 1992. *Basics of grounded theory: Emergence vs. forcing.* Mill Valley, CA: Sociology Press.

Glaser, B. G. 2001. *The grounded theory perspective: Conceptualization contrasted with description.* Mill Valley, CA: Sociology Press.

Gonzalez-Guarda, R. M., Vasquez, E. P., Urrutia, M. T., Villarruel, A. M., & Peragallo, N. 2011. Hispanic women's experiences with substance abuse, intimate partner violence, and risk for HIV. *Journal of Transcultural Nursing: Official Journal of the Transcultural Nursing Society/Transcultural Nursing Society*, 22, 46–54.

Hutchinson, S. A. 1993. People with bipolar disorders quest for equanimity: Doing grounded theory. In P. Munhall & C. Boyd (Eds.), *Nursing research: A qualitative perspective* (pp. 213–236). New York: National League for Nursing Press.

Ingram, E. M. 2007. A comparison of help seeking between Latino and non-Latino victims of intimate partner violence. *Violence against Women*, 13, 59–171.

Klevens, J. 2007. An overview of intimate partner violence among Latinos. *Violence against Women*, 13, 111–122.

Page, R. L., Chilton, J., Montalvo-Liendo, N., Matthews, D., & Nava, A. 2017. Empowerment in Latina immigrant women recovering from interpersonal violence: A concept analysis. *Journal of Transcultural Nursing*, 28(6), 531–539.

Perilla, J. L. 1999. Domestic violence as a human rights issue: The case of immigrant Latinos. *Hispanic Journal of Behavioral Science*, 21, 107–122.

Pitts, K. M. 2014. Latina immigrants, interpersonal violence, and the decision to report to police. *Journal of Interpersonal Violence*, 29(9), 1661–1678.

Reina, A. S., Lohman, B. J., & Maldonado, M. M. 2014. "He said they'd deport me": Factors influencing domestic violence help-seeking practices among Latina immigrants. *Journal of Interpersonal Violence*, 29, 593–615.

Rodriguez, E. R. August 1999. *Embarazadas y maltratadas: Domestic violence among Latinas*. Occasional Paper No. 94, Julian Samora Research Institute.

Sherry, L., Raul, C., Craig, A. F., & Gregory, L. L. 2006. The role of intimate partner violence, race, and ethnicity in help-seeking behaviors. *Ethnicity & Health*, 11, 81–100.

Shetty, S., & Kaguyutan, J. 2002. Immigrant victims of domestic violence: Cultural challenges and available legal protections. *Minnesota Center against Violence and Abuse*. Retrieved March 20, 2004, from www.vaw.umn.edu/documents/vawnet/arimmigrant/arimmigrant.pdf.

Strauss, A., & Corbin, J. 1998. *Basics of qualitative research: Techniques and procedures for developing grounded theory* (3rd ed.). Newbury Park, CA: Sage Publications.

Swatt, M., & Sabina, C. 2013. *Summary report: Latino intimate partner homicide* (No. Grant No. 2013-IJ-CX-0037). Washington, DC: National Institute of Justice.

U.S. Census Bureau. 2018. Population estimates. Retrieved October 28, 2018, from www.census.gov/topics/population.html.

United States Department of Justice (USDJ). 2016. Bureau of Justice Statistics. Criminal Victimization. Retrieved May 7, 2019, from https://www.bjs.gov/index.cfm?ty=tp&tid=317

Vidales, G. T. 2010. Arrested justice: The multifaceted plight of immigrant Latinas who faced domestic violence. *Journal of Family Violence*, 25, 533–544.

WEAVE. 2019. Domestic Violence. Retrieved May 7, 2019, from https://www.weaveinc.org/get-informed-domestic-violence

Zadnik, E., Sabina, C., & Cuevas, C. A. 2016. Violence against Latinas the effects of undocumented status on rates of victimization and help-seeking. *Journal of Interpersonal Violence*, 31, 1141–1153.

4 Gendered oppression within African-initiated Christian churches in Europe

The case of Amsterdam

Justice Richard Kwabena Owusu Kyei

Defining the problem

The purpose of the study is to understand how African-initiated Christian churches (AICCs) in Amsterdam sanction certain forms of discrimination against women in the religious field. The research investigates the diversified gendered dynamics of oppression within the religious field, especially with the children of immigrants. This chapter contributes to the literature on AICCs (Kyei and Smoczynski 2016; Kyei, Setrana and Smoczynski 2017) as it explores the intersection between migration, gender, and religious oppression within AICCs in Europe in the case of Amsterdam. Adasi and Frempong (2014: 63) noted in their study of female pastors in the Presbyterian Church of Ghana that these women are confronted with socio-cultural setbacks in the execution of their duties. Ndeda (2005) also concluded in her study of the Nomiya Luo Church in Kenya that women battle oppression as female subordination is multifaceted in the church setting. Agadjanian (2015) also concluded in his work on women's leadership in a Christian setting in Mozambique that, in spite of some traits of leadership by women, most women continuously face gendered challenges that deprive them of access to formal leadership. Inglehart and Norris (2003), in their analysis of the World Values and European Values Surveys that took place between 1995 and 2001, noted that gender inequality was limited not only to economic growth and legal-institutional reforms but also to religiosity in particular.

The violence executed in the religious field has not attracted as much attention in gender studies because of research interest in interpersonal violence such as domestic and/or sexual abuse (Morgan and Björkert 2006: 441). Michel Foucault held that power is not a possession that is unequally shared in society but rather an attribute that is constantly negotiated in small, ceaseless, real-time interaction between individuals. For Foucault (1998: 63), power is everywhere and comes from everywhere, so it is neither an agency nor a structure. The theme of power has not attracted much discussion in the literature on religion (Beckford 1983), although classical sociologists like Weber (1992) dealt with religion and economic power; religion and political power have been addressed by Inglehart and Norris (2004). The literature on gender fundamentally holds that females are disadvantaged and disempowered relative to men across the globe (Connell 2002: 97–114). Feminist theorists further argue that difference is not only reproduced but also generates unequal distribution of power based on gender (Walby 1997).

This research focuses on violence that is symbolic and interactional but systematically structured in the social system in ways that make it difficult to identify the effect on female–male relationships. The research asks how second-generation female migrants in AICCs in Amsterdam are oppressed in terms of accessing the religious field. How do second-generation Ghanaians respond to the issue of oppression? Religion is traditionally considered patriarchal and hegemonic due to male dominance in representation, irrespective of female dominance in participation. The chapter is interested in examining how AICCs in Europe in the case of Amsterdam are able to perpetuate gender inequality irrespective of Dutch society's continuous propagation of equal rights of participation and representation for its members.

According to assimilation theorists (Gordon 1964; Portes and Rumbaut 2006), one of the pertinent factors that influences immigrant integration in the host country is immigrants' religion. Studies have established that religious organizations were one of the first institutions established by immigrants (Portes, Guarnizo and Landolt 1999). Ghanaians in the Netherlands, like most immigrant groups, carried their religion with them to the destination country. As some European countries like the Netherlands continue to experience secularization (Knippenberg 2010), there has been an influx of non-Western immigrants for whom religion remains pertinent in both the public and private sphere. Secularization is used here heuristically to mean a low level of church participation and decrease in institutionalized forms of religion. With the consistent fall in the institutionalized religiosity of native Dutch citizens shown in recent surveys in the Netherlands (Bernts, Dekker and De Hart 2007: 14, 17; Becker and De Hart 2006: Annex B3), there is the perception that the proliferation of immigrant religions in the Netherlands will also come to a halt with time.

Immigrant integration studies have for some time identified religion as a stepping stone in the process of immigrant integration; consequently, the long-term contribution of immigrant churches to the socioeconomic and socio-cultural integration of second-generation migrants into the host country was questioned (Alba 2005; Alba and Nee 1997; Alba, Raboteau and DeWind 2009; Gordon 1964). Migration scholars tend to focus on the secular nature of some European countries while downplaying the persistence of religion in the integration process of second generation individuals. Widespread secularization in mainstream European societies (Bruce 2011) has, however, been challenged by counter-developments (see: Berger 1999), especially by the proliferation and persistence of immigrant religious groups (Yip and Nynäs 2012). The interplay between immigration and immigrant Christian churches does not terminate with the search for refuge among first-generation immigrants, but second generations also seek respect and resources (Hirschman 2004) from immigrant religion in the host society. As such, immigrant Christian churches are more likely to survive beyond the initial stages of immigrant settlement in the host country (Ambrosini and Caneva 2009; Baffoe 2013; Portes and Rumbaut 2006; Warner 2007).

Formation of AICCs in the Netherlands

Mass immigration of Ghanaians to the Netherlands is a relatively new phenomenon compared to the massive number of Turkish, Moroccans, Antilleans, and Surinamese immigrants who entered the country from the late 1960s onwards, but the number of Ghanaians has grown steadily in the last three decades (Statistics Netherlands 2015a). According to the Amsterdam Bureau for research and statistics, Ghanaians in the Netherlands numbered about 12,480 in 1996 but as of 2014, the total Ghanaian population had increased to 22,556 (Statistics Netherlands 2015b). The total number of second-generation Ghanaian migrants in the Netherlands has more than doubled. In 1996, there were 3,056 second-generation Ghanaian migrants in the Netherlands, but as of 2014, this had gone up to 8,871 (Statistics Netherlands 2015b). More than half of Ghanaians live in Amsterdam, and they are the fifth largest immigrant group in Amsterdam after the Moroccans, Turkish, Antilleans, and Surinamese (Gemeente Amsterdam 2013: 62).

Most Ghanaian immigrants settled in the Bijlmer district of Amsterdam and, to a lesser extent, in The Hague (Dietz, Mazzucato, Kabki and Smith 2011). Ghanaians in Amsterdam became well known in the Netherlands after a plane crashed into buildings in the southeast of Amsterdam in September 1992, claiming many Ghanaian lives and injuring others (Dietz, Mazzucato, Kabki and Smith 2011; Knipscheer, de Jong, Kleber and Lamptey 2000). Ghanaians in the Netherlands are from different ethnic groups in Ghana, but most of them are Akans and consist of Asantes, Khawu, and the Fante. Ghanaians are visible in the Netherlands through their churches, shops (food, clothing), media (television and radio broadcasting), and magazines. In spite of the medium education level of Ghanaians in the Netherlands, they are employed in semi-skilled and unskilled jobs mainly due to low proficiency in the Dutch language and discrimination in the labor market (Choenni 2002) as well as the cumbersome process of foreign diploma recognition by the Dutch government.

In the Netherlands, a growing number of African-led churches were initiated, mostly by Ghanaians, in the 1990s (Ter Haar 1995). According to Ter Haar (1998: 6), as of 1995 there were about 17 Ghanaian-led churches and as of 1997 40 African-led churches in Amsterdam alone. African-led churches in Amsterdam had grown to about 150 as of 2013 (Van den Bos 2013). There are two main types of Christian churches among Africans in the Netherlands; Mensah (2009) has noted similar divisions in his study of Ghanaian Christian churches in Canada. The first group consists of traditional missionary churches like the Catholic, Methodist, Presbyterian, and Seventh Day Adventist (SDA) churches. The second category consists of those churches that are Pentecostal/Charismatic in nature that were initiated by Africans rather than foreign missionaries; these are referred to in the literature as African-initiated churches (AICs) (Asamoah-Gyadu 2010; Baffoe 2013; Turner 1979).

In this research, AICC is defined as any Christian denomination that was initiated or newly formed in or transplanted to the host country by immigrants of African descent. The presence of co-ethnic churches in the host country provided an avenue for new arrivals to meet people with similar language and worldviews. AICCs in Amsterdam provided the opportunity for some first-generation African migrants to meet and share their experiences, with the aim of helping to shed the stress and trauma that their migration trajectories might have generated. Some AICCs in Amsterdam therefore tried to provide psychosocial well-being services to first-generation African immigrants, which consequently might have influenced their integration into the Netherlands.

Intersecting gendered oppression, religion, and migration

Gender is conceptualized as a system that is culturally constructed in the power relations produced and reproduced in the interactions between and among men and women (Bourdieu 2001). Bourdieu (in Bourdieu and Wacquant 1992: 170) perceives gender domination as "the paradigmatic form of symbolic violence." For Bourdieu, gender results from social classification. This understanding provides the space for a discussion of gender that is not static and stagnant, with the limitation of the biological features of sex rather enriched with socio-cultural and socioeconomic variables. Women are "separated from men by a negative symbolic coefficient which like skin colour for blacks . . . negatively affects everything that they are and do" (Bourdieu 2001: 93). Bourdieu (2001: 42–49) provides the example of marriage in the institution of family, whereby females are objects of exchange rather than subjects; as such, women have to conform to the androcentric ideal of femininity. Historical relations of agents and institutions have maintained and perpetuated the concept of gender, especially in the institutions of church, state, family, and education (Bourdieu 2001: 82). The interest of this research rests on how gender continues to direct relations in the institutions of AICCs in spite of their presence in more liberalized European societies like the Netherlands.

I adopt Bourdieu's (1985) concept of field to facilitate discussion on the multidimensional relations that occur within AICCs in Amsterdam. The terms "field" and "social field" are used here interchangeably. Bourdieu argues that the groups of people within a social field have their own set of beliefs and distinctive "logic of practice," which is not fixed, however, but flexible (Bourdieu and Wacquant 1992: 97). Bourdieu defines field analytically as a

> network, or a configuration, of objective relations between positions. These positions are objectively defined, in their existence and in the

determinations they impose upon their occupants, agents or institutions, by their present and potential situation in the structure of the distribution of species of power whose possession commands access to the specific profits that are at stake in the field.

(Bourdieu and Wacquant 1992: 97)

The field is a social arena in which people maneuver, develop strategies, and struggle over desirable resources, just as in a game (Bourdieu and Wacquant 1992: 97). Bourdieu talks of the academic field, the religious field, the economic field, and the field of power. This research examines the religious field of AICCs in Amsterdam. In migration studies, the concept of social field (see Glick Schiller 1999, 2003; Fouron and Nina 2001) has been widely used in the discussion of transnationalism. Social field is defined here as "a set of multiple interlocking networks of social relationships through which ideas, practices, and resources are [. . .] exchanged, organized and transformed" (Levitt and Glick Schiller 2004: 1009). Female and male members compete for the resources within the religious social field as they seek to achieve full religious citizenship. Bourdieu (Bourdieu and Wacquant 1992) explains that male dominance in the religious social field has engendered competition for capital resources and, in consequence, access to religious citizenship is embedded with gender relations.

Within the religious field of AICCs, women and men struggle and operate within structured systems that are defined by social positions (Jenkins 1992). These struggles are enshrined in symbolism and meanings that are executed through indirect cultural mechanisms of order and restraint rather than direct and coercive control (Jenkins 1992). Bourdieu argues that the symbolism and meanings are imposed in ways accepted as legitimate by the social actors (Jenkins 2002: 104). The legitimate authority and domination (Weber 1968) is systemic because it is institutionalized within the religious field. There is a kind of violence in the process of institutionalizing certain forms of behaviors to be accepted as norms within a particular field, which Bourdieu refers to as symbolic violence (Bourdieu 1990: 27). Symbolic violence is defined as the "violence which is exercised upon a social agent with his or her complicity" (Bourdieu and Wacquant 1992: 167). Within the religious field, the various actors experience the systems of meanings as legitimate, but reality is misrepresented through the transmission of ideologies and values.

Some of the social actors in the religious field are manipulated to embrace culturally accepted ways of behavior, which is an indication of oppression. Oppression is defined as "the imposition of the will of a certain person or group upon another person or group which may take [. . .] structural (repressive cultural customs) or more personalized form" (Ndeda 2005: 51). This chapter argues that the power relations between and among men and women's interactions are not neutral but are rather embedded with the imposition of the will of one group over the other. The process of moving beyond superficial discourse and entering the realm of discovering the agents that impose their will over others in the social interaction is described as gendering oppression. Ramodibe argues that

> there can be no argument that the church is one of the most oppressive structures in society today, especially in regard to the oppression of women. About three-quarters of the people in the church are women, but men make decisions affecting them alone (with very few exceptions). Once women are acknowledged as pastors, as the body of Christ, we can build a new church [. . .]. I say a new church because the church as we have it today is a creation of male persons. As women, we have always felt like strangers in this male church.
>
> (1996, cited in Ndeda 2005: 51)

Religious socialization in AICCs

The study adopts the concept of religious socialization in the discussion of the dynamics and manifestation of religiosity. Religious socialization further guides the understanding of the motivation for the interiorisation of religiosity among second generation Ghanaians in Amsterdam. Religious socialization is defined as "an interactive process through which social agents influence individuals' religious beliefs and understandings" (Sherkat 2003: 157). Religious socialization is the process whereby people come to accept religious preferences. Religious preference is defined as the acceptance of supernatural explanations about the purpose, meaning, and origins of life that go beyond human reasoning (Sherkat 2003). The strength of religious preferences determines the intensity of religiosity in terms of religious devotion, affiliation to a religious organization, and participation in religious activities. People tend to hold on to the religions they are used to, and so religious preferences are reinforced through continuous religious practices (Sherkat and Wilson 1995).

Decision-making in religious preferences is influenced by social pressure. Individuals think and act in ways that are expected of them, and with time they internalize these norms as their own (Sherkat 1998; Sherkat and Wilson 1995); the study refers to this process as "religious indoctrination." Parents are the first agents of socialization for infants; as such, their religious preferences guide and direct the religious beliefs of their children as they grow up (Myers 1996; Cornwall 1989; Sherkat 1998). Immigrant churches may serve as extended families to their members, compensating for the families far away from the host society (Levitt 2006). As crucial agents of socialization among immigrants, immigrant churches implement sanctions in the form of rewards and punishments for compliance of the norms in the church, or lack thereof, so as to ensure effective socialization (Sherkat 2003).

Data and method

Data are drawn mainly from in-depth interviews, participant observation, and informal interviews in Amsterdam between January 2014 and January 2015. Life history interviews were conducted with 50 second-generation migrants within AICCs in Amsterdam, out of which 33 were female and 17 were male. Semi-structured in-depth interviews were also conducted with nine AICCs in Amsterdam, represented by the head pastor or a founding member. Four of the AICC representatives interviewed belonged to mainline Protestant churches; three came from Pentecostal/Charismatic churches; one belonged to a Charismatic church; and the last came from a Pentecostal church. Other sources of data are from records of church meetings, constitutions, annual programs, and websites; videos; the website of the Dutch statistical office; books and online scholarly journals; and search engines like Google Scholar and the JSTOR database. A snowball sampling technique was used to recruit second-generation Ghanaian migrants, mainly due to the age limitation in this study. A purposive sampling technique was used to recruit Ghanaian Christian churches based on the dominant churches attended by the second-generation Ghanaian migrants interviewed.

The interviews were audio recorded and transcribed verbatim. Line by line, the data were manually categorized into analytic units under descriptive words or category names. The information was organized into themes and subthemes (Rossman and Rallis 1998: 171). The documentation process immensed me in the data and prompted additional questions for follow-up interviews. The themes and subthemes were analyzed for each participant; they were also connected to other interviewees with quotations. Descriptive and inferential analyses of data have been employed in this work (Guba and Lincoln 1982; Hammersley 1992). The interpretations are based on state of the art and personal interpretations. The voluntary nature of the research participation and the possibility of withdrawing as a participant at any moment were clearly specified in the informed consent (Daly and McDonald 1996). This research does not seek to draw representative and generalized conclusions from the research findings but instead paves the way for future research.

Religiosity of second-generation respondents

The institutional mode of religiosity is the public manifestation of one's religiosity. The study takes into account time of membership, participation, baptism, and church denomination. Out of the 50 respondents, 48 declared themselves to be members of AICCs in Amsterdam, while two are lapsed-members. Thirty-five (35) of the respondents attend Pentecostal/Charismatic churches, while nine (9) of them attend mainline Protestant churches and four (4) are Catholic. The predominance of members of Pentecostal/Charismatic churches among the respondents is not surprising given that Pentecostal/

Charismatic churches were the first to respond to the pastoral needs of Ghanaian immigrants compared to the mainline Christian churches.

Participants were asked about their church participation. The study built a typology and asked the respondents if they attend church services twice a week or more; once a week; twice a month; once a month; or once in a while. Twenty (20) participants identified themselves as attending church services more than once a week; twenty (21) respondents attended church services once a week; five (5) respondents attended church services twice a month; two (2) attended church services once a month; and two (2) participants attended church services once in a while. Forty-four (44) of the respondents joined AICCs in infancy, while six (6) of the respondents started frequenting AICCs during adolescence. Forty (40) of the participants indicated that they had been baptized, of whom 25 of them were baptized as children (10–12 years of age), four (4) during infancy (0–4 years of age), and 11 in early adulthood. Some of the respondents converted from other religions to Christianity. Others were not religious but developed interest in religion with time, while others were lapsed Christians who later revived their Christian faith and moved to different Christian churches.

Assimilation theorists (Alba and Nee 1997; Park 1930) claim that second-generation migrants are likely to abandon the culture and religion of their parents due to the theory of the melting pot. Most of the respondents, however, held that the religious field of AICCs is an integral part of their life. A respondent recounted that

> *at birth my parents were members of the Resurrection Power and Living Bread Ministries. I have been attending this church since childhood and even as a young adult I still belong to this religious group. I have friends here in church and I consider the elders as my foster aunts and uncles.*
> (interview on 03–01–2015)

Another respondent narrated:

> *I discovered this church myself because my parents were not attending any church. I had a friend who attended the church and it was close to my house so I decided to join her. I have been a member since then . . . it is about fifteen years ago and I am one of the leaders in the youth group.*
> (interview on 12–09–2014)

Gendered oppression in the religious field

This section discusses the lived experiences of oppression by second-generation Ghanaians in AICCs in Amsterdam. The gendered nature of the religious field cannot be ignored because it is pertinent in social interactions. The symbolic violence in the religious field is androcentric, affecting the ability to enjoy rights and even responsibilities. During the life history interview, I asked participants about the extent to which second-generation female migrants could rise in terms of leadership compared to second-generation male migrants in AICCs. Alice, a 25-year-old second-generation female migrant, noted that

> *it is a good question but I have never thought of it. I know that there are some male second generation migrants who are deacons and even one of the guys I work with within the youth group is an elder[1] in the church. I know of women who are deaconesses but none is an elder in the church. It has never occurred to me to question this practice. I need to find out from the church authorities.*
>
> (interview on 18–09–2014)

Another second-generation female migrant, Ann (age 22), recounted that:

> *Oh yes. We have females that are deaconess but we do not have any elder as female. I think it is possible for women to be elders but only that we do not have them. I know that the elders are all men. I do not even know why it is so. I have not really thought about it.*
>
> (interview on 19–09–2014)

Data from the fieldwork show that some of the AICCs exclude women from church governance, as they are restricted from taking part in higher ecclesiastical duties and the occupation of leadership and positions of authority. This may result from the domination of the male perspective and male-centered worldview in some of the AICCs in Amsterdam, which silence the voices of some women and devalue or ignore female perspectives and contributions. The research shows that the judgment of women by models of masculinity (Rosicki 2012: 9) in the hierarchical structure of some AICCs keeps most females at the lowest level of the religious hierarchy. The shifting nature of the religious field does not provide women in most of AICCs with equal opportunities to compete in the religious field of their churches due to structural constraints embedded in the norms and practices. Androcentric discourse in the religious field is translated into oppressive actions against women.

Silencing women in the religious field

Internalizing the oppression on the part of most of the respondents might make them somehow victims as they accept the gendered norms and practices in AICCs. This internalization of oppression could pose challenges for the majority of the female respondents, as they may find it difficult to disentangle themselves from the oppressive bondage and therefore seek equal right to representation in the religious social field. Ndeda (2005: 52) notes that "internalized oppression becomes something of a vicious circle since once women accept the judgments of androcentrism or patriarchy they are unable to critique it" as these are perceived as legitimate practices in the religious field. The social agents in the religious field are not coerced into accepting the dominant culture and values; rather, they do it with their complicity (Rosicki 2012). Legitimacy, however, obscures the existing unequal power relations in the religious field.

Joan, 29, another second-generation female migrant, explained that

> *in the church's hierarchy, women could rise to the level of deaconess or they could be leaders of the women ministry. I am aware that there is a kind of discrimination in this instance but unlike the secular sphere where one could argue for such rights, in the church one has to accept certain customs without complaint.*
>
> (interview on 18–04–2014)

Lucy, a 28-year-old second-generation female migrant, also recounted that

> *the highest position that a woman could attain is deaconess or maybe national women's leader or maybe national youth leader. In our church a woman cannot be a pastor. We do not do that. So from a male's side one could start as a member then rise to deaconship then to an elder. Even as the elder based on how active the male is, he could become a leader of one of the ministries like witness or men or youth or children. From an elder the male could become a presiding elder then a pastor and the highest rank is an apostle [. . .]. I think with time these laws will change.*
>
> (interview on 23–04–2014)

Oppression may result from religious socialization in AICCs. Religious socialization is the "interactive process through which social agents influence individuals' religious beliefs and understandings" (Sherkat 2003: 157). The gradual and systemic patriarchal teachings in the religious field may result in the interiorization of the exterior. On the one hand, the study shows that some of the analyzed second-generation female migrants are aware of the gendered discrimination and inequality in the exercise of religious citizenship within the religious social field. Through religious socialization, some of the respondents interiorize the rules, restrictions, and standards of the AICC religious social field in ways that are accepted as the rules of the game. As a result, about 20 of the studied second-generation female Ghanaians failed to acknowledge the discrimination meted out to them. Rather, they justified the religious indoctrination that results in the perpetuation of the gendered leadership within most of the AICCs in Amsterdam.

On the other hand, some of the respondents may not be aware of the gendered discrimination inherent in their right to representation as religious citizens in the religious field of their churches. The mode of religious socialization is imbued with oppressive features that may not permit some of the female respondents to recognize the gender imbalance or bias of representation in their churches. The data show that a few of the female respondents perceive themselves as qualified and aspire to attain leadership positions in their churches due to their active involvement in AICCs. A respondent noted, "I hope to be an elder or even a pastor in the church and I am capable of performing well." They are, however, likely to be confronted with structural impediments that will curtail or challenge their access to representation in the religious field of their churches. Structural impediments against female respondents exist when it comes to competition with their male counterparts for leadership positions in the religious social field. The situation may result in the subordination of some of the analyzed female respondents. However, religious socialization may form and inform some of the studied second-generation respondents about the neutrality of the citizenship rules that could prevent them from exercising agency.

The data show that half of the studied second-generation female interviewees saw the patriarchy and androcentrism in their churches as divinely ordained. In Marxist parlance, there is a demonstration of false consciousness that is perpetuated in ideologies and values. A female respondent observed that

> *the church is governed by faith so not all things of the church could be understood by mere reasoning. The church is patriarchal but it is divinely instituted by God through the leaders of the church and we cannot fight God.*
>
> (interview on 20–11–2014)

Another female participant also recounted that:

> *No I do not feel discriminated because it is more from the Biblical perspective so personally I do not feel discriminated. I have not given it a thought because I see it as normal. In the Netherlands there is a saying that church and state are separate so the things that are done in the church are different from those done in the state and I have all the respect for church issues. It is in the women's movement where a woman can become a chair lady.*
>
> (interview on 12–09–2014)

Data from the research show that the oppression in some of the AICCs could be generated through a process of social reproduction that acts behind a "veil" to ensure the reproduction of social order (Rosicki 2012: 15). Religion is itself a system of power that involves the interaction between "sacred" and "secular" (Woodhead 2004). The sacred manifests or exhibits its power through the secular. The secular powers in religion reinforce and legitimize dominant power interests (Woodhead 2013: 61) through the invocation of the sacred powers in religion. By means of symbolic and material ways of acting, religion has the capacity to reinforce existing gendered social practices within a given community. The study found that AICCs have strengthened hegemonic relations in the religious field by drawing on divine powers to buttress the gendered oppression and thus avoid interrogation of gendered power relations.

Conclusion

Drawing on ethnographic research carried out in AICCs in Amsterdam, the chapter highlighted gendered oppression in the religious field. The chapter sought to examine how relations in the religious field are gendered. Bourdieu's concept of field provided the arena for understanding gendered interactions in AICCs. The chapter revealed that the genderedness of relations in the religious field manifests oppressive features because of the manipulative laws that govern the rules of the game. From these findings, religious socialization in most of the analyzed AICCs in Amsterdam is likely to perpetuate gendered discrimination against women, which is a manifestation of symbolic domination and hegemonic display of power.

The chapter demonstrated that the level of gendered consciousness in the religious field among female respondents were not on par, as most of the female respondents were aware of the gendered oppression and discrimination but, as a result of indoctrination, could not identify the imbalanced power structure in the AICCs. Such respondents were said to consolidate the gendered order (Woodhead 2013) in the religious field as they reified without questioning the hegemonic power relations. The chapter also showed that a few of the female respondents were not conscious of the patriarchal oppression in the AICC religious field, and therefore were likely to be confronted with the problem of discrimination in some hierarchical positions when the time comes to contest or present their candidature. The imposition of Christian religious teachings of male hegemonic power and domination upon females is experienced in manipulative rather than coercive manner.

Note

1 In the Pentecostal/Charismatic churches, the hierarchy (presbytery) follows deacons/deaconesses – elders – pastor in ascending order.

References

Adasi, G. S. and Frempong, A. D. 2014. Multiple roles of African women leaders and their challenges: The case of the Presbyterian Church of Ghana. *Research on Humanities and Social Sciences*, 4 (11): 63–68.

Agadjanian, V. 2015. Women's religious authority in a sub-Saharan setting dialectics of empowerment and dependency. *Gender & Society*, 29 (6): 982–1008.

Alba, R. 2005. Bright vs. blurred boundaries: Second-generation assimilation and exclusion in France, Germany, and the United States. *Ethnic and Racial Studies*, 28 (1): 20–49.

Alba, R. and Nee, V. 1997. Rethinking assimilation for a new era of immigration. *International Migration Review*, 31 (4): 826–874. Alba, R., Raboteau, J. A. and DeWind, J. 2009. *Immigration and religion in America: Comparative and historical perspectives*. New York: New York University Press.

Ambrosini, M. and Caneva, E. 2009. Le Seconde Generazioni: nodi critici e nuove forme di integrazione. *Sociologia e Politiche Sociali*, 12: 25–46.

Asamoah-Gyadu, J. K. 2010. Mediating spiritual power: African Christianity, transnationalism and the media. In *Religion crossing boundaries: Transnational religious and social dynamics in Africa and the new African Diaspora*, edited by Adogame, A. and Spickard, V. J., pp. 87–103. Leiden and Boston: Brill.

Baffoe, M. 2013. Spiritual well-being and fulfillment, or exploitation by a few smart ones? The proliferation of Christian Churches in West African immigrant communities in Canada. *Mediterranean Journal of Social Sciences*, 4 (1): 305–316.

Becker, J. and De Hart, J. 2006. *Godsdienstige veranderingen in Nederland. Verschuivingen in de binding met de kerken en de christelijke traditie*. The Hague: Sociaal en Cultureel Planbureau (Social and Cultural Planning Office of the Netherlands).

Beckford, J. A. 1983. The restoration of "power" to the sociology of religion. *Sociological Analysis*, 44 (1): 11–31.

Berger, P. L. 1999. *The desecularization of the world: Resurgent religion and world politics*. Grand Rapids, MI: William. B. Eerdmans Publishing Company.

Bernts, T., Dekker, G., and De Hart, J. 2007. *God in Nederland 1996–2006*. Kampen: Ten Have.

Bourdieu, P. 2001 [1998]. *Masculine domination*. Trans. R. Nice. Stanford, CA: Stanford University Press.

Bourdieu, P. 1990. *The logic of practice*. Stanford, CA: Stanford University Press.

Bourdieu, P. 1985. The forms of capital. In *Handbook of theory and research of the sociology of education*, edited by Richardson, J. G., pp. 241–258. New York: Greenwood.

Bourdieu, P. and Wacquant, L. J. D. 1992. *An invitation to reflexive sociology*. Chicago: University of Chicago Press.

Bruce, S. 2011. *Secularization: In defence of an unfashionable theory*. Oxford: Oxford University Press.

Choenni, C. 2002. *Ghanazen in Nederland. Een Profiel*. Den Haag: Ministerie van Binnenlandse Zaken en Koninkrijkszaken.

Connell, R. W. 2002. *Gender*. Cambridge: Polity.

Cornwall, M. 1989. The determinants of religious behaviour: A theoretical model and empirical test. *Social Forces*, 68 (2): 572–592.

Daly, J. and McDonald, I. 1996. Introduction: Ethics, responsibility and health research. In *Ethical intersections: Health research, methods and researcher responsibility*, edited by Daly, J. Sydney: Allen and Unwin.

Dietz, T., Mazzucato, V., Kabki, M., and Smith, L. 2011. Ghanaians in Amsterdam, their good work back home and the importance of reciprocity. *Journal of Global Initiatives: Policy, Pedagogy, Perspective*, 6 (1): 7.

Foucault, M. 1998. *The history of sexuality, Vol. 1: The will to knowledge*. London: Penguin Books Limited.

Fouron, G. and Schiller, N. G. 2001. All in the family: Gender, transnational migration, and the nation-state. *Identities Global Studies in Culture and Power*, 7 (4): 539–582.

Gemeente Amsterdam. 2013. *Amsterdam in Cifers 2013*. Amsterdam: O+S Research, Gemeente Amsterdam. [online]. Available at: www.ois.amsterdam.nl/media/Amsterdam%20in%20cijfers%202013/HTML/#62/. [Accessed on March 20, 2015].

Gordon, M. 1964. *Assimilation in American life*. New York: Oxford University Press.

Guba, E. G. and Lincoln, Y. S. 1982. Epistemological and methodological bases of naturalistic inquiry. *Educational Communication and Technology Journal*, 30 (4): 233–252.

Hammersley, M. 1992. *What's wrong with ethnography? Methodological explorations*. London: Routledge.

Hirschman, C. 2004. The role of religion in the origin and adaptation of immigrant groups in the United States. *International Migration Review*, 38 (3): 1206–1233.

Inglehart, R. and Norris, P. 2004. *Sacred and secular: Religion and politics worldwide: Cambridge studies in social theory, religion, and politics*. Cambridge: Cambridge University Press.

Inglehart, R. and Norris, P. 2003. The true clash of civilizations. *Foreign Policy*, pp. 63–70.

Jenkins, R. 2002. *Pierre Bourdieu* (Rev. Ed.). London: Routledge.

Jenkins, R. 1992. *Key sociologists: Pierre Bourdieu*. London: Routledge.

Knippenberg, H. 2010. Secularisation and the rise of immigrant religions: The case of the Netherlands. *Acta Universitatis Carolinae. Geographica*, 44(1–2): 63–82.

Knipscheer, J. W., de Jong, E. E. M., Kleber, R. J., and Lamptey, E. 2000. Ghanaians in the Netherlands: General health, acculturative stress and utilization of mental health care. *Journal of Community Psychology*, 28 (4): 459–476.

Kyei, J. R. K. O., Setrana, M. B., and Smoczynski, R. 2017. Practising religion across national borders: A study of Ghanaian Christian churches in Amsterdam. *Interdisciplinary Journal for Religion and Transformation in Contemporary Society: J-RaT*, 3 (1): 148–182.

Kyei, J. R. K. O. and R. Smoczynski 2016. Building bridges or bonds: The case of Ghanaian second generation migrants in Ghanaian churches in Amsterdam. *Romanian Journal Anthropological Research and Studies*, 6: 13–24.

Levitt, P. 2006. Redefining the boundaries of belonging: The transnationalization of religious life. In *Everyday religion: Observing modern religious lives*, edited by Ammerman, N. T., pp. 103–120. Oxford: Oxford University Press.

Levitt, P. and Schiller, N. G. 2004. Conceptualizing simultaneity: A transnational social field perspective on society. *International Migration Review*, 38 (3): 1002–1039.

Mensah, J. 2009. Doing religion overseas: The characteristics and functions of Ghanaian immigrant Churches in Toronto, Canada. *Societies Without Borders*, 4: 21–44.

Morgan, K. and Björkert, S. T. 2006. "I'd rather you'd lay me on the floor and start kicking me": Understanding symbolic violence in everyday life. *Women's Studies International Forum*, 5 (29): 441–452.

Myers, S. M. 1996. An interactive model of religiosity inheritance: The importance of family context. *American Sociological Review*, 858–866.

Ndeda, M. A. J. 2005. The Nomiya Luo Church: A gender analysis of the dynamics of an African independent church among the Luo of Siaya district. In *Gender, literature and religion in Africa*, edited by Ndeda, M. A. J., Nyamndi, G., Senkoro,

F. E. M. K., and Ssetuba, I., pp. 49–78. Dakar: Council for the Development of Social Science Research in Africa.

Park, R. E. 1930. Assimilation social. In *Encyclopedia of the social sciences*, edited by Seligman, E. and Johnson, A., Vol. 2, p. 281. New York: Macmillan.

Portes, A., Guarnizo, E. L., and Landolt, P. 1999. The study of transnationalism: Pitfalls and promise of an emergent research field. *Ethnic and Racial Studies*, 22 (2): 217–237, DOI: 10.1080/014198799329468.

Portes, A. and Rumbaut, R. G. 2006. *Immigrant America: A portrait*. Berkeley, CA: University of California Press.

Ramodibe, D. 1996. Women and men building together the church in Africa. In *With passion and compassion: Third World women doing theology*, edited by Fabella, V. and Oduyoye, M. Maryknoll: Orbis.

Rosicki, R. 2012. Public sphere and private sphere: Masculinity and femininity. In *Some issues on women in political, media and socio-economic space*, edited by Andruszkiewicz, I. and Balczyńska-Kosman, A., pp. 9–19. Poznań: WNPiD UAM.

Rossman, G. and Rallis, S. F. 1998. *Learning in the field: An introduction to qualitative research*. Thousand Oaks, CA: Sage.

Schiller, N. G. 2003. The centrality of ethnography in the study of transnational migration: seeing the Wetland instead of the Swamp America arrivals. In *American arrivals: Anthropology engages the new immigration*, pp. 99–128. Santa Fe: School of American Research Press.

Schiller, N. G. 1999. Transmigrants and Nation-States: Something old and something new in the U.S. immigrant experience. In *The handbook of international migration: The American experience*, edited by Hirschman, C., Kasinitz, P., and DeWind, J., pp. 94–119. New York: Russell Sage.

Sherkat, D. E. 2003. Religious socialization: Sources of influence and influences of agency. In *Handbook of the sociology of religion*, edited by Dillon, M., pp. 151–163. Cambridge: Cambridge University Press.

Sherkat, D. E. 1998. Counterculture or continuity? Examining competing influences on baby boomers' religious orientations and participation. *Social Forces*, 76: 1087–1115.

Sherkat, D. E. and Wilson, J. 1995. Preferences, constraints, and choices in religious markets: An examination of religious switching and apostasy. *Social Forces*, 73: 993–1026.

Statistics Netherlands 2015a. *Population; sex, origin and generation*. The Hague and Heerlen: Statistics Netherlands, January 1 [online]. Available at: http://statline. cbs.nl/StatWeb/publication/?DM=SLEN&PA=37325ENG&D1=0&D2=a&D3= 0&D4=0&D5=0,85&D6=11-17&LA=EN&HDR=G2,G3,G4,T&STB=G1,G5& VW=T. [Accessed February 22, 2015].

Statistics Netherlands 2015b. *Population dynamics; birth, death and migration per region*. The Hague and Heerlen: Statistics Netherlands. http://statline.cbs.nl/Stat web/publication/?DM=SLEN&PA=37259ENG&D1=0,25,30&D2=0&D3=0,2-5&D4=0,10,20,30,40,52-53&LA=EN&HDR=T&STB=G1,G2,G3&VW=T. [Accessed March 22, 2015].

Ter Haar, G. 1998. *Halfway to paradise: African Christians in Europe*. Cardiff: Cardiff Academie Press.

Ter Haar, G. 1995. Strangers in the promised land, African Christians in Europe. *Exchange*, 24 (1): 1–33.

Van den Bos, D. 2013. *Kerken in de Bijlmer zijn parels in Amsterdam-Zuidoost.* www. refdag.nl/kerkplein/kerknieuws/kerken_in_de_bijlmer_zijn_parels_in_amster dam_zuidoost_1_749924. [Accessed June 27, 2013]. Reformatorish Dagblad.

Walby, S. 1997. *Gender transformations.* London: Routledge.

Warner, S. R. 2007. The role of religion in the process of segmented assimilation. *Religious Pluralism and Civil Society*, 612: 102–115.

Weber, M. 1992. *The protestant ethic and the spirit of capitalism.* Translated by T. Parsons with an introduction by A. Giddens. London and New York: Routledge.

Weber, M. 1968. *Economy and society.* Totowa, NJ: Bedminster Press.

Woodhead, L. 2013. Gender differences in religious practice and significance. *International Advances in Engineering and Technology*, 13: 58–85.

Woodhead, L. 2004. *An introduction to Christianity.* Cambridge: Cambridge University Press.

Yip, A. K. and Nynäs, P. 2012. Re-framing the Intersection between religion, gender and sexuality in everyday life. In *Religion, gender and sexuality in everyday life*, edited by Nynäs, P. and Kam-Tuck Yip, A., pp. 1–16. London, UK: Ashgate.

5 The Paradox of Cultures

Violence against women and the German immigration debate before and after New Year's Eve 2015 in Cologne

Petra Klug

On criticizing "the other"

On New Year's Eve 2015 in Cologne, Germany, several groups of young men sexually assaulted, robbed, and in some cases even raped women. Over 1,000 incidents have been reported to the police. That the perpetrators were described as of North African or Arabic descent caused a months-long debate over sexism and racism. One side used a critique of Islamic gender norms and a discriminating view of women seemingly shared by these immigrants in order to argue against accepting refugees and granting asylum in Germany. The other side condemned this as an abuse of sexism for the purposes of racist ideology. They pointed out the existence of widespread sexual violence in German society and how this is shielded by projecting it onto Islam and Muslim immigrants. What was overlooked in this *circle of abuse and denial* was the fact that that immigrant women, and those who do not conform to their communities' gender norms, were those most affected by disrespect towards women and the harmful cultural practices of some immigrants. It is not a coincidence that the debate became so heated only when native German women were the victims of this sexism. The violence against and murder of immigrant women within their own communities was ignored or even tolerated for decades by almost all political groups in Germany. While the Right has generally shown little interest in the well-being of immigrants, the majority of the Left defended all aspects of immigrant culture in the name of anti-racism. German academics finally deconstructed the notions of "culture" and "religion"[1] and, through this, delegitimized the critique of harmful cultural and religious practices altogether. The racist and (post-)colonial division of humanity into those who demand and live an emancipated life and those whose rights are violated without causing indignation has thereby been reproduced.

In order to focus attention on the most vulnerable among the immigrants, I use an intersectional approach that reveals that the voices of immigrant women, queers, and critics have been muted in Germany's immigration debate, especially ironically by those German intellectuals who consider themselves feminist, anti-racist, queer, and critical. Against the racist idea of culture as determined through origin, culture has been presented as a matter of identity that is internally plural, fluid, and can be chosen or changed freely. But cultures exist not only as a matter of choice but also as a set of norms and practices that can limit and harm people. Given this *Paradox of Cultures* – that they don't exist in a deterministic way but rather exist in a way that affects people's lives – I want to propose a possibility of criticizing harmful cultural or religious practices without stigmatizing all adherents. With regard to the ongoing immigration process, I've modeled an integration approach based on individual human rights as a guideline for future policies. But first, let me outline the events of Cologne and the debate about them as an example for the problematic developments in German integration policies since the second half of the twentieth century.

The circle of abuse and denial

The events of New Year's Eve 2015 in Cologne, although internationally discussed, have still not been entirely reconstructed. As is usual given the date, a large group of people gathered in front of the dome and the train station in order to light fireworks. Out of this mass, several smaller groups sexually attacked and robbed women. Altogether, the police counted over 1,000 charges, almost half of them sexual offenses. The perpetrators were often described as of North African or Arabic ethnicity. Among the suspects were Algerians and Moroccans (the majority), as well as Tunisians, Germans, Syrians, an Iraqi, a Libyan, an Iranian, and someone from Montenegro. Some of them were minors, asylum-seekers, or illegal immigrants, and some were people already known to the police from previous criminal activity (Flade, Pauly, and Frigelj 2016). It took the media a couple of days to report the events, partly due to the slow reaction of the police. Although there were over 100 charges in the same night, the police first reported a "frisky atmosphere" and that the party was "predominantly peaceful" (Polizeipräsidium Köln 2016). Further investigations revealed similar sexual attacks and robbery with the same tactics in many other cities, too (Kampf 2016). When the events became known to the public and the media, this started an unprecedented societal debate about immigrants and their gender norms and, of course, about how many immigrants are tolerable for German society.

For the one side, the incidents in Cologne confirmed their racist fears. Although many refugees, especially from Syria, publicly distanced themselves from the attacks on women and demonstrated against sexism (see Syrians against Sexism 2016), the events fueled resentments and violence against immigrants. Days after New Year's Eve, a group of hooligans, rockers, and bouncers met in the center of Cologne in order to "clean up" and go "hunting for humans," as they themselves announced on Facebook. Two Pakistanis and a Syrian were injured (n-tv.de 2016). The violent attacks on immigrants, which in 2015 had already reached notably high levels, escalated even further in 2016 (Rühle 2016). Right-wing movements that had grown after the arrival of larger numbers of asylum-seekers, like Pegida (Patriotic Europeans against the Islamization of the Okzident) or the AfD (Alternative for Germany), used the events to spread hate and promote violence against refugees; to attack German chancellor Angela Merkel, whom they blamed for immigration; and to accuse the media of lying about the events (Meisner and Wischmeyer 2016; Gensing 2016). The founder of Pegida, Lutz Bachmann, posed in a T-shirt with the text "Rapefugees not welcome" on it (Zeit Online 2016). AfD leader Frauke Petry asked on Facebook: "Ms. Merkel, after the wave of crimes and sexual offenses, is Germany 'open und colorful' enough for you?" She also compared the events with the rapes of German women by soldiers of the Red Army in 1945 (cited after Weiland 2016). Some of the so-called asylum-critics went so far as to suggest that anti-racist politicians and activists should have been in Cologne themselves, or even that they be raped (Günther 2016; Schwesig 2016b). The mainstream media also used racist stereotypes and imagery. FOCUS magazine illustrated its cover "Women Accuse" with a photo of a naked blonde woman with black hand-prints on her skin (FOCUS 2016). As for the state reaction, after it became clear that the majority of the suspects were not recent refugees but immigrants from Maghreb states who had been in Germany for a long time and had repeatedly committed crimes, the German government restarted negotiations with Morocco, Tunisia, and Algeria in order to facilitate deportation to these countries (Süddeutsche.de 2016). In addition, the government plans to declare the Maghreb states as "safe states of origin." For immigrants from states that are declared "safe," getting asylum in Germany is much harder (ProAsyl 2018).[2] On New Year's Eve 2016, the situation in Cologne remained under control. The police registered about 2,000 persons whom they categorized as of North African or Arabic descent in front of the train station. Although 674 of them were stopped, held, and controlled, neither their nationalities nor the reasons for their gathering in Cologne were totally clear. Accusations of racial profiling were refused through the police, who said that there was an "aggressive atmosphere" among the people (Zeit Online 2017a).

On the other side, the debate showed the racism, Islamophobia, and sexism of German society,[3] which discusses gender violence only if it's committed by non-Germans. Under the hashtag #ausnahmslos, which means "without exception,"[4] Muslim and non-Muslim anti-racists and feminists pointed out that

> it is harmful for all of us if feminism is exploited by extremists to incite against certain ethnicities, as is currently being done in the discussion surrounding the incidents in Cologne. It is wrong to highlight sexualized violence only when the perpetrators are allegedly the perceived "others": Muslim, Arab, black or North-African men, i.e., those who are regarded as "non-Germans" by extremists.
>
> (#ausnahmslos 2016)

They point out that sexualized violence must also be taken seriously if the victims are not white cis-women,[5] but they warn that the problem cannot be "Islamized" and attributed in a generalized way to a religion. Editorial staff of media "should avoid lurid and stigmatizing interpretations" (#ausnahmslos 2016). The call gathered 11,000 signatures in just one week and was also supported by Manuela Schwesig, the Federal Minister for Family, Senior Citizens, Women, and Youth (Schwesig 2016a). Many commentators compared the incidents to Oktoberfest or Carnival, where sexual violence is quite common but usually goes unnoticed by the public. Queer journalist Hengameh Yaghoobifarah wrote that "experience shows that in these situations women are not believed, accused of having sent the wrong signals while they were drunk and unalert or of just having imagined the incidents." As many others had, she pointed out that some of the politicians who are concerned about the security of women now were anti-feminists before men of color were the perpetrators and the events could be used for their racist agenda (Yaghoobifarah 2016). Feminists in Germany have long criticized the fact that many forms of gender violence are not punishable, and that Germany has signed but not ratified the Istanbul Convention on preventing and combating violence against women and domestic violence. Christina Clemm, a lawyer with a focus on sexual crime legislation, points out that

> the events were grave sexual offenses [. . .]. But I don't think they are punishable under the current law in Germany, because nonconsensual sexual acts are punishable only if they are carried out with violence, under immediate threats toward body or life, by taking advantage of the helplessness of a person, or if the person is not capable of resistance.

If a woman does not struggle, for example out of fear, she is not protected by the law (Clemm and Hark 2016).[6]

The connection between the events and the potential Islamic background of the suspects was discussed with great controversy. In a much noted article, journalist and anti-Nazi activist Simone Rafael was quick to state that perpetrators were "not refugees or Muslims, but criminals that broadened their criminal intentions towards sexual offenses" (Rafael 2016).[7] The Chairman of the Central Council of Muslims in Germany, Aiman Mazyek, rejects every connection to the Islamic view of women: "The perpetrators have nothing in common with Islam. If they were Muslims they would have committed a deadly sin" (Mazyek 2016). Muslim journalist Khola Maryam Hübsch points out the "thinly veiled racism," the "cultural chauvinism," and the Orientalist tradition of the projections about Islam and gender relations.

> Of course one may be permitted to wonder whether the image of women in parts of the so-called Islamic world doesn't favour problematic behaviour toward them. But right-wing populist opinion-makers who now feel they have to conjure up a cultural war must be made to

realize that Islam can also be a partner rather than a problem in the fight against a misogynist mentality. After all, the perpetrators evidently do not really follow the commandments of the Koran – in any case, they had certainly flouted the tenet of no-alcohol.

(Hübsch 2016)

The radical Salafist preacher Pierre Vogel, who otherwise is of the opinion that most of the people in hell are women (Vogel 2011), also said women are more respected in Islam than in Western cultures, and that in Islam sexual contact without marriage is forbidden even if consensual. In Islamic countries, "asocial crimes" like that of New Year's Eve would be punished by jail or whipping (Vogel 2016).

But while a broad variety of Muslim public figures as well as many anti-racist activists rejected the violence as having connections to Islamic gender roles, there also were Muslims who confirmed this connection. Sami Abu-Yusuf, the imam of a Cologne mosque, blamed the victims. According to media reports, he said that the women provoked the attacks because they wore perfume and were "half-naked" (Abu-Yusuf, cited after Bild.de 2016).[8] Similarly, the website MuslimStern (MuslimStar), which was founded to raise awareness of rising hostility towards Islam and Muslims, criticized that way that the events were exaggerated through media and instrumentalized in order to spread hate against minorities. They blamed the incidents on the consumption of alcohol and the women, who went out lightly dressed and tipsy. "The Woman, because of her constitution, in general bears responsibility when leaving the house. One cannot put a naked antelope in front of a lion and expect that nothing happens" (MuslimStern 2016).[9]

But Muslim observers weren't the only commentators who recommended that women change their behavior. The major of Cologne, Henriette Reker, caused indignation and ridicule (see #einearmeslaenge) when she answered the question of how women can protect themselves with the tip that they should stay at more than "an arm's length" distance from people who they don't know, and go out exclusively in groups (Spiegel Online 2016).

In addition to the large number of right-wingers who disguised their racism as a "critique of Islam," among the critics of Islamic gender roles were also some feminist activists, including Alice Schwarzer, Germany's most well-known women's rights activist. She called the events in Cologne the consequence of integration that has failed, or was never really sought.

These young men [. . .] are the product of a false tolerance in which almost everyone – people, media, churches, and politicians – questioned our democracy, juridical system, and equality, and allowed them to be spurned. Spurned in favor of "other mores" or an ominous "freedom of religion" in whose name parallel societies were allowed and integration ignored. As if this fanaticism would have anything to do with belief.

She reminds the reader that she was criticized as racist when her journal EMMA demanded better protection of female refugees and children, as well as respect from male refugees for the juridical system in Germany and for women's rights (Schwarzer 2016). Necla Kelek, a Turkish-born feminist critic of Islam, who was also criticized for her support of more strict integration policies, worries about the number of refugees from Islamic countries with war or Islamic dictatorship: "Their socialization was minted by violence, oppression of women through men, homophobia, anti-Semitism, and the subjection of the individual under the religious community." Of course, she adds, many refugees fled these exact same "plagues," but all of them come with a cultural heritage that is different from a libertarian idea of freedom, and this culture-shock unloaded itself in violence. "Everyone who knows just a little bit about the circles of Muslim immigrants knows that this problem is not qualitatively new. New are the scale and the visibility of the event" (Kelek 2016). Another critic of Islamic gender roles was Ali Toprak, chairman of the Kurdish Community and Immigration Councils, who criticized the "thought control" of white left feminists. In his view, the denial of the misogyny of Muslim men is a betrayal of the victims: women in Islamic countries. It is this "post-colonial arrogance" that is stronger than the empathy for the victims of Islamism (Toprak 2016).

The response towards these critiques – not surprisingly – comes from people who negate any idea of a connection between the incidents and Islamic gender roles. The already mentioned Salafist preacher Pierre Vogel said it would be wrong for "Islam-haters" like Necla Kelek to be allowed to associate the acts with Islam because, even if the perpetrators were Muslims, their motives were not Islamic (Vogel 2016). Spiegel commentator Jakob Augstein, who accused politicians of adding fuel to the fire by referring to the events as abominable, "as if the women were eaten and not robbed and molested," calls the debate racist.

> In the past, biological racism was more prevalent, in the present it is the cultural racism. [. . .] The racists of the past would have said that the Muslims are born to be criminal. Today's racists say that they were socialized that way.
>
> (Augstein 2016)

And journalist Charlotte Wiedemann finds the debate about Islam as a religion of harassment and molestation much like what it criticizes: "It lacks respect towards the women that adhere to this religion, the millions of proud and educated Muslimas" (Wiedemann 2016).

It is not possible to sum up a debate like the one about Cologne in full. The positions that I include here, are, of course, a subjective and selective choice. And, of course, I wasn't able to reproduce more than fragments of each article. Nevertheless, I hope to have given a rough overview of the most important positions. But my concern here is actually not to repeat those who have made themselves heard already, but to point out what has not been heard in this debate and has created a blind spot in the German integration debate since the second half of the twentieth century: a critique of Islamic gender norms and immigrants' cultural traditions that puts the situation of immigrant women, queers, and nonconformists at the center of attention.

Immigrants who refuse these gender norms, or even confront their religious foundations, are marginalized not just through the majority society but also through those who are dominant in their communities and through the allegedly anti-racist discourse that calls the critical debate about Islamic gender norms "anti-Muslim racism" or Islamophobia. Their critique is either used for the racist discourse or rejected because it can be used for the racist discourse. This circle of the abuse of critique, and its rejection because it can be abused, was put on the spot by Muslim-raised Algerian author Kamel Daoud and the Western responses towards him. Daoud published texts about the incidents in Cologne and "The Sexual Misery of the Arab World" in the Italian newspaper *La Repubblica*, the French newspapers *L'Hebdo* and *Le Monde*, and the *New York Times*. Later translations also appeared in the German newspaper *Frankfurter Allgemeine Zeitung* (Daoud 2016a, 2016b, 2016c). Daoud criticizes the "phantasm" of the Right that equated refugees with rapists before it was even clear what had happened in Cologne. But he also points out the naiveté in ignoring the culture that the refugees bring with them.

> When he has made it to the West, the refugee has saved his life. But one happily overlooks that he won't give up his culture so easily. Given the uprooting and the shock of his new environment, his culture is all he has left.

Daoud suggests that for the average male refugee, this change in his relationship towards women will be difficult and precarious (Daoud 2016e). For him, the events of Cologne have

> led people in the West to realize that one of the great miseries plaguing much of the so-called Arab world, and the Muslim world more generally, is its sick relationship with women. In some places, women are veiled, stoned and killed; at a minimum, they are blamed for sowing disorder in the ideal society.

He describes how Islamic preachers restrict sexuality and the freedom of women, and how as a result "people fantasize about the trappings of another world: either the West, with its display of immodesty and lust, or the Muslim paradise and its virgins." Until this sickness spread to their societies through migration, Westerners denied it:

> The West has long found comfort in exoticism, which exonerates differences. Orientalism has a way of normalizing cultural variations and

of excusing any abuses: Scheherazade, the harem, and belly dancing exempted some Westerners from considering the plight of Muslim women. But today, with the latest influx of migrants from the Middle East and Africa, the pathological relationship that some Arab countries have with women is bursting onto the scene in Europe.

(Daoud 2016d)

After his article, Daoud was accused by a group of 19 predominantly Western-based academics of "recycling orientalist clichés" and cultural-ism. The authors argue that the "self-declared humanist" reduces a bil-lion inhabitants to a homogenous mass that is defined only through their relationship towards religion.

(Collectif 2016)

This construct is then contrasted with a happy and emancipated moder-nity, thus ignoring the "multiple forms of inequality and violence towards women in Europe and North America" (Collectif 2016). By psychologizing this sort of sexual violence, he blurs, in their opinion, the social, political, and economic conditions that fuel it, like the collective housing and the con-ditions of migration that favor the immigration of male youth. Furthermore, this creates an image of a wave of potential sexual predators, which benefits the right-wing movement Pegida. When Daoud suggests that the refugees should be convinced to change their relationship towards women, they refer to that as a disciplinary project. This is scandalous, in their opinion, not just because it evokes the insupportable routine of the mission of Occidental civilization and superiority, but because it also affirms that the "culturally unadapted and psychologically deviant" Muslim masses are a threat for Europe (Collectif 2016). Daoud, against whom a death-fatwa was issued in 2015 accusing him of being an apostate and an "enemy of religion" (cited after Carvajal 2015), calls the accusations of Islamophobia "an inquisition." As the petitioners, who enjoy the security of the West, do not have to live his life, he criticizes their post-colonial pretensions of defending the indigenous. As a result of their accusations, he pulls back and stops journalism (Daoud 2016f). In France, Daoud received support from, among others, the French Prime Minister Manuel Valls. One of his first and most outspoken defend-ers was the Franco-Tunisian feminist writer Fawzia Zouari, who confirms Daoud's criticism of the gender norms in the Islamic world, points out the similarity of the accusations to that of the Islamists, and calls the tendency of anti-Islamophobe Western intellectuals – to mute Arab voices that are criti-cal of their own traditions – "neocolonialism" (Zouari 2016; Symons 2016).

Daoud's warning sounds generalized and stigmatizing towards the refu-gees. It is by no means clear that most of them will cling to the patriarchal traditions of their home countries. The people in Islamic societies are not one homogenous mass, and he himself is the best example for that. But even if one doesn't share his thesis, Daoud has pointed out what is actually at stake in this debate. The matter, which is carefully avoided by most of its participants, is the situation of those who actually do suffer from patriarchal gender norms within their culture, whether as refugees here or in the countries where they live or from which they flee. In order to place the struggle of these people at the center of the analysis, we need to overcome ritualized discussions such as those surrounding Cologne and apply an approach that incorporates the intersections of racism, sexism, and religion.

Racism, sexism, and religion in the German immigration debate

The concept of intersectionality goes back to the legal scholar Kimberle Crenshaw, who developed it out of a criticism of anti-discrimination laws that "treat race and gender as mutually exclusive categories of experience and analysis" (Crenshaw 1989, 139). This

> single-axis framework erases Black women in the conceptualization, identification, and remediation of race and sex discrimination by limiting inquiry to the experience of otherwise-privileged members of the group. In other words, in race discrimination cases, discrimination tends to be viewed in terms of sex- or class-privileged Blacks; in sex discrimination cases, the focus is on race- and class-privileged women. But this focus on the most privileged group members marginalizes those who are multiple-burdened and obscures claims that cannot be understood as resulting from discrete sources of discrimination.
>
> (Crenshaw 1989, 140)[10]

Crenshaw even describes how it was controversial to portray domestic violence within the Black community because it was felt that this would reproduce racist stereotypes of the Black male. "The struggle against racism seemed to compel the subordination of certain aspects of the Black female experience in order to ensure the security of the larger Black community" (Crenshaw 1989, 159–163). This results in the problem that anti-discrimination laws protect Black women only where their experiences equal those of either Black men or white women. The specific experience as Black women falls through this grid (Crenshaw 1989, 143). When "*white* women speak for and as *women*," white feminists ignore their privileges and how they mitigate aspects of sexism, as well as how this perpetuates their domination over other women. So, the feminist theory that focuses on the experiences of white women fails to analyze and address the situation of non-privileged women (Crenshaw 1989, 154). Re-reading Crenshaw's article is – despite the obvious differences in time, place, and subject – very helpful in describing the debate about Muslim immigrants and the cultural and religious impact on gender roles in Germany.

The German debate about the incidents in Cologne, about immigration, religion, and gender violence in general, follows two narratives: protecting

German women against the sexism of Muslim immigrants, on the one hand, and fighting racism against Muslim immigrants – particularly as it involves the critique of gender norms – on the other. The fight against the sexism experienced by immigrant women within their communities falls through that grid. Sexism is addressed as the sexism against the native German woman, which she experiences through the Muslim immigrant or through German society. Racism is addressed as the racism towards the Muslim male or against the male or female spokespersons of their communities. Critiques that actually address the situation of those who do not conform to the norms of their communities are denied. This ignorance has a history that is perpetuated throughout the immigration debate in Germany. An intersectional analysis can help to point this out if it focuses not on identities and cultures but rather on the intersections of different forms of oppression. It can help then, if not in tracing the voices of those who are not heard, at least in "measuring the silence" (Spivak 1994, 82).

Racism, not just in Germany, has always had a gender component. As its main rationale is the continuity or expansion of what is thought of as the indigenous "race," the focus on reproduction is a crucial aspect of it. In Germany, one of the biggest racist concerns was a native society that had fewer and fewer children, as opposed to an immigrant one that was younger and had more offspring. The "Heidelberger Manifest" of 1981, one of the most prominent examples of German postwar racism, argues in a biologistically way that the German people ("Volk") are endangered through immigration: "Only the living and intact German family can preserve our people in the future. Only our own children are the basis of the German and European future" (Heidelberger Manifest, cited after Elfferding 1983, 256). A significant part of the outrage against the gender violence in Cologne is linked to that old racist fear that the immigrants are taking away "our women." As the main mechanism of racism is to associate a certain origin or ethnicity with certain cultural or mental characteristics, the "culture" of the immigrants has always played a role in this. The veil was maybe the most visual marker of Islam, which was the religion of most Turkish immigrants. Therefore, the alleged cultural difference was closely linked to gender roles. Behavior scientist Irenäus Eibl-Eibesfeldt summed up the contrast: "Christianity here – Muslims there. Here: the emancipation of women – there: humble submissiveness" (Eibl-Eibesfeldt cited after Herbert 2003, 259). But, of course, the intention behind this accentuation was not to improve the situation of Muslim women, but to get rid of the Turks altogether. The radical right-wing party NPD (National-Democratic Party of Germany) showed posters with veiled women carrying heavy bags. The slogan: "We wish a good trip home!" (NPD 2007 [2006]).

Huge parts of the Left, the Liberals, and intellectuals responded to this by defending the idea of multiculturalism and a multicultural society, in which different cultures can live together peacefully and be accepted in their own ways. After the German government still hadn't acknowledged the fact that

Germany is a country of immigration, the term "multiculturalism" became a tool not just to acknowledge and describe this new reality (Leggewie 1990, 7–20) but also to appreciate it. The differences between cultures should be experienced as "enrichment, not as a threat." According to that view, societal norms and power structures must be changed in order to reach equality of cultures (Butterwegge 1992, 11). Gender aspects of immigration and the situation of women or nonconformists within minority cultures have been largely ignored. The traditional gender norms under which many women have suffered were accepted as "their" culture or religion. Violations of women's rights such as forced marriages, honor killings, and domestic violence were taboo both inside and outside immigrant communities (Ateş 2007, 48–51). Seyran Ateş, a feminist lawyer who grew up under the patriarchal regime of a Turkish-Kurdish family in Berlin, looks back on the decade-long toleration of honor killings and violence in the immigrant communities: "Neither the media, nor the official politics or the German Left, who was busy fighting the 'pig-state,' were thinking about the Human Rights-violations in their own neighborhoods." She especially criticizes the Leftist activists, who through several collaborations with Turkish and Kurdish projects knew about these problems but did not want to give up their black-and-white ideology, in which the immigrants were per se good, and the Germans were per se bad (Ateş 2007, 62). They conflated tolerance towards immigrants with tolerance towards their patriarchal traditions. Attempts to scandalize the violence in Turkish or Kurdish culture failed because of the fear of fostering hostility towards migrants (Ateş 2003, 163–174).

But the feminist movement was also barely interested in the situation of immigrant women. While student revolts in the 1960s and 1970s lifted restrictions on sexuality and the second wave of the women's movement fought for sexual freedom and autonomy for women and homosexuals, the situation of female immigrants and sexual minorities within the immigrant communities was seldom addressed, if at all. Although the women's movement claimed to have a broad critique of subjection that included sex, race, and class, many of its topics focused on the emancipation of the well-educated, politically active German female. Those were sometimes very different from that of immigrant women. While, for example, the feminist movement fought for and in all-female organizations where women could find themselves or make politics without the patriarchy of male-dominated structures (Nave-Herz 1997, 50–84), many immigrant women fought patriarchy within their families and communities, and for the freedom to meet with male friends or to go out at all (Ateş 2007, 42–44). The state's gender equality policies also did not recognize the problem that lay in the patriarchy of some immigrants' cultural practices. German politicians saw immigrants as workers who weren't part of German society. As a consequence, they had little interest in their affairs. The investigation-committee about women and society, which was initiated to inquire about the situation of women and pointed out inequalities in a broad range of societal fields, did not even mention immigrants (see Ausschuß für Jugend, Familie und Gesundheit 1986). So, despite the increasing sensibility for women's rights issues and the negative spotlight on immigrant culture, the problems of immigrant women were ignored.

As a reaction, immigrant and black women questioned patriarchal structures within immigrant cultures and within the majority culture, as well as the racism and ignorance of the German feminist movement. They formed their own groups, which fought for their rights and called for solidarity between German and non-German women. The "Committee of Women from Turkey" stated:

> It is clear that we all live in a society in which the women's question (no matter from which country we are) is not solved. But the question is even bigger and more severe if it is about women from Turkey. To live and to work in the BRD [Federal Republic of Germany, PK] as a non-German – with other words: as a non-German worker who is a second class human anyway – and additionally to be a non-German woman means: the woman from Turkey is a third class of humans.
>
> (Komitee der Frauen aus der Türkei 1981, cited after Lenz 2010a, 714–715)

They also worked together with German feminists – often those who had non-German partners or children from relationships with non-Germans, and therefore were themselves indirectly affected by racism. In the Call for the First Joint Women's Congress, they declared that as immigrant women, they are the "female slaves of slaves"[11] and that the German immigration policy towards immigration abets this. For example, if women immigrated as part of a family reunion, they had no working permit. That meant that they had to leave the country in the case of a divorce, or even a separation that forced them to live on welfare. As they had no living base back in their home countries, especially as many of them had been in Germany for more than 15 years, this made them more vulnerable to domestic violence. Sometimes this was even used by violent husbands or their own families as a threat that held women in marriage (Lenz 2010b, 709).

> Through the denial of material existence, of a secure residence permit, and of support for our independence, we non-German women are relinquished. Thereby we are bound to our husbands, although we are already very dependent upon them because of the lack of communities of women, which we had in our home countries, because of the social isolation, and the foreign language and environment. Additionally, our children assimilate themselves faster and alienate from us. Our own home can become a prison, and clinging to tradition often becomes the last foothold but also a special chain. This is a burden especially for the girls of the "second generation." They are dragged into a grueling

fight where they are torn between the creation of a life-perspective of their own and the traditional role expectations, watched by fathers and brothers as the guards of morality.

(Arbeitsgruppe Frauenkongress 1984, cited after Lenz 2010a, 716–719)

With the shift in immigration since the late 1970s from guest workers to asylum seekers, it became obvious that the German criteria for the grant of asylum were also gender biased and hetero-normative: the flight reasons of women and homosexuals were often not accepted as valid. Women-specific forms of persecution include, for example, forced marriages, honor killings, or abduction, the practice of sati in India, or the practice of female genital mutilation in many countries in Africa, some of Asia, and the Middle East. In many countries, strict gender roles, certain dress codes like the veil, or virginity before marriage are violently enforced. Rape is a common form of torture against women. Mass rapes are systematically part of warfare (Gahn 1999, 19–35). Homosexuality was and is forbidden in many countries, and in some it is even punished by death (Rupar 2014). However, the right of asylum in Germany was restricted to "Persons persecuted on political grounds" (Basic Law for the Federal Republic of Germany, Art. 16a (1)). It is not exactly defined what political means here, but violence against women was usually interpreted as a private affair. And even where the persecutor was clearly the state, as in cases where women violated gender dress codes in Iran and faced a whipping, they were denied asylum because the punishment is supposed to maintain the Islamic legal order and therefore had to be accepted. Furthermore, it was stated that these gender rules apply to all women in Iran and do therefore not present a sufficient reason for asylum (Gahn 1999, 61).

Gender-specific persecution or violence against women – which are often based in cultural or religious traditions – were not seen as political persecution but as something that somehow belongs to these countries. This cultural relativism was directly used to argue against the asylum rights of women. In the early 1980s, women's rights groups began demanding the recognition of gender-specific reasons for granting asylum (Gahn 1999, 58). But it took an EU decision to force Germany to finally include them in 2005 (Deutsches Rotes Kreuz 2012, 9; Pelzer 2009). For a long time, persecution because of sexual orientation was not necessarily accepted, either, even when homosexuality was illegal in the state. The argument of the Federal Administrative Court (Bundesverwaltungsgericht) was again relativistic. As the ban on homosexuality in Iran was similar to the ban that had been in place in Germany 20 years earlier, "it is not the purpose of the asylum-right to implement the changing moral views of the Federal Republic of Germany in other countries" (BVerwGE 79, 143, cited after Markard 2013, 75). Homosexuals had to prove that it was not possible for them to restrain their sexual desire; otherwise, asylum was denied and asylum-seekers were advised to hide their homosexuality in order to avoid persecution (Markard 2013, 75). This rule was applied to religious communities, too, until members of the Ahmadiyya religion in Pakistan won their case in the Court of Justice of the European Union, which ruled that the potential to hide religious orientation is irrelevant for the asylum laws (Markard 2013, 76–77). After a British court ruled that it is possible to apply this to homosexuality, too, Germany followed: the possibility of living a discreet life is no longer a reason to refuse asylum-seekers (Markard 2013, 82). However, this positive development would be contradicted by the post-Cologne attempts to declare Tunisia, Algeria, and Morocco "safe states of origin," which would facilitate deportations. The situation for women and homosexuals in North Africa is anything but safe (Meiritz 2016). It is not clear how such a law would be handled in practice, but there is the apparent risk that the muting of critique of gender norms and harmful cultural practices in order to avoid accusations of racism and Islamophobia might turn against those who seek asylum because of gender persecution.

Religion in general and Islam – as the religion of most of the immigrants in Germany – in particular became the central topic of the immigration debate only after 9/11. After the Islamist terrorist attacks and the discovery that a part of the terrorist group had lived in Germany, it became shockingly clear that in the past little had been done for the integration of Muslims. In the following debate, we can observe a similar dynamic to the one regarding religion and gender violence: one side instrumentalizes the attacks to argue against migration in general. The other side wants to avoid the potentially dangerous stigmatization of Muslims and therefore denies any connections between Islam and terrorism. Former German chancellor Gerhard Schröder, for example, said in his government statement in the German Parliament (Deutscher Bundestag): "We all know that the attacks of New York and Washington have absolutely nothing to do with religion. They are an expression of criminal intents" (Schröder 2001). Critique of Islam or of the religious background of the terror was called Islamophobia, which was categorized as a form of heterophobia or "hostility towards humans" (Leibold and Kühnel 2003). But this terminology was problematic itself, because it erased the possibility of differentiating whether the intention was racist or, for example, condemning Islamic patriarchy or human rights violations supported through religious doctrines (Seidel 2003). Critique of Islam can have at least three different reasons: it could be invoked because it is experienced as the religion of the immigrants, which would make it racist or nationalistic. It can be invoked because it is a religion that is different from that of one's own, which is common in interreligious relationships, demarcation, or conflict. Finally, it can be criticized because it is a religion, and as a result brings religious norms back into the public realm, which would give it a secular or ideology-critical aspect (see Klug 2010, 21–27). The undifferentiated disqualification of critique as racist or Islamophobic created a political taboo, which in turn was used in arguments by racists, who pointed out the Islamist motivation of the terrorists or the cultural differences in terms of gender roles. The Right also used feminist authors with a Muslim Background like Necla Kelek, Seyran Ateş, and Ayaan Hirsi Ali in order to give its racist rejection of immigrants a legitimate aspect. These authors criticize the gender norms that are prevalent in many Islamic societies and Islamic communities in the West, like arranged or forced marriages, honor killings, the extreme focus on female virginity and moral conduct, the requirement to separate genders and veil women, female genital mutilation, the submission of women under the rules of their male family members, and the widespread disdain for apostates, non-Muslims, and modern democracy. They call the Western ignorance towards these practices "misunderstood tolerance" (Kelek 2006, 253), ask for "help from the liberal West" in order to reform Islam (Hirsi Ali 2006, 12–14), and call the idea of multiculturalism a "mistake" (Ateş 2007).

Germany has also witnessed many successful and educated Muslim women who actively counter the picture of the oppressed women in Islam because they find that discriminating or stigmatizing towards their religion and towards themselves. Fereshta Ludin, the teacher who (with the financial support of Islamic groups) fought for a teacher's right to wear the Islamic headscarf in public school classrooms, claimed that wearing it was a personal decision and that veiled women can also be emancipated. She said that it would take away her "dignity" if she would have to take it off in the classroom and that she would feel "naked" without it (Ludin cited after Leffers 2003). And there are also Muslim women who are engaged in the feminist reinterpretation of Islam. Projects like the Cologne-based *Center for Islamic Women-Research* claim, for example, that the message of the Qur'an is "freeing for and supporting of women" (Zentrum für Islamische Frauenforschung s.a.). And the project *Nafisa* wants to bring to mind the active role that women played in early Islam as scholars, which they see as a "model" for participation in public life and intellectual discourse (Nafisa s.a.). While this stream of more women-friendly interpretations of Islamic scripture and tradition, which was internationally promoted by Fatima Mernissi and Leila Ahmed, was widely acknowledged in academia (see for example Rommelspacher 2009) and some academics even misunderstood it as an actual description of Islamic societies (see for example Braun and Mathes 2007), feminist critics of Islam and Islamic gender roles were either ignored or even actively fought by the academic discourse. In a petition by a group of 60 German academics, Necla Kelek, Seyran Ateş, and Ayaan Hirsi Ali were heavily criticized for "inflating their own experiences and singular cases as a societal problem" in order to have success in the book market.

The academics criticized the fact that their (partly autobiographic) books were not scientific and used "cheap clichés" about Islam or Turks that were at odds with the findings of German academic literature about migration (Karakasoglu and Terkessidis 2006). The culture-relativists Christina von Braun and Bettina Mathes even suggest that the topic of Islamic gender roles itself is the problem as it distracts attention from the problems in Western society (Braun and Mathes 2007, 429–435). For them, the bikini equals the burka and plastic surgery is the Western version of female genital mutilation. The Islamic veiling of women's faces is comparable to the practice of photography; both are "the art of seeing without being seen" (Braun and Mathes 2007, 24, 9–31). They state that

> such relativism does not mean to ignore or even support the violence against the female body. [. . .] But it allows us to ask for the cultural background of such a difference and questions the Western view of women along the way.
>
> (Braun and Mathes 2007, 18)

This speaks volumes about the racist culturalism and (neo-) colonialism of many Western academics. Even where the spotlight is on the intersection of gender, religion, and race or immigration, the focus often remains the sexism of Western societies. The actual situation of women in Islamic contexts or their concerns are largely ignored, especially where they contradict the image of Islam that Western academics draw.

But the difference between plastic surgery in the West and female genital mutilation (FGM) is that, as an anonymous refugee has put it, in the latter "women were being forced to have FGM performed on their fragile, innocent bodies" because the girls are very young (Anonymous 2016, 49). And Bintou Bojang, a victim of female genital mutilation who sought asylum in Germany because she was persecuted for speaking out against the practice in her home country of Gambia, asks international organizations for solidarity in order to "stop cutting our girls" (Bojang 2016, 92). The difference that has been pointed out here is the use of institutionalized physical force and the lack of legal protection. An intersectional approach has to acknowledge the hardship that non-Western women endure, often in addition to the sexism that is typical for the Western world. Even if Western culture is still patriarchal, it provides women and homosexuals with a minimum of legal and actual protection against violence – as incomplete and precarious as it may be.[12] Pointing out this difference is not about denying the sexism and the violence in the West. It is about solidarity with those who are in a situation that is even worse. It is about fighting for their right to find asylum here. It is about fighting with them to end violence against women and queers. And it is about overcoming the ethnocentrism and colonialism of a Western feminist culture that ignores the harmful cultural practices that women and queers in and from other parts of the world are exposed to.

Going through different aspects of the debate in German history shows that the discussion about Cologne is by no means new. The positions that were expressed had been formed in German society long ago. That most of the New Year's Eve victims were women without a Muslim or immigrant background was just one more reason for the Right to use the critique of Islamic gender roles for their racist discourse, and just one more reason for the Left to reject this critique and to focus on sexism in Western societies. These are the two sides of the same culturalist and racist coin.

The Paradox of Cultures

Not only the incidents of Cologne but also the violence towards immigrant women, homosexuals, and nonconformists that had already been happening in Germany for decades made it clear that we desperately need a debate about the connection between religion, culture, and patriarchal gender norms and practices. But how can we express the problem that there are religious or cultural traditions that legitimize, institutionalize, or even prescribe the violation of human rights without generalizing and stigmatizing all who live in the countries or communities where these traditions are common?

It is important to keep in mind that this is not just a debate about Islam or about immigrant culture. Cultural practices that violate human rights in general and women's and queer rights in particular are found in many different cultures and subcultures. So, we not only discuss the sexual assaults of Cologne and how much they are based on Islamic gender norms but also speak about honor killings as they are also practiced by Yezidis, about arranged or forced marriages that also occur among Evangelical Christians and Orthodox Jews, about polygamy as also practiced among Mormons, about female genital mutilation as it is also practiced by some Christians in Africa, about circumcision of small boys as it is also common in Judaism and in the United States, about the burning of widows in India, foot-binding in China, witch-hunts in Africa, intersex surgeries in the West, the persecution of homosexuals in several countries of the world, and all other culture-based violations of human rights. While many human rights groups actually advocate addressing these "Harmful Cultural or Traditional Practices" (see e.g. Women's Legal Centre s.a.; Terre des Femmes s.a.; United Nations Human Rights Office of the High Commissioner s.a.; Stop Violence against Women 2010), in Western academia the debate about gender roles and different cultures usually is framed as the relationship between "us" and "the others," whether the dominant West versus the colonialized or the majority versus the minority. Critiques of traditional gender roles among immigrants or in non-Western cultures are discredited as "Homonationalism" (Puar 2007) or "Femonationalism" (Farris 2012) and are seen as a form of cultural imperialism. In order to avoid the stigmatization of marginalized cultural or religious groups and their members, patriarchal or sexist cultural practices are denied or ignored and the critique is pointed back at the Western culture. The underlying assumption is that religion and culture are matters of identity, of a self-chosen commitment: something that is lived, performed, and upheld. And if cultural practices are something that people are free to choose, then they do not present a problem for human rights. But cultures and religions are more than a matter of choice: they are sets of convictions, norms, and practices that entail power structures and can be enforced through sanctions.[13] Cultures also limit personal choices, especially where they shape law and custom. As Iranian Canadian feminist Haideh Moghissi has reminded us,

> in supporting the rights of minority cultures and indigenous traditions, we should ask ourselves: do we know with any precision whose cultures and whose rights to self-expression we are supporting? What are the social and political contexts and power relations behind particular forms of cultural expression? Who has assumed the authority for cultural representation in particular cases and why?
>
> (Moghissi 1999, 59)

Cultures and traditions always implicate hierarchies, create exclusions, and institutionalize power-relations.

My overview about the German integration debate has shown that the problem of gender violence in immigrant cultures and cultural and religious traditions goes beyond the degradation of the "other" in order to preserve a superior image of the "we." If we consider that religions and cultures entail power structures and establish gender norms, the first people concerned are those who are aggrieved through those power relations or deviate from those norms. In order to acknowledge that, we need to focus not just on *the other* but also on *the other of the other*.

In the German integration debate, the term "culture" has been used in a way that sees cultures as homogenous entities that determine people's behavior according to their origin. This classical biological racism has been mirrored by the multi-culturalists and culture-relativists who defend cultural practices in every aspect in the name of anti-racism, assuming that the defense of "their" cultural norms and practices is in the interest of the immigrants. As this is more and more contested, especially through cases in which the cultural or religious norms of one group also affect people who do not belong to the group – like in the events in Cologne – the idea of cultures and religions as homogenous and generalized entities has finally been given up completely, especially among academics, the media, and in parts of the Left. This deconstruction of culture is compelling in the sense that there is no such thing as a culture that determines all its members in the same way. Cultural or religious groups – especially those as big as world religions – are diverse within themselves. But not only do they have as many interpretations as members, but it is also highly contested as to whose interpretations are authoritative and who belongs to the group at all. And yet, this argument fails to acknowledge that there are cultural or religious legitimations for gender violence nevertheless. Gender norms and roles are prescribed in religious texts and performed in cultural practices. That cultures are diverse and plural, that norms are shifting and contested, and that they are not shared by everybody in the same way does not contradict that. Quite the opposite! It creates an obligation to acknowledge the problem, to address discriminatory practices, and to act in solidarity with those who want to change, to stop, or to flee them. We cannot fight violence if we ignore the motives and the rationales of the perpetrators.

On March 13, 2016 in Hannover, 21-year-old student Shilan H. was shot to death at her own wedding. The perpetrator was her cousin, with whom Shilan's uncle had arranged an engagement while her father was working in Iraq. When the father came back, he dissolved the forced bond and allowed his daughter to marry someone else. After Shilan was shot, he wrote in her obituary that this had been an honor killing and that his daughter had become a "victim of traditions" (cited after Prüfer 2016). A few newspapers reported. A societal debate, like after the incidents in Cologne, was not even started. The death of Shilan was just one of countless such incidents that happen in Germany every year. I chose it because it provides an example of the quintessential paradoxical situation that I have described: we have to acknowledge that there are no homogenous entities called "cultures" or "religions" that determine everyone with the same origin or all of its adherents. But, at the same time, we have to acknowledge the existence and power of certain norms and convictions and traditions in certain groups, and that they can lead to the violation of human rights. So, in a way, cultures don't exist, and yet they do. This is what I call the *Paradox of Cultures*.

Creating immigration policies based on human rights

The ongoing migration to countries in Europe creates a challenge, especially for Germany. After a long history of denying being an immigration country at all, and after decades of very diffident integration policies that have been characterized by ignoring harmful cultural practices within immigrant communities, German policies after 9/11 have turned integration more and more into a matter of Islam instead of economic or political rights. The focus has been on the acknowledgment of religion and culture, without questioning whether these are in line with human rights or whether they violate them (Klug 2011). New Year's Eve in Cologne made it clear that ignoring these problems can easily have repercussions for native Germans, too. The calls for action that followed the events have typically come from the Right or Conservative side, which has discovered feminism as a means to argue against immigration. The other side focused mainly on sexism and discrimination within German society. But refusing to be taken in by racist instrumentalization cannot mean ignoring sexism and harmful cultural practices among immigrants. Therefore, I want to offer some proposals for basing integration policies on the principles of human rights instead of nationalism or the dialogue of cultures.

The first goal of immigration policies must be the protection of those who are threatened with the violation of their human rights. These are, of course, people in dangerous situations like wars, authoritarian regimes, and natural or economical catastrophes, but these are also victims of harmful cultural traditions and practices. We need to be sensitive to flight-reasons that relate to gender or sexual orientation. That persecution or cultural practice is common or legal in a country does not present a reason to deny asylum. To the contrary: as it makes it more unlikely to find protection within one's country of origin, the legal or widespread existence of such practices should guarantee asylum for all who are in danger. This would also encourage the governments of the host countries to fight these practices in the countries where they are performed.

The subjects of human rights are individuals, not cultures or religions. To ban hate speech and racism cannot mean to delegitimize critique. The critique of cultural and religious practices is protected by the right to freedom of expression. As the line between the two is often contested, I want to propose a mode of differentiation, which can help to shape nondiscriminatory policies: something can be categorized as racism or hate speech if it is directed towards people based on their identity, and to cultural or religious practices that apply to them individually. But as soon as their practices affect other individuals, including minors in the care of the practitioners, they must be open to critique. Furthermore, we need to be sensible of the fact that religion always includes processes of othering and that this creates outgroups that are vulnerable to violence, particularly in times of religious radicalization.

Immigration policies need to break the cycle of using the critique of gender violence or cultural practices in immigrant culture in order to spread racism, and the subsequent rejection of that critique in the name of anti-racism and tolerance. Although there are no such things as homogenous cultures or religions that determine all their adherents, we need to be aware of cultural and religious practices that are harmful, even if it may seem paradoxical. Women, and people who do not conform to gender norms, are affected by both racism *and* the cultural or religious gender violence. In order to determine whether human rights violations occur, we need to pay attention not only to the communities' leaders and spokespersons but also to those who criticize their communities from within or after they've left them. An intersectional analysis that focuses on those who have "no space from which [they can] speak" (Spivak 1994, 103) can help to detect victims that are absent from our attention. The situation of minors and other vulnerable groups, like women and people who do not conform to heterosexual norms, needs to be monitored and improved. This must include not only the situation in the public sphere but also environments of limited protection, like in collective housing or the private sphere.

Integration in the host country should not be based on national cultures, which can be equally discriminating, but on human rights standards. Racism and hostility towards strangers need to be fought more effectively in order to secure safety for refugees.

The responsibility for human rights is shared internationally – human rights violations are never domestic issues! This is of special importance for people who are fleeing their country and seeking asylum in another one.

Although Western societies themselves are not free of gender violence and discrimination, they have to extend their protective measures, like human rights instruments, towards other cultures and towards immigrants, while at the same time expanding and improving them.

Human rights are not neutral; they are a normative frame by themselves. But there is an important difference between the idea of human rights and other cultures and traditions. The latter establish norms that limit people in their personal expression or even harm their physical integrity. Human rights do not limit individual expression or collective cultural expression, where it is based on individual consent. It is not possible to impose human rights on someone. The only freedom that they limit is the limiting of the freedom of others. Therefore, immigration and integration policies need to be based on human rights and not on the dialogue of cultures or religions. While human rights can be criticized for allowing only incomplete protection or emancipation (see e.g. Gouges 2003 [1791]; Marx 1976 [1843]; Arendt 2013 [1962]), critiques should not fall back behind the standards that the human rights frame provides.

Notes

1 I often use the terms "cultural" and "religious" interchangeably depending on the context. Religion is part of culture, which is legitimized through a reference to the supernatural. In general, the differentiation is fluid, though.

2 In March 2018, an attempt by the economically liberal opposition party FDP to declare those state as safe states failed in the German Parliament (Bundestag), despite the fact that members of both of the governing parties CDU and SPD agreed on the subject, because they do not see a majority in Germany's Federal Assembly (Bundesrat) – a legislative council, which consists of representatives of the 16 German states – and will work on an even broader proposal themselves (Deutscher Bundestag 2018). However, the discussion is ongoing.

3 It is telling that the racism in accusing someone of being of North African or Arabic descent – as if one could easily identify this – is mirrored by the racism in pointing to German society instead, as if it would not contain immigrants, too!

4 The group itself translated its name as "noexcuses." As there are other significant differences between the German and the English version of their texts, and in Germany the German version was the basis of the discussion, I have used my own translation of the German text.

5 The term "cis"-women stands for women whose sexual identity fits with the common gender norms in a society.

6 In 2016, that law was changed, and in 2017, Germany finally ratified the Istanbul Convention.

7 After it became known that there were refugees among the suspects, the article was updated and stated that there is no causal connection between the crimes and the question of if the perpetrators were refugees or Muslims. "Crimes are committed by criminals, by individual people, not by groups or religions" (Rafael Update 2016).

8 After Volker Beck, a politician of the Green Party in Germany, filed charges against Abu-Yusuf because he saw this as a public incitement to criminal behavior, the imam defended himself by saying that his comments were taken out of context. He repeated that one reason why the North African men attacked the women

was because of the way they were "almost naked" with mini-skirts or tight pants and because they wore perfume. However, he said that the attacks were not legitimate and that Muslims are not even allowed to look at those women, let alone to touch them. Native German women, "who live here since centuries," use to dress like that. Any visitor who can't accept that should go to another country (Abu-Yusuf 2016).

9 After the post was criticized, the website stated that it did not intend to suggest that women who are raped are responsible for that crime. They concede that men should always control their desires. But they refer to this as a "utopian" concept, because not all men are Islamic or rational. Therefore, women for their own safety should dress modestly and avoid places where alcohol flows in masses. Later the post and the discussion were deleted.

10 While I follow Crenshaw in her analysis, I find the term "privilege" of little help here, because it implies that not to be subjected to a certain form of discrimination is an unjust advantage that needs to be overcome. Rather than pointing to the "privilege" of Western women, I would point to the different forms of discrimination against non-Western women as well as to a system that inevitably implies power structures and needs to be criticized in its totality (see also Fischer 2017).

11 In German: "Sklavinnen der Sklaven." While the German language makes a distinction between the female and the male form of a term, mixed groups are called by the male term. In the example of slaves, the female form is Sklavin, the male form is Sklave, and the mixed plural would be Sklaven, which is called the generic masculine. Only, as is the case here, if a group is explicitly addressed as women, is the plural form "–innen" used. This not only excludes the females from the plural term and makes them invisible but also causes problems for translation. In order to translate appropriately, I add "female" when the female form is used in German.

12 How precarious those freedoms are can be seen in the fact that the events of Cologne were not punishable under German law at the time, but also in the misogynist view of women that has been expressed in the "Locker Room Talk" of Donald Trump.

13 This has been internationally discussed through the debate about Susan Moller Okin's essay "Is Multiculturalism Bad for Women?" (see Okin 1999 and for the debate the articles in Okin et al. 1999). For an overview about the current debate about feminism and human rights in Germany, see Leicht et al. (2015). For the term "religion," I have shown that – although usually defined as something that is important primarily for its adherents – religion can also have an impact on nonbelievers, religious minorities, and nonconformists (Klug 2015a, 2015b).

References

Where not otherwise noted, the German and French texts have been translated by Petra Klug.

#ausnahmslos. 2016. "#ausnahmslos: Gegen sexualisierte Gewalt und Rassismus. Immer. Überall." Accessed March 04, 2016. http://ausnahmslos.org/.

#einearmeslaenge. "Twitter." Accessed March 09, 2016. https://twitter.com/hashtag/einearmeslaenge.

Abu-Yusuf, Sami. 2016. Interview with *Kölner Express*, 21.01.2016. Accessed May 30, 2017. www.express.de/koeln/koelner-silvester-mob-interview-sorgt-fuer-wirbel – jetzt-redet-der-imam-bei-express-23423742.

Anonymous. 2016. "It is about freedom of movement." *International Women Space*: 43–58.

Arendt, Hannah. 2013 [1962]. *The origins of totalitarianism.* [7th ed.]. Meridian Books, MG 15. Cleveland: World Pub. Co.

Ateş, Seyran. 2003. *Grosse Reise ins Feuer: Die Geschichte einer deutschen Türkin.* Berlin: Rowohlt.

———. 2007. *Der Multikulti-Irrtum: Wie wir in Deutschland besser zusammenleben können.* Berlin: Ullstein.

Augstein, Jakob. 2016. "Lust der Angst." *Spiegel Online*, January 11. Accessed March 05, 2016. www.spiegel.de/politik/deutschland/koeln-wenn-sexismus-und-rassismus-sich-treffen-kolumne-a-1071403-druck.html.

Ausschuß für Jugend, Familie und Gesundheit. 1986. "Beschlußempfehlung und Bericht des zu dem Bericht der Enquete-Kommission Frau und Gesellschaft gemäß Beschluß des Deutschen Bundestages vom 5. Mai 1977*) – Drucksache 8/305-: Drucksache 8/4461." http://dip21.bundestag.de/dip21/btd/10/056/1005623.pdf.

Basic Law for the Federal Republic of Germany: *English Version.* With the assistance of C. Tomuschat and D. P. Currie. Accessed May 04, 2016. www.gesetze-im internet. de/englisch_gg/basic_law_for_the_federal_republic_of_germany.pdf.

Bild.de. 2016. "Weil sie Parfüm trugen | Kölner Imam: Opfer von Sex-Mob selbst schuld." Accessed March 05, 2016. www.bild.de/regional/koeln/sex-uebergriffe-silvesternacht/imam-gibt-frauen-mitschuld-an-sex-taten-44243172.bild.html.

Bojang, Bintou. 2016. "I am a victim of Female Genital Mutilation." *International Women Space*: 87–95.

Braun, Christina V., and Bettina Mathes. 2007. *Verschleierte Wirklichkeit: Die Frau, der Islam und der Westen.* Schriftenreihe der Bundeszentrale für Politische Bildung Bd. 652. Bonn: Bundeszentrale für Politische Bildung.

Butterwegge, Christoph. 1992. "Thesen zur 'multikulturellen Gesellschaft'." *Der Rechte Rand* (18): 11.

Carvajal, Doreen. 2015. "An Algerian author fights back against a Fatwa." *New York Times*, January 4. Accessed March 10, 2016. www.nytimes.com/2015/01/05/books/an-algerian-author-fights-back-against-a-fatwa.html?_r=0.

Clemm, Christina, and Sabine Hark. 2016. "Sexismus: Sind wir über Nacht zu einer feministischen Nation geworden?" *Die Zeit*, January 18. http://pdf.zeit.de/kultur/2016-01/feminismus-uebergriffe-koeln-clemm-hark-10-nach-8.pdf.

Collectif. 2016. "Nuit de Cologne: Kamel Daoud recycle les clichés orientalistes les plus éculés." *Le Monde*, February 11. Accessed March 09, 2016. www.lemonde. fr/idees/article/2016/02/11/les-fantasmes-de-kamel-daoud_4863096_3232.html.

Crenshaw, Kimberle. 1989. "Demarginalizing the intersection of race and sex: A black feminist critique of antidiscrimination doctrine, feminist theory and antiracist politics." *University of Chicago Legal Forum* (1): 139–167. http://chicagoun bound.uchicago.edu/cgi/viewcontent.cgi?article=1052&context=uclf. Accessed March 12, 2016.

Daoud, Kamel. 2016a. "Colonia: Il corpo delle donne e il desiderio di libertà di quegli uomini sradicati dalla loro terra." *La Repubblica*, January 10. Accessed March 09, 2016. www.repubblica.it/esteri/2016/01/10/news/colonia_molestie_capodanno_un_articolo_dello_scrittore_algerino_daoud-130973948/?ref=search.

———. 2016b. "Viol et fantasmes sur 'Europe'." *L'Hebdo*, January 14. Accessed March 09, 2016. www.hebdo.ch/hebdo/id%C3%A9es-d%C3%A9bats/detail/viol-et-fantasmes-sur-%C2%ABeurope%C2%BB.

———. 2016c. "Cologne, lieu de fantasmes." January 31. Accessed March 09, 2016. www.lemonde.fr/idees/article/2016/01/31/cologne-lieu-de-fantasmes_4856694_3232.html.

———. 2016d. "The Sexual Misery of the Arab World." February 12. Accessed March 09, 2016. www.nytimes.com/2016/02/14/opinion/sunday/the-sexual-misery-of-the-arab-world.html?_r=0.

———. 2016e. "Islam und Körper: Das sexuelle Elend der arabischen Welt." *Frankfurter Allgemeine Zeitung*, February 18. Accessed March 09, 2016. www. faz.net/aktuell/feuilleton/islam-und-koerper-das-sexuelle-elend-der-arabischen-welt-14075502.html?printPagedArticle=true#pageIndex_2.

———. 2016f. "Kamel Daoud et les 'fantasmes' de Cologne, retour sur une polémique." *Le Monde*, February 23. Accessed March 09, 2016. www.lemonde.fr/idees/article/2016/02/20/kamel-daoud-et-les-fantasmes-de-cologne-retour-sur-une-polemique_4868849_3232.html.

Deutscher Bundestag. 2018. "Algerien, Marokko und Tunesien bleiben keine sicheren Herkunftsstaaten." October 18. Accessed December 18, 2018. www.bundestag.de/dokumente/textarchiv/2018/kw42-de-herkunftsstaaten/573208.

Deutsches Rotes Kreuz. 2012. "Erläuterungen zum Asylverfahrensgesetz – Vorgerei chtliches Verfahren." Accessed March 18, 2016. www.asyl.net/fileadmin/user_upload/redaktion/Dokumente/Arbeitshilfen/2012-11-DRK-Erlaeuterungen_AsylVfG.pdf.

Elfferding, Wieland. 1983. "Notiz zum Diskurs des 'Heidelberger Manifest'." *Das Argument* 138: 254–260. Accessed May 03, 2016.

Farris, Sara R. 2012. "Femonationalism and the 'regular' army of labor called migrant women." *History of the Present* 2(2): 184–199. doi:10.5406/historypresent.2.2.0184.

Fischer, Leo. 2017. Repression für alle. In L'Amour Lalove, Patsy (Ed.) *Beissreflexe. Kritik an queerem Aktivismus, autoritären Sehnsüchten, Sprechverboten*. Berlin: Querverlag, 104–110.

Flade, Florian, Marcel Pauly, and Kristian Frigelj. 2016. "Silvester: 1054 Strafan-zeigen nach Übergriffen von Köln." *Die Welt*, February 10. Accessed March 03, 2016. www.welt.de/politik/deutschland/article152018368/1054-Strafanzeigen-nach-Uebergriffen-von-Koeln.html?config=print.

FOCUS. 2016. "Die Nacht der Schande." *FOCUS*, January 8. Accessed March 04, 2016. www.focus.de/politik/focus-titel-die-nacht-der-schande_id_5198275.html, see also: http://images.google.de/imgres?imgurl=http%3A%2F%2Fp5.focus.de%2Fimg%2Ffotos%2Fcrop5197352%2F5832718137-w1200-h627-o-q75-p5%2Ffocus 02-2016.jpg&imgrefurl=http%3A%2F%2Fwww.focus.de%2Fpolitik%2Ffocus-titel-die-nacht-der-schande_id_5198275.html&h=627&w=1200&tbnid=HxDo 6LSfUaYTwM%3A&docid=RgbEPz2A0JJuKM&ei=FtTZVrzuHMXv6QSNgZf 4Aw&tbm=isch&iact=rc&uact=3&dur=1672&page=1&start=0&ndsp=25&ve d=0ahUKEwi80c_j1KfLAhXFd5oKHY3ABT8QrQMIMDAG.

Gahn, Catrin. 1999. *Adäquate Anhörung im Asylverfahren für Flüchtlingsfrauen? Zur Qualifizierung der "Sonderbeauftragten für geschlechtsspezifische Verfolgung" beim Bundesamt für die Anerkennung ausländischer Flüchtlinge*. Schriftenreihe des Instituts für Bildung und Kommunikation in Migrationsprozessen (IBKM) an der Carl von Ossietzky Universität Oldenburg Nr. 4. Oldenburg: Bibliotheks-und Informationssystem der Universität Oldenburg. Accessed March 18, 2016. http://oops.uni-oldenburg.de/622/13/gahada99.pdf.

Gensing, Patrick. 2016. "Rechtsextreme nach Köln-Übergriffen: 'Rache für unsere Frauen'." *tagesschau.de*, January 12. Accessed March 03, 2016. www.tagesschau.de/inland/koeln-rechte-gewalt-101.html.

Gouges, Olympe de. 2003 [1791]. *Déclaration des droits de la femme et de la citoyenne: Suivi de Préface pour les dames ou Le portrait des femmes*. With the assistance of E. Gaulier. Mille et une nuits 416. Paris: Éd. Mille et une nuits.

Günther, Judith. 2016. "Streit über Facebook-Entgleisung: Claudia Roth nimmt AfD in die Mangel." *n-tv.de*, January 29. Accessed March 11, 2016. www.n-tv.de/poli tik/Claudia-Roth-nimmt-AfD-in-die-Mangel-article16884851.html?service=print.

Herbert, Ulrich. 2003. *Geschichte der Ausländerpolitik in Deutschland: Saisonarbe-iter, Zwangsarbeiter, Gastarbeiter, Flüchtlinge.* Schriftenreihe/Bundeszentrale für Politische Bildung Bd. 410. Bonn: BpB.

Hirsi Ali, Ayaan. 2006. *Ich klage an: Plädoyer für die Befreiung der muslimischen Frauen.* Ungekürzte Taschenbuchausg. Serie Piper 4791. München [u.a.]: Piper.

Hübsch, Khola M. 2016. "Cologne: New Year's Eve mob: Thinly veiled racism." Accessed May 02, 2016. https://en.qantara.de/content/cologne-new-years-eve-mob-thinly-veiled-racism.

International Women Space, ed. 2016. *In our own words: Refugee Women in Ger-many tell their stories.* International Women Space, accessed at https://iwspace. wordpress.com, May, 2019.

Kampf, Lena. 2016. "BKA-Bericht zu Silvester: Übergriffe in zwölf Bundesländern." February 24. Accessed March 04, 2016. www.tagesschau.de/inland/silvester-uebergriffe-bka-101.html.

Karakasoglu, Yasemin, and Mark Terkessidis. 2006. "Gerechtigkeit für die Muslime! Die deutsche Integrationspolitik stützt sich auf Vorurteile. So hatsie keine Zuku-nft." *Die Zeit*, February 1. Petition von 60 Migrationsforschern. Accessed March 24, 2016. http://pdf.zeit.de/2006/06/Petition.pdf.

Kelek, Necla. 2006. *Die fremde Braut: Ein Bericht aus dem Inneren des türkischen Lebens in Deutschland.* 4. Aufl. München: Goldmann.

———. 2016. "Die Übergriffe von Köln und die Folgen: Kaum einer hat sich Gedan-ken gemacht, wer da ins Land kommt." *Rheinische Post*, January 10. Accessed March 07, 2016. www.rp-online.de/nrw/staedte/koeln/gastbeitrag-zu-koeln-und-den-folgen-es-gibt-kein-schluessiges-konzept-fuer-integration-aid-1.5680719.

Klug, Petra. 2010. *Feindbild Islam? Der Diskurs über Muslime in Bundestagsdebat-ten vor und nach dem 11. September.* Marburg: Tectum-Verl.

———. 2011. "Die Kulturalisierung der deutschen Integrationspolitik: Grundannah-men der politischen Auseinandersetzung im Bundestag nach dem 11. September." *Politik und Kultur. Zeitung des Deutschen Kulturrates*: 8–9. www.kulturrat.de/ dokumente/puk/puk2011/puk05-11.pdf. Accessed April 14, 2016.

———. 2015a. "Der Religionsbegriff der Religionswissenschaft im Spiegel von Nich-treligion und Nonkonformität: Religiöse Normierung als blinder Fleck eines implizit emischen Religionsverständnisses." *Zeitschrift für Religionswissenschaft* 23(1): 1–19.

———. 2015b. "The blind spot in the study of religion: Religion's impact on the nonbeliev-ers." *Nonreligion and Secularity, NSRN-Blog.* Accessed May 02, 2016. https://blog. nsrn.net/2015/03/25/the-blind-spot-in-the-study-of-religion-religions-impact-on-the-nonbelievers/.

Leffers, Jochen. 2003. "Kopftuch-Kontroverse: Kulturkampf in Karlsruhe." *Spie-gel Online*, September 24. Accessed March 27, 2016. www.spiegel.de/unispiegel/ studium/kopftuch-kontroverse-kulturkampf-in-karlsruhe-a-266826.html.

Leggewie, Claus. 1990. *Multi Kulti: Spielregeln für die Vielvölkerrepublik.* 1. Aufl. Rotbuch Taschenbuch 28. Berlin: Rotbuch.

Leibold, Jürgen, and Steffen Kühnel. 2003. "Islamophobie: Sensible Aufmerksam-keiten fürspannungsreiche Anzeichen." In Heitmeyer 2003, 100–119.

Leicht, Imke, Christine Löw, Nadja Meisterhans, and Katharina Volk, eds. 2015. *Feministische Kritiken und Menschenrechte: Reflexionen auf ein produktives*

Spannungsverhältnis. 1. Aufl. olitik und Geschlecht – kompakt 27. Leverkusen: Budrich, Barbara.

Lenz, Ilse, ed. 2010a. *Die neue Frauenbewegung in Deutschland: Abschied vom kleinen Unterschied; ausgewählte Quellen*. 2. aktualisierte Aufl. Wiesbaden: VS-Verl.

———. 2010b. "Differenzen in der Frauenbewegung: MigrantInnen und schwarze Frauen fordern Anerkennung und Rechte." In *Die neue Frauenbewegung in Deutschland: Abschied vom kleinen Unterschied; ausgewählte Quellen*, edited by Ilse Lenz. 2. aktualisierte Aufl., 707–714. Wiesbaden: VS-Verl.

Markard, Nora. 2013. "Sexuelle Orientierung als Fluchtgrund – Das Ende der 'Diskretion': Aktuelle Entwicklungen beim Flüchtlingsschutz aufgrund der sexuellen Orientierung." *Asylmagazin* (3): 74–84. Accessed March 18, 2016. www.asyl.net/fileadmin/user_upload/beitraege_asylmagazin/Beitraege_AM_2013/AM2013-3beitragmarkard.pdf.

Marx, Karl. 1976 [1843]. "Zur Judenfrage." In Karl Marx and Friedrich Engels. *Werke*. 1, 347–377. Berlin: Dietz Verlag.

Mazyek, Aiman. 2016. "Nach den Schandtaten am Kölner Hauptbahnhof: Todsünde im Islam." *islam.de*, January 6. Accessed March 07, 2016. http://islam.de/27092.

Meiritz, Annett. 2016. "Sichere Herkunftsstaaten: So begründet die Regierung, warum sie Nordafrikaner nicht möchte." *Spiegel Online*, February 2. Accessed April 18, 2016. www.spiegel.de/politik/deutschland/sichere-herkunftsstaaten-bundesregierung-will-ausweitung-schon-am-mittwoch-beschliessen-a-1075224.html.

Meisner, Matthias, and Nils Wischmeyer. 2016. "Nach der Silvesternacht: Rechtsextreme nutzen Köln für rassistische Hetze." *Tagesspiegel*, January 5. Accessed March 03, 2016. www.tagesspiegel.de/politik/nach-der-silvesternacht-rechtsextreme-nutzen-koeln-fuer-rassistische-hetze/12790838.html.

Moghissi, Haideh. 1999. *Feminism and Islamic fundamentalism: The limits of postmodern analysis*. London and New York: Zed Books.

MuslimStern. 2016. "+++Stellungnahme+++ Handlungsanweisungen+++." Accessed March 05, 2016. www.facebook.com/MuslimStern.

Nafisa. s.a. "Warum Nafisa?" Accessed March 27, 2016. www.nafisa.de/ueber-uns/warum-nafisa/.

Nave-Herz, Rosemarie. 1997. *Die Geschichte der Frauenbewegung in Deutschland*. Bonn: Bundeszentrale f. politische Bildung.

NPD. 2007 [2006]. "Gute Heimreise: Feldzug gegen Multi-Kulti." Accessed March 15, 2016. www.npd-stuttgart.de/gute-heimreise-feldzug-gegen-multi-kulti/. n-tv.de. 2016. "'Auf Menschenjagd' in Köln: Gewalttäter verletzen mehrere Ausländer." January 11. Accessed March 05, 2016. www.n-tv.de/politik/Gewalttaeter-verletzen-mehrere-Auslaender-article16735566.html?service=print.

Okin, Susan M. 1999. "Is multiculturalism bad for women?" In *Is multiculturalism bad for women?*, edited by Susan M. Okin, Joshua Cohen, Matthew Howard, and Martha C. Nussbaum, 7–24. Princeton, NJ: Princeton University Press.

Okin, Susan M., Joshua Cohen, Matthew Howard, and Martha C. Nussbaum, eds. 1999. *Is multiculturalism bad for women?* Princeton, NJ: Princeton University Press.

Pelzer, Marei. 2009. "Geschlechtsspezifische Verfolgung findet in vielen Fällen im Privaten statt." Accessed March 22, 2016. www.bpb.de/internationales/weltweit/menschenrechte/38734/interview-fluchtursachen.

Polizeipräsidium Köln. 2016. "Ausgelassene Stimmung – Feiern weitgehend friedlich: POL-K: 160101–1-K/LEV." Accessed March 03, 2016. www.presseportal.de/blaulicht/pm/12415/3214905.

ProAsyl. 2018. "Die Maghreb-Länder: Noch immer keine 'Sicheren Herkunftsstaaten'." July 13. Accessed December 19, 2018. www.proasyl.de/news/die-maghreb-laender-noch-immer-keine-sicheren-herkunftsstaaten/.

Prüfer, Benjamin. 2016. "'Meine Tochter wurde Opfer von Traditionen': Vater von Ehrenmord-Opfer schreibt bewegenden Nachruf." *Huffington Post*, March 16. Accessed April 9, 2016. www.huffingtonpost.de/2016/03/16/meine-tochter-wurde-opfer_n_9475344.html.

Puar, Jasbir K. 2007. *Terrorist assemblages: Homonationalism in queer times*. Next wave. Durham: Duke University Press.

Rafael, Simone. 2016. "Silvesternacht in Köln: Sexuelle Gewalt ist keine Frage der Ethnie." January 5. Accessed March 05, 2016. www.netz-gegen-nazis.de/artikel/silvesternacht-k%C3%B6ln-organisiertes-verbrechen-nicht-enthemmte-fl%C3%BCchtlinge-10812.

———. Update 2016. "Silvesternacht in Köln: Sexuelle Gewalt ist keine Frage der Ethnie." Accessed May 03, 2016. www.netz-gegen-nazis.de/artikel/silvesternacht-k%C3%B6ln-organisiertes-verbrechen-nicht-enthemmte-fl%C3%BCchtlinge-10812.

Rommelspacher, Birgit. 2009. "Zur Emanzipation 'der' muslimischen Frau | Bundeszentrale für politische Bildung." Accessed April 4, 2016. www.bpb.de/apuz/32234/zur-emanzipation-der-muslimischen-frau?p=all.

Rühle, Marc O. 2016. "Immer mehr Attacken auf Asylheime: Der Atlas der Angst." *Bild*, March 2. Accessed March 04, 2016. www.bild.de/politik/inland/fremden feindlichkeit/atlas-der-angst-dokumentiert-uebergriffe-auf-fluechtlinge-bisher-in-2016-44658446.bild.html.

Rupar, Terri. 2014. "Here are the 10 countries where homosexuality may be punished by death." *Washington Post*, February 24. Accessed March 21, 2016. www.washingtonpost.com/news/worldviews/wp/2014/02/24/here-are-the-10-countries-where-homosexuality-may-be-punished-by-death/.

Schröder, Gerhard. 2001. "Regierungserklärung Terroranschläge in den USA und Beschlüsse des Sicherheitsrates der Vereinten Nationen sowie der NATO." In *187. Sitzung*, p. 18301B. Deutscher: Bundestag.

Schwarzer, Alice. 2016. "Die Folgen der falschen Toleranz." January 12. Accessed March 07, 2016. www.aliceschwarzer.de/artikel/das-sind-die-folgen-der-falschen-toleranz-331143.

Schwesig, Manuela. 2016a. "Botschaft ist klar und deutlich: #ausnahmslos. Aufruf hat meine Unterstützung." *twitter*, January 11. Accessed March 12, 2016. https://twitter.com/ManuelaSchwesig/status/686520954776883200.

———. 2016b. "Diese und andere Reaktionen auf #ausnahmslos zeigen das Problem!" *twitter*, January 12. Accessed March 12, 2016. https://twitter.com/ManuelaSchwesig/status/686934902588203008.

Seidel, Eberhard. 2003. "Die schwierige Balance zwischen Islamkritik und Islamophobie." In Heitmeyer 2003, 261–278.

Spiegel Online. 2016. "#einearmlaenge: Oberbürgermeisterin Reker verärgert mit Verhaltenstipps für Frauen." January 5. Accessed March 04, 2016. www.spiegel.de/panorama/justiz/koeln-oberbuergermeisterin-henriette-reker-gibt-verhaltens tipps-fuer-frauen-a-1070650-druck.html.

Spivak, Gayatri C. 1994. "Can the subaltern speak?" In *Colonial discourse and post-colonial theory: A reader*, edited by Patrick Williams and Laura Chrisman, 66–111. New York: Harvester and Wheatsheaf.

Stop Violence against Women. 2010. "Types & prevalence of harmful practices." Accessed April 11, 2016. www.stopvaw.org/harmful_practices_types_prevalence.

Süddeutsche.de. 2016. "Migration: Auch Tunesien kooperiert bei Abschiebungen aus Deutschland." March 1. Accessed March 04, 2016. www.sueddeutsche.de/news/politik/migration-auch-tunesien-kooperiert-bei-abschiebungen-aus-deutschland-dpa.urn-newsml-dpa-com-20090101-160301-99-45647.

Symons, Emma-Kate. 2016. "The Daoud Affair: Arab feminist defends writer accused of fueling Islamophobia with 'sexual misery'." *New York Times*, March 7. Accessed March 09, 2016. http://nytlive.nytimes.com/womenintheworld/2016/03/07/arab-feminist-defends-writer-accused-of-fueling-islamophobia-with-sexual-misery-op-ed/.

Syrians against Sexism. 2016. Accessed March 11, 2016. www.syrergegensexismus.org/.

Terre des Femmes. s.a. "Focus Areas." Accessed April 10, 2016. www.frauenrechte.de/online/index.php/our-work/focus-areas.

Toprak, Ali. 2016. "Bevormundet uns nicht!" *EMMA*, February. Accessed March 11, 2016. www.emma.de/artikel/hoert-endlich-auf-uns-zu-bevormunden-331467.

United Nations Human Rights Office of the High Commissioner. s.a. "Harmful traditional practices affecting the health of women and children." *Fact Sheet No. 23*. Accessed April 10, 2016. www.ohchr.org/Documents/Publications/FactSheet23en.pdf.

Vogel, Pierre. 2011. "Mehrzahl der Höllenbewohner sind Frauen? Diskriminierung?" June 8. Accessed March 07, 2016. www.youtube.com/watch?v=eedR5kYkIIU.

———. 2016. "Die asozialen Frauen-Grapscher von Köln!" January 6. Accessed March 07, 2016. www.youtube.com/watch?v=RCxClhh-00s.

Weiland, Severin. 2016. "Rechte Hetze: Wie die AfD die Übergriffe von Köln instrumentalisiert." *Spiegel Online*, January 8. Accessed March 04, 2016. www.spiegel.de/politik/deutschland/koeln-afd-instrumentalisiert-uebergriffe-politisch-a-1070895-druck.html.

Wiedemann, Charlotte. 2016. "Sexualisierte Gewalt gegen Frauen: Für einen Feminismus der neuen Allianzen." February 3. Accessed March 07, 2016. https://de.qantara.de/print/22620.

Women's Legal Centre. s.a. *Harmful cultural practices in South Africa: A women's rights perspective*. Accessed May 04, 2016. www.wlce.co.za/images/HarmfulCultural.pdf.

Yaghoobifarah, Hengameh. 2016. "Gewalt gegen Frauen: Willkommen in der Hölle, Ladys." January 6. Accessed March 04, 2016. www.taz.de/!5263311/.

Zeit Online. 2016. "Lutz Bachmann: Pegida-Chef wegen Volksverhetzung angezeigt." *Die Zeit*, January 10. Accessed March 04, 2016. www.zeit.de/gesellschaft/zeitgeschehen/2016-01/lutz-bachmann-pegida-anzeige-volksverhetzung-juergen-kasek-fluechtlinge-koeln.

Zeit Online. 2017a. "Polizei korrigiert Angaben zu Nationalität der Kontrollierten." *Die Zeit*, January 13. Accessed May 31, 2017. www.zeit.de/gesellschaft/zeitgeschehen/2017-01/silvester-koeln-polizei-neue-erkentnisse-kaum-nordafrikaner?print.

Zentrum für Islamische Frauenforschung. s.a. "Hermeneutische Konstrukteim islamisch weiblichen Theologieverständnis (sic!)." Accessed April 4, 2016. www.zif-koeln.de/7538.html.

Zouari, Fawzia. 2016. "Au nom de Kamel Daoud." *Libération*, February 28. Accessed March 10, 2016. www.liberation.fr/debats/2016/02/28/au-nom-de-kamel-daoud_1436364.

6 Cultures in contrast

LGBTQ movements and post-Soviet religious resurgence in the Republic of Georgia

Susan C. Pearce

Introduction

In June of 2013, a group of 50 activists gathered in a central public space in the capital of the Republic of Georgia, Tbilisi. These young Georgians were members of the LGBTQI community. With their allies, they planned to march peacefully to mark an annual transnational event, IDAHOT (International Day Against Homophobia and Transphobia). This march did not go peacefully as planned. In reaction to their gathering, a massive crowd of approximately 40,000 people, organized by Orthodox Christian leaders, violently descended on this small group (IDAHOT Report 2014). According to Amnesty International, the mob attack included an attempted lynching of an IDAHOT activist. One of the marchers, leader of the Georgian LGBT organization Identoba, observed: "They wanted to kill all of us" (Amnesty International 2013).

This chapter reviews the country conditions of Georgia regarding the rights and freedoms of LGBTQI individuals, as "contexts of exit," or rationales for individuals who find the need to out-migrate from their home countries. Sociologists of immigration have argued, based on research, that a combination of the "context of exit" and the "context of reception" in a new host country is a key component to understanding the full scope of a migrant's experience (Portes and Rumbaut 2014). As I have written elsewhere, gender- and sexuality-based violence are common contexts of exit for migrants globally, but this motivation is yet to be fully integrated into research on migration (Pearce and Sokoloff 2013). Further, for a full analysis of these contexts, scholars must reach beyond migration theory and research and incorporate the lenses of other relevant sociological subfields, including social movements, religion, and culture. As an illustration, for women and LGBTQI people in a number of countries in Central and Eastern Europe and beyond, organized religion has played a major background role in the context of exit with regard to exacerbating gender-based violence, whether intended or unintended, as illustrated in this opening example. The category of "organized religion" is far from a monolithic or transhistorical entity. Rather, religious meanings and expressions are temporally and spatially contingent. While more complex than either Marx's "opium of the people" (Marx 1843) or Weber's elective affinity with the development of Western capitalism (Weber [1905] 1930), religions make themselves known and experienced in reference to the societies in which they are embedded.

When Georgia gained its independence from the Soviet Union in 1991, the country embarked on its own political and economic reconstructions, which arguably remain in a fluid process as of this writing. Those reconstructions were simultaneously cultural. In this chapter, I review the major societal–institutional players that help define the migration situation for LGBTQI people, and the dynamic relationships between those players. In this analysis, I draw on theoretical paradigms from the sociology of immigration, social movements, gender studies, religion, and culture to outline the current country conditions in Georgia.

Theoretically, I demonstrate here that the cultural constructions and reconstructions that characterize post-Soviet-era Georgia are symbiotically interrelated with their institutional and extra-institutional carriers (see Pearce and Sojka forthcoming). Those institutions include – among others – state, transnational, and international governmental institutions; state institutions such as courts; and religious bodies. Extra-institutional bodies include activist networks and their "routinized" forms, to use the language of Weber (Weber 1978, 246–254), which, despite their routinization, remain distant from societal power, as they do not have the force of rule or cultural control of institutions such as a religious body. At the individual lifeworld level, these social, group-level dynamics carry implications for individuals regarding financial livelihoods, domicile options, and sheer survival. The structures of relationships cross-influence one another, although at uneven levels due to clear imbalances of power between these entities.

Religion-nation

With the collapse of the Soviet Union and the hold of Moscow over Georgia's governance and culture, religious freedom returned along with other civil–society liberties that had previously been suppressed, ushering in what scholars have termed "return to self." Part and parcel to this "return to self" was the release from a state-communist-imposed atheism that had commenced with Georgia's designation as a Soviet republic in 1922. Ironically, Georgian national Joseph Stalin, who would become the multi-decade-long Soviet dictator beginning in 1929, initially studied to become a Georgian Orthodox priest, but became attracted to Marxist ideas and would eventually rise to the center of the Soviet politburo. Mirroring the same processes as other Soviet Republics, organized religion had been abolished and religious places repurposed for secular ends. Today, among the remaining relics of the former system in the Georgian landscape are secular civic halls established for ceremonies such as weddings; former religious buildings, in contrast, had been de-sacralized and used for other secular purposes.

For Georgia and its neighboring countries of the Caucasus (Armenia and Azerbaijan), post-1991 independence involved a revival of the religious identity that had been historically bound up with each particular nation and national culture. The histories of these three countries consist of population waves that migrated, conquered, and settled in their regions, resulting in three distinct religious traditions that define the majority of each national population residing in their home countries. Today, 89% of Georgians identify as Georgian Orthodox Christians, 89% of Armenians identify as Armenian Apostolic Christians (Pew Research Center 2017), and 96.9% of Azeris identify as Shia Muslims (Pew Research Center 2012, 95).

As sociologist of religion José Casanova has written (1994), the task of constructing a polity and society built upon modern democratic values involves, critically, that institutions such as religion reemerge and rebuild as members of civil society – outside of the realm of the state. This is a model that sociologist Émile Durkheim proposed as he observed modernization of political and economic systems in Europe and elsewhere: the differentiation of spheres into their specializations (Durkheim [1893] 1984). Religion, for example, would no longer be an intertwined function of political governance – its limits as well as its freedom would be the result of inhabiting its own sphere, with its own institutional logic, values, norms, leadership, and entrance requirements. Sociologists have named this process of privatization of religion "secularization," which is distinct from secularism as a world view or ideology (Casanova 2009, 1050–1051). In modernizing societies such as the United States, the result was what Peter Berger termed a "marketplace of religion" that replaced the former model of a "sacred canopy" that encompassed all community members, and where the state represented a particular religion and enforced its operations (Berger 1967).

Post-communist transformations across Eurasian countries demonstrates a variety of patterns, but many are moving toward a sacred-canopy modern rather than a (pluralistic) religious marketplace. The country of Georgia particularly stands out in this regard, as reported in a 2017 publication by the Pew Research Center of a survey of 17 Central and Eastern European countries. Among those, Georgians reported the highest positive opinion of religious institutions in society. As noted, 89% of Georgians are Orthodox Christian, and 80% of surveyed Georgians said that religion strengthens morality in society. Further, 52% of those surveyed agreed that "governments should promote religious values" (Pew Research Center 2017), the second highest percent in the survey, second to neighboring Armenia. According to the US Department of State, "laws and policies favor the Georgian Orthodox Church (GOC), granting it privileges not accorded to any other religious group" (U.S. Department of State 2015, 1).

For Georgia, the strong correlation between national identity and particular religious tradition indicates that the "return to self" has simultaneously been one of mono-nationalism wedded to mono-religiosity. Ewa Ochman (2009, 393) observed that the process varied from across nations, but a visible pattern occurred in each state: the nationalization of the past was achieved by utilizing traditions of independence, referring to military victories and endorsing a national martyrology, with the identity of victim, collaborator, or oppressor defined along strict ethno-national lines.

In Caucasus and other post-communist countries of the region, in recent years especially, a vitriolic nationalism has moved from the fringes to the center, giving mono-nationalist narratives a modicum of power. Further, those narratives define the nation as one *against:* against not only the foreign other but the internal other, what Georg Simmel termed the "stranger," who "comes today and stays tomorrow" (Simmel 1950). When nationalist narratives incorporate a push to reproduce the nation physiologically, the result is commonly a pro-natalist, insistent norm that both scripts women's options and reinforces heteronormativity.

LGBTQI movements and Georgian society

Just as a revitalization of religious adherence and institutions has returned to Georgia, a reconstituted civil society offers opportunities for freedom of association, and thus the potential for social movement activism. As a result, members of marginalized communities, including women and LGBTQI people, began to establish their own networks, gathering places, and organizations to work to advance their needs, including legal protections. Part and parcel to this organizing has been an "NGO-ization" across the region: the establishment of NGOs for a range of causes, some initiated by grassroots groups from the bottom up, and others as satellite offices of transnational NGOs or INGOs (International NGOs) (Pearce and Cooper 2014).

In Georgia, this has involved the birth of organizations such as Equality Georgia, a Tbilisi-based organization that has recently developed satellite offices in provincial locations. The staff of Equality Georgia engage in activism and services, including health screenings and information distribution. A second prominent Georgian LGBTQI advocacy organization is Identoba, which also provides services such as HIV/AIDS awareness and legal and psychological services. Given the repression of almost all independent civil society activities under the Soviet Union and in the Eastern Bloc, such activism was not allowed to begin to develop until 1989/1991. Further, homosexuality was criminalized in the Soviet Union, and in Georgia it was not decriminalized until 1991.

More recently, Georgia and neighboring countries in the region have been formally changing their criminal and civil laws to include protections for sexual minorities to conform to European Union and Council of Europe human rights guidelines and laws. Although Georgia is not yet in the EU accession process, it is now a member of the Council of Europe and is a border country that falls within EU's Neighbourhood Policy. These developments exemplify what Keck and Sikkink have termed a "boomerang effect": the dependence of small, disenfranchised activist groups on transnational pressure on their home governments and societies (Keck and Sikkink 1998).

Such legal changes have been largely welcomed by activists in the respective countries, although some have feared that they could invite societal backlash. These new legal protections have, in fact, been countered by a strong backlash wave that has resulted in right-wing parties moving into political office and gaining power in a number of countries (see O'Dwyer 2013, 103). Such parties arise or benefit from the growing base of nationalist sentiment that usually intersects with religious belief or affiliation, as mentioned above. In fact, the most recent results from the World Values Survey indicate high levels of public aversion to LGBTQI people across all three Caucasus countries. When respondents from a representative sample were asked who they would not like to have as neighbors and were given a list of various groups from which to choose, high percentages of the populations of each country answered that they would not like to have "homosexuals" as neighbors. In 2011, 94.4% of Azeris mentioned homosexuals, as did 92.7% of Armenians. The latest results from Georgia are for 2014, when 86.6% answered "homosexuals" (World Values Survey 2018).

Comparing attitudes within Georgia to those in other countries, the Pew Research Center has found that in Christian Orthodox-majority countries, views on sexual and gender norms are more traditional and conservative than in Catholic-majority or religiously mixed countries. Adults in Orthodox countries are more likely than those elsewhere to reject homosexuality and to oppose same-sex marriage and legal abortion. Only 3% of surveyed Georgians said that same-sex marriage should be legal, which was the lowest percentage across surveyed countries. Further, 93% of Georgians said that homosexuality should not be accepted by society, again the second highest percentage in the survey, behind Armenia (Pew Research Center 2017). A 2013 study reported similar findings in an analysis of the World Values Survey: across 21 post-communist countries (which did not include Armenia), Georgian respondents were the most likely to say that "homosexuality is never justified in society" (O'Dwyer 2013, 113).

Georgian religiosity carries a particular intensity and pride, given the country's history. Christianity was founded in the first century CE, and by the fourth century, it was adopted as the official state religion: an early marriage of church and state that imbues Georgian cultural identity as a Christian one. Reports from LGBTQI people indicate that this narrative is often experienced in homophobic tones. In the seaside city of Batumi, for example, there is a gay bar named "Secret Bar" because, according to one observer, "it's not safe, because there's strong anti gay attitude in the country which is proud to be one of the first nations in the world to adopt Christianity" (Gay Batumi 2016).

Public performances and clashes

This chapter began with an anecdote of an event in 2013: an annual activist marking of the International Day Against Homophobia and Transphobia (IDAHOT).[1] It was reported that "the priests entered, the priests broke the fences and the police didn't stop them, because the priests are above the law in Georgia" (Rothmay 2013). Amnesty International also observed that the police were "woefully unprepared" and observed that "by failing to take effective measures and hold these accountable to justice, the Georgian authorities are allowing the intolerance and impunity to grow and fester" (Amnesty International 2013). And Human Rights Watch concluded: "Although police evacuated rally participants to safety, they failed to contain the mob, which threw stones and other objects at a van carrying participants" (Human Rights Watch 2016).

As they prepared for the annual event the following year, 2014, anti-homophobia activists feared for their safety, due to threats by the public and the police. Instead of a rally, activists organized a day of "Invisibility," placing 100 shoes in the public square where the violence had taken place in 2013. Approximately 4,000 counter-protesters appeared, to honor "Strength of Family and Respect for Parents" on a newly instituted "Family Protection Day" by the Orthodox Church to counter IDAHOT. Each year since, Georgian Church leaders have organized the counter-events and demonstrations. By 2016, anti-homophobia activists' request to hold an IDAHOT event on the main thoroughfare in Tbilisi was denied, as authorities responded that it was reserved for the Orthodox groups' Family Protection Day observations. IDAHOT organizers held several unannounced "flash events," such as placing a rainbow-colored stool outside of the meeting place for the World Congress of Families, which was removed by police. Police arrested ten LGBTQI protestors for painting graffiti on a fence, stating "all love is equal." Activists reported that these officers were not uniformed and spoke to them in homophobic terms. Due to safety concerns, the anti-homophobia activists held their rally in a secret location and were escorted to and from the event with police surveillance. The church-organized Family Protection Day event drew several thousand people.

The reaction of Georgia's Orthodox Church to institute a new Family Protection Day to counter LGBT activism has been bolstered by international support. In 2016, the annual meeting of the World Congress of Families was held in Tbilisi to show their alliance with the Georgian Church's resistance to homosexuality in society, drawing Christian church leaders from around the world. And on May 17, 2018, Georgian Orthodox clergy again used the annual date slated for the IDAHOT event to process through the public center of Tbilisi in defiance. Central to that defiance was the organized performance of mass (heterosexual) weddings, numbering at least 400, across churches and the central cathedral of Tbilisi. In a May 17 sermon, Archbishop Shio, who is the Catholicos-Patriarch of All Georgia and the spiritual leader of the Georgian Orthodox Church, warned that "the war against family and its values is a war against God" (Eurasianet 2018). Advancing the message that Church leaders had broadcast across the years of this particular culture war, this rhetoric clearly referenced mass violence, even if the word "war" was intended as a trope. LGBTQI activists countered with an insistence of their own national belonging. As one activist stated, "we are citizens of this country and we are members of this family. We are not going anywhere" (Eurasianet 2018), an insistence that the ruling mono-national/mono-religious hegemony cannot claim to be a sacred canopy.

Notably, in 2015, the European Court of Human Rights ruled against the government of Georgia in a case brought before them by the organization Identoba (and others), who had organized the IDAHO (International Day Against Homophobia) on May 17, 2012. The transcript of the case indicates that counter-protesters, mobilized by two religious organizations, shouted that the marchers "should be burnt to death" and "crushed." Marchers were violently attacked. The Court ruled in favor of most of the claimants and claims in this case, concluding that the state of Georgia and its police had violated several articles of the Convention for the Protection of Human Rights and Fundamental Freedoms. This case was groundbreaking, because for the first time, this Court ruled that Article 3, "no one shall be subjected to torture or to inhuman or degrading treatment or punishment," was violated in conjunction with violating Article 14, that

> the enjoyment of the rights and freedoms set forth in [the] Convention shall be secured without discrimination on any ground such as sex, race, colour, language, religion, political or other opinion, national or social origin, association with a national minority, property, birth or other status.
>
> (European Court of Human Rights 2015)

This effectively means that states that are party to the Convention must adequately protect LGBTQI people from "hate speech and serious threats" and "physical abuse" that arouse "fear, anxiety and insecurity" (European Court of Human Rights 2015). The Court stated that the Georgian authorities had not adequately investigated and prosecuted the cases filed by victims (European Court of Human Rights 2015).

Religious cultures, institutions, and backlash

A key institutional player in the unfolding dramas of a rising culture of LGBTQI activism and a resurgent nationalist–religious awakening is the (presumably secular) state. Following the much-publicized 2013 attacks in Tbilisi, the European Union required that Georgia pass an anti-discrimination law as a condition for a more liberal visa process for Georgians. Although that law did pass the Georgian parliament in 2014, it was met by skepticism by activists. One activist leader representing Identoba responded, "since the law was passed, things are actually worse now for LGBT people. When they make a complaint about something, people just say, 'what more do you want? You've got your rights now in law'. It's really obnoxious" (Stracansky 2014). And in 2015, there were reported threats against Identoba, prompting Georgia's Public Defender to call for their protection (Public Defender of Georgia 2015).

This skepticism over the anti-discrimination law was borne out. In 2015, the Romanian Center for European Policies reported that following the 2013 attacks in Tbilisi, "no effective investigation was conducted and perpetrators have not been brought to justice for violence against LGBT persons and their rights defenders" (Haller et al. 2015). Further, in 2017, a Democracy & Freedom Watch report stated: "but the LGBT community and rights activists claim that the anti-discrimination law has barely been implemented in practice" (DFWatch Staff 2017). And, in 2016, the US State Department acknowledged that despite anti-discrimination language in Georgia's constitution and criminal code, "according to NGOs, the government rarely enforced the law, and law enforcement authorities lacked training in hate crimes" (U.S. Department of State 2016, 43). In general, a 2017 report by the Georgian organization Coalition for Equality stated that "the LGBT community is the most marginalised group in the country – with politicians politicising LGBT rights, a clearly hostile and homophobic environment has been formed towards the community" (Coalition for Equality 2017, 10).

Human Rights Watch reported that during 2015, the Tbilisi City Court acquitted a priest and three other men against charges that they disrupted the May 17, 2013 rally, citing lack of evidence. This report further noted another acquittal by a Georgian court, of a man accused of murdering a transgender woman and lighting her apartment on fire to cover up the crime. Instead, he was sentenced to four years in prison for "violence and property damage." Rights groups contested this outcome (Human Rights Watch 2016). The US State Department reported in 2016 that "victims of discrimination and violence also were reluctant to report incidents to police due to fear of disclosing their sexual orientation or gender identity to family members and of homophobic reactions by police" (U.S. Department of State 2016). According to an interview that I conducted with one activist, "there are very few odds that they will get justice by the police or the courts. Most police are super homophobic and express it openly."

The political party ruling the country as of this writing, Georgian Dream – Democratic Georgia, the largest of a six-party coalition, won elections to control the Parliament in 2012 and 2016 with opposition to same-sex marriage as a key platform in its campaign, although it is a center-left party. The government is currently moving forward to implement a proposed constitutional change to declare marriage to be a "union between a man and a woman," even though LGBTQI activists had not yet mobilized a same-sex marriage campaign (Pertaia 2017). In the words of the watchdog organization Human Rights Watch,

> Prime Minister Giorgi Kvirikashvili vowed to pursue a constitutional definition of marriage after the October elections, arguing that this would help counter alleged Western efforts to spread same-sex marriage "propaganda" in Georgia. Local rights groups feared this effort would further marginalize the LGBT community and intensify anti-LGBT prejudice.
>
> (Human Rights Watch 2017)

In reference to the current state of justice within the Georgian court system, the Council of Europe and the European Union issued a report in April 2017 regarding Georgia's application of the European Convention on Human Rights (ECHR) and decisions of the European Court of Human Rights (ECtHR) by Georgia's common courts. In that meeting, the Director of Human Rights, Directorate General Human Rights and Rule of Law of the Council of Europe, Christos Giakoumopoulos, summarized the study's findings in the following way: "Common Courts of Georgia are ready and capable to apply in practice and introduce the judgments rendered by the ECtHR," but "the study also identified cases when national courts applied the practice of the ECtHR incorrectly or incompletely" (Council of Europe 2017). A 2016 report on the judiciary by the Open Society Foundation Georgia concluded that "the courts do not function as a lead actor in the fight for human rights and fundamental freedoms, particularly as far as the rights of vulnerable groups are concerned" (Open Society Foundation Georgia 2016). This study found that Georgia has not yet implemented judicial reforms required by the EU–Georgia Association Agreement.

Further, among the four cases from Georgia that were argued before the European Court of Human Rights in 2016, all four were given judgments with at least one violation; one was the right to a fair trial (European Court of Human Rights 2016a, 2016b). Although other countries had numerically more judgments in 2016, Georgia was one of a handful of countries that were handed down violations in 100% of their cases. Between 1959 and 2016, the Court handed down at least one violation in 52 of 68 Georgian cases argued before the Court. Based on observations and documentation, a current Georgian jurist stated that despite LGBTQI rights protections on the books, "the existence of Constitution or other laws does not guarantee the realization of the norms in reality, when the regime that governs the country disregards and in many occasions intentionally violates the requirements of law" (European Court of Human Rights 2016a, 2016b). The jurist also emphasized: "The Government in Georgia is unwilling to secure the rights and freedoms of LGBT persons" (European Court of Human Rights 2016a, 2016b).

This chapter opened with the example of violence in the Georgian capital of Tbilisi. However, LGBTQI people are reportedly in greater danger outside of the capital, and there are no cities or regions where their safety could be taken for granted or guaranteed. As one Georgian activist living outside of Georgia confirmed, "it is not at all safe outside of Tbilisi. There are no strong LGBT communities." More rural areas are less likely to have been exposed to an LGBT community and could harbor more fear and hostile feelings. The Georgian regions of Abkhazia and South Ossetia, for example, claim independence, but Georgia views them as territories under Russian military rule, giving the central government less oversight into the protection of their residents' rights (U.S. Department of State 2015, 10). As Russia has increasingly voiced anti-Western views on such issues as LGBTQI rights, passed homophobic legislation, and banned LGBTQI public gatherings, those opinions have also gained traction in Georgia, with a number of pro-Russian groups publicly expressing their opposition to gay rights (Applebaum 2014). There is one city in Georgia that had begun to develop a gay scene for leisure gatherings, the Black Sea coastal city Batumi, but my interview respondents indicated that LGBTQI people need to remain closeted there.

LGBTQI community activists and hundreds of allies made their opinions of the ruling party clear in May of 2018. This followed a 2018 police raid on Tbilisi nightclubs that victimized LGBTQI people and many others. One highly popular music club that was particularly targeted, the BASSIANI/HOROOM club, presents itself as a movement "that stands at the forefront of the social changes and speaks loudly regarding the inequality in the country, high level of injustice and discrimination" ("UPDATE . . ." 2018). Just weeks after street protestors in neighboring Armenia won the resignation of their prime minister, several hundred young people protested in the streets of Tbilisi against the nightclub raids as well as the lack of justice in the deaths of two teenagers earlier in the year. Calling their actions "a RAVE-olution," protestor complaints encompassed charges of high-level government corruption. Angry counter-demonstrators responded by lighting candles on the scene, reciting the Lord's Prayer, and attempting to rush a protective police line (Pertaia 2018). These protests forced the resignation of the Georgian Prime Minister and his cabinet (Pertaia 2018).

Contexts of reception: migration and asylum

LGBTQI people in Georgia reportedly confront three choices: remain in Georgia and continue to advocate for change, remain closeted in Georgia, take on a heterosexual identity, or migrate elsewhere. Untold numbers are choosing to do the latter, often due to repeated acts of violence against them during Pride events or in more quotidian public incidents. The domain of asylum law, therefore, is a potential human rights player in the mix of institutional players involved here. What are the potential contexts of reception for those who seek to find legal asylum in another country? There are two trending waves that are helping to determine those contexts, which continue to be in flux. The first is that one element of the European Union's

mainstreaming of LGBTQI rights into its human rights policies and requirements for new member states is the opening of asylum to those escaping
homophobic violence. Simultaneously, the United States and other countries
have increasingly granted asylum in such cases. Asylum and refugee laws
in the United States follow the standards of the United Nations, specifying
that the laws are to protect individuals who have suffered persecution or
fear that they will suffer persecution due to their race, religion, nationality,
membership in a particular social group, or political opinion. After years of
activist work, US judges are now considering gender, sexual orientation, and
gender identity to constitute "a particular social group." Like other asylum
applications, however, only a minority are approved. Overall, in fact, in
the United States, there were 65,218 asylum cases open in 2016; 8,726, or
13%, were approved (U.S. Department of Justice 2016). And yet, a second,
opposing trending wave is a tightening of borders and growing restrictions
on the numbers, national origins, and contexts of exit that a receiving country allows. That wave is evident in both the United States and the European
Union, the key international contexts most relevant for Georgian LGBTQI
asylum seekers.

Here, I provide an example of a recent case of a gay male Georgian who
applied for asylum in the United States. I researched his experiences and
served as an expert witness on the country conditions of Georgia for an
immigration court hearing during 2017 to appeal his prior deportation
order. Therefore, this applicant walked into a judicial culture that had set
precedents of asylum for LGBTQI persons. Nevertheless, asylum was far
from automatic. This applicant had attempted to cross into the United States
on the Florida border, via a boat trip from Cuba with fellow Georgians.
Unlike Cubans, who have automatic rights to refugee status upon arrival,
this Georgian was apprehended by border patrol and sent immediately to
detention in Florida. He pressed forward with his asylum application, with
support from his sisters who had settled in New York. His first experience
with an immigration judge resulted in a denial. That judge reviewed Georgian country conditions such as the new legal anti-discrimination measures
passed in recent years and deemed that this man's rights would be protected if he returned. However, due to mistakes made during the hearing, the
Board of Immigration Appeals re-opened the case with a new attorney. In
the meantime, this applicant was moved across detention centers in several
states, and eventually returned to Florida. He suffered the psychological
effects of imprisonment, a novel host country, and separation from family.
The eventual appeal was successful, due to the information that his attor-
neys gathered and presented, and due to the US government attorney failing
to identify a location across Georgia where this man could live safely. With
his release, he was able to move to New York to live in the company of his
sisters and other family members, although the physical and mental toll of
his 18-plus months in detention would likely require a long recovery time.
Since his release in 2017, the United States government has made gestures

toward ending gender-based asylum, leaving an open question about the continued role of asylum as a player in LGBTQI rights movements.

In safe passage to another country, if indeed a life is spared, much is lost, from the domicile of a citizen national for that individual, to the disruption of an activist network that is critical for moving human rights provisions and practices forward. That individual does have the opportunity to continue to pressure their home country on LGBTQI rights and practices. Historically, there are clear patterns of politically displaced individuals joining diaspora politics, boosting a potential boomerang effect (Keck and Sikkink 1998; Koinova 2012). Not every asylee and refugee is able to involve themselves in boosting those networks, however. For the gay Georgian man who won asylum in the United States, his treatment in detention centers and uncertain fate in immigration courts, combined with his repeated hunger strikes to protest his conditions, can deter hope and sap energy. Some may view the situation in their home country as desperate and beyond repair. Others may have been burned out or disillusioned from their years of activism. Such was evidently the case for a lesbian couple who had to flee violence against them at a Pride event in a Balkan country. In my interview with this couple, one of them reflected: "We used to be activists. Now we're gardeners."

Conclusions

As this chapter has illustrated, the country of Georgia exemplifies the tensions between various players within a society in a particular state of transformation, as well as ancillary players outside of the country such as regional courts and transnational governmental bodies. On particular dates and places, the volatility of those relationships erupts, opening a sociological window into the quotidian dynamics around questions such as human rights, marginalized groups in a polity, and norms regarding morality and behavior. Returning to the contrast between a sacred canopy and a religious marketplace, and to the political–theoretical formulas for democratic institutions inhabiting separate spheres, Georgia exemplifies the challenges of post-Soviet countries in a similar position. As we have seen across this chapter, a dynamic interplay between individual, group, and institutional actors, often involving transnational parties, indicates that the place of LGBTQI people in a democratizing polity and civil society is an unsettled one. Risks to their safety and livelihoods that will be present even in welcoming contexts of reception are especially magnified within the home country, one where a "return to self" that merges national and religious identities carries a potent appeal. The result is contestation not only arising out of a hegemonic religious body and a marginalized sector of civil society, but also between state and civil society, when the state has divided allegiances: international human rights law and protection of citizenry on the one hand, and representative of the nation as defined by voices with historic and current cultural power on the other. While LGBTQI activists point to holes in the sacred canopy, that canopy continues to be revered.

LBTQI people in Georgia, as elsewhere, have looked to a transnational context both for boomerang effects and as a sanctuary when the domestic situation does not appear to hold hope. And yet, the transnational context is a mixed one. On the one hand, it consists of legal rulings and watchdog organization shaming that could potentially bolster the community's rights and safety. And on the other, it offers ambiguity regarding asylum possibilities and actual influence on the application of human rights norms within the country's borders. Further, the incursion of the Kremlin into Georgian cultural and governmental realities appears to the LGBTQI community as furthering homophobic hostility within Georgia. Although future directions remain unclear, given developments in and beyond Georgia, the LGBTQI rights movement shows no signs of a full retreat, as illustrated by the RAVE-olution protests of May 2018. Making claims on polity based on their membership in the political body, this community defies any characterization of the LGBTQI person as the "stranger."

Acknowledgments

I would like to express my appreciation to the Woodrow Wilson International Center for Scholars and the Open Society Institute for their support, which made this research possible; to attorney Aygul Charles; and to Jacqueline Hagan and the Migration Working Group of the Department of Sociology at University of North Carolina, Chapel Hill for their contributions to the draft of this chapter.

Note

1 Across the years that this chapter spans, the acronym for this day has expanded. It is now IDAHOTB, or International Day Against Homophobia, Transphobia, and Biphobia.

References

Amnesty International. 2013. "Georgia: Homophobic Violence Mars Tbilisi Pride Event." May 17, 2013. www.amnesty.org/en/latest/news/2013/05/georgia-homophobic-violence-mars-tbilisi-pride-event/

Applebaum, Annie. 2014. "Russia's Anti-Western Rhetoric Is Spreading, and President Obama Is Wrong to Ignore It." *Slate*, March 28, 2014. www.slate.com/articles/news_and_politics/foreigners/2014/03/ukraine_and_georgia_we_can_t_ignore_the_building_anti_western_sentiment.html

Batumi, Gay. 2016. "Blog Post." https://gaybatumi.wordpress.com

Berger, Peter L. 1967. *The Sacred Canopy*. New York: Anchor Books.

Casanova, José. 2009. "The Secular and Secularisms." *Social Research* 76, no. 4 (Winter): 1049–1066.

Casanova, José. 1994. *Public Religions in the Modern World*. Chicago: University of Chicago Press.

Coalition for Equality. 2017. "The Right to Non-Discrimination in Practice for Various Groups in Georgia." www.osgf.ge/files/2017/Publications/Diskriminacia_ENG_WEB.pdf

Council of Europe. Newsroom Georgia PCF ECHR. "Application of the Standards of the European Convention on Human Rights by the Common Courts of Georgia." April 5, 2017. www.coe.int/en/web/national-implementation/-/application-of-the-standards-of-the-european-convention-on-human-rights-by-the-common-courts-of-georgia

DFWatch Staff. 2017. Four Years after Violence, Tbilisi's LGBT Activists Meet Under Tight Security. May 18, 2017. http://dfwatch.net/violence-tbilisi-lgbt-activists-security-48516

Durkheim, Émile. [1893] 1997. *The Division of Labor in Society*. New York: Simon and Schuster.

Eurasianet. 2018. "Small Gay Rights IDAHOTB Rally Held in Tbilisi Amid Fears of Violence." International Day against Homophobia, Transphobia, and Biphobia Website. May 17, 2018. https://dayagainsthomophobia.org/georgian-activists-activists-cancel-17-may-demonstration-after-threats-from-far-right-groups/

European Court of Human Rights. 2016a. "Violations by Article and by State (2016)." www.echr.coe.int/Documents/Facts_Figures_2016_ENG.pdf

European Court of Human Rights. 2016b. "Violations by Article and by State (1959–2016)." www.echr.coe.int/Documents/Stats_violation_1959_2016_ENG.pdf

European Court of Human Rights. 2015. "Case of Identoba and Others v. Georgia." http://hudoc.echr.coe.int/eng#%7B%22languageisocode%22:[%22ENG%22],%22documentcollectionid2%22:[%22JUDGMENTS%22],%22itemid%22:[%22001-154400%22]%7D

Haller, Istvan, Aurora Martin, Roxana Albisteanu, and Tamar Dekanosidze. 2015. "The Anti-Discrimination System in the Context of the EU Visa Liberalization Action Plan." Romanian Center for European Policies, CRP Policy Memo 60. www.osgf.ge/files/2015/Publication/Binder_CRPE_AntiDiscriminare_Georgia.pdfv

Human Rights Watch. 2017. "Georgia: Events of 2016." www.hrw.org/world-report/2017/country-chapters/georgia

Human Rights Watch. 2016. "Georgia: Events of 2015." www.hrw.org/world-report/2016/country-chapters/georgia

IDAHOT Report. 2014. http://dayagainsthomophobia.org/idahot-report-2014-georgia/

Keck, Margaret E. and Katherine Sikkink. 1998. *Activists Beyond Borders*. Ithaca and London: Cornell University Press.

Koinova, Maria. 2012. "Autonomy and Positionality in Diaspora Politics." *International Political Sociology* 6, no. 1 (March): 99–103.

Marx, Karl. [1843] 1970. *A Contribution to the Critique of Hegel's Philosophy of Right*. Trans. Annette Jolin and Joseph O'Malley. Ed. Joseph O'Malley. Cambridge: Cambridge University Press.

Ochman, Ewa. 2009. "Municipalities and the Search for the Local Past: Fragmented Memory of the Red Army in Upper Silesia." *East European Politics and Societies* 23, no. 3: 392–420.

O'Dwyer, Conor. 2013. "Gay Rights and Political Homophobia in Postcommunist Europe: Is There an 'EU Effect'?" In *Global Homophobia: States, Movements, and the Politics of Oppression*, edited by Meredith L. Weiss and Michael J. Bosia, 103–126. Champaign, IL: University of Illinois Press.

Open Society Foundation Georgia. 2016. "Judicial Reform in Georgia and the Association Agreement: Old Wine in a New Barrel: What Has Changed?" *Policy Brief*. www.osgf.ge/files/2016/EU%20publication/Angarishi_A4_Policy_Brief_Eng.pdf

Pearce, Susan C. and Alex Cooper. 2014. "LGBT Movements in Southeast Europe: Violence, Justice, and International Intersections." In *Handbook of LGBT Communities, Crime, and Justice*, edited by Dana Peterson and Vanessa R. Panfil, 311–338. New York: Springer Publishing.

Pearce, Susan C. and Eugenia Sojka, eds. Forthcoming. *Cultural Change from Central and Eastern Europe to Central Asia.* Cham, Switzerland: @Springer International Publishing Switzerland AG.

Pearce, Susan C. and Natalie J. Sokoloff. 2013. "'This Should Not Be Happening in This Country': Private-Life Violence and Immigration Intersections in a U.S. Gateway City." *Sociological Forum* 28, no. 4: 784–810.

Pertaia, Luka. 2018. "Making Sense of Georgia's Raveolution." https://iwpr.net/global-voices/making-sense-georgias-raveolution

Pertaia, Luka. 2017. "Georgia's Constitutional Changes Explained." *OC-Media*, April 18. http://oc-media.org/georgias-constitutional-changes-explained/

Pew Research Center. 2017. "Religious Belief and National Belonging in Central and Eastern Europe." www.pewforum.org/2017/05/10/views-on-religion-and-politics/

Pew Research Center. 2012. "The Global Religious Landscape: A Report on the Size and Distribution of the World's Largest Religious Groups as of 2010." www.pewforum.org/2012/12/18/global-religious-landscape-exec/

Portes, Alejandro and Rubén G. Rumbaut. 2014. *Immigrant America: A Portrait.* 4th ed. Berkeley: University of California Press.

Public Defender of Georgia. 2015. "The Public Defender Statement Regarding Threats against Organization 'Identoba' and Its Former Head Irakli Vacharadze." January 9. www.ombudsman.ge/en/news/the-public-defender-statement-regarding-threats-against-organization-identoba-and-its-former-head-irakli-vacharadze.page

Rothmay, Andrew. 2013. "Crowd Led by Priests Attacks Gay Rights Marchers in Georgia." *The New York Times*, May 17, 2013. www.nytimes.com/2013/05/18/world/europe/gay-rights-rally-is-attacked-in-georgia.html?_r=0

Simmel, Georg. 1950. *The Sociology of Georg Simmel.* Compiled and Trans. Kurt Wolff. Glencoe, IL: Free Press.

Stracansky, Pavol. 2014. "New Anti-Discrimination Law Could Worsen Situation for Georgia's LGBT Community." *InterPress Service News Agency*, September 9. www.ipsnews.net/2014/09/new-anti-discrimination-law-could-worsen-situation-for-georgias-lgbt-community/

"UPDATE: Hundreds Protest Police Raid of Tbilisi Night Clubs." 2018. *Agenda.ge*, May 12. http://agenda.ge/en/news/2018/1017

U.S. Department of Justice. 2016. "Executive Office for Immigration Review Office of Planning, Analysis, and Technology Immigration Courts: Asylum Statistics FY 2012–2016." www.justice.gov/eoir/file/asylum-statistics/download

U.S. Department of State. 2016. "Georgia 2016 Human Rights Report." www.state.gov/documents/organization/265634.pdf

U.S. Department of State. 2015. "Georgia 2015 International Religious Freedom Report." www.state.gov/documents/organization/256403.pdf

Weber, Max. 1978. *Economy and Society: An Outline of Interpretive Sociology.* Vol. 1. Eds. Guenther Roth and Claus Wittich. Berkeley: University of California Press.

Weber, Max. [1905] 1930. *The Protestant Ethic and the Spirit of Capitalism.* Trans. Talcott Parsons. London: George Allen & Unwin.

World Values Survey. 2018. www.worldvaluessurvey.org/wvs.jsp

7 Religion, gender-based violence, and the rights of the girl child in Kenya

Mary Nyangweso and Mansi Trivedi

Introduction

In a little village in the western part of Kenya, Chepkorir, a 28-year old Pokot who dresses like a woman, struggles with her identity. She is grateful for surviving the death that most of her kind are exposed to, thanks to her mother's pleas to her father to spare her life. This is because, although she has large, well-formed breasts, she has not menstruated since she was born. She has a normal-sized penis and "rudimentary testes" located above her otherwise normal-appearing vagina. She is often referred to as *sererr*, a Pokot word for individuals that are "neither male nor female." Because of her appearance, she is referred to as a woman, preferable to being a *sererr*, which is an insult in her Pokot community. When Chepkorir was born, in Sook location, her father, Kurupirra, wanted her killed. Her life was saved because of her mother's plea to her father not to kill her. Kurupirra explains how he agonized over the fact that his child was a *sererr* and how his thoughts led him consider killing his own child. "What use could such a person be?" he contemplated. "I would have to feed 'it' for 'its' whole life as it could never marry and what would I get in return? . . . It could never bring me bride wealth. So, I thought it would be better to kill this *sererr*," he concluded. But Chepkorir's mother intervened, saying, "no, no – do not kill it. It is a child like any other – it can help me with work and I will feed it." Fortunately, Kurupirra spared Chepkorir's life. He explains: "I did not kill the *sererr*. I did not want to annoy my wife so I let her have this child" (Edgerton, 1964: 1293).

Although Chepkorir's life was spared, she has not had an easy life like her sister and two brothers, who are completely normal. As a small child, she was often teased and called *sererr* by other children. As Edgerton (1964: 1292) explains, "sometimes the little boys would catch her and . . . examine her genitals." Chepkorir would cry and try to fight back, but the boys would laugh and taunt her. They would mock her, saying "she should be happy, because she was equipped to have intercourse with herself." When Chepkorir realized that she could not experience sexual activities her age mates were experiencing in their teenage years, she would say,

> God made a mistake. I am neither a boy nor a girl. My penis will not stand up as a boy's and my vagina is no good either. If anyone ever

asks me to have sex with them, I will fight – I will absolutely kill such a person.

Her older brother, Syatugei, noticed how this depressed her. He explains:

> When the rest of us were enjoying playing with girls, she wanted only food and sleep. She worked all the time – in the fields and herding the cattle. She worked very hard; when I wanted to run off to have sex with a girl she would do my work for me.
>
> (Edgerton, 1964: 1292)

At age 17, when most of her age mates were circumcised in preparation for marriage, she could not be circumcised since she did not fit either gender. At age 28, she continues to live on her father's homestead. Her father, who is now very fond of her because of her hard work, says that "she is good for me to have – she works more than my wife and sons and daughters together." Because she can never marry, or permitted to adopt children, she is to live in her father's home until she dies (Edgerton, 1964: 1292–1293).

Josephine (pseudonym), a Samburu girl, is 12 years old and several months pregnant. Josephine explains how her pregnancy resulted from a sexual encounter she had with a relative. She engaged in a culturally sanctioned practice known as "beading" that is common among the Samburu of Kenya. The Samburu live in a small village in a remote part of Isiolo in the Eastern Province of Kenya. According to the beading culture of the Samburu, girls are encouraged to engage in sex with a relative in exchange for beaded neck-laces. A close male family relative from the family is permitted to approach a girl's parents, and with their permission, he may place the beaded neck-lace around the girl's neck as a declaration of engagement; this act is called "beading." Once the declaration is made, the man is granted permission to have sexual intercourse with the girl in question. As Josephine Kulea, an activist and member of the Samburu community that embrace beading explains, when a man beads a girl, he has essentially "booked her, . . . he can then have sex with her" (McKenzie, 2011a). Since beading is an early promise of marriage to the family, girls may be beaded as early as 6 years old (McKenzie, 2011b).

The experiences of gender-based violence that Chepkorir and Josephine were exposed to are not unique to their communities, to Kenya, or to Africa in general. Their experience is similar to that of Piah Njoki, whose eyes were gouged out by her husband for bearing him only female children. Betty Kavata was beaten senseless in the same year by her husband, who inflicted such serious head injuries that she was hospitalized (Ondicho, 2000: 21). The list is endless, in a country that has initiated significant efforts to combat this behavior, including designing and enacting laws and policies. Current data from a demographic and health survey (KDHS) of Kenya indicate that one out of every four women experiences intimate partner violence. Of 612 women surveyed, 58% reported experiencing beatings often or sometimes. About 40% reported having experienced physical violence, 16% of whom experienced sexual violence. Existing data from the police headquarters indicate that 2,005 women and children were raped in the year 2002, a figure that increased to 2,908 in 2004. It should be noted that most rape survivors don't report rape due to ignorance about their basic rights and an inability to negotiate the legal system. Due to stigma, fear of being blamed, rejected, and even abandoned, and a general cultural attitude that blames the woman for sexual assault, most survivors of rape refrain from going public.

Studies also show that child marriage remains rampant in Kenya, with an estimated 23% of girls being married before they attain their 18th birthday. The World Health Organization (WHO) documents higher percentages in some counties. For instance, Kilifi county has the highest prevalence of child marriage at 47%, followed by Homa Bay at 38%, Kwale at 38%, Bondo at 29.5%, and Tharaka at 25% (Center for Human Rights, 2018: 22). Many parents, especially in the rural areas, continue to marry off their daughters at ages as young as 12 years old. Further, it is estimated that about 37% of girls continue to be exposed to genital cutting (Momoh, 2005: 6). Although statistics indicate that there has been a decline in the practice over the past two decades following the illegalization of the practice in Kenya, the rate of those circumcised is still significant. In fact, the United Nations Population Fund statistics show that female genital cutting is on the rise. The rate of this practice is higher in some communities, such as those of the Somali, the Kisii, and the Maasai, where over 90% of the population embraces the practice.[1] Levels are lower among communities such as the Kikuyu (34%) and Kamba (27%).[2] The prevalence of gender-based violence in Kenya was alluded to during the Gender Forum on Sexual Gender-Based Violence held on February 28, 2014 in Nairobi by the Heinrich Boell Foundation in conjunction with the African Women's Development and Communication Network (FEMNET). The persistence of cultural norms and practices that legitimize violence through homophobia, child marriage, female genital cutting, and widow cleansing is a concern and an obstacle to gender equality.

In this chapter, we draw from existing data to highlight how gender-based violence is constructed and informed through culture and religious values in select communities in Kenya. We explore the moral rationale behind these practices to highlight patriarchal and sexist norms behind gender-based violence and especially how social equality and human rights are undermined. While acknowledging the often-compelling arguments for the practices, we highlight the controversial discourse that surrounds these practices due to moral universality and cultural relativist viewpoints. It is the objective of this chapter also to explore efforts by the government of Kenya to minimize human suffering that results from gender-based violence through the development and enactment of effective human rights-based policy.

Gender-based violence in Kenya

The term gender-based violence (GBV)[3] was officially used by the United Nations in 1993 in reference to any act of violence that results, or is likely to result, in physical, sexual, or psychological harm or suffering by women; this may include threats of such acts, coercion, or arbitrary deprivations of liberty, whether occurring in public or in private life.[4] To understand the roots of gender-based violence in Kenya, it is important to interrogate cultural values, including religious norms that influence behavior. This is because, in most societies, women's subordinate status, coupled with general acceptance of interpersonal violence as a means of resolving social conflict, has often rendered women disproportionately vulnerable to violence at all levels of social interactions. As Andrea Cornwall states:

> Men's violence is a key determinant of the inequities and the inequalities of gender relations that both disempower and impoverish women. Violence is a fundamental dimension of human poverty. Yet, men's natural aggression is often invoked as a defining characteristic of an essential gender difference and as an explanation for gendered hierarchical arrangements in the political and economic contexts of richer and poorer countries alike (Cornwall, 1997/2001: 1997).

It is for this reason that Chepkorir's fate must be understood within her community's worldview. Among the Pokot of Kenya, intersexuality is acknowledged as a natural phenomenon that is found in both human and animals. Often, intersexed children are put to death because they are perceived to be an unfortunate occurrence or a freak that does not deserve to live. As Edgerton explains, to some Pokot, such a child was "a useless thing" because "it could never be a real person" (Edgerton, 1964: 1291). Although there are instances, however, where some individuals' lives are spared because they are viewed as "God's wish," violence against intersexed individuals commonly known in modern society as belonging to the LGBTQ community is rampant beyond Kenya.

Josephine's experience also makes sense within the Samburu culture. Beading is essentially a form of child marriage that is culturally sanctioned by the Samburu, a nomadic pastoralist ethnic group that resides in the northern parts of Kenya. To the Samburu, for instance, beading is a culture that prepares young girls for marriage, while ensuring that the warriors, known as the *morans*, do not seduce the wives of the elders, and is thus, as Kangara has argued, a way of preventing social conflict between the men in the communities (McKenzie, 2011). The warrior, who often seeks the permission of the girl's family to engage in sexual union with their daughter, is expected to present to them with red beads that he specifically bought for her. Most often the girl's consent is not sought during the negotiation of the beading relationship. Negotiations are held between the warrior, the mother, and the brothers of the chosen girl. If the mother approves the beading relationship, she is required to build a hut (*Singira*) for her daughter and for the warrior. The beads, which are often colorful, are an important part of the Samburu culture. They signify beauty and wealth for women and men. The patterns and colors of the beads have their own meanings. For instance, the color red signifies strength and power of the community. Blue and green represent the natural vegetation (water and grass), which are vital for the welfare of the livestock of the community. Black is a reminder of the hardships of their pastoralist lifestyle.

At the commencement of the sexual relationship, the warrior gives the girl special white and black beads to signify that she is taken. This means that no one else is to have an intimate relationship with her, except for her suitor. Since the *moran* and his beaded girl are often related, and the girl is often uncircumcised, sexual encounter is not to result in pregnancy or marriage. In case of a pregnancy, it must be terminated. If the beaded girl chooses to keep the pregnancy, the child, after birth, is either given away to a neighboring community – often the Turkana, who neighbor the Samburu – or, often, is killed as she/he is rendered illegitimate and therefore an outcast.

The Samburu, like some communities that embrace child marriage, also practice female genital cutting. While widely practiced in some communities in Kenya, female genital cutting is not embraced by all Kenyan communities. Female genital cutting involves either partial or total removal of the external female genitalia or other injury to female organs for cultural reasons.[5] As discussed in chapter 14, female genital cutting is generally classified into four typologies to reflect its severity. Type 1, known generally as clitoridectomy, involves the removal of the prepuce (clitoral hood), leaving a part of the clitoris (aka *sunna* circumcision). Type 2, referred to as excision, involves the removal of the entire clitoris together with part or all of the labia minora (the inner vaginal lips). Type 3, known as infibulation, involves the genital cutting as well as the stitching of the raw edges to allow for the formation of scar tissue around the vaginal opening. As indicated earlier, this is the most severe form of female genital cutting because of the repetitive process of de-infibulation and re-infibulation. Finally, type 4 designates all other unclassified procedures that inflict some kind of pain on the female genitalia.

In cultural settings, female genital cutting is undertaken according to traditional requirements, as an initiation into adulthood (Rahman and Toubia, 2001: 8; Spencer, 2002: 2). Beading is an example of many widespread socially accepted forms of gender-based violence. Although this culture is commonly featured as a symbol of Kenyan cultural pride, the violence against children and women that is legitimized in the name of culture should counter any pride claimed. Children's and women's integrity and ultimately rights are undermined by the legitimization of underage sexual encounters that are essentially rape and that often lead to unwanted pregnancies. This practice exposes young girls to reproductive health issues such as STIs, child mortality, fistula, and other health complications. Studies indicate that some of the girls and their babies end up dying due to health complications.

Child marriage and female genital cutting are not only a problem among the Samburu but are widespread practices in several communities in Kenya. As indicated earlier, child marriage is a rampant problem, with an estimated 23% of girls being married before their 18th birthday. The effects of this on school drop-out rates is astounding. Among the Maasai of Kenya, for instance, only 11% of girls graduate from elementary school, a reflection of how valuable marriage is compared to education (UNFPA, 2000–2011). Although reasons for embracing child marriage and female genital cutting may be compelling culturally, they ought to be understood beyond cultural expressions.

Construct of gender-based violence

To understand gender-based violence, it is important that perceptions about human behavior are highlighted. In Kenya, gender-based violence is a complex issue because it is rooted in the structural inequalities between men and women that result in the persistence of power differentials between the sexes. In most societies, women's subordinate status, coupled with a general acceptance of interpersonal violence as a means of resolving social conflict, has often rendered women disproportionately vulnerable to violence at all levels of social interactions, a fact that is clearly illustrated in Cornwall's argument above (Cornwall, 1997/2001).

Gender relations are not only a social construct; they are also influenced by social institutions such as the family, religion, law, economy, and medicine that embrace these norms as such. Social behavior such as heterosexuality, homosexuality, celibacy, monogamy and polygamy, child marriage, female circumcision, and widow inheritance are culturally sanctioned by social norms embraced in the community. According to Foucault, power or political forces include the religious influence of attitudes and behavior. Feminists such as Catharine Mackinnon have argued that where gender occurs is where "dominance defines the imperatives of masculinity," and "submission eroticized defines femininity" (Mackinnon, 1989: 69). In other words, the status of women as second class must be understood within the dynamics of inequality of sexes.

Gender as a social construct is reinforced through socialization and the distinction of patterns that are different for males and females. Where observed, transition rites form an integral part of the socialization process. Often, gender-based violence sanctioned by the community is embraced by all as the norm. In African communities where norms and modes of ethical conduct are perceived in communal terms, living entities and experience not only are interconnected but also supplement and complement each other. Every social phenomenon is perceived as dependent and interrelated and is therefore defined by other social phenomenon. Without one entity, the other is not only devalued but also loses its validity and meaning. Implicitly, therefore, social behavior must be understood as part of the whole, often in relation to social needs of a community. Although Western notions of behavior are gaining ground in contemporary Africa, indigenous values remain persistent.

Often, femininity is often associated with reproduction, caretaking, generosity, modesty, and the dignity of perseverance, obedience, submissiveness, conformity, and dependence. Masculinity, on the other hand, is associated with virility, strength, authority, power, leadership, and the ability to bear physical pain and offer protection and economic sustenance as the breadwinners. Deviant lifestyles are considered inappropriate and are discouraged, stigmatized, or severely punished. These values, generally inculcated in the individual from early childhood, are expected of boys when they are told that "men don't cry," while girls are told not to insult boys or show the aggression often associated with males. Attitudes toward men's strength and women's weaknesses usually translate into marriage such that even in sexual relations, the woman's sexual role is expected to be more or less marginal or passive. She is not expected to take initiative in sexual activities such as courtship, to show desire for sexual intercourse, or even to indicate that she is enjoying sex without taking the risk of being branded a prostitute.

Among the Kikuyu, for instance, when a child is born, his or her gender is announced by the mother's screams; four screams for a girl and five screams for a boy. From birth onwards, the parents and the community at large instill into children gender expectations. In most cases, girls are brought up to embrace household duties such as house care, fetching water and firewood, and treating boys and men as superior entities. Boys, on the other hand, are taught to embrace masculine duties such as hunting, sitting with elderly men to learn leadership wisdom, and protecting their families (Mbiti, 1990). At puberty, a sharp distinction is made between maleness and femaleness. While men enter into the world of power, girls are instructed in matters of womanhood such as sexual games, menstruation taboos, and the "secret" of childbirth. For instance, a girl is taught moral values about the sanctity and purity of her body and how to remain clean and undefiled sexually until marriage. Emphasis on maintaining one's virginity is a common method used by most communities to maintain purity among women. During the circumcision ritual, one of the excisers ensures that initiates are virgins. Those who are not virgins during this time are considered a disgrace to their families and are often excluded from attending important initiation rituals. Apart from references to sex organs and sexual activities, which are usually made through admonition and ridicule of initiates and in songs sung during puberty rituals, the initiate is introduced to themes revolving around subordination, power, authority, and challenge. After marriage, chastity is expected from married women with infidelity receiving severe punishment. Most women fear divorce, not only because it is a stigma but also because a divorced woman and her parents are often required to go through the painful ordeal of returning the dowry, which most often has already been shared and utilized by family members and extended relations.

It is important to note that while virginity is stressed in most communities, some communities allow premarital sex as preparation for adult life. Among the Kikuyu and the Akamba, for instance, premarital sexual activities known as *ngwiko*, which include for instance the fondling of each other's genitals, is allowed as a means of instilling self-control in the youth without actual penetration. Virginity is maintained in spite of this. As Davison (1995: 11) observes, "newly initiated youth of both sexes were allowed to sleep together and engage in sexual play and experimentation without intercourse under a strict code of behavior in a communally controlled environment designed to prohibit premarital pregnancy" (Davison, 1996: 11).

Early marriages are encouraged to ensure virginity until the wedding night. In case a girl becomes pregnant before marriage, the man responsible is obliged to marry her (Amour, 1996). Among the Maasai, for instance, marriages are arranged for daughters as young as 12 years. In marriage, power is displayed by granting the man exclusive rights over his wife's body and sexuality. Practices such as domestic violence are justified in these communities to help subdue the wife and to keep her in her proper position. Rape in marriage is unheard of simply because sex is believed to be a husband's right at all times. Men expect sex on demand and enforce this privilege through a variety of means. In some communities, denying your husband sex is a good reason for wife-beating. Among the Kikuyu, for instance, men are encouraged to beat their wives at least once, otherwise the curse of their ancestors will catch up with them (Bukenya, Kabira and Okoth-Okombo, 1994: 77–84). Among the Kalenjin and the Maasai, a narrative is told about how to discipline a wife who refuses to be subordinate. Ciarunji Chesaina explains:

> Two friends were coming from a beer party. Rero told his friend "These days, these women of ours are behaving differently from long ago. They are becoming too inquisitive. Every time we go anywhere they must ask where we have been. I think it is high time we disciplined them." On hearing this, Arap Suge was angry because he knew his wife was a friend of Rero's wife and he knew that whatever Rero was experiencing from his wife had been discussed by the two women. Above all, Arap Suge believed strongly that a woman had no right to question her husband. He therefore supported Rero that they discipline their wives that night by beating them severely. They agreed to lock the doors before starting on the beating so that the wives would not . . . run away. . . . Arap Suge beat his wife almost to death.
>
> (Chesaina, 1994: 64–65)

While some practices such as child marriage and female genital cutting are essentially culturally legitimate, others are often linked, albeit indirectly, to religious practice. In some cases, norms about gender behavior are transmitted through religious stories, myths, folktales, and songs that caution about the consequences of non-adherence or resistance to such practices. Traditionally, for instance, female genital cutting is rooted in indigenous notions of natural androgynies, bisexuality, and hermaphroditism, notions that are expressed in various mythologies that link it to claims of extraordinary characteristics of the gods. According to these mythologies, the human genitalia is linked to the human soul, which reflects the extraordinary bisexual nature of the gods, manifest in the bisexual nature of all humans at birth (Griaule, 1965: 21; Griaule, 1970: 17).[6] While it is not mentioned in the Bible, some Jews and Christians have used biblical narratives to make a case for female genital cutting. It is argued, for instance, that the justification of male circumcision as given to Abraham in the Old Testament extends to female circumcision. Studies have referenced the existence of the practice among the 1,000 tribes of Eastern Jews for the reasons of reduced sexual sensitivity. Others have referenced claims that Mary, mother of Jesus, was a virgin (Mt 1:23; Lk 1:27) to argue that virginity values are often accompanied by practices of child marriage and female circumcision. In other words, Mary, mother of Jesus, must have been circumcised for her virginity to have been established. While the term female circumcision does not appear in the Qur'an, the practice is widely associated with Islam. Although the practice was prevalent in pre-Islamic Arabia, advocates of female circumcision have often referenced religious teachings of purity as well as the tradition of the prophet – *khitan al-sunna* or *al-sunna* (Abu-Sahlieh, 2001: 11). To most advocates, the mention of the practice in the *Hadith* (sayings and actions of the prophet), the factual report of its prevalence during the time of Prophet Muhammad, and the fact that Imam Ali endorsed it is enough justification of the practice as Islamic.

Beliefs that the fall of man was caused by a woman, and the description of a woman as the tempter, deceiver, and seducer of Adam reinforce stereotypes about gender. To blame a woman for the fall of humankind was to associate femininity with evil. This not only reinforced the mindset that men should always be dominant, it also expressed the idea that women are "oversexed" and incapable of controlling themselves. This view creates the perception that the woman must be protected from herself and that men should be protected from women. The belief that woman was created for man, as taught in the Judeo-Christian and Muslim religions that have been embraced in Kenya, help to reinforce male dominance and female subordination. As Riffat Hassan explains, *Sura* 4:34 and *Sura* 2:288 of the Qur'an are often cited in support of male dominance (Hassan, 110). Abdul A'la Maududi translates these Suras thus:

> Men are the managers of the affairs of women because Allah has made the one superior to the other and because men spend all of their wealth on women. Virtuous women are, therefore, obedient; they guard their rights carefully in their absence under the care and watch of Allah. As

for those women whose defiance you have cause to fear, admonish them and keep them apart from your bed and beat them. Then, if they submit to you, do not look for excuses to punish them: note it well that there is Allah above you, who is supreme and great.

(Maududi, 1979)

To present cultural practices as sacred and religious is to grant them a sacred veil that communicates to the individual that these practices are intended by a God, gods, or some supernatural divine. This attitude elevates these practices beyond the rational discourse and demands that they be accepted without question in a powerful process of socialization and construction of behavior. When such practices involve violence, such violence is then justified. Such legitimation undermines basic individual rights. It is therefore important that initiatives to address gender-based violence recognize how gender-based violence is constructed and legitimized by such values, including religious ones. To employ a social functionalist approach toward legitimizing such a practice is to ignore how respect for cultural values and heritage can undermine basic individual rights to integrity, health, and education. Unchecked social functionalism has infringed upon the rights of children and women in the name of culture and religion. The need to reconcile this is the objective of this chapter. It is apparent from the foregoing that the concepts of gender in Kenya not only conform to the holistic, corporate, and functional roles of the society but are also reinforced by foreign ideologies. While a holistic approach is and should be admired for its emphasis on the importance of functionalism, interrelatedness, and most importantly complementarity, virtues that are indigenous to an African country such as Kenya, when unchecked, holism can subsume and infringe upon the rights of some individuals in any society. It is on this basis that female circumcision, widow inheritance, and polygamy find critique in feminist and human rights discourse.

It is, therefore, important that attitudes towards gender in Kenya and Africa as a whole should be interrogated within the complex values and norms that influence social behavior. It is important to recognize that these practices do not operate independently of each other and that they are embedded in patriarchal, structural systems that sanction male dominance and female subordination. It is for this reason that scholars such as Ellen Gruenbaum have described female genital cutting as a cultural practice that is part of a social structure that promotes similar practices such as polygamy, child marriage, bride price, and widow inheritance, all of which are designed to limit women's self-realization and enjoyment of life (Gruenbaum, 2001: 133). Nancy Bonvillain describes female genital cutting as a procedure that is sexually disfiguring because victims are forced to avoid sex because of intercourse is painful as a consequence of the procedure. She argues that this practice interferes not only with the right to sexual pleasure but also with reproductive health since the victim loses part of her sexual organs in the process (Bonvillain, 2001: 277). To Barbara S. Morrison, "the clitoris removal serves to create pain in the female body and also to permanently obliterate one of the sites of pleasure that constitutes the female body"(2008: 126). In a patriarchal system, gender is understood from a dualist mindset that views reality as consisting of two basic opposing elements – typically the mind and matter (or mind and body), or good and evil, or God and the devil. The dualist ideology has been expanded to justify social structures, including patriarchal hierarchies, to the point of identifying masculinity with transcendence, rationality, and logos and femininity with immanence, emotionality, and eros (Makoye, 2013). It is the general assumption that the higher reality often identified with the male must dominate and control the lower reality – the female. It is believed that the female threatens the male domain. The influence of this dualist ideology on African thought contributes significantly toward challenges for transforming attitudes to women's experiences.

Towards ending gender-based violence

Critics of beading, child marriage, and female genital cutting consider these to be instances of gender-based violence and violations of the basic rights of children and women due to moral and health concerns. While beading and female genital cutting are legitimate forms of cultural heritage that are valued by the Samburu, they are norms that find critique because they sanction gender-based violence such as genital mutilation, sexual assault, and the rape of minors. Kenya, like other modern societies, has initiated significant steps to protect the rights of children by insisting on girl child education. As a member state of the United Nations, an organization that has criticized gender-based violence as stipulated in the Universal Declaration of Human Rights, Kenya has declared that each and every person has the basic rights to education, shelter, and food, including children. As statistics clearly show, countries with the highest child marriage rates have the lowest rates of educated women. A country that denies women education not only denies these women a healthy and better livelihood but also denies itself human power that would have gone into its development. This fact is reiterated in the UNICEF statement that most of these child brides end up in poverty, are less educated, and experience serious health issues for themselves and their children. Studies also indicate that girls age 15–19 are twice as likely to die during pregnancy or childbirth compared to those over age 20. Girls younger than 15 are five times more likely to lose their lives during childbirth. When a woman is under 18, her child is 60% more likely to die in its first year of life than a baby born to a mother over 18 years. While it is common for families in communities that engage in child marriage to use this practice as a tool for alleviating poverty, the practice perpetuates a cycle of impoverishment at the familial as well as the national level.

Moral concerns relate to human rights values. These practices are considered not only an expression of patriarchy, sexism, and sexual control of sexuality but also a violation of the human rights of children and women (Gruenbaum, 2001: 133; Hite, 1976: 99). Human rights principles are embedded in the moral universalist framework to argue for the basic rights inherent to all human beings regardless of their nationality, race, gender, and origin. They were instituted in the 1940s order to protect humans from atrocities that violated their humanity, including protection from violence. The establishment of human rights principles was meant to discourage discriminatory practices, including female genital cutting. The United Nations Declaration of Human Rights and its issuance of the Convention on the Elimination of All Forms of Discrimination Against Women (CEDAW) in 1979 served as a way to protect women from all forms of violence, including culturally legitimate ones such as female genital cutting (Steiner and Alston, 1996: 244–245). Human rights and the moral universalist rationale are used to condemn all practices considered to be gender-based violence. It is for these reasons that those who have advocated practices such as female genital cutting have insisted on the necessity of informed consent, which in many countries is the age of 18. As Fuambai Ahmadu has argued, informed consent should be sought before any female genital cutting procedure is administered, and that age of consent should be 18 years of age (Ahmadu, 2000: 284). The same argument has been made for child marriage.

Moral concerns are embedded in two theoretical frameworks: (1) moral universalism, a theoretical framework that advocates for human rights; and (2) cultural relativism, a theory that has advocates for group rights (Billet, 2007). Moral universalism rationalizes its position through various theories. First, it draws on the theory of natural law to argue that human beings possess a certain degree of sovereignty with regard to ideals such as freedom and honor and that all human beings possess this sovereignty equally. Therefore, imposing any restriction on human sovereignty is morally wrong (Perry, 1997: 478–481; Billet, 2007: 16). Second, they use the theory of rationalism to argue that all humans, as rational beings, are sovereign beings equal to each other (Billet, 2007: 1). Third, they draw from the theory of human capabilities to argue for the need to recognize that the fundamental characteristics that define what it means to be human occur across diverse societies, and that these include the basic needs for food, drink, shelter, and mobility as well as the capacity for pain and pleasure. Fourth, they use the doctrine of positivism to argue that countries with representative forms of government should promote universal norms of behavior (Billet, 2007: 6).

Although human rights serve as the ideal moral tool of cultural analysis, it was not accepted by cultural relativists who have defended female genital cutting based on "group rights," cultural diversity, or multiculturalism. The need to preserve group identity and cultural diversity is intended to defend the preservation of traditional values. Central to the cultural relativist discourse is the need to correct and prevent misconceived imperialist attitudes. Questions of difference, which characterized the 1994 Cairo Conference on Population and Development, continue to challenge the concept of human rights, deeming it a Western imperialist ploy (Afkhami and Fridi, 1997). By invoking cultural imperialism and intellectual colonialism, the universality of human rights is questioned as a moral principle suitable for adoption by non-Western cultures (Kalev, 2004: 345; Afkhami and Fridi, 1997). In defense of female genital cutting, cultural relativists critique advocates of moral universalism for exaggerating health issues associated with the practice and for disregarding the cultural values associated with it. For instance, Fuambai A. Ahmadu, who experienced the procedure, is an ardent defender of cultural relativism. She criticizes the use of the Western norms of sexuality to critique cultural patterns that structure another society. Ahmadu argues that the assumption that women in all societies desire sexual fulfillment is misleading, since sexuality is socially defined (Ahmadu, 2000: 284; Shweder, 2000).

The cultural relativist argument has, however, received criticism from scholars such as Iris Young, Francis Beckwith and Gregory Koukl, W. Kymlicka, Sebastian Poulter, Henriette D. Kalev, and Chandran Kukathas, among others. Beckwith and Koukl assert that the cultural relativist argument promotes a form of cultural romanticism that is resistant to the reality of cultural critical appraisal, which is a critical reflection of cultural values to determine what should be discarded or retained (Beckwith and Koukl, 1998). They state that cultural relativism can be interpreted as a form of extreme relativism, an approach that is likely to lead to a world in which nothing could be considered to be wrong (Beckwith and Koukl, 1998). Such an approach presupposes a world in which justice and fairness are meaningless concepts, since not only is accountability impossible, but there is also no possibility of moral improvement or moral discourse and tolerance in such a society (Beckwith and Koukl, 1998: 69). While presenting a compelling argument for social identity, as a discourse this approach poses certain social implications for women's rights (Parekh, 1999: 121). Iris Young argues that although social difference as espoused by group rights is a multicultural value that is a source of power, recognition, identity, and emancipation for the marginalized, it can also be a tool of oppression (Young, 1990: 39–63, 163). She argues that unchecked claims of multiculturalism may lead to cultural romanticism and the stifling of social justice. Cultural tolerance should not be a "cloak" for promoting oppressive and unjust practices, argues Poulter (1986: 593).

Health concerns include immediate consequences such as severe pain, urine retention, shock, hemorrhage, and infection, as well as death in some cases; long-term consequences include cysts, abscesses, keloid, scarring, damage to the urethra, dyspareunia, difficulties with childbirth, and sexual dysfunction. Other consequences can be psychological, such as feelings of anxiety, terror, humiliation, and betrayal. A study undertaken by Africans and international researchers indicates that female genital cutting can have adverse effects on birth outcomes. In this study, in which Professor Emily Banks of the National Center for Epidemiology and Population Health at

Australian National University was involved, 28,393 women were studied in 28 obstetric centers in six African countries: Burkina Faso, Ghana, Kenya, Nigeria, Senegal, and Sudan. The findings of the study indicate that women who have had female genital cutting are significantly more likely to experience difficulties during childbirth and that their babies are more likely to die as a result of the practice. Childbirth complications include the need to perform a Caesarean section, dangerous bleeding after childbirth, and prolonged hospitalization following the birth. According to the study, women who have had severe forms of FGC are on average likely to have a 30% greater likelihood of undergoing a Caesarean section compared with those who have not. Seventy percent of these women are more likely to suffer hemorrhage after birth. The need to resuscitate babies born to these women is not only high, but the death rate for these babies during and immediately after birth is also higher compared to those whose parents have not had female genital cutting (Vangen et al., 2004; Varol et al., 2016; WHO, 2006). The degree of complications increases in relation to the severity of the procedure. According to Professor Banks, this collaborative study provides the first reliable evidence of the impact of female genital cutting. Due to these health consequences, the WHO, United Nations Children's Fund, and UN Population released a joint statement in 1996 condemning the practice. In part, the statement reads:

> It is unacceptable that the international community remain passive in the name of a distorted vision of multiculturalism. Human behaviors and cultural values, however senseless or destructive they may appear from the personal and cultural standpoint of others, have meaning and fulfill a function for those who practice them. However, culture is not static but it is in constant flux, adapting and reforming. People will change their behavior when they understand the hazards and indignity of harmful practices and when they realize that it is possible to give up harmful practices without giving up meaningful aspects of their culture.[7]

Due to the controversial positions and norms that surround the cultural sanctioning of some violent gender-based practices, attempts to outlaw and eradicate them have proven to be unsuccessful. Social resistance is complicated by challenges related to the enforcement of established policies. This attitude accounts for the persistence of gender-based practices such as child marriage, female genital cutting, and even domestic violence. In order to effect behavior change, it is important that intervention programs target attitude change for the realities various communities deal with. The World Health Organization (WHO) and Appropriate Technology in Health (PATH) have recommended that effective intervention programs be broad in the sense of targeting both the men and women who play a role in the persistence of the practice. These programs must (1) establish strong and capable institutional programs at national, regional, and local levels, (2) support these programs with strong policies, laws, and resources, (3) ensure that female genital cutting is institutionalized as an issue to be addressed by national reproductive health and development programs, (4) ensure effective coordination between governments and nonprofit organizations in addressing female genital cutting, (5) ensure that health providers are trained in order to effectively recognize wounds and complications associated with female genital cutting, and (6) promote effective advocacy that fosters positive policy enactment and legal measures against female genital cutting. These community-based initiatives can effect behavior change, if properly executed. Community-based initiatives are said to be most successful not only because they seek to promote community education and awareness of the problem at the grassroots level but also because they are often culturally sensitive in their approaches. Any behavior change strategy must acknowledge that the meaning and value of what is to be changed is more meaningful to those who seek such a change.

Conclusion

In this chapter, we have described how some forms of gender-based violence are legitimately sanctioned by culture and religion. We have argued that in some communities, gender-based practices such as beading, child marriage, and female genital cutting are embraced. We have described the origins of and reasons given for these practices and highlighted how religious explanations can be offered for their origin, practice, and persistence. We have described reasons and values behind these practices and argued as to why they are categorized as gender-based violence despite being they are culturally legitimate in the communities in which where they are found. Drawing on social, ethical, and holistic theoretical frameworks, we have highlighted the basis for arguments from human rights and cultural relativist perspectives. While we recognize the cultural values within which these practices are embedded, we have highlighted health and moral concerns that arise from the practices. Utilizing an intersectionality approach, we have demonstrated how complex these practices are given that they are rooted in holistic frameworks that must be appreciated when examining the origin, reasons, and norms behind them and even perceptions regarding eradication.

It is argued that while these practices have been declared human rights violations, attempts to eradicate them have generated controversial feelings and sometimes dilemmas that result from valid perceptions of such attempts. We recognize that while arguments for human rights draw on concerns embedded within moral universalism, which categorize these practices as violations of children's and women's rights, this position has not successfully argued for the eradication of these practices because moral universalism is often undermined and overshadowed by imperialist and post-colonial sentiments. Similarly, we argue that while cultural relativism as an approach presents a compelling argument for the need to respect group rights and individual identities as an approach it is undermined by romanticism and other biased tendencies that are likely to fail the individual who tries to claim and protect their basic needs and rights. Efforts to promote diversity and multicultural-ism with respect to identities, values, and cultural heritage, can sometimes undermine basic human rights values. While each position on the matter is compelling, we argue for the need to respect the strengths and weaknesses of each position as this relates to the basic needs and rights of the individual. The plight of the girl child or the needs of the woman involved should over-ride cultural and imperial concerns associated with these approaches.

The chapter ends by developing the argument for eradication of the prac-tice. We argue that efforts to end the practice must ensure that strategies are employed that are likely to be effective. We recognize that efforts to eradicate child marriage and female genital cutting have encountered seri-ous challenges leading to the persistence of these practices, despite long a history of strategies aiming toward eradication. We argue in support of the World Health Organization's recommendations that effective strategy must be community-based. We give a brief description of community-based initia-tives and how effective they are in engaging grassroots communities through contextualization and an empowerment approach that educates, inspires, and encourages the community itself to reexamine its values vis-à-vis the basic human rights of its people. We argue that its approach is effective because it is not holistic and inclusive of all members of the community; by including youth, men, and women, traditional birth attendants and edu-cators, it recognizes that cultural practices such as child marriage, female genital cutting, and other gender-based forms of violence do not operate in a vacuum. Empowering all agents is key to transforming behavior since all members in the community are called upon to engage in cultural appraisal of the values they embrace from the insider's perspectives and to engage in attitude transformation as necessary. Behavior change is socially con-structed, but it can also be socially deconstructed if proper cultural appraisal is ensured.

Notes

1 n. 16 above, 251.
2 As above.
3 Important to note is the fact that the terms gender-based violence (GBV) and sexual and gender-based violence (SGBV) are often used interchangeably.
4 See Article 1 of DEVAW. Article 2 of the Declaration states that the definition should encompass, but not be limited to, acts of physical, sexual, and psychological violence in the family, community, or perpetrated or condoned by the state, wherever it occurs. These acts include: spousal battery; sexual abuse, including of female children; dowry-related violence; rape, including marital rape; female genital mutilation/cutting and other traditional practices harmful to women; non-spousal violence; sexual violence related to exploitation; sexual harassment and intimidation at work, in school, and elsewhere; trafficking in women; and forced prostitution.
5 (n 16 above) 250.

6 Griaule, Marcel. 1965. "Second Day," "Third Day," and "Fourth Day," *Conversations with Ogotemmeli*, International African Institute, Oxford University Press, New York.; Griaule, Marcel. 1970. Conversations with Ogotemmeli: An Introduction to Dogon Religions, Oxford: Oxford University Press.
7 Joint statement by the World Health Organization, UN Children's Fund (UNICEF) and UN Population Fund, February 1996.

References

Abu-Sahlieh, Sami Awad Aldeeb. 2001. *Male and Female Circumcision: Among Jews, Christians and Muslims: Religious, Medical, Social and Legal Debate*. Warren Center, PA: Shangri-La Publications.

Afkhami, M. and Fridi, E. (eds.). 1997. "Introduction." In *Muslim Women and the Politics of Participation: Implementing the Beijing platform*. Syracuse: Syracuse University Press.

Ahmadu, Fuambai. 2000. "Rites and Wrongs: An Insider/Outsider Reflects on Power and Excision." In *Female "Circumcision" in Africa: Culture, Controversy and Change*. eds. Bettina Shell-Duncan and Ylva Herlund, 283–312. London: Lynne Reinne Publishers.

Amour, Elizabeth. 1996. "Violence and Women's Bodies in African Perspective." In *Women Resisting Violence: Spirituality for Life*. eds. Mary John Mananzan, Mercy Amba Oduyoye, Elsa Tamez, J. Shannon Clarkson, Mary C. Grey, Letty M. Russell, and Orbis Books, 91. New York: Maryknoll.

Beckwith, Francis, J. and Gregory Koukl. 1998. *Relativism: Feet Firmly Planted in Mid-Air*. Baker Books.

Billet, L. Bret. 2007. *Cultural Relativism in the Face of the West: The Plight of Women and Female Children*. New York: Palgrave Macmillan.

Bonvillain, N. 2001. *Women and Men Cultural Constructs of Gender* (3rd ed.). Grand Rapids, MI: Upper Saddle River, NJ, Pearson.

Bukenya, Austin, Wanjiku Mukabi Kabira and Duncan Okoth-Okombo. 1994. *Understanding Oral Literature*. Nairobi: University of Nairobi Press.

Center for Human Rights. 2018. "A Report on Child Marriage in Africa," http://www.chr.up.ac.za/images/researchunits/wru/news/files/2018_child_marriage_report_en.pdf

Chesaina, Ciarunji. 1994. "Images of Women in African Oral Literature: A Case Study of the Kalenjin and the Maasai Oral Narrative." In *Understanding Oral Literature*. eds. A. Bukenya, M. K. Wanjiku, and O. Okombo, 85–92. Nairobi: Nairobi University Press.

Cornwall, Andrea. 1997/2009. "Men, Masculinity and 'Gender Development'." *Gender and Development*, 5(2), https://www.tandfonline.com/doi/abs/10.1080/741922358

Davison, Jean. 1996. *Voices From Mutira: Change in the Lives of Rural Gikuyo Women, 1910-1995*. Boulder: Lynne Rienner Publishers.

Edgerton, Robert B. 1964. "Pokot Intersexuality. An East African Example of the Resolution of Sexual Incongruity." *American Anthropologist*, 66(6): 1288–1299, https://anthrosource.onlinelibrary.wiley.com/doi/pdf/10.1525/aa.1964.66.6.02a00040

Gruenbaum, Ellen. 2001. *The Female Circumcision Controversy: An Anthropological Perspective*. Philadelphia, PA: University of Pennsylvania Press.

Hassan, Riffat. 1990. "An Islamic Perspective." In *Women, Religion and Sexuality: Studies on the Impact of Religious Teachings on Women*, edited by Jeanne Becher, 93–129. Geneva: World Council of Churches Publications.

Hite, Shere. 1976. *The Hite Report: A Nationwide Study of Female Sexuality*. New York: Macmillan Publishing Co., Inc.

Kabira, Wanjiku Mukabi. 1994. "Images of Women in African Oral Literature: An Overview of Images of Women in Gikuyu Oral Narratives." In *Understanding Oral Literature*, edited by A. Bukenya, M. K. Wanjiku, and O. Okombo, 77–84. Nairobi: Nairobi University Press.

Kalev, Henriette Dahan. 2004. "Cultural Rights or Human Rights: The Case of Female Genital Mutilation." *Sex Roles*, 51(5/6): September.

Mackinnon, Catharine. 1989. *Toward a Feminist Theory of the State*. Cambridge, MA: Harvard University Press.

Makoye, Kizito. 2013. "Gender-Based Violence Rising in Tanzania." *Thomas Routers Foundation News*, http://news.trust.org/item/20130725231724-ijt3z

Mbiti, John S. 1990. *African Religions and Philosophy*. London: Heinemann Educational Books.

McKenzie, David. 2011a. "Activist Battles Kenyan Tradition of Rape 'Beading'," *CNN*, May 11, http://www.cnn.com/2011/WORLD/africa/05/11/kenya.children.beading/index.html

———. 2011b. "School 'Pays Dowry' to Save Girls from Being Child Brides," *CNN*, June 16, http://www.cnn.com/2011/WORLD/africa/06/16/kenya.school.maasai/index.html

Momoh, Comfort. 2005. *Female Genital Mutilation*. Oxford: Radcliffe Publishing.

Morrison, Barbara S. 2008. "Feminist Theory and the Practice of Female Genital Mutilation," https://www.academia.edu/7780610/Feminist_Theory_and_the_Practice_of_Female_Genital_Mutilation

Ondicho, Tom G. 2000. "Battered Women: A Socio-legal Perspective of their Experience in Nairobi." *African Studies Monograph*, 21: 35–44.

Parekh, Bhikhu. 1997. "Rethinking Humanitarian Intervention." *International Political Science Review*, 18(1), 49–69.

Perry, Michael J. (1997). "Are Human Rights Universal? The Relativist Challenge and Related Matters." *Human Rights Quarterly*, 19: 461–509.

Poulter, Sebastian. 1986. *English Criminal Law and Ethnic Minority Customs*. London: Butterworths.

Rahman, Anika and Nahid Toubia (Eds.). 2001. *Female Genital Mutilation: A Guide to Worldwide Laws and Policies*. New York: Zed Books.

Shweder, Richard A. 2000. "What About FGM: And Why Understanding Culture Matters in the First Place." *Daedalus*, 129(4): 209–233.

Spencer, Zara. 2002. "The Criminalization of Female Genital Mutilation in Queensland," *Murdoch University Electronic Journal of Law*, 9, no. 3 (September), accessed at http://www5.austlii.edu.au/au/journals/MurUEJL/2002/16.html, on June 15, 2017.

Steiner, Henry J. and Alston, Philip. 1996. *International Human Rights in Context: Law, Politics, Morals*. Oxford: Clarendon Press.

Vangen, Siri, Johansen R. Elise, Sundby, Johanne, Traeen, Bente and Stray-Padersen Babill. 2004. "Qualitative Study of Perinatal Care Experiences Among Somali Women and Local Health Care Professionals in Norway." *European Journal of Obstetrics and Gynecology*, 112, 29–35.

Varol, Nesrin, Angela Dawson, Sabera Turkmani, John J. Hall, Susie Nanayakkara, Greg Jenkins, Caroline S. E. Hormer and Kevin McGeechan. 2016. "Obstetric Outcomes for Women with Female Genital Mutilation at an Australian Hospital, 2006–2012: A Descriptive Study." *BMC Pregnancy Childbirth*, 16, 328.

WHO. 2006. "Female Genital Mutilation and Obstetric Outcomes: WHO Collaborative Prospective Study in Six African Countries." *The Lancet*, 367, 1835–1841.

Young, Iris Marion. 1990. *Justice and the Politics of Difference*. Princeton: Princeton University Press.

8 Religion, culture, and family violence among the Yoruba of Nigeria

Enoch Olujide Gbadegesin and Elizabeth Ayoola Adeyemi-Adejolu

Introduction

In spite of its importance to the formation and shaping of an individual's personality and character, and in spite of the views of the majority that family is the first institution to which they are exposed, the family has been negatively affected from ancient to modern times. Family is not just experiencing crisis or violence; it is an age long phenomenon. Needless to say, the family has undergone and continues to undergo changes precisely as a result of modern social change. It is not only in bad shape but also continues to experience deep crisis in the contemporary world. In fact, the family is experiencing a growing problem.

In recent times, Nigeria, just like elsewhere in the world, has seen a proliferation of problems and perils bedeviling the family. At times, the number of women who are abused, humiliated, and battered by their husbands or boyfriends is increasing to an alarming degree; indeed, around 50% of Nigerian women are assaulted each year by their husbands and boyfriends (AfrolNews, 2007). A National Demographic and Health Survey in 2008 showed that gender-based violence (GBV) cuts across all socioeconomic and cultural backgrounds. Twenty-eight percent of all women, and almost one-third of all women in Nigeria, are reported to have experienced gender-based violence.[1] Unfortunately, this violent and abusive behavior has also been extended to children within many family settings in Nigeria, with stories of child abuse, neglect, and maltreatment have been constantly reported in paper and electronic media. GBV is more than what happens only between husband and wife. According to scholars, "violence within families includes child abuse and neglect, intimate-partner violence and elder abuse" (Phinney & de Hovre, 2003: 67). The only difference is that spousal abuse is of greater concern than other types of violence in the family. Of course, spousal abuse can be two-way, from husband to wife and from wife to husband. Although a high incidence of violence and abuse is experienced from men (husbands) against women (wives) (UNICEF, 2000: 2), incidences of violence against men are also a reality. This chapter, however, will concentrate more on the abuse and violence women suffer from their husbands and intimate male partners.

This chapter argues that apart from other factors, religion and culture have contributed to GBV not only in Nigeria but also all over the world. Ironically, on the one hand, religion and culture have contributed and continue to contribute to the promotion of healthy families (depending on how positive the majority of people's attitudes are toward this important aspect of social life). On the other hand, however, religion and culture have also contributed and are still contributing to the perpetuation of GBV cross-culturally (Asay, DeFfrain, Metzger & Moyer, 2014). Religion and culture share a lot in common; according to cultural anthropologists in particular, religious belief systems and values can only be properly appreciated when situated within their cultural context. Religion is a product of culture, or, as Clifford Geertz argues, religion is a cultural system (2000: 90), implying that religion is culturally constructed. As a result of this connection, we contend that a particular societal religion and cultural outlook often reflect a society's views, interpretations, and actions.

Any given culture, without its religion, is replete with norms, customs, or values that are to be not only believed but also internalized. Nevertheless, some cultures have actually identified themselves by their religion; i.e. their religion is the center that has held their culture together. The complex relationship between religion and culture can lead to the use of religious explanations for cultural practices, particularly among populations with high illiteracy rates. Such common cultural events as farming, relationships, marriage, birth, and death often have religious significance. As with culture, religion serves as a means by which to judge behaviors and appropriate responses to them. Therefore, because of the importance of religion and culture to human sociality, there is a need to reexamine these with respect to the family and especially GBV in a contemporary Nigerian society.

Our focus is on the Yorùbá society, using Ado-Ekiti in Ekiti State and Ile-Ife in Osun State as our case study. Aside from the introduction and conclusion, this chapter is organized into four different but interrelated sections. In the first section, above, we have examined religion and culture. In the second section, we look at family and how it is constituted. In the third section, we use empirical (ethnographic) data gathered from 120 victims and survivors as well as reportage from print and electronic media and a review of literature to critically analyze the roles that religion and culture have played in either promoting or reducing gender-based violence. Finally, in the fourth section, we suggest ways GBV could be reduced or totally eradicated by reexamining religious and cultural values among the Yorùbá in light of contemporary social reality. We adopt socio-anthropological and ethnographic approaches to analyze theories of GBV with respect to the family. We use pseudonyms for all our respondents throughout this chapter.

In turning to the definition of family, Pierre Bourdieu argues that "the family is a set of related individuals linked either by alliance (marriage) or filiation, or, less commonly, by adoption (legal relationship), and living under the same roof (cohabitation)" (Bourdieu, 1998: 64). Bourdieu shows further how this definition could be expanded. First set of properties: through a kind of anthropomorphism in which the properties of an individual are attributed to a group. The family is seen as a reality that transcends its members, a transpersonal person endowed with a common life and spirit and a particular vision of the world. Second set of properties: definitions of family are seen as having in common a separate social universe, engaged in an effort to perpetuate its frontiers and oriented toward idealization of the interior as sacred, *sanctum* (as opposed to the exterior) (Bourdieu, 1998). Bourdieu thinks that "the sacred, secret universe with its doors closed is to protect its intimacy, separated from the external world by the symbolic barrier of the threshold, perpetuates its own separateness, its *privacy*, poses an obstacle to knowledge, turning itself into a private secret, 'backstage'" (1998: 65).

Due to its variations, the family is never structured and does not function the same way cross-culturally; rather, it is expressed differently from one culture to another. While in some cultures family is patrilineal; in others, it is matrilineal; and in others still, it is virilocal. In Yorùbá society, marriage is patrilocal (Bascom, 1969; Fadipe, 1970). Clarification of these terms is in order: patrilineal means descent is traced only through male lines, while matrilineal indicates descent is traced through female lines. In patrilocal societies like the Yorùbá, the bride comes to live in one of the many rooms of the groom's father, while the opposite is true in virilocal societies. What is most important, however, is that the norms, customs, values, and moralities governing these families are often dictated by the kind of religions being practiced by the members of the household. In many cultures all over the world, religion is at the core of legal, political, economic, family, and social decisions.

The family in particular is a legitimating and perpetuating site of religious and cultural norms, customs, and values. Kate Millet argues that "the family is the main institution of patriarchy" (1970: 35), meaning that the family is where gender inequality is encoded. According to Aborisade Olasunkanmi, the term "family means 'the rule of the father'; more broadly, it refers to a society ruled and dominated by men over women" (2013: 2). No doubt, Yorùbá has a traditional patriarchal family structure; the man is regarded as the head of the family while women play a subordinate role. Women are indoctrinated into playing along with the male dominant role by the religious and cultural teachings of African societies in general and the Yorùbá society in particular. Domestic responsibilities, household chores, and ultimate responsibility for children are still more women's tasks than men's (Fadipe, 1970). In the Yorùbá culture we find similar patterns of perception as those Morris E. Opler observed many years ago during his research into Chiricahua Apache culture. In this culture, women were charged with being more excitable and unstable than men and more likely to say or do things to cause domestic or interfamily strife (Opler, 1945:199). Unfortunately, this is not the judgment of men only but an appraisal, which a majority of Yorùbá women accept and help perpetuate as well. Perhaps violence towards and abuse of women do not just suddenly happen to any family they actually start with the premise of negatively evaluating women.

Brief history of the Yorùbá and their family structure

The Yorùbá people are one of the major ethnic groups occupying Southwestern Nigeria. According to the CIA World Factbook, they represent about 21% of the total population, or over 35 million people.[2] They are one of the largest ethnolinguistic groups on the African continent.

In Yorùbá cultural life, a family is constituted through the coming together of two different persons from two different families who have agreed to be husband and wife. Family life in the Yorùbá setting, however, is a bit complex in that marriage is not only between two consenting individuals but also includes the extended family structure. While it is true that modernity and urbanity are changing this (many married couples now live away from their extended family), there is not yet a total separation of the nuclear family from that of the extended one. The fathers and mothers of the two consenting individuals still have a little say in the affairs of their children who are either about to get married, or who married, who are now procreating. In this kind of Yorùbá setting, apart from father and mother, the married couple's siblings and relations in the form of uncles, aunties, cousins, etc. also contribute in no small measure to the stability or disintegration of the family structure. It is, however, good to note that millions of Yorùbá get married, stay married, and live happily married for life. We do not want make a hasty generalization that suggests all Yorùbá families experience crises and violence. Even many Yorùbá men and women who divorced have remarried and continued to enjoy their marriage. Our oral interviews with many people of different religious traditions – namely: Christianity, Islam, and Indigenous Yorùbá Religion – have shown that family is still a very important aspect of Yorùbá social life. It is also true that family has historically been of high priority for the average Yorùbá person. Most young people still aspire to get married and have a family of their own. The question we raise here is: why are those few individuals able to maintain good families, or to put it another way, what are the factors responsible for those few stable and happy families, given so many others are neither? The answer to this question will be our main focus in the next section.

History, causes, and incidences of gender-based violence

Inherent in human nature is the manifestation of violent behavior from one person towards another. GBV is not an exception; it even seems to be the most common of all violence in human society, with evidence for it even in the Holy Scriptures. Anthropological evidence also shows that violence generally, and GBV in particular, is endemic to human society. Social research has also shown GBV to be a global phenomenon that varies from one society to another only in its magnitude (UNFPA, 2016: 1; UNICEF, 2000). Some scholars once argued that in traditional Yorùbá society, family crises/ violence leading to divorce was also present (Fadipe, 1970: 90), but claimed that this was not as prevalent as it is now. One of the reasons Bascom (1969: 65) and Fadipe (1970: 90) gave is that virtually all married couples lived among their relatives in a big and extended family compound. Members of the larger compound apart from the immediate family of the husband and his wife often served as mediators when there were arguments, misunderstandings, fighting, and the like. Either in the traditional Yorùbá past, or in contemporary Yorùbá society, many factors have been assumed to be responsible for GBV, especially between husbands and wives. Before going into that, we need to familiarize ourselves with what GBV means.

GBV has been defined by the World Health Organization (WHO, 2011) as the range of sexually, psychologically, and physically coercive acts used against women by current or former male intimate partners. While women, men, boys, and girls can be victims of gender-based violence, women and girls are disproportionately affected. Furthermore, the UN General Assembly, in adopting the 1993 Declaration on the Elimination of Violence Against Women, its article 1 defined GBV as an act of violence that results in physical, sexual, or psychological harm or suffering of women; including threats of such acts, coercion, or arbitrary deprivation of liberty, whether occurring in public or private life (Population Reference Bureau, 2001) in an Interfaith Resource Guide (IRG). IRG stands for the Interfaith Resource Guide, which documents examples of family violence and how religion is implicated in the process in the United States of America (Volcano, CA: Volcano Press, 1995). Titled *Family Violence and Religion* edited by David Charlsen, domestic violence is defined as

> the mistreatment of one family member by another. Most often perpetrators of abuse and battering are: a spouse, ex-spouse, boyfriend, ex-boyfriend, or lover. Most often victims of abuse are women and children. The abuse can be physical, sexual, verbal, emotional and psychological.
>
> (Charlsen, 1995: 11)

Perhaps we can add financial abuse to the list. In this same book, it is recorded that

> abuse in couple relationships may include intense criticisms and put-downs, verbal harassment, sexual coercion and assault, physical attacks and intimidation, restraint of normal activities and freedoms, and denial of access to resources.
>
> (As Charlsen demonstrates, contrary to, 1995)

Physical abuse is the use of physical force in a way that injures the victim or puts him/her at risk of being injured. It includes beating, kicking, knocking, punching, choking, and confinement. As Charlsen demonstrates, contrary to society's concept of violent victimization as focused on assaults occurring between acquaintances and strangers, women's greatest risk of assault is from their intimates (husbands or boyfriends) (1995: 11–12). More than 65% of the women we interviewed confessed that their husbands were always using physical force against them, including beating, punching, or pushing them against the wall on regular occasion. Mrs. B. Adubi, who is in her fifties), said that her husband had subjected her to constant beatings beginning barely three months after their wedding in 1987. She told us that she had been rushed to hospital more than five times after suffering serious injuries from her husband physically assaulting her. She also said that she had reported those incidences to police officers (cops) at their station more than three times and that police officers (especially female officers) had warned her husband to stop beating her or risk being jailed. But because her husband was not prepared to change, and her life was already in danger, she had to move out of her matrimonial home and had already started living elsewhere in Ibadan as of February 2015. When she was questioned further as to what could have been responsible for her husband's constant physical assault, she claimed that her husband was full of envy and always suspicious upon seeing any other man with her. Even if people (men especially) came to buy household materials in her shop (she is a petty trader), her husband would trail after them, feeling that there must be something going on between them and his wife. A marriage that had been blessed with four children had already run into a hitch.

Cases like this one above are very common and are increasing on a daily basis in Nigeria in general and in the Yorùbá community in particular. Many people tend to believe that women who are physically assaulted are responsible for their husbands physically assaulting them. The majority of people's opinion is that women tend to be very abusive, proud, unreasonable, non-submissive, and aggressive, leading to physical assault from their husbands. Research has shown, however, that while both men and women can be physically and verbally aggressive, many men have been found to be more aggressive, intolerant, and impatient with either their wives or their children. Men are even said to be the primary perpetrators of violence in intimate relations (IRG, 1995:53). Incidences of physical assaults leading to death are constantly being reported in the daily news (both print and electronic media). In the months of April and May 2016 alone, around ten cases of women murdered by their husbands were reported. For example, a man named Lekan Shonde, accused of allegedly killing his wife on May 5, 2016, was remanded in police custody in Ikeja, Lagos (Usman, 2016). Mr. Shonde, who claimed he loved his wife, said that he did not have any hand in his wife's death. He confessed that he and his wife had actually only argued as a result of his wife's infidelity. He confessed that after the wife begged him, he still pushed her away. The pushing away of the wife eventually led to her death.

Some of our respondents told us that many men are in the habit of abusing them sexually. That is, their husbands are in the habit of forcing them to have sexual intercourse; if they (wives) refused, the husbands often resorted to rape. At least 40% of our informants confessed to having been raped by their husbands at one time or another. Unfortunately, three people were almost moved to tears when confessing they had been raped by their fathers.

> Sexual abuse has been defined by the National Centre for Injury Prevention and Control (2012) as forcing a partner to take part in a sex act when the partner does not consent. This includes all forms of sexual assaults, harassment or exploitation. It also involves using a child for sexual purposes including child prostitution and pornography.
>
> (Igbokwe et al., 2013:28)

Charlsen claims that "most sexual assault of women is perpetrated by male intimates" (1995:52). It even says, further, that "rape by male partners seems to occur most frequently in relationships in which other forms of physical aggression are ongoing" (1995:52–53).

Causes of gender-based violence

Many causes have been cited as responsible for the aggressive and violent behavior of spouses in nations around the world. No doubt there are variations from one culture to another; however, many of these causes are likely to overlap in most societies of the world. Even though our concern is Yorùbá society, insights from other societies help to highlight how rampant this problem is. A few of them will be highlighted here. Traditional (cultural) attitudes towards women depicting them as inferior, dependent, untutored, and unrefined can found almost everywhere in the world, creating an avenue for devaluing women and contributing to many men's aggressive behavior towards women. For example, it has been observed that "stereotypical roles in which women are seen as subordinate to men constrain a woman's ability to exercise choices that would enable her end the abuse" (Igbokwe et al., 2013: 28). The GBV perpetrated on Yorùbá women is fundamentally rooted in the assumption that they occupy a subordinate status. The patriarchal nature of African society in particular enables men to discipline their wives at will without any interference from social institutional structures already put in place. Less educated men and women in remote villages and settlements of the Yorùbá society are most likely to support discipline of and/or violence against women on the grounds of matters like the burning of food, arguing with one's husband, going out without asking for permission, neglecting the children, and refusing to have sexual intercourse. As Anne Kingston explains, the introduction of "the notion that women are in any way responsible for being beaten or mistreated might appear only to add to their violation" (Kingston, 2004: 158). Yorùbá culture seems to define the "good wife" by her willingness to submit to her husband's unreasonable demands and rules or through fulfilling her marital obligations even if she has long ceased to enjoy the marital union.

Another cause of violence against women is rooted in thinking that a woman is a man's property, an object that can be used and dispensed with at will. As Alokan Funmilola Bosede and Harvey and Gow explain, some historians believe that the history of violence against women is tied to the history of women being viewed as property and a gender role assigned to be subservient to men and also other women (Alokan, 2013: 101; Harvey & Gow, 1994). The more unfortunate side of it is that the typical Yorùbá man often assumes that any children born within the marriage belong to him only and not to both himself and his wife. Many Yorùbá women who suffer in silence in their marriages often are constrained to continue to endure ill-treatment and abuse because they believe they have everything to lose if they walk away from their marriages, as this would mean they would no longer have free access to their children. Worse still, the force of custom, as it has been argued, makes many Yorùbá wives content to share their husbands' affections with other women (Fadipe, 1970), even if they are not satisfied with the arrangement. While women who engage in extra-marital affairs are given all sorts of negative names, so much so that their parents often disown them, men are permitted to have as many concubines as they want (Fadipe, 1970).

Another important cause of GBV is uncontrolled substance abuse or excessive consumption of alcohol by men. A drug addict or a drunkard is more likely to assault his wife or even kill than a person who does not engage in any of this. Many drunkards and those on drugs excuse their violent behavior on their lack of knowledge of what happened once they were drunk. As explained in IRG, some have argued that they did not know what happened arguing that "I was really wrecked last night," "It only happens when I drink," "I just blacked out," "I am not myself when I'm drinking." Others have argued that they lost control saying "I just lost it," "something snapped inside of me," "I was so angry I didn't know what I was doing" (Charlsen, 1995). It has also been found that "alcoholism and drugs that have made their ways into many homes have exacerbated family tensions and they are often used to excuse violent behavior" (Charlsen, 1995). As evidence of this, at least 25% of our responders claimed that their spouses are drunks and that they have no doubt that their husbands also smoke Indian hemps based the way they behave at home to them as wives and the children. Problems with alcohol are linked to a confused and disorderly life. This kind of life leads to less closeness and more conflict within a family. The confusion of a life with a drinking problem makes it harder to be a good parent.[3] Possible solutions might include seeking help from a psychiatrist, psychotherapist, or a pastor who has counseling and deliverance gifts.

Infertility is another cause of GBV in a few homes, especially when a man continues to accuse his wife of being barren. A number of less educated and even a few educated men and women in Yorùbá society often think along these lines, too. Traditional Yorùbá culture does not help, either; quite often, women who are barren are accused of past wayward lives. They are usually blamed for their past misdeeds of abortion and prostitution rather than consideration being given to other medical underlying factors such as gynecological problems on the part of the woman or urological problems on the part of the man. Husbands' extended families have been found on many occasions to have forcefully removed the luggage of wives assumed to be barren and arranged for new wives for their sons. More than 20% of respondents to our questionnaire and those we personally interviewed admitted to being victimized as a result of infertility. Of these, 3% claimed that they eventually reconciled with their spouses after a temporary separation. The reason, according to them, was that their spouses had later discovered that they had falsely accused and violently treated their wives. The majority of the 20% vowed not to have anything to do with any man any longer.

Mrs. S. Adekiite (aged 35) was interviewed by one of the authors of this chapter on April 5, 2016 in Ado-Ekiti, Ekiti State. She said that because of her infertility problem, her husband and his extended family members have continued to frustrate her and have made her marriage unbearable and unenjoyable. According to her, a few of her husband's extended family members were fond of threatening her with all kinds of afflictions if she did not leave their son alone. She finally left her matrimonial home.

The above example illustrates how culture, specifically Yorùbá culture, contributes to GBV. As we have already mentioned, traditional Yorùbá society is known for its communitarian ethic of collective social action as compared with privatized, individualized life of the Western society. The problem with this culture, however, is demonstrated by the fact that when a woman gets married, she does not merely marry to her husband but instead marries into a complex web of her husband's relations – father, mother, siblings, cousins, uncles, aunties, nephews, and nieces. A woman very unfortunate enough to be married into a family where she has little or no control over her life and her immediate family stands the risk of becoming a perpetual victim of GBV.

Modernization and globalization can also have corrosive effects on marriages and families. Here we see that the force of globalization comes not only from the movement of people but also from the ideas, habits, and behaviors of people in other nations that are now being absorbed, emulated, and circulated around the world. In a technologized environment, the forms, functions, and structures of the family are also largely altered and are badly affected. Theologian and social scientist Don Browning rightly argues that in spite of

> the ample improvements to many families – higher incomes, better education and health care, more equality for women, greater protections and opportunities for children [. . .] these positive consequences are unevenly distributed, and they are frequently accompanied by negative consequences, such as the collapse of communal controls; the impoverishments of mothers and their children due to abandonment, divorce, and nonmarital births; increase violent of youth; aggressive new forms

of coerced prostitution and illegitimacy; sharp increases in transient nonmarital cohabitation; and the growing absence of fathers from their children.

(Browning, 2005: 269–285)

This observation is apt in the sense that many violent behaviors that are being witnessed and practiced all over the world today, including those of the family, can be traced in part to the negative effects of globalization and modernization as expressed through the internet, television, social media such as YouTube, etc.

As already discussed above, it is expected that relatives of both husband and wife could come and stay either for a short period or for a longer period, depending on the situation that brings such people to the couple's home. Often-times, the wife must be careful about how she treats her husband's family members, especially if the husband is not tactful or wise enough to protect his wife from his extended family's insults, assaults, and unreasonable demands.

Mrs. A. Ajagbe (aged 35) in Ado-Ekiti, Ekiti State, told us that her hus-band went as far as impregnating her own sister, and yet still beat her (the wife) for daring to challenge him for engaging in such ugly behavior. The woman claimed that she had to move out of her matrimonial home because her husband not only turned against her but also succeeded in turning her sister against her. Mrs. B. Abatan (aged 42) at Obafemi Awolowo University, Ile-Ife, Osun State, told us that she has been humiliated by her husband's younger brother so much that he developed the habit of slapping her when-ever she had occasion to quarrel with her own husband. She said that, worse still, her husband would not do anything about it but continued to behave as if nothing had happened. She said that neighbors whom she thought could help always counseled her to endure the insults and assaults because of her children. When she was asked if she had reported the incidents to her hus-band's parents, she said she was afraid that they might support their sons. There is a cultural force at play here. While it is true that some families in Yorùbá society will allow this to happen, the fact is that most will not. We again need be aware that modern family values within the Yorùbá culture emphasize secrecy and confidentiality, which discourages members from dis-closing private matters to outside parties. Perhaps due to the tendency for gossip from those people around them, victims of GBV prefer suffering in silence to exposing themselves to public ridicule.

In some Yorùbá towns, the sudden death of a husband is often first blamed on the wife. The situation is so bad that the woman is forced not only to swear before a family deity but also to drink a concoction prepared by mixing the water used to bathe the dead husband. It is expected that after drinking the "ritual water," she would also die if she were the cause of her husband's death. This inhumane treatment of women stems from the fact that in Yorùbá society, women may be accused of witchcraft, especially if they happen to be very outspoken and principled and refuse to be subordinated by their culture.

It seems that the Yorùbá cultural orientation that symbolizes women as evil continues to condition the way some academics think at Obafemi Awolowo University, Ile-Ife. In this university community, some people are fond of saying that women are "evil," thus leading to the feminization of evil as is perhaps found in many African societies as well. A good example can be shown here. In 1989, Mrs. C. Adebun, who was in her late twenties at the time (around 29 years), married to an Edo man. They continued to enjoy their marriage until suddenly, in 1997, the husband was involved in a ghastly motor accident along Ife-Ibadan highway. He was rushed to the University College Hospital (UCH), Ibadan for emergency treatment but, after a few days, the husband died. As soon as the news of the death of her husband reached his family, they came with the intention of making Mrs. Adebun undergo what is considered "rites of proof of innocence." The rite forced the woman to drink some concoctions so that if she were responsible for her husband's death, she would also die, seven days after his death. But her husband's family did not stop at that; they also violently carried off all of their son's belongings as well as those of his wife and their two children. They even went so far as refusing to accept their son's death, thinking that she should do whatever she wanted with the dead body. Mrs. Adebun was fortunate that the Pentecostal/Evangelical church they were attending was a great deal of help to her. The church not only protected her from cultural humiliation by taking it upon itself to bury the dead on church land but also agreed to rehabilitate the woman and took up the responsibility of catering to the welfare of the two children.

In the case of religion, the situation is the same, if not worse. Many religious leaders, pastors, imams, and indigenous religious priests have not helped the matter either with regard to GBV. For example, we like to submit that Islamic culture, which subjects some women to wearing purdah, is a form of abuse and violence against them, no matter how it may be argued religiously. The same argument applies when, Islam also legitimizes beating an erring woman after other options have failed (Opeloye, 2014). With respect to Christianity too, there are many scriptural passages that priests and marriage counselors use to perpetually keep abused women in their abusive and violent relationships. It seems some Christian women have internalized those scriptural passages and use them to rationalize inexcusable abuse (Charlsen, 1995).

Many of our respondents complained bitterly that whenever they reported their spouses' violent behavior to their pastors, Bible passages like these were often quoted to them so that they could continue to suffer in their homes. Mrs. O. Akeju (aged 45) told one of the authors of this chapter that after she discovered that her husband was hiding under the "sacred canopy" in order to continue to beat and ill-treat her, she took her life in her own hands and walked out of their marital union. Surprisingly, she exclaimed,

> the man I thought loved me never came looking for me and our two children, he instead went ahead to marry another wife. [. . .] Worse still, some of the pastors I talked with asked me to go back and beg him. That I have vowed not to do.

Another woman's (Mrs. R. Danmola) story is even more affecting. She got married at the age of 45 in 2004. Her ex-husband, who was a few years younger and who had initially claimed that God specifically told him to marry her, later abandoned her and went after another woman. But the very short time they were together, Mrs. Danmola said he was always nagging, abusive, and shouting her down during any conversation between the two of them. She said that she continued to endure untold hardships until one day when, her husband began to accuse her of being barren because of her past wayward life. According to her, he did not stop at this but went about telling everybody in the church they attended that it was because of his wife's ugly past that they had no children.

GBV can occur when a woman denies her husband sexual intercourse. Of course, there may be many underlying reasons for doing this that are not usually disclosed as a result of the Yorùbá culture of silence. Unfortunately, many pastors and perhaps imams might not bother to probe into the reasons behind a woman's refusal of sex for her husband; these priests always jump to the conclusion that the wife has a secret lover or is promiscuous. We suggest that there are many reasons why a woman might deny her husband sexual intercourse, such as that he may be depriving his wife of financial support does not appreciate her. Another reason might be that the man is promiscuous and his wife is afraid of contracting a sexually transmitted disease (STD) or HIV. One of our respondents (Mrs. J. Akesan, in her late thirties) from Osun State claimed that her husband has many sexual partners. As a result, she has continued to deny her husband sexual intercourse because she fears for her life, especially due to the fact that her husband always refused to use condom as a protective measure against sexual diseases. As a result of her refusal, her husband often resorted to beating and hitting her with objects that could harm her. She said her husband did not stop at that but also called her all kinds of negative names.

Perhaps we might add one further, but not least, point about how religion could contribute to GBV. Many churches, especially Aladura churches, which are fond of seeing (funny) visions and dreams, always view women in a negative light. In some of these churches, visions have been seen that show many women as witches whose husbands needed to divorce before they could enjoy or progress in their lives. Unfortunately, too, women prophetesses in these churches contribute in no small measure to breaking many homes through their negative visions and revelations. A good example happened many years ago at Obafemi Awolowo University, where three pastors/prophets told a professor that his wife's witchcraft was responsible for his misfortunes. The professor was gullible enough that he walked out of his matrimonial home and even abandoned their three children. About a year ago, a professor/pastor at the same university boasted in his office that he was convinced beyond reasonable doubt that Mrs. O. Ajekuleje was a witch and that he was one of the pastors who had counseled her husband to leave her when she refused to be delivered from her practice of witchcraft. On the indigenous traditional religious side, too, priests have also succeeded in breaking many homes by casting women in a bad light through their divinations.

Consequences of GBV

There are many effects of GBV; they have been divided by social scientists into the categories of physical, psychological, social, financial, and negative effects on children. We shall look at few of them here. According to Angela Browne's contribution to the IRG book, physical outcomes of partner violence can lead to "typical injuries rang[ing] from bruises, cuts, black eyes, concussions, broken bones, and miscarriages to permanent injuries, such as damage to joints; partial loss of hearing or vision; scars from burns, bites, or knife wounds, or even death" (Browne, 1995: 67). Many of the women we interviewed showed evidence of physical assault on their bodies. A woman's left eye was presented with a permanent red-shot sign. Another woman had a permanent deep scar on her upper left hand as a result of an iron object the husband used to wound her years earlier.

According to F.B. Alokan, psychological effects could lead victims of violence to develop high amounts of stress; fear and anxiety are commonly reported. Depression is also common, as victims are made to feel guilty for "provoking" the abuse and are frequently subjected to intense criticism (Alokan, 2013). Bard and Sangrey claim that "assaulted women, post-attack, may become dependent and suggestible and may find it difficult to carry out long-range planning or to make decisions alone" (Bard & Sangrey in Browne, 1995: 58). Cumulative effects of trauma have been found to lead to post-traumatic stress disorder (PTSD) in many female sufferers (Browne, 1995).

With respect to children, the effect is even more complicated. Alokan also asserts that "some emotional and behavioral problems that can result due to GBV include increased aggressiveness, anxiety, and changes in how a child socializes with friends, family, and authorities. Problems with attitude and cognition in schools can start developing, along with a lack of skills such as problem-solving (Alokan, 2013: 102). We found at Obafemi Awolowo University that many female children who come from homes where their mothers were abused or violently treated often exhibit morbid fear towards the opposite sex, including male lecturers. It has also been found that children who witness mother-assault are more likely to exhibit symptoms of PTSD (Lehmann, 1995: 57).

Rethinking religion and culture in GBV

Given the negative effects of GBV and the roles culture and religion have played in perpetuating it, it is our opinion that there are positive roles religion and culture could play in stemming the tide of GBV, especially against women. There is no doubt that other measures to achieve this same aim have already been suggested by well-meaning people. At least in Nigeria, history was made in March, 2013 when the 360-member House of Representatives of the National Assembly of the Federal Republic of Nigeria passed the Violence Against Persons (Prohibition) Bill, a law which aims to eliminate, or reduce to a minimum, cases of GBV.[4] However, we feel that religion is potentially a powerful force in the fight to strengthen Yorùbá families, and, hence, religious leaders of all traditions have lots of roles to play in this regard. We highlight those roles in this section.

First, the negative roles that have been played by both religion and culture with respect to GBV need to be revised given the connection between religion and culture is so interwoven that religion has an important function in reinforcing and maintaining cultural values. As a result of the abusive power and male violence that has been encouraged by some religious and cultural teachings about an image of God whose "maleness" is authoritarian, patriarchal, jealous, and vengeful, many Western feminist writers have asked whether violence toward women would be as prevalent if these images of God were challenged (Nelson-Pallmeyer, 1996: 102). Perhaps it is not the image of God that is at stake here but rather how religious leaders interpret that image to suit their own biased and patriarchal positions. We contend here that any religion or cultural teachings that show commitment to defending the traditional masculine role of husbands within a traditional family setting will continue to promote violence against women.

Second, while the communitarian ideal of the Yorùbá society extended family structure should be upheld, there is a need to check unnecessary intrusion into the privacy and manipulation of the nuclear family by the extended family. Yorùbá society and indeed religious leaders should encourage entirely new forms of communal living arrangements in which couples are allowed to manage their own private affairs with little or no intervention from their parents or extended relations. This becomes inevitable if GBV is to stop in our own modern dispensation.

Third, it is important for religious leaders to develop listening ears for the women who are so often victims of GBV, instead of denying them the opportunity to express their emotional feelings or their aversion towards the misbehavior of their spouses. Not allowing victims of GBV to reveal what triggered the violence in the first instance but merely appealing to them to be patient devalue these women and perpetuates more violence against them. Because many priests hold to the idea that women are the primary cause of GBV and are responsible for stopping the violence against them, this may further many women's reluctance or refusal to consult with priests to find a solution to their family problems. According to the Domestic Violence Project, "only the perpetrator has the ability to stop the violence. Many women who are battered make numerous attempts to change their behavior in the hope that this will stop the abuse. This does not work" (Charlsen, 1995: 19).

Fourth, religious leaders should be able to counsel battered and beaten women to stay away from their abusers on either a temporary or permanent basis, depending on the assessment of the situation, instead of telling them to continue to endure their suffering because of their children. Enabling battered women to leave the environment that endangers them often allows them to become active on their own and able to move on with their lives. The often-quoted biblical verse "God condemns divorce" (Malachi 2:16 KJV) will further heighten the pain suffered by victims of GBV and cause more damage instead of healing. Priests and marital counselors should be aware that batterers can kill their wives at any time. Many cases of men killing their wives reported in Nigerian dailies point to this fact.

Fifth, constant teaching and education by priests and stakeholders on those values that make for a good family, as already embarked upon by a few Christian organizations,[5] can go a long way in stemming the tide of GBV in the Yorùbá society. Other churches and religious organizations should emulate this tactic. Religious and cultural values, as seen in Yorùbá society, overemphasize children as the necessary outcome of marriage and put undue pressure on women, who might not be the actual cause of the delay in having children. The negative Yorùbá word *àgàn* (which can be interpreted to mean barrenness or lack of productivity) is often used for the delay of fertility and will continue to make women subject to cultural humiliation and even embarrassment from the public. It is very important that priests of any religious organization not only be educated but also aware that children can be gotten through many other means: adoption, surrogacy, and test-tube or in-vitro fertilization are potential solutions for families suffering from infertility. Besides this, however, it is our candid opinion that a lack of children in marriage does not make a couple barren; maybe they are reproductively, but they are not socially and spiritually.

Sixth, the religious leaders of any religious organization should concentrate their teachings on virtues such as love, forgiveness, temperance, and caring for one another through compassion, kindness, etc. These kinds of teachings often promote healthy relationships in any social setting, including family life. According to Robert Wuthnow, "religious resources and programs concerned specifically with family problems often do significantly mitigate the ill effects of family disruption" (Wuthnow, 2005: 80).

Seventh, religion can also offer help to mitigate GBV if members of particular religious organization regularly attend weekly religious programs and use religious resources that can aid in improving healthy family relationships. In their jointly held research, Ellison and Anderson compared the responses of people who attended religious services more or less often in America and found significant differences. According to them,

> among women, the odds of having been a victim of domestic violence
> among those who said they attended religious services at least once

a week were only about half as great as among those who said they attended religious services once a year or less. Among men, the difference was almost the same.

(Wuthnow, 2005: 85)

We also assume that if religious leaders motivate couples by getting them involved in programs that can prevent, heal, and promote marriage, family, and parenting, this would go a long way in stemming the tide of GBV.

Another point that has been suggested, which we assume might also help, is that people should marry within their faith tradition rather than outside of it (Wuthnow, 2005). For example, Muslims marry Muslims, Christians marry Christians, and indigenous religious worshipers marry people of their own faith, instead of intermarriages with people outside of one's faith community. At least, the marital injunction in Islam is that a Muslim man should not intermarry with women of other religious faiths except Christian and Jews. Even with those, the women convert to Islam, which is violence in itself. Mrs. D. Abike, a Christian (aged 35) in Ado-Ekiti who responded to our questionnaire, said she was constantly harassed, assaulted, and abused due to the fact that she refused to convert to Islam after her marriage to a Muslim based on their agreement before marriage. This might not have happened if the woman had married a Christian like herself. We are not unaware that many traditional Yorùbá marriages have followed the pattern of interreligious marriage systems and are getting along well, but the modern situation, wherein religious identity is becoming a sensitive issue, may not permit that peaceful marital relation any longer.

Last but not least, priests or religious leaders of victims of abuse should endeavor to "work through" the process of healing with assaulted and battered women instead of neglecting them. Proper arrangements could be made for female members of the congregation to visit with victims (women) of GBV. Financial intervention might also be necessary to rehabilitate those women who as full-time housewives have been deprived of making a livelihood, which has now thrown them into financial embarrassment as a result of divorce or separation. It has been observed that "the practice from Christian tradition of providing sanctuary for those in danger of further harm is a clear ethical mandate for ministry in the face of family violence" (Charlsen, 1995: 258).

Conclusion

In this chapter, we have argued that family is in further serious danger of disintegration through GBV if negative attitudes of religion and culture are not revisited with a view to changing them. Apart from defining and analyzing what religion, culture, and family are, we also critically looked at gender-based violence (GBV). We have been able to show through ethnographic evidence and a literature review how family has continued to suffer disintegration due to the effect of GBV or intimate partner violence. After looking at the causes of GBV, especially from a religious and cultural dimension with concrete examples of

GBV through ethnographic and questionnaire methods, we offered some valuable suggestions not only for mitigating causes of GBV in the family but also for eradicating GBV itself altogether. We believe that GBV in the family needs constant positive intervention from religious leaders and needs to be rescued from those religious and cultural beliefs and attitudes that can undermine healthy family relationships in our present dispensation. We believe that religion and culture, if they are transformed, can help in transforming family life and build not only men and women into maturity but also a strong society. We contend that when family is negatively affected, so is society.

Notes

1 See Domestic Violence and Abuse Center website: http://domesticviolence.com.ng/research-statistics/ (accessed May 20, 2016).
2 www.cia.gov/library/publications/the-world-factbook/geos/ni.html (accessed November 18, 2014).
3 www.ptsd.va.gov/public/problems/ptsd-alcohol-use.asp updated 2015 at PTSD: National Center for PTSD.
4 See Repila, Jacky. "History is made as Nigeria passes domestic violence law." http://policy-practice.oxfam.org.uk/blog/2013/05/nigerias-new-domestic-violence-law (accessed April 15, 2016).
5 Churches like Christ Way Ministries International, which has its headquarters in Ile-Ife, hold family life conferences every year and look for every opportunity to teach about marital happiness on every one of their important quarterly programs. Deeper Life Bible Church's *Women Mirror's Magazine* is equally a very good avenue that has helped Christian couples deal with marital challenges.

Bibliography

AfrolNews. 2007. "Half of Nigeria's women experience domestic violence," Retrieved May 20, 2016 from www.afro.com/ articles/16471.

Alokan, Funmilola Bosede. 2013. "Domestic Violence against Women: A Family Menace," A paper presented in the 1st Annual International Interdisciplinary Conference, AIIC 2013, April 24–26, Azores, Portugal and was published as conference proceeding, 100–107.

An Interfaith Resource Guide. 1995. *Family Violence and Religion*. CA: Volcano Press.

Asay, Sylvia M., John DeFfrain, Marcee Metzger and Bob Moyer (eds.). 2014. *Family Violence from Global Perspectives: A Strength-Based Approach*. Volcano, London and Los Angeles: Sage Publication.

Bard, Morton and Dawn Sangrey. 1986. *The Crime Victim's Book* (2nd ed.). New York: Brunner and Mazel.

Barnard, Frederick M. and Johann Gottfried. 1969. *Herder on Social and Political Culture*. Translated, edited and with an Introduction by F.M. Barnard. Cambridge: Cambridge University Press, 117–178.

Bascom, William. 1969. *The Yoruba of Southwestern Nigeria*. New York, Holt, Rinehart and Winston, William Russell Bascom.

Bourdieu, Pierre. 1998. *Practical Reason: On the Theory of Action*, Stanford CA: Stanford University Press.

Browne, Angela. 1995. "Violence against Women by Male Partners: Prevalence, Outcomes, and Policy Implications." In *Family Violence and Religion: An Interfaith Resource Guide*, compiled by the Staff of Volcano Press. CA: Volcano Press, 49–81.

Browning, Don. S. 2005. "The World Situation of Families: Marriage Reformation as a Cultural Work," in Steven M. Tipton and John Witte Jr. eds. *Family Transformed: Religion, Values and Society in American Life*. Washington DC, Georgetown University Press.

Charlsen, David. 1995. *Family Violence and Religion: An Interfaith Resource Guide*. Volcano: Volcano Press.

Fadipe, Nathaniel Akinremi. 1970. *The Sociology of the Yorùbá*. Ibadan Volcano: Ibadan University Press.

Geertz, Clifford. 2000. *Interpretation of Culture*. New York: Basic Books.

Harvey, Penelope and Peter. Gow. 1994. *Sex and Violence: Issues in Representation and Experience*. London: Routledge.

Igbokwe, Chima, C., Michael Chijioke Ukwuma and Kelechi Juliet Onugwu. 2013. "Domestic Violence against Women: Challenges to Health and Innovation." *JORIND*, 11 (2) December. ISSN 1596–8303, Retrieved May 16, 2016 from www. transcampus.org/journals; www.ajol.info/journals/jorind.

Jones, Richard, 1997. "The American College of Obstetricians and Gynecologists: A Decade of Responding to Violence against Women." *International Journal of Gynecology and Obstetrics*, 58 (1), 43–50.

Kingston, Anne. 2004. *The Meaning of Wife: A Provocative Look at Women and Marriage in the Twenty first Century*, Toronto: Harper Collins.

Lehmann, P.J. 1995. "Children Who Witness Mother-Assault: An Expander Post-traumatic Stress Disorder Conceptualization." (Unpublished M.A. Thesis), Wilfrid Laurier University. Retrieved from http://scholars.w/u.ca/etd/193.

Nelson-Pallmeyer, Jack. 1996. *Families Valued: Parenting and Politics for the Good of All Children*. New York: Friendship Press.

Olasunkanmi, Aborisade. 2013. "Subordinated by Culture: Constraints of Women in Elective Politics in Nigeria," LexHumana Petropolis, 6 (1), 1–8.

Opeloye, M.O. 2014. *The Qur'an and the Bible: Common Themes for Peaceful Co-Existence*. Ibadan: Spectrum Books Limited.

Opler, Morris Edward. 1945. "Themes as Dynamic Forces in Culture," American Journal of Sociology Vol. 51(3).

Phinney, A. and S. de Hovre. 2003. "Integrating Human Rights and Interpersonal Violence." *Journal Health and Human Rights*, 6 (2), 65–87.

Repila, Jacky. 2016. "History is made as Nigeria passes domestic violence law." Retrieved April 15, 2008 from http://policy-practice.oxfam.org.uk/blog/2013/05/nigerias-new-domestic-violence-law Demographic and Health Survey, Retrieved April 10, 2016 from www.measuredhs.com/pubs/pdf/GF15/GF15.pdf.

Schoenmakers, Hans. 2012. *The Power of Culture: A Short History of Anthropological Theory about Culture and Power*. Globalization Studies. Groningen: University of Groningen.

Scruton, Roger. 2009. *Modern Culture*. New York: Continuum.

Tipton, Steven M. and John Jr. White. 2005. *Family Transformed: Religion Values and Society in American Life*, Washington DC, Georgetown University Press.

UNICEF. 2000. "Behind Closed Doors: The Impact of Domestic Violence on Children," accessed at https://www.unicef.org/protection/files/BehindClosedDoors.pdf, on January 2016.

Usman, Evelyn. 2016. "Egbeda Murder: I loved my wife, I did not kill her: Husband." *Vanguard Newspaper*. Retrieved May 10 from www.vanguardngr.com/2016/05/egbeda-murder-not-kill-wife-hypertensive-husband/.

Wuthnow, Robert. 2005. "The Family as Contested Terrain." In Steven M. Tipton and John Witte Jr. (eds.), *Family Transformed: Religion, Values, and Society in American Life*. Washington, DC: Georgetown University Press, 71–93.

9 Gender-based violence

The case of the Babukusu of Bungoma Kenya

Sychellus Wabomba Njibwakale

Introduction

Various ways have been devised to keep women subordinated to men in patriarchal communities. For instance, "foot binding was used by the Chinese to cripple women for over 1,000 years" (Martin, 1981: ix). Purdah, the practice of secluding women from contact with men outside of the immediate family, is still widespread today among the Muslim populations of the Middle East, North Africa, and Asia (ibid.). There are other uncivilized traditions still going on among young girls; for instance, clitoridectomies (excision of the clitoris) are still practiced on millions of pre-pubescent girls in Egypt, Sudan, Somalia, Kenya, Yemen, Saudi Arabia, Iraq, Guinea, and Ethiopia (ibid.). The reality of domestic violence is that while these stereotypes fit some situations, they do not even begin to touch upon the scope of the problem. Many health facilities have clients who have experienced some form of domestic violence, and some are traumatized due to the shame associated with domestic violence. Holden writes that domestic violence refers to "assaultive and coercive behaviors that adults use against their intimate partners" (Holden, 2003: 151–160).

The lifetime prevalence of physical domestic violence has ranged from "seventeen to forty-eight percent among various women in Africa" (Coker and Richter, 1998: 61–72), while about "one-third of ever-married Egyptian women have reported being beaten since marriage" (El-Zanaty, 1995). Although research on domestic violence has concentrated on cultural practice, results show that domestic violence affects persons in every community, regardless of age, economic status, race, religion, nationality, or educational background. In domestic violence, the characteristic of controlling behavior is prevalent, which creates a system of dominance and control. Serious consequences associated with domestic violence include physical injury, psychological trauma, and family separation as well as sometimes death. Interestingly, despite widespread domestic violence against women, tests of competing presuppositions about its causes have been limited outside of the West.

This chapter seeks to examine domestic violence among families, and particularly how this violence affects the lives of women and children. It is argued that men's brutality against women, including the battering of wives, rape, and femicide, is based on the general assumption that brutality is a natural consequence of women's feebleness. This should not be understood as blaming women for their weakness contributing to them being battered. But by nature, women were created with fragile bodies that need to be touched tenderly with love rather than with brutality as if they were dangerous animals. In this chapter, the author will examine the causes, effects, and prevention measures of domestic violence and the position taken by religious groups to put a cap on the menace. Before getting into the main matter of the chapter, let this question be answered first: who are the Bukusu people, and what values do they have that promote patriarchy?

The Bukusu community and their values

The Bukusu people are one of the 17 Kenyan tribes of the Luhya Bantu people of East Africa. They refer to themselves as BaBukusu and are the largest of the Luhya tribes, making up about 34% of the Luhya population. Their medium of communication is Bukusu dialect. Like many other African ethnic communities, "the Bukusu are said to have originated from an area which is only remembered as Esibakala" (Wafula, 2006: 10). Makila argues that "this place appears to have been somewhere in the present-day northern Sudan or the southern region of present-day Egypt" (ibid).

The Bukusu myths state that the first man, Mwambu (the discoverer or inventor), was made from mud by Were Khakaba at a place called Mumbo (which translates to "west"). It is believed that God created a woman called Sela as a wife for Mwambu. Mwambu and his descendants moved out of Mumbo and settled in the foothills of Mount Elgon (known to them as Masaba), from where their descendants grew to form the current Bukusu population.

Wafula Msaja says, "Mwambu was the son of Muntu wa Entebbe who was a warrior. Muntu was defiled by the people of Misri (now Egypt)" (Wafula, 2011) goes on to say that

> his son Mwambu married Sela the daughter of Wasiela the son of Samba Ambarani who is believed to be Abraham the Hebrew. Mwambu founded the cities of Kush, Nabibia (Nubia), Namelu (Meroe), Rwa (Alwa) and others including Soba and Balana.
>
> (ibid.)

They moved into Central Uganda as part of a much larger group of people, mainly forming the eastern extension of the great Bantu migration out of central Africa. The Bukusu clan include a subdivision called *ekholo*. The subdivision includes Bakibeti, Bakibumbi, Batilu, Babichachi, Baengele, Batukuika, Batecho, Bachemai, Bakoi, Balunda, and Bakobolo, among others.

Along with other Luhya sub-tribes, the Bukusu are believed to have first settled north of Lake Turkana at a place called Enabutuku. From here they settled in Cherangani Hills at a place called Embayi, later to be called Sirikwa. After the evil and bad omen befell them, they dispersed, taking six different routes, five going around the western side of Mount Elgon and one via the eastern side of Mount Elgon. The groups that went via the western side of Mount Elgon included Basilikwa, Banabayi, Baneala, Bakikayi, and Bamalaba. Mwalie cluster took the eastern side route and settled at Mwalie hills. This area was already inhabited by some Kalenjin sub-tribes like the Laku, Sabiny, Bongomek, Sebei, Ndorobo, etc. The bad omen was because of disobedience to their God Khakaba, and so he sent a giant boulder from the sky that hit the land of Mbayi, causing an earthquake followed by swarms of stinging insects that spread all over the land.

Currently, the Bukusu mainly inhabit the counties of Bungoma, Trans Nzoia, part of Uasin Gishu, and Lugari in the former Western Province of Kenya. The Bamasaba of Uganda are very closely related to the Babukusu, with many shared customs and a closely related dialect. Previously, the Bukusu were referred to as the "Kitosh" by the colonialists; this was a word derived from the Nandi and Kwavi people, who used the word derogatively to describe the Bukusu. *Kitosh* means the terrible ones; they called the Bukusu the terrible ones because Bukusu warriors were ruthless and decisive on the battlefield. With vigorous campaigns by community leaders, "the name Kitosh was eventually substituted with Bukusu in the mid-1950s" (http://immigrantnationusa.us/wp-content/uploads/2013/08/DER-20).

One of the well-known cultural practices among the Bukusu people is male circumcision. It is believed that the circumcision practice "was revived by a man known as Mango, during their migratory movements, the Bukusu were said to have either lost or relaxed the male circumcision practices" (Wafula, 2006: 10). Wafula goes on to observe that "while the Bukusu had temporarily settled at Mwiala, an area around Tororo hill near the present Kenya–Uganda border, there lived a monstrous serpent known as Khururweyabebe that used to terrorize the surrounding communities and their livestock" (ibid.: 10).

Mango was a courageous and brave man. He used a machete to kill the fiery serpent. To honor him for a job well done, the Barua, who were neighbors with the Bukusu people, circumcised Mango, a practice they (Barua) had kept since the time of migration from northern Africa. Mango was an adult and married with several children by the time he killed the serpent and got circumcised. As Wafula observes, "this marked the new phase of the Bukusu male ritual circumcision" (ibid.: 10).

Like most African communities that practice circumcision, circumcision among Bukusu people plays an important role in the life of a person. Male circumcision serves as training for the Bukusu boys to transition from childhood to manhood. After circumcision, the boy is considered an adult and therefore begins to be useful in the community as a man. As Boston Soko understands, these rites are "a high school of learning" for the adolescents (as quoted in M'Passou (in Cox, 1998: 15). Ritual circumcision for an African boy is a significant time. This is the time when the identity of the boy is defined in the community.

Ritual circumcision in most African communities is done in various stages. For instance: pre-ritual preparation, the operation, and seclusion into lonely places. In all of these stages, the candidates (eventually initiates) undergo instructions on how to withstand the process and how to behave in order to heal quickly. The climax of the process is the reintegration into the community. At this stage, the initiate is referred to as an adult. The normal age of circumcision used to be between 15 and 18 years of age. But in recent years, and with changes in community life that mean children are attending schools, the age limit is now set as low as 8 to 12 years. The point is to circumcise the boy before he joins high school. This has also reduced the period of seclusion from 9 to 12 months to only four weeks. This is done so as not to interfere with the school system, which only allows four weeks of holiday.

Although circumcision was universal among the Bukusu, the form of the ceremony varied according to the clan. The festivities and ceremonies accompanying the final stage of initiation were not the same. Each community had its own activities. During the time when the initiates came out of seclusion to rejoin their families as men, the process they pass through varied from one clan to another, and these processes have been handed down largely intact to the present day. Among the Bukusu community, just as among other African traditional communities, "a circumcised male is perceived or at least is expected to be worthy, desirable, and respected in a public square as opposed to the uncircumcised" (Wafula, 2006: 68).

Female circumcision (clitoridectomy) is not a Bukusu practice. However, some clans are said to have practiced it. This is especially the case around Mount Elgon, where the neighboring Kalenjin tribes also practice a form of female circumcision. This practice of female circumcision among the Bukusu female ended before World War II. Both male and female initiates were given lessons during their seclusion period that enabled them to face marriage with knowledge.

Unfortunately, this male ritual circumcision is the key factor that promotes patriarchy among the Bukusu people. As the boys go through the stress and pain of the circumcision ceremony, they feel more superior to women. Patriarchy, from the Latin "Patriarchia," means the "rule of the father." The term is often used to refer to the "rule of men over women." As Jones writes, the term "refers to the web of economic, political, social, and religious regulations that enforces the domination of women by men throughout the ages" (Jones, 2000: 77). Since all circumcised Bukusu boys think of becoming fathers after seclusion, they think of ruling over their women and children. This notion has a long history that has bound women for centuries.

Marriage contract

Boys got married at about the age of 18–20, while girls got married at about the age of 16–17. There were two types of first-time marriage: arranged marriages and enforced eloping. Some qualities that men and the community have considered in a girl fit for marriage are the ability to cook well, bear children, and work on the farm. In the marriage contract, the historical roots of our patriarchal family models are ancient and deep. To have a formula of tearing them up and forming more equitable human relations is a formidable task. Yet, new ideas for marriage and family must be created, since domestic violence against women grows naturally out of ancient, patriarchal traditions.

Martin writes, "in the beginning, human beings lived in a state of promiscuity, which by its nature made all certainty regarding paternity impossible. Lineage in these early days could only be reckoned through the female line" (Martin, 1981: 25). Martin further states that "women, as mothers, were the only discernible parents and received a high degree of consideration and respect" (ibid.). This statement partly clarifies the idea of men, especially in the Bukusu community, who would describe themselves as sons of women, not sons of men. For instance, my father would tell us, I am the son of Namukhosi – Namukhosi being his mother – but not the son of Njibwakale, his father.

Fredrick Engels recounts, "all primitive societies passed through this initial stage of human relations; it was the precursor to all other stages of social development" (Engels, 1948: 420). "Women were not only free, but they held a highly respected position in the early stages of civilization and were the great power among the clans" (ibid.).

In Bukusu culture, as in most African "tribes," marriage is organized around traditional kinship. Kimuna and Djamba note that "Kenyan society was organized around kinship groups with strong structural patterns of interaction. The system of exchange was the most important unifying system that tied kinships together and to neighboring groups" (Kimuna and Djamba, 2008: 23, 333–342). Once a girl was identified, an emissary was sent to her parents to ask for her hand. The girl had no say whatsoever in the whole matter: bride price would be discussed, and then once it was paid, she would be sent off to live with her new husband. As a result of this exchange system, marriage constituted a covenant between two families. These two families established a set of rights and duties that bound the two groups together.

Marriage among the Bukusu clan, like any other "tribes" in Kenya, is accompanied by vows and payment of bride price by the groom's family to the bride's family. Sue Ellsberg et al. observe that in Kenya,

> marriage vows and payment of bride wealth by the groom's kinship family to the bride's kinship family were interpreted within and among

kinship families as granting rights for a man to have unconditional sexual access to his wife for reproductive purposes, which also included other services from the woman's family to the husband's family.

(Heise et al., 2001: 1–16)

However, it is argued by the Bukusu elders that payment of bride wealth is an appreciation to the bride's family for the care they have given to their daughter. The man is not buying the woman as a property; rather, the woman is willingly joining the man as an equal partner to form their new family. It should be remembered that without the bride price, the two people can still stay if they love each other. It may be argued that the man has the right to control his wife as he deems best. In the case of violence where the man exercises his right, the family intervenes. The family presumes that one does not indeed act in any manner without the threat of consequences for one's character. In other words, the man disciplines the wife within the norms as set up by the community of elders. Based on such an argument, as (Kimuna and Djamba, 2008: 333–342) note, "the ideological framework within which Kenyan ethnic groups function constitutes a strong male dominance and female subordination." This notion of "male dominance and female subordination," on the other hand, is caused because a woman has left her maternal home to join the man in his maternal home.

In a culture where there is strong gender inequality, not only in the Bukusu "sub-tribe" but also in Kenya as a whole, women function as second-class citizens. With the new constitution, women have a voice, but customary laws are still in force over their status in families. The very people who drafted the new constitution are the same people emphasizing customary practices. This puts the constitution in an awkward situation, where the constitution fails to be reinforced when it comes to matters of the family.

The institution of marriage compels women to forcibly comply with the demands of their husbands, even forced sex, for any resistance will lead to violence. Since girls in Kenyan culture, like any other African culture, are considered the property of parents, once they marry and the parents receive their share of the bride price, they become the property of their husbands. This notion is wrongly interpreted, and it has made women live in fear in the new home. It makes women unable to have the capacity for decision-making in family matters.

After interviewing five elders from the Bukusu people who have sons and daughters married, they reject the interpretation of dowry as a way of selling their daughters as properties of their husbands. In fact, these elders have given their daughters to cultures outside of their own Bukusu culture, and have had their sons marry other outside cultures, too. All the same, while the system of dowry is different, the interpretation is the same. According to these elders, marriage vows and the payment of bride wealth is meant to strengthen the relationship between the couples as well as between the two families of the bride and the groom. Bride prize cements the relationship, for it to be lived on a firm foundation. In the event of any problem, like death to the woman, the family of the woman will claim the body of their deceased daughter if the bride price was not paid. Bride wealth gives the power of ownership to the property acquired by the two couples. When a man dies, the widow has full right to the property of her home.

History of violence

Observing the histories of domestic violence, those who engage in violence often witnessed violence in their homes between their parents when they were young children. Most husbands who batter their wives very often were battered children from broken or dysfunctional families. The other category of violent husbands, as studies show, is the one who has been in military service or law enforcement. In their study, Eisenberg and Micklow find that "a number of wives specifically mentioned that their husbands had learned how to inflict nonvisible injuries while in service" (Eisenberg and Micklow, 1974: 24). Although there has not been a correlation study between wife-abuse and military service or law enforcement, there is evidence that men in these categories of service are wife-abusers. Living under the tight control of an authoritarian, hierarchical, and highly disciplined system, men learn how to maim and kill other human beings. They become immune to the cruelty and horror of what they are doing not only because it is done for a supposedly righteous cause, but also because he must live with it on a day to day basis.

In their article entitled "Violence in the Family," Suzanne K. Steinmetz and Murray A. Straus believe that "violence-prone persons have a willingness and ability to use physical violence as a resource, and that family member can use this resource to compensate for lack of other resources as money, knowledge, and respect" (Steinmetz and Murray, 1974: 9). In other words, when a man has no job, does not make enough money, or is otherwise dissatisfied with his job, he will take out his frustration on his wife. When there is no income in the family, there is a significant increase in wife-beating because men want to evade the responsibility of providing. In a conversation with wives/victims, I found out that men suffer less from a lack in their own education than they do when their wives are better educated than they are.

Martin, in her book, asks these questions: "What kind of man beats up his wife? What are the underlying psychological and social causes of wife-beating, and what triggers this behavior? Are men naturally violent creatures? Or is aggressive behavior learned?" (Martin, 1981: 44). It is not easy to get the answers to these questions. Most men who beat their wives do not admit to their cruel and violent behavior. However, a few of them, after the incident, will come to their senses and accept their bad behavior. A typical Bukusu man, especially the one traditionally circumcised (vowing *bakheba* [circumcise]), rarely sees the problem in what he does and seeks help. He claims to be right in what he does in his home as a man and that nobody should question him.

A random sample describing domestic violence against women shows that wife-abuse may come from any walk of life. As Erin Pizzey observes, one wife described her husband as "a cultured man who had graduated, started his own business, and was rapidly becoming a successful business-man" (Pizzey, 1974: 11). Claudia Dreifus notes that a woman once said her husband had the "male violence in him. He was right. He was indisputable" Dreifus, 1973: 71). Another woman in the church described her former battering, deceased husband to me as "handsome, charming. Everybody likes him. He can give out all the money he has to whoever asks him, but I do not question it."

Husbands who batter their wives are described as angry, resentful, suspicious, moody, and tense. These battered women further state that though their husbands are terrifying, they often have about them an aura of helplessness, fear, inadequacy, and insecurity. This guy is angry with himself and frustrated in life. He may hide his shame in public by putting on a good face, but in privacy as well as the intimacy of his home he may not hide, either from his wife or himself, his feelings of inadequacy and low self-esteem. Martin writes, "the man who is losing his grip on his job or his prospects may feel compelled to prove that he is at least the master of his home. Beating his wife is one way for him to appear a winner" (Martin, 1981: 45). Pizzey says that "wife-beaters are alcoholics, psychotics, or plain and simple bullies. This is exactly why he is aggressive, dangerous, plausible, and deeply immature" (Pizzey, 1974). These descriptions suit any wife-abuser across cultures.

Women who have been battered say that when the husband erupts in a volcanic rage, he uses his fists, not his open hand. The man who batters knows how to aim his blows at the places that do not show bruises. Women say he goes for the breasts, the stomach (even when the wife is expecting), the base of the spine, and parts of the head where bumps and bruises will be covered by hair. Richard Gelles says, "slapping, scratching, or grabbing are most common when both parties actively participate in a fight, but that husbands predominate when it comes to pushing (downstairs, for instance), choking, shoving, punching, kicking – even throwing things" (Gelles, 1972: 36). Threats of violence may be as frightening as actual violence. Most men threaten by punching holes in the wall, breaking down doors, or smashing TV sets or radios to demonstrate their potential destructiveness. Little is noted in terms of threats by women, though in her observations, Mirra Komarovsky (1940: 227) found that wives threatened their husbands with other possibilities: that they would withhold sexual favors, call the police, or leave and take the children.

In Kenya, like any other part of Sub-Saharan Africa, the causes of domestic violence against women have not yet been comprehensively explored. In this chapter, I suggest some levels and factors associated with wife battery among the Bukusu community that also affect other communities in Kenya. By so doing, I will shed some light on this cruel, demeaning, and retrogressive behavior that has robbed women their freedom to economic development in communities and the country at large. I suggest some of these causes here but the possibilities are not limited to those mentioned in this chapter.

Causes of gender-based violence

Arguments/war of words

In most research, professionals believe that physical battles grow out of verbal arguments. They point out that during intimate fighting,

> each party knows the other well, is all too aware of the vulnerable spots in the mate's coat of armor and can easily resort to below-the-belt comments that are deeply wounding to the other's self-esteem. When this happens, the quarrel becomes heated, and the potential for violence is unleashed.
>
> (Martin, 1981: 50)

In fact, the war of words appears so sharp, the feeling of betrayal and loss so great, that redress must be physical and destructive. The person who wins the war of words is often a woman since she is ordinarily perceived more verbally facile. In his article entitled "Force and Violence in the Family," William J. Goode (1971) states, "The person who is least fair may be the most competent in a verbal attack." Middle-class wives probably feed violence-prone situations in a less passive manner than lower-class wives. Middle-class wives have a more highly developed verbal capacity and are less willing to play the subservient role, thereby provoking their husbands' violent responses, states Robert N. Whitehurst (1974: 78).

The sentiments of these two professionals conjure up stereotyped images of a nagging Bukusu woman whose husband has to hit her to shut her up, or the strong, silent type who shows forbearance, up to a point, in the face of the little woman's bickering. We have some men who see their wives' concerns as minor and their complaints as provocation for a family quarrel. However, Goode and Whitehurst's take of women as verbally superior to men seems unaccountably female-chauvinistic. At the same time, they may be true but unsure if the assumption of the class system determines verbal capacity.

Martin reiterates that the male attitude about the power of "fighting words" is related to the ancient and very peculiar belief that when a man was insulted, he could retain his "honor" only by challenging his insulter to a duel to the death. Even in such instances, strict etiquette was observed with regard to the challenge and the duel itself. But when a husband feels insulted by his wife, no warning or rules apply. She is often treated as fair game (Martin, 1981: 51). Based on this ancestral ideology, Bukusu men are advised to provoke their newly married women so that the women will insult them and men can thereby institute violence against them early in their marriage. This happens in the first four weeks of marriage. If the woman withstands violence without walking out of marriage in the first four weeks of violence and insults, then it is a sign that she is a woman who is capable to live in all marriage circumstances.

Drunkenness and alcoholism

The habits of drunkenness and alcoholism are stigmas that trigger most domestic violence in families. Conversations with women who have been beaten by their husbands point to instances of drunkenness and alcoholism. A woman said in her conversation with me while I was her pastor that when the husband is sober, he is pleasant and charming, but when he is drunk, he is a monster or a bully. Many women who have been beaten say that their husbands beat them only when they are drunk. When I was serving as a pastor, one woman who was a member of my church told me that her husband would never slap her when he was sober, no matter how angry he was. Women believe that if their husbands do not drink, they would not be violent.

Law enforcement and social scientists have similar views that many dysfunctional or broken families are a result of the use of alcohol by one or both partners. Drunkenness leads to violence, in many instances, because alcohol sets off a primary conflict over drinking; it can also extend to arguments over how money is spent and cooking as well as sex. On the other hand, drinking serves as a trigger for long-standing marital quarrels. Though those in the drinking category may deny this, the truth is, it is not easy to separate violence from drinking. A person who is potentially violent can drink with the sole purpose of providing himself with a timeout in which he can lay the blame for his violent behavior on the alcohol. After the violence, the individual may deny or plead for forgiveness because he did so when he was not in his true senses.

Some women have tried to stop their husbands from drinking and have succeeded. But they have not stopped the violence. Anything can cause violence from the batterer. It can be alcohol, the baby crying, a bad mood, or an animal that was not well fed. Alcohol is one of the many factors that causes violence in marital relationships. It may be used as an excuse for violence, and it may trigger arguments that lead to violence.

Jealousy

In some cases, and to certain people, wife-battering is associated with underlying quality or feeling of romance in lifestyle. Any man is jealous when his wife is found engaging in extra-marital affairs. Martin says, "the romantic interpretation of the archetypal situation is that the trust of a loving man is betrayed by the unfaithful wife, and he is therefore unable to hide his pain and control his anger" (Martin, 1981: 58). In a more realistic manner, not only has the trust of the husband been betrayed, but his territory (home) has also been invaded and his possession (wife) has been handled by an outsider.

Women in Kenya, as in any other African culture, are possessed by men and men are possessed by women. They acquire each other through a price, and therefore both men and women will feel jealousy when someone else illegally enters their marital relationship. Although in developed countries like the United States of America the family structure has moved away from what has been termed as the out-and-out slave market method of marriage, the principle of ownership still operates: the family system is such that male dominance demands absolute faithfulness from the woman; if she did not agree to be controlled, the system would fall apart. On the other hand, as Martin says, "unfaithful women have been portrayed throughout history and literature as degraded seductresses – they have not been forgiven for daring to besmirch the holy marriage vows and humiliate the husband" (ibid.). In modern times, the woman is described as oversexed for caring enough about sexual fulfillment to seek it outside her marriage.

On the other hand, the unfaithful husband has been described as a player of the whole game. A man is exhorted to develop his extra-marital style to such a level that, in this millennial period, he is viewed somewhat ridiculous for remaining faithful to his woman. Some cultures have mock men who are faithful to their women for being weak and hiding behind the skirts of their women. When a woman is unfaithful to her man, the man feels he does not control his possession well, and vice-versa.

In their article on jealousy, Joan and Larry Constantine conclude that "sex is almost never the real issue, only the arena" (Constantine and Constantine, 1974: 59–60). Sex is viewed like alcohol, which affords the husband a socially accepted excuse for venting a violent mood that erupts over the loss of control of his wife as his possession. More ironically, as Martin observes,

> women who marry violent men are rarely allowed to use contraception because along with the batterer's violent nature goes tormented jealousy that can barely let his woman out of sight and which finds security in keeping her pregnant and thus captive.
>
> (Martin, 1981: 60)

Men beat their wives if they find them with pills, and some even beat their wives when they become pregnant. Those who beat their pregnant wives are perceived to be expressing jealousy toward the newcomer and resentment against the change it will bring to their lives. The larger picture is that they may be reacting directly against the tremendous pressure the community places on men to marry and sire children. A man is expected by the community at-large to accept his roles as husband and father; often his joy for these roles is a sign of his responsibility. Another factor that promotes jealousy is the type of marriage. The type of marriage affects the probability of physical and sexual abuse. Women in polygamous marriages are more likely to be victims of physical abuse than those in monogamous relationships. Jealousy is intense in polygamous marriages and results in constant complaints that end in physical abuse.

Social economic variables

Another significant cause of domestic violence against women is the socioeconomic variables. These include "social position, employment status, financial circumstances, self-concept, and personal and community values" (Gelles, 1972: 186). Most people would agree that domestic violence is linked to class and social status. Others believe that it is a direct result of poverty and low social status. McCloskey states that "education and higher occupational status are key factors of female empowerment" (McCloskey et al., 2005: 124–130).

Observations show that since lower-class families have fewer resources and less privacy, they are more apt to contact public social agencies like the police, which compile domestic-disturbances statistics. With middle-class families, they have greater access to private support services, such as marriage counselors and psychiatrists (especially those in urban centers), who compile the data per their work ethics. When an injury occurs during the violence, lower-class women will obtain a police form (P-3) and are sent to emergency rooms in public hospitals, while middle- or working-class women can afford to go to a private physician or hospital for treatment. Such differences make lower-class family domestic violence more visible as police and emergency room data are readily available for studies.

The type of marriage also contributes to domestic violence. For instance, those in polygamous marriages experience more battering than those in monogamous marriages. At the same time, the number of children born in a family creates anxiety and may cause more abuse to the woman. In addition, these children are prone to more abuse. Male children are more welcome in the family than female children. Boys are considered by the Bukusu community as the source of protection against any attack. As such, a woman who bears female children only risks higher chances of abuse than a woman who bears male children or mixed gender. As Kimuna and Djamba reiterate, "the number of children can exacerbate a woman's economic dependency on her husband and consequently lead to the woman tolerating violence" (Kimuna and Djamba, 2008: 336). But when the children grow up, they become a threat to the father abusing their mother in their presence. The age of the children has a positive effect on the mother's abuse. I now turn to examine the effects of domestic violence.

Effects of domestic violence

Nothing happens without cause and effect. Domestic violence has many potential effects on the life of its victims. Most men and women who are victims of intimate domestic violence do not disclose it, because of either fear or shame. The reach of domestic violence is extensive: stress, economic hardship, psychological illness, and addiction. Like other forms of trauma, domestic violence has a number of effects on the victims. However, the impact of domestic violence varies enormously between individuals. As a matter of fact, domestic violence is a family matter in the sense that it also affects the children in the family. The reactions vary depending on the child's gender and age. Children exposed to family violence are more likely to develop social, emotional, psychological, and/or behavioral problems compared to those who are not. Children in families where domestic violence is a norm show more anxiety, low self-esteem, depression, anger, and temperament problems than those who grow up in families where there is no violence.

People who live with domestic violence experience emotional pain expressed through physical pain. Victims of domestic abuse exhibit a number of severe symptoms, some of which are seen and others that may not be noticed. The stress of being in an abusive relationship often has a physiological effect, as well as the common physical and psychological effects, and it increases one's vulnerability to illness that cannot be cured. Other than the unexplained physical problems, such as chronic pain or migraine headaches, there are other symptom-based syndromes that are caused by domestic violence. These include "fatigue syndrome, multiple chemical sensitivity, temporomandibular disorder, irritable bowel syndrome, and Tinnitus" (Richardson and Engel, 2004). Because most of the victims hide their sufferings, these problems are discovered late when they have advanced in ends stages and the victims succumb to death.

According to the studies carried out by Briere and his team, "domestic abuse and other related violence are associated with increased risk for developing a range of psychiatric conditions like depression, anxiety, and post-traumatic stress disorder" (Briere et al., 1997: 95–101). Also, in connection with domestic violence, "the victim has a problem of eating disorders, sexual difficulties, and psychotic episodes." As stated above, when someone is depressed, the family will assume the person is bewitched, and if they reach such a conclusion, no medical attention is sought.

Religious values and domestic violence

Just like most Kenyan communities, the Bukusu community is a religious community. Whether in childhood or adulthood, most people have had some association with a faith tradition. For some it has been positive, and for others, negative. But many families retain and rely on values and faith doctrines that they have received within a faith community. Unless otherwise stated, two different faith traditions exist among the Bukusu people: Christianity and Islam. I have not heard of any Jews, Hindus, or Buddhists among the Bukusu people, for these traditions mostly establish themselves in cosmopolitan areas. There are many varieties of Christians, including Roman Catholics, Evangelicals, mainline Protestants, Pentecostals, and many others. Bungoma County, like other areas of Western Kenya, also benefited from missionary explorations of the region in the early twentieth century. It is a region with strong religious traditions. This chapter will examine how Christians and Muslims deal with domestic violence among their members.

The problems of domestic violence affect people physically and psychologically as well as spiritually. These dimensions ought to be addressed both for victims and those in the family that instigates the abuse. There are certain issues that are left out when the problem is addressed from the secular or religious perspectives only. In other words, it is important to develop a shared responsibility and cooperation between secular and religious leaders while addressing the problems of domestic violence.

Religious teachings, traditions, and practices represent a fundamental aspect of culture for most of the Bukusu people as well as for most Kenyans. For instance, a Roman Catholic may not going to mass but may still identify as Roman Catholic and honor the ritual of prayer and other Roman Catholic values. For many people, their family/clan heritage is linked to their faith history, such as with Muslims. For this reason, cultural competency in addressing domestic violence must include some awareness and appreciation of religion as well as faith traditions. Those working as social workers and psychotherapists sometimes wonder, why they should bother with religious concerns while dealing with domestic violence. The simple response here is that religious issues that surface for people during times of problems are primary issues. If they are not addressed in time, they will at some point erupt into stumbling blocks for the victim's effort to deal with the problem. Furthermore, an individual's religious beliefs and faith community, like the church or mosque, provide an initial support system for a person and his/her family while experiencing domestic abuse.

The religious leader, like the secular counselor, has a vital role to play when facing the issue of domestic violence. Families in which there is domestic abuse need the support and encouragement as well as expertise of the clergy in times of crisis. The pastor or the imam can be of great help to the victim of domestic violence by working closely with reference to secular resources. Combining the two, i.e. secular and religious resources, provides a well-balanced approach that deals with specific physical, external, and emotional needs in confronting wider religious, ethical, and philosophical problems. Some pastors may also be victims or perpetrators of abuse themselves, and when faced with such a case in the congregation, due to lack of expertise, he will say, "these people just need to get right with God and everything will be okay." Such an understanding overshadows the significance of practical issues. Marie M. Fortune et al. explain:

When approached about domestic violence, the minister or imam/rabbi should be aware of the dynamics of domestic violence and utilize this understanding for evaluating the situation; use one's expertise as a religious authority and spiritual leader to illuminate the positive value of religious traditions, while clarifying that they do not justify domestic violence; and identify the parishioner/congregant's immediate needs and refer to secular resources to deal with the specifics of abuse, advocacy, intervention and treatment

(Fortune et al., 2010: 1–17).

Marriage relationships from both Christian and Muslim perspectives do not support violence against women. For instance, Ephesians 5:21–29 is commonly used in marriage ceremonies, primarily used to instruct husbands. Nine of these verses address husbands' responsibilities in marriage; three verses refer to wives' responsibilities; and only one addresses both husband and wife. Due to lack of expertise and knowledge of biblical interpretation, modern interpreters often focus on wives, misusing the texts to justify wife-abuse. Similarly, "the Qur'an provides the equal nature of men and women and reminds each gender that God is a witness to the fulfillment of their mutual rights" (Qur'an 4:1). The Qur'an also refers to spouses as garments for one another (Qur'an 2:187).

In his role as a leader, "a husband must remember his accountability to God and his responsibility to lead his family in accordance with Islamic values, which include justice, compassion, and equity" (Fortune, 2010: 1–17). While spousal abuse may be a common pattern in a number of religious marriages, it certainly cannot be legitimized through religious teaching and values. In sum, as Fortune states, "in ignorance and oversight, we can do much harm. In awareness and action, however, we can contribute a critical element to the efforts to respond to domestic violence in our communities" (ibid.).

Prevention of domestic violence

The consequences of domestic violence can move across generations and last a lifetime if care is not taken. But with the care of the suffering, all forms of wife-battering are preventable. Preventing domestic violence requires addressing difficult issues associated with the violence. This involves addressing the underlying causes of problems by using strategies and approaches known to be effective. Habitually occurring violence disturbs the peace of the immediate family and the neighbors as well; as such, the family should question if there is any way to help end the violence.

George R. Bach and Peter Wyden believe that if married disputants could overcome inhibitions and express their emotions directly, it would eliminate disturbing tensions and foster deeper and more cordial relationships. In their book *The Intimate Enemy – How to Fight Fair in Love and Marriage* (Bach et al., 1969), the authors explain a technique of verbal conflict in which the couple talk about their feelings and explain their emotional reactions. The presupposition for these authors is that the husband regards the wife as an individual in her own right. Otherwise, if the husband regards the wife as chattel, negotiations and compromises are futile. However, most husbands who beat their wives believe they have the right to make all decisions for the family and to institute punishment if their demands are not met.

In his studies, Whitehurst reminds us that men are not programmed to be other than aggressive and that much of the aggressive hostility vented on wives must be seen as a product of our sexually schizoid culture. He says, "our culture teaches men to also become tender lovers and responsive husbands seem to be asking more than logic can allow" (Whitehurst, 1971: 41). Ultimately, I agree with Whitehurst; we sometimes expect too much if we think these changes will come about by themselves. It is a huge task involving nothing less than a cultural revolution of attitudes and values. But those men who batter their wives argue that they are acting within their cultural values.

Experts identify three stages of prevention: primary, secondary, and tertiary. These labels are used to distinguish interventional strategies and do not reflect any one strategy as being more effective than another. In their discussions to describe a public health model of preventing domestic violence, Wolfe and Jaffee (2016) discuss primary, secondary, and tertiary interventions that can be applied to children, adolescents, and adults.

Primary prevention efforts aim to prevent the onset of a targeted condition. In the case of intimate partner violence, primary prevention aims at preventing the initial occurrence of domestic violence. Methods of primary prevention include public awareness campaigns and educational programs concerning domestic violence. Such types of campaigns have been used locally and nationally, as domestic violence is not located in one community but is all over Kenya. Unfortunately, men who are perpetrators of domestic violence do not attend such meetings. Primary prevention also focuses on changing environments so that they are safer for the women who are most often the victims of domestic violence. The approach of victim-oriented appeals provides the public-at-large, including potential victims of domestic violence, with information about the nature of what constitutes domestic violence; ways to help keep them safe, including self-protection techniques; ways to report domestic violence; and resources that can be used to help them.

Secondary prevention targets persons who are at risk for domestic violence or are experiencing early signs of domestic violence. Understanding these risk factors helps to frame interventions and select appropriate responses. In any case, the presence of these risk factors does not mean that an individual will become a victim of domestic violence or an offender. These risk factors include age/gender, socioeconomic status, race, etc. Females who are between the ages 18 to 25 are at the highest risk for domestic violence.

This is because men want to exercise their authority over women early in marriage life so that as they progress in marriage, the women may know that men are to be feared and obeyed.

Men who are socioeconomically low have a high risk of causing abuse, and this increases if the woman is employed or has higher income. Men of this sort evade responsibility by inflicting violence on their wives. Couples of the same ethnic community experience higher rates of victimization than those in mixed marriages. This is because all come from the system of violence. But if one is of another race or country, they will take off if any form of wife-abuse is initiated. Another risk factor of domestic violence is verbal abuse. Wives whose husbands are jealous or tightly controlling are at risk of intimate violence and stalking. In their survey, Tjaden and Thoennes conclude that "there is a strong link between threats of domestic violence and perpetration of domestic violence, suggesting that abuser threats should be taken seriously" (Tjaden and Thoennes, 2000).

Tertiary prevention is aimed at victims and perpetrators after domestic violence. These services are different from primary and secondary in a way that they are mandated rather than voluntary. Family-based intervention includes involving law enforcement, court, and family collaboration to address situations of severe domestic violence. Victims may receive an array of services to support future prevention, and perpetrators may be warned of dire consequences in case of any further violence. The programs for perpetrators target behaviors and recidivism.

Conclusion

This chapter has examined domestic violence against women among the Bukusu people of Bungoma County in the Republic of Kenya as a larger picture of wife-abuse in Kenya as well as elsewhere that the cruel act of wife-beating is taking place. The Bukusu people, with their diversity in traditions and culture, is a good community for carrying out such a study because they argue that ancestral cultural traditions find violence against married women to be a normal practice. The growth in population, changes in socioeconomic development, health, and the conditions of marriage and family life in Kenya provide an opportunity to explore these questions in a cross-cultural context. Also examined in this chapter were the effects of domestic violence, prevention measures, and the values of religion in married families.

By and large, if the Bukusu community, like any other community in Kenya, is to achieve the 2030 vision, women should be equal partners in economic development, able to make independent decisions that help the family to achieve its economic goal. Women are equal partners in family matters not pegs in corners where they just sit and wait to be given. Marital violence is a social disaster, and its victims have the same desperate need for relief and support just as the victims of a natural disaster. The problem of wife-battering has robbed many families of their joy. What is your response?

References

Bach, George R., and Wyden, Peter. 1969. *The Intimate Enemy*. New York: Morrow.

Briere, John, Woo, Rose, Folz, James, and McRae, Bonnie M. 1997. "Lifetime Victimization History, Demographics, and Clinical Status in Female Psychiatric Emergency Room Patients." *Journal of Nervous and Mental Disorders* 185, 95–101.

Coker, Ann L., and Richter, Donna L. 1998. "Violence against Women in Sierra Leone: Frequency and Correlates of Intimate Partner Violence and Forced Sexual Intercourse." *African Journal of Reproductive Health* 2, 61–72.

Constantine, Joan, and Constantine, Larry. 1974. "Jealousy: The Marriage Killer." *Penthouse Forum*, 59–60.

Dreifus, Claudia. 1973. Vol. 3(6), *Woman's Fate*. New York: Bantam.

Eisenberg, Sue, and Micklow, Patricia. 1974. "The Assaulted Wife: Catch 22' Revisited." Unpublished, University of Michigan, Ann Arbor, 24.

El-Zanaty, Fatma, Hussen, Enas M., Shawky, Gihen A., Way, Ann A., and Kishor, Sunita. 1995. *Egypt Demographic and Health Survey*. Cairo, Egypt: Macro International, Inc.

Engels, Fredrick. 1948. *The Origin of Family, Private Property and the State*. Moscow: Progress.

Fortune, Marie M., Abugideiri, Salma, and Dratch, Rabbi Mark. 2010. *A Commentary on Religion and Domestic Violence*. Faith and Trust Institute. Lebanon: Lebanese American University Beirut.

Gelles, Richard. 1972. *The Violent Home*. Beverly Hills: Sage.

Goode, William J. 1971. "Force and Violence in the Family." *Journal of Marriage and Family* 33, 624–36.

Ellsberg, Mary, Heise Lori, Pena Rodolfo, Agurto Sonia and Winkvist, Anna. 2001. "Researching Domestic Violence against Women: Methodological and Ethical Considerations." *Studies in Family Planning* 32 (1), 1–16.

Holden, George W. 2003. "Children Exposed to Domestic Violence and Child Abuse: Terminology and Taxonomy." *Clinical Child and Family Psychology Review* 6, 151–160.

Kimuna, Sitawa R., and Djamba, Yanyi K. 2008. "Gender-Based Violence: Correlates of Physical and Sexual Wife Abuse in Kenya." *Journal of Family Violence* 23, 333–342.

Komarovsky, Mirra. 1940. *Blue Collar Marriage*. New York: Vintage.

Jones, Serene. 2000. *Feminist Theory and Christian Theology: Cartographies of Grace*. Minneapolis: Fortress.

Makila, Fred K. 1978. *An Outline History of the Babukusu*. Nairobi, Kenya: Kenya Literature Bureau.

Martin, Del. 1981. *Battered Wives*. New York: Volcano, 25.

McCloskey, Laura Ann, William, Corrine, and Larsen, Ulla 2005. "Gender Inequality and Intimate Partner Violence among Women in Moshi, Tanzania." *International Family Planning Perspectives* 31 (3), 124–130.

M'Passou, Dennis. 1998. "The Continuing Tension between Christianity and Rites of Passage in Swaziland." In Cox, J. L., ed., *Rites of Passage in Contemporary African*. London: Cardiff.

Msaja, Wafula. 2011. *A History of the Bukusu*. 15–33.

Pizzey, Erin. 1974. "Violence Begins at Home." *London Spectator*, November 23.

———. 1974. "The Cultured Graduate Who Became a Thug." *Manchester Daily Express*, October 29, 11.

Richardson, Ralph, and Engel, Charles C. 2004. "Evaluation and Management of Medically Unexplained Physical Symptoms." *The Neurologist* 10(1).

Steinmetz, Suzanne K., and Murray, A. 1974. "General Introduction: Social Myth and Social System in the Study of Intra-Family Violence." In *Violence in the Family*. Suzanne Steinmetz and Murray A. Straus, eds. New York: Harper and Row 9.

Tjaden, Patricia, and Thoennes, Nancy. 2000. *Extent, Nature, and Consequences of Intimate Partner Violence: Findings from the National Violence against Women Survey*. Washington, DC: National Institute of Justice and the Center for Disease Control and Prevention.

Wafula, Robert J. 2006. "Male Ritual Circumcision Among the Bukusu of Western Kenya: An Indigenous African System of Epistemology and How it Impacts Western Forms of Schooling in Bungoma District." PhD Dissertation, Ohio University, Athens, OH.

Were, Gideon S. 1967. *A History of the Abaluyia of Western Kenya: c. 1500–1930*. Nairobi, Kenya: East African Publishing House.

Whitehurst, Robert N. 1974. "Violence in Husband-Wife Interaction." In *Violence in the Family*. Suzanne Steinmetz and Murray A. Straus, eds. New York: Harper and Row.

———. (1971). "Violently Jealousy Husbands." *Sexual Behavior*.

Wolfe, David. A., and Peter G. Jaffee. 2016. "Emerging Strategies in the Prevention of Domestic Violence." Retrieved June 13, 2016 from http://futureofchildren.org.

10 Religion and reproductive health in Africa

An exploration of Christian ethics with a focus on abortion

Precious Nihorowa

Introduction

Generally, in Africa, religion is intertwined with all aspects of people's life. This relationship originates from African Traditional Religion (ATR), to which Africans belonged before converting to Christianity and Islam, the most dominant religions in Africa at the moment. Thus, in ancient Africa, everything was viewed in light of one's religion or relationship with God. If anything were to be characterized as good, it had to be in line with what God willed for his people. Similarly, all that was not in line with God's will was considered morally, socially, and politically wrong. Years after converting to modern religions, many Africans seem to be attached to the roots of their traditional religion. It is not surprising, therefore, that the modern religions seem to clash with some of the beliefs of the traditional religions, a phenomenon that is known as syncretism. Olowola affirms that "the continuing revival of traditional African religiosity in our day presents a great unavoidable challenge to Christianity in Africa" (Olowola, 1993: 7). Such traditional values have also withstood the test of foreign cultures for a long time. Thus, Olowola further argues that "while Africans are being exposed to Western education, traditional thought is still the source of the basic world-view of most of the people" (Olowola, 1993: 7). Nevertheless, not all beliefs in ATR clash with beliefs in Christianity. Actually, there are some aspects of ATR that aided Christianity in easily setting its roots in Africa. These aspects include respect for human life as well as the vibrant religiosity among Africans that has prompted John Mbiti to describe Africans as notoriously religious (Mbiti, 1989: 1).

Africans do all they can to safeguard human life. Anything that tampers with human life is considered a threat to the community and is eliminated immediately. Moreover, Africans have a broader view of life. They believe that those who have died, some of whom are called ancestors, are still alive and that their spirits are felt among the people. This is why these ancestors are sometimes called the living-dead. Africans also believe that death is not the end of life. As part of showing the importance of life, in Africa, everyone is expected to marry with the primary aim of bearing children who will ensure the continued existence of the community. This is why those who choose not to marry for no tangible reason face some sort of rejection from society. Worse still, those who marry but fail to bear children are ridiculed and face social stigma. All this shows how Africans revere life. Why am I beginning by tracing the social function of religion as well as the reverence of life in African society?

For a long time, it has been taken for granted that abortion is un-African and that advocating for it was a fruit of Western influence, based on the fact that Africans revere human life. And so, it was commonly held that Africans could not opt for abortion and end the life of an unborn child. This is why issues of abortion have sparked controversies in most African countries, mostly around resistance. Christianity, and the Catholic Church in particular, has for a long time taken advantage of this pro-life attitude to deliver its teaching on abortion, which basically teaches against the act of abortion. However, recently there has been a new phenomenon among Africans in terms of reproductive health as well as sexuality issues as far as morality is concerned. There has been a more or less a liberal attitude that finds issues such as abortion justifiable. This is contrary to the resistant attitude that Africans used to be known for. Why has there been a shift in attitude among Africans? Why do some Africans no longer see the value of life that they have been known for? And why is there a moral dilemma or a moral panic among many Africans about having to choose between adhering to their traditional values and seizing Western values?

While some people may simply feel that the Universal Declaration of Human Rights in 1948 triggered and facilitated this shift, this chapter argues that the main cause is cross-cultural contact between Africa and people of other cultures. This contact comes from multiple dimensions such as migration and globalization. Due to mixture with other cultures, Africans have changed mindsets on some issues. They have come to be a bit liberal on some issues that they could not previously tolerate. In recent times, the Church has faced resistance in imparting its moral teaching in Africa, which is not how it used to be. This has made some people think that Christian ethics needs updating to suit the changing times. However, the chapter argues that the current scenario does not render Christian ethics irrelevant or outdated. The Church is facing resistance in imparting its moral teaching simply because it has not read the signs of the changing times. It has continuously used old means in the face of new problems and phenomena. This chapter, therefore, holds that there is a problem in the methodology. This is why there is a clash between the Christian doctrine and contemporary pastoral reality. The Church needs to adopt a more dialogical approach. This chapter proposes the theory of intersectionality as a better approach to the morality of abortion in contemporary Africa. This theory argues that the differences among people in the society should be considered unitary in order to progress in society. The paper shall mainly use Malawi as a case study.

African view of reproductive health and abortion

The issue of reproductive health is not new in Africa. Africa had its own way of handling such issues even though they were not as modern as those that it has adopted from the West today. For a long time, the refusal to accept the legalization of abortion in Africa was based on the premise that abortion is un-African or unusual to African culture. However, research has shown, and Benezet Bujo affirms, that even in traditional Africa, abortion existed. But it was not as widespread as it is today (2009: 148). Moreover, abortion was a secret between the woman and those close to her, especially women. Most of the time, even the husband was not aware that his wife wanted to commit or had committed abortion. Similarly, the community was not aware of her act of abortion (Bujo, 2009: 148). This seems to imply that the woman knew how life was valued in African society and that letting the people know about her act of killing the unborn baby would lead to unbearable consequences for her (Bujo, 2009: 148). Bujo also asserts that the woman concealed the act because "she was aware of the fact that the community certainly will not tolerate such a killing" (Bujo, 2009: 148). This points to the communitarian morality for which Africans used to be known. Such morality was a manifestation of *ubuntu*, a philosophy that one exists in connection with others.

Evaluating all this, Bujo concludes that

> in general, it can be said that abortion is not acceptable to traditional African society. [. . .] African people see their survival in the bearing of many children. Abortion goes against this. A woman who will be suspected of practicing abortion will be told *Ni ko tsitsi* (you are uprooting us).
>
> (Bujo, 2009: 148)

In other words, the picture we get here is that in traditional Africa, abortion was not tolerated and was heavily punished. But why was abortion considered immoral in Africa? The main reason for considering abortion immoral was the fact that it was against life, which Africans value very much. However, Bujo further gives a three-fold explanation for this reverence of life. He argues that

> abortion was rejected for three reasons: it is against God as the base of life; it is against the ancestors whose existence is guaranteed by the not-yet-born; and it is a form of suicide for the couple because only when they reject any attitude hostile to life will they find their identity as husband and wife.
>
> (Bujo, 2009: 148)

All three reasons still point to the fact that Africans regard life very highly. But Bujo mentions one captivating thing in the third reason. He calls abortion suicide for the couple. Thus, for the couple, killing the unborn child is like killing themselves. This conception seems to be strictly African, because modern and Western conceptions do not regard abortion as suicide for the couple. This may also entail that, if the community recognizes, tolerates, or legalizes abortion, it would be suicide for the whole community: by allowing the killing of the unborn, they are diminishing the community and, consequently, the ancestral line.

Women whose act of abortion was known to the community received punishment for it. Alluding to Nyeme Tese, Bujo asserts that,

> a mother who intentionally provokes abortion will be condemned by the Tetela clinging to the ancestral traditions. They will treat her as a *"jokaloka,"* that is, a witch and enemy of life, hostile to the mission of humans in the world. Her situation is judged as absurd since even if the child's father were unknown, or its biological father does not want to take care of it, it may without the slightest difficulty be adopted by the clan and will then enjoy equally all the rights of children regarded as "legitimate."
>
> (Bujo, 2009: 148)

What Bujo raises here as reasons for divorce are the same as those used by modern pro-abortion activists as "excuses" for permitting and legalizing abortion in Africa and indeed the world. Thus, they suggest that abortion should be permitted in cases such as rape or a girl who might wish to pursue her education and yet falls pregnant. Except in cases of a minor, which Bujo's argument does not clearly state, such excuses as getting pregnant out of wedlock and other arguments of a similar kind were not viewed as sufficient reason to end the life of an unborn child. Among the Lhomwe of Malawi, when it was known in the community that a woman or a girl had aborted, she suffered social stigma from the community, shamed her parents, and was considered immature, one who was afraid of the responsibility of taking care of a child. To this, Bujo adds that "a husband who causes miscarriage by physically abusing his wife is held responsible and is obliged to make reparation to the community" (Bujo, 2009: 148).

Bujo, however, acknowledges that there were some elements in Africa that implied abortion. He therefore suggests that "if Africa wants to continue the joyful welcome of life rooted in the tradition of ancestors without contradiction then negative elements have to be done away with immediately" (Bujo, 2009: 149). In other words, Bujo seems to say that there is no way Africans can keep on saying that they value life and yet retain cultural elements that suggest the opposite. Bujo is very right, but what has to be remembered is that no culture is free from impurities. This, however, does not mean to justify the African contradiction referred to here.

Influence of religion in Africa

In Africa, there has always been a thin line between culture and religion. These two seemed to be synonymous because Africans believed that God was always with them in all activities. This is why Mbiti argues that "religion is part of the cultural heritage" (Mbiti, 1975: 10). He views religion as part of the African way of life. He further acknowledges that religion was by far the richest part of the African heritage and that it was found in all areas of human life (Mbiti, 1975: 10). But what influence has religion had on African society? Mbiti contends that religion "has dominated the thinking of African peoples to such an extent that it has shaped their cultures, their social life, their political organizations, and economic activities" (Mbiti, 1975: 10). In other words, religion penetrated all aspects of life. Kunhiyop concurs with Mbiti but stresses that in traditional Africa, life was not dissected. That is, it was not conceived as having multiple aspects but was rather one whole interrelated dimension. Referring to the present dissection of life, he argues that

> this compartmentalization was fundamentally alien to Africa. Life to the African is basically interpreted holistically. The radical split between the now and then, body and soul, religion and morality/economics is alien to Africa. A study of God which is removed from the reality of life or just mere academics does no good for Africa.
>
> (Kunhiyop, 2017: 68)

In talking about African morality, "it is believed in many African societies that their morals were given to them by God from the very beginning. This provides an unchallenged authority for the morals" (Mbiti, 1975: 174). To someone who does not understand the African system, this may be thought of as a way of justifying some moral behavior by appealing to God as an unchallenged authority. However, this explains how influential religion is in Africa.

The notion of Christian ethics on life

Generally, ethics is defined as "well-founded standards of right and wrong that prescribe what human beings ought to do, usually in terms of rights, obligations, benefits to society, fairness or specific virtues" (Velasquez, et al., 1987: 3). Such standards act as a yardstick for separating right from wrong. Ethics and morality are related but often considered separate by different scholars. However, this chapter uses these terms interchangeably. Christian ethics is based on divine revelation as well as the Bible, especially the New Testament. The Christian notion of ethics as it relates to life is based on the biblical maxim "do not kill" (Ex. 20:17). This means that anything that has to do with taking away human life is considered a sin against God, and, consequently, immoral. This is why the Catholic Church, and other Christian churches, has maintained that the killing of innocent persons through acts of abortion cannot be supported because such acts are direct attack on life as an absolute good from God (Ssekyanzi, 2011: 96). This teaching is based on the Church's view of life as beginning at the moment of conception.

The *Catechism of the Catholic Church* (CCC) also states that

> human life must be respected and protected absolutely from the moment of conception. From the first moment of his existence, the human being must be recognized as having the rights of a person – among which is the inviolable right of every innocent being to life. . . . Direct abortion, that is to say, abortion willed either as an end or a means, is [thus] highly contrary to moral law (CCC art. 2270-2271).[1]

In other words, induced abortion, which is voluntary and intentional, is considered morally wrong. However, an abortion that happens naturally and is not directly induced is not considered morally wrong as it is not voluntary. An example of this is miscarriage.

Abortion in Malawi

The Catholic Church in Malawi holds an important place in the history of the country. Apart from the fact that it has helped to set up reliable facilities for education at all levels and health facilities, it also plays an influential role in the socio-political life of the country. For a long time now, the Episcopal Conference of Malawi (ECM), which is a body comprising all the Catholic Bishops of Malawi, has issued pastoral letters to all its faithful and to people of goodwill in Malawi to sensitize them and confront leaders on matters of national relevance. The first time the Catholic Church hit the headlines in Malawi was in 1992 when the ECM took the bold step of confronting the autocratic government of the time, which was by then ruled by the first native president of Malawi, the late Dr. Hastings Kamuzu Banda. This was a time when talking about the president and political matters, let alone confronting him, was an offense similar to treason and was punishable by death. Disregarding all this, the Bishops issued a letter entitled *Living Our Faith* that directly addressed issues that the president was mishandling and pleaded with him to consider changing them and to adopt a system of leadership that had the people at heart. In reaction to this, the ruling elite, under the order of the president, threatened to kill all the Bishops, an idea that was later revoked. People praised the Bishops for their courage and for addressing relevant issues that affected many Malawians. Since then, the Bishops have always enjoyed a prophetic influence when they talk on social, moral, and political issues. Another historical event for ECM was in 2011, when they issued a pastoral letter called *Reading the Signs of the Times*, which, just like *Living Our Faith*, condemned government efforts in different sectors and also confronted the leadership on issues that needed serious consideration. The general reaction seemed that the president of the time, the late Bingu wa Mutharika, was not happy at being exposed and confronted by men of God.

The Bishops have commented on not only political affairs but also other issues in line with the doctrine of the Church. Another area they tackled is morality. In 2013, they issued a letter that reaffirmed the Church's moral teaching on abortion, contraceptives, and homosexuality. Recently as well, the Church planned and held a pro-family and pro-life march that sought to emphasize the Church's teaching, especially on abortion and homosexuality, both of which were described as threats to the Christian family and life in general. The march, which was called a "citizen march for life and family," was held on December 6, 2016 in all districts across the country. The ECM, together with the Evangelical Association in Malawi (EAM), organized the march when the Malawi parliament was planning to retable and review the abortion law and make it tolerant of some cases of abortion. The Church meant to speak against this move. Thus, according to Fr. Henry Saindi, the Secretary-General for ECM, and Rev. Francis Mkandawire, Secretary-General for EAM, the march was meant to serve as a reminder to all people and institutions that human life is sacred and that the dignity of the human being is the foundation of the moral vision for the society (Nankhonya, 2016). Even the document that the two Church bodies issued and distributed a few days before the march stated in part that

> from the moment of conception a life began that is neither of the father nor the mother. It is rather a life of a new human being with its own growth. It is, therefore, important that we all safeguard, preserve and protect life with extreme care from conception.
>
> (Nankhonya, 2016)

Thus, the march was not meant to impart any new doctrine but simply to reiterate and emphasize what the Church had already taught previously. To further prove the validity of its doctrine, the Church added that it was not true that legalizing abortion would result in a drop in maternal death rate during conception as research and reality has proved that the countries where abortion was legalized had not faced any drop in the rate. Rather, countries which have not yet legalized abortion, such as Egypt, have their maternal death rate in check (Nankhonya, 2016). In other words, the Church sought to show that the arguments suggested by the parliamentarians for reviewing the abortion law were unreasonable.

However, for the first time in the history of the Church's take on social, political, and moral matters, there was a division among Malawians concerning the move of the Church. While some people sided with Church bodies and took part in the march, others viewed it as unjustified and felt that the Church had gone out of its way in holding the march. The accusations evaluated not only about the method that the Church used to disseminate its teaching but also the Church's teaching itself, with most people describing it as inconsiderate. Even though the Church held the march to voice objections to both abortion and homosexuality, the issue that was picked up by most Malawians was abortion, and not homosexuality. This caused some people to call the march an "anti-abortion march" and not a "citizen march for life and family" as it was meant to be. Even though the reasons for this are not known, it seems many Malawians are unanimous that homosexuality should not be legalized, even though a few people have arisen to defend the rights of such people. Therefore, they felt that the issue was not debatable as it was "obvious" that homosexuality is not acceptable. The debate on abortion was picked up by different people after the Church's march.

Arguing from a medical perspective, Dr. Rodney Kalanda, Vice President of the Christian Medical Dentist Fellowship, agreed with the Church that the argument that legalizing abortion would reduce the maternal death rate was not true. Thus, he contended that, "we would like to bring to the attention of the public that the notion that we shall see a decrease in maternal mortality rate is misleading. In fact, there is no country that has achieved that" (Nankhonya, 2016). This was contrary to the government's position and a reason for deciding to review the abortion law. It argued that denying women legal access to abortion was leading to health complications among women, including death, and that this was costing government more money to treat such complications. In Kalanda's view, the reasons on the government side for reconsidering the law were medically unsupported, at least for the reasons given.

Dissatisfied with the Church's march, Pilirani Kachulu wrote in one of the country's newspapers, *The Nation*, that, "I find it absurd for the Catholic Church to demonstrate against the liberalization of abortion in the country. The Church has diverted from its spiritual means of achieving its goals to secular ones. It seems the Church has lost trust in prayer and preaching as a way of convincing people on what is good for the society" (Kachulu, 2016). For Kachulu, the Church had got the methodology of imparting their teaching wrong. For her, the Church was supposed to pray or to preach in the church or issue a pastoral letter as it had been known for. Arguing in favor of abortion, Kachulu stated that she believed in empowering women to make decisions about their bodies. She concluded by saying that "although the Church has an obligation to preach what is right according to them, they have to respect other people's views and decisions" (Kachulu, 2016). Here Kachulu provides the second problem of the Church, which is tolerance of other views. Thus, even though the Church is obliged to impart its teaching, it has to take into account other voices on the issues of concern. Responding to Kachulu, Maxwell Mezuwa Banda wrote that "the churches, and not just the Catholics, have a right to demonstrate like any Malawian. Whenever the church comes together regardless of its differences, it means there is something worth communicating to the public" (Banda, 2017). By arguing in this way, Banda sought to dismiss Kachulu's argument about the methodology used by the Church. For him, there is nothing wrong with the way the

Church conducted itself. Alluding to the Holy Scripture, he further argued that even Jesus himself led a march to Jerusalem and later cleansed the temple. Martin Luther King Jr. also led a civil rights activism, and the Israelites marched around the city of Jericho until it fell (Joshua 6:1–5). Banda concluded that the Church had acted within its mandate (Banda, 2017).

Winnie Nyakadoda, however, was of the view that women should be given a voice in the debate on abortion. For her, the abortion debate was dogged by lies, assumptions, and religious dogma and confirmed how people deliberately or ignorantly ignored crucial facts in the debate (Nyakadoda, 2016). Thus, people were busy taking matters into their own hands and excluding those directly affected by abortion. She argues that

> as a woman I feel sad that it is men who are on the forefront opposing the liberalization of laws that affect women's health and rights. Who drafted the petition to block women from enjoying their reproductive rights to safe abortion? Men. Who received the petition? Men! Who organized the demonstration? Men [in robes]. Why do impregnators, who do not get pregnant and do not even induce abortions, want to make laws that directly affect women. This is all about male chauvinism and gender discrimination.
>
> (Nyakadoda, 2016)

Nyakadoda, it seems, would have loved it if women were included in the decision-making process that involves their own reproductive health rather than talking about it all without hearing from their side and including their voices.

Arguing along the same lines, Sellah Singini also expressed concern over the exclusion of women from the debate. She wrote that

> since the debate started, conspicuously missing has been the loud voice of women. Apart from few who have done so on social media, many women have kept quiet. I am not sure whether that is a silent protest by women. I have no problem with people or institutions debating however, I have a problem with men and institutions that try to control a woman's body. The choice of whether to abort or not, lies with the one carrying the pregnancy. It's her womb and she is in charge of it, not men, institutions or morality.
>
> (Singini, 2017)

While Singini partly argues with Nyakadoda on the idea of including women in the debate and in the process of decision-making about abortion, she adds that the decision on whether to abort or not should be left to the bearer of the pregnancy to decide what is right for her.

The views given above on the abortion debate are some of the reactions that people raised concerning the Church's march. Reading between the lines of these arguments, it is clear that people have divided opinions on the matter. This is obvious based on the media battle that erupted after the march. What used to be a clear-cut issue is now debatable. Thus, what Malawians easily considered as unacceptable, as in the case of abortion, now has sympathizers. And the Catholic Church, which used to carry authority when it spoke on most matters, has now been openly challenged by different people suggesting opposing views on the matter. So, what led to the change in viewing matters of morality in Africa? Here are some of the factors suggested.

The causes: migration and other factors

According to Magesa, "in the African moral and ethical sphere, there have been huge changes [. . .] although in most cases people cannot articulate them clearly, most feel them and, for many, they are threatening" (Magesa, 2010). Thus, even Magesa acknowledges that things are no longer the same in Africa as far as morality is concerned. While diverse reasons have been given as explanations for the change in the moral life of Africans, and particularly Malawians, this chapter suggests cross-cultural encounters as the main reason. Given that Africans had their own culture with its own values that hardly tolerated abortion and public talk about sexual issues, mixing with other cultures has made them review their moral values, often considering them irrelevant, and adopt the influential ones that, unfortunately, have a liberal view of most moral issues. Cross-cultural encounter embraces multiple dimensions. One of the dimensions that is becoming a common phenomenon in Africa is migration, especially international migration, which involves moving from one country to another.

There are a lot of issues that lead to migration in Africa, including civil wars and looking for job opportunities, among many other related issues. Alluding to UNHCR statistics from January 1, 2004, Diane B. Stinton argues that Africa has about 4,285,100 refugees and major exoduses from countries such as Sudan, Liberia, Democratic Republic of the Congo, Cote de Ivoire, Somalia, and Central African Republic (Stinton, 2008). These migrated people, most of whom are called refugees, settle mostly in African and European countries. In the countries where they are hosted, the refugees get in contact with citizens of the hosting countries as well as other nationals being hosted by the same country. For instance, South Africa as a country is seen as a source of greener pastures for most Africans. As a result, due to lack of job opportunities in their home countries, different African nationals migrate to South Africa to look for means of survival. When people intermix with other cultures in such instances, they learn from each other's way of life.

What Queen Elizabeth I did in 1601 proves how cultural values can be influenced or can change when people mix through migration. She proclaimed that "Negroes and blackamoors" should be deported from England because they were "infidels" and were contributing to social and economic problems such as poverty and famine (Haralambos and Holborn, 2008: 143). Queen Elizabeth I felt that those she referred to as Negroes and blackamoors were transmitting undesirable cultural values to the natives of England. She was afraid that their cultural values would be assimilated or would undergo change through the intermixture of the cultures. Cultural exchange among people is inevitable due to the very fact that they stay together and are able to learn from one another some ways of doing things. Their cultures dialogue with one another, and this leads to shedding some elements that seem irrelevant and adopting those that seem convincing. Such adopted ideas include those pertaining to morality.

Citing the historian Philip D. Curtin, Haralambos and Holborn assert that "in the eighteenth century some 9.5 million Africans were transported across the Atlantic to become slaves in North and South America and the Caribbean" (2008: 143). Already, this entailed an intermixture of cultures. However, there were unbalanced and inferiority claims characterizing the Africans. For instance, "John Taylor, a writer and traveler, described the black slaves in Jamaica as 'these ignorant pore souls' who differed 'from brute beast', only by their shape and speech" (Haralambos and Holborn, 2008: 143). Such claims may make the inferior culture feel suppressed and resort to adopting the lifestyle of the host country in order to feel some belonging. Adolf Hitler's idea of establishing a pure race, which led to the extermination of millions of Jews, was also based on the premise that these foreign cultures and races were corrupting the natives. Whenever there are differences among the people, there is often a feeling of some group doing things or having a better view of life than the others.

Migration comes with new social relationships and social changes among the people. One of the models that tends to conceive of the relationship between immigrant groups and the host country is the immigrant–host model. It posits that "the immigrant group will adapt to the way of life of the host society and will be assimilated into it" (Haralambos and Holborn, 2008). Even if this view is true of some instances, it does not fully explain the relations between immigrants and host nations in so far as issues of cultural influence are concerned. It is not always the case that the host nation assimilates the immigrant's way of life. Sometimes the host could even be assimilated by the immigrant minority. An example of this is Africa. When colonialists came to Africa, they were few in number but managed to convince Africans that their white race was superior to the black one of the Africans. Similarly, some of the first missionaries managed to convince most Africans that their beliefs were pagan and that they had no belief in God. Such kind of characterization definitely may lead, and perhaps led, Africans to be assimilated and adopt the way of life of their colonial masters and the missionaries.

When Africans who migrated to other countries go back to their countries, either through repatriation or the normal way, they influence people and advocate for strange cultural values such as Western ideas or views of life that are contrary to their own. Countries with refugee camps that host foreign nationals are also more prone to such influence than those that do not. For example, Malawi has Dzaleka camp, which hosts refugees from a number of countries, mostly African. The country started hosting refugees in 1985 with the start of civil war in Mozambique, when some 1.2 million Mozambican refugees sought refuge in Malawi. After the successful repatriation of the Mozambican refugees, Malawi continued hosting other refugees (UNHCR, 2015: 9). Since then, a number of foreign nationals have been hosted at the refugee camp. According to a United Nations Higher Commissioner for Refugees (UNHCR) 2014 report, by December 2014 Malawi had 20,398 refugees and asylum seekers, most of whom are hosted at Dzaleka camp. The report further stated that 2014 recorded the highest number of refugees, which reached 400 people entering Malawi per month.[2] But why is the number of refugees in the country so high?

The report states that,

> Malawi is on a migration route and the refugee camp continues to receive transiting migrants from the Horn of Africa, estimated at between 5,000–10,000 persons per annum [. . .] They turn up at the camp for rest and recuperation before they continue to South Africa.[3]

Given the large number of people going to South Africa from elsewhere in Africa to seek their fortunes, a lot of people pass through the camp. This is why the report acknowledges that "there are no accurate statistics, as many do not enter through formal migration and border points."[4]

The report further revealed that the traditional leaders of the hosting community have tried their best to meet the refugees together with the whole host community to discuss with them what constitutes acceptable behavior in the community, but the refugees have been reluctant to turn up for such meetings.[5] The hosting community complains that the refugees display unacceptable behavior in the community, showing that there is a clash in culture with the hosting community. Malawi is just one example among many other countries that host refugees, not only from the Horn of Africa[6] but also elsewhere in Africa, of how the mixture of cultures affects the morality of the people. There are also many Africans going to Europe almost every day (Stevens, 2016).

The second dimension of cross-cultural encounter is globalization. For Magesa, globalization is the main root cause of moral–ethical change, especially in Africa. Thus, he argues that "the source for the moral–ethical change today can be put down to one major movement: globalization" (Magesa, 2010: 50). He further defines what he means by globalization. According to him, "in its basic meaning, globalization implies simply cross-cultural contact and influence and the consequences in political, economic and social structural organization, and human attitudes that go with it" (Magesa, 2010: 50). Here, again, Magesa acknowledges that even globalization basically involves contact between cultures. However, Magesa adds that globalization is not a new phenomenon and has been around since the beginning of humanity. It only appears to be a new phenomenon in our world today because of its speed and reach and, therefore, weight and power, the degree of which has up until now been unknown and unimaginable (Magesa, 2010). Just like migration, one of the areas that globalization has impacted is ethics, or the moral life of Africans.

So, Magesa asks, "what have been the effects of globalization on African moral-ethical life?" He points out that African morality has been trampled by other dominant moralities, particularly Western. He further argues that "imposition is the best general term we can use to describe the situation. Whether positive or negative, imposition stifles the creative imagination of peoples since it does not encourage self-identity and dialogue. It does violence to people's selfhood" (Magesa, 2010: 50). Magesa seems to acknowledge that in the contemporary world, one cannot avoid the impacts of globalization. However, he bemoans the fact that there has been no dialogue between African moral values and Western ones. That is why he refers to such cultural contact as imposition. He further contends that "in moral ethical terms in Africa, the power of globalization forces upon the general public almost blind imitation of Western cultural values, spread through the media of mass communication, some of which are clearly destructive" (Magesa 2010: 51). It is African culture that has suffered unbearable consequences, resulting in near-assimilation of its traditional values. Commenting on morality and abortion in particular, Bujo concurs with Magesa and asserts that

> today the situation has worsened; the world is a global village, people know other people and cultures and are hugely influenced by them often to their detriment [. . .] in the old days, abortion was done in secret, something not accepted by the community. Nowadays a woman may have an abortion legally because, as the western world says, she has a right to it.
>
> (Bujo, 2009: 150)

This shows how globalization has impacted the abortion talk, especially in Africa. Another consequence, now obvious in the moral talk in Africa, is a liberal mentality towards sex talk as compared to traditional silence about such matters, which, in a way, safeguarded the moral values of the people. "This is most apparent, perhaps nowhere else than in the area of sexual ethics among the youth" (Magesa 2010: 51). Today in Africa, people can freely talk about and debate sexual issues on media platforms. This has resulted in a high rate of HIV/AIDS victims; by many accounts, including the United Nations World Health Organization (WHO), Sub-Saharan Africa is the statistically the most affected by this pandemic (Magesa, 2010: 51).

Another dimension of cultural encounter is mass communication through media. Media can refer to a variety of things, such as technologies, modes of communication, and methods of disseminating messages to audiences (Haralambos and Holborn, 2008: 711). The media has an impact on how people think and view some issues. Since it can accommodate a wide range and a number of people, it acts as a site for intercultural encounters. The media as a tool of communication is very influential on its audience. Some horrors of society, such as the Rwandan genocide, were aggravated by messages communicated through media. Most of the time, the media has a great ability to communicate its agenda to its mass recipients. For Bujo,

> not only has the media and consumerism contributed to the loss of but unjust socio-economic structure in time of globalization has also played a part. If we can complain that western countries, in general, maintain oppressive structure in the southern hemisphere, many African dictators were supported by those same western powers, all of which has led to bloody revolts and chaos.
>
> (Bujo, 2009: 150)

In other words, the media has been manipulated by the West to send wrong moral signals that clash with African values. In Bujo's view, Westerners have often ignited and fanned flames of conflict, including guns, in Africa, resulting in wars that have lasted for decades. He adds that through such wars, people lose any ethical orientation and their sense of life, and the command not to kill becomes meaningless (Bujo, 2009: 151). Thus, he connects the liberal attitude towards abortion to this loss of the sense of sacredness of life. So, in the face of witnessing moral degradation as evidenced in the issue of abortion, what can Africa do to get out of this grip of cultural influence?

Towards a solution: engaging intersectionality

Our exploration of the issue of abortion in the light of Christian ethics has revealed that there is lack of consensus between Christian moral principles and the current conception of abortion in Africa. There seems to be a clash where there was initially harmony. So, what is the problem? Is Christian ethics outdated or has it outlived its usefulness? This chapter argues that Christian ethics is as relevant to Africa as it has been in past years. However, there is a problem with the methodology that is used to impart Christian moral values. According to Magesa, "methodology is not only an academic question involving the teaching of ethics in schools. It is also, and I think, supremely, a pastoral issue touching on the central question of following Christ" (Magesa, 2010: 47). What Magesa mainly puts forward here is that methodologies of Christian ethics should not just remain dogmatic but should go out of their way to dialogue with the situation at hand. Magesa, however, does not propose a change in ethical principles. He simply contends that existing Christian moral principles should be flexible enough to adapt to the changing times. Just as the Vatican II council fathers taught, theology "should not lose contact with its own times, so that experts in various fields may be led to a deeper knowledge of the faith."[7] This, again, is in line with what Magesa has already proposed. Assessing the impact of Christian ethics in Africa, Magesa concludes that "the truth is that here is where the method of Christian pedagogy has almost totally failed to make an impact on the ground" (Magesa, 2010: 49). Since there seems to be a gap between Christian ethical principles and the moral life of the people, what can bridge this gap in order to produce the desired impact? This chapter suggests there should be an intersection between the church and the life of the people. Hence, this chapter proposes the theory of intersectionality as a solution.

According to Patricia Hill Collins, "the term intersectionality references the critical insight that race, class, gender, sexuality, ethnicity, nation, ability, and age operate not as unitary, mutually exclusive entities, but rather as reciprocally constructing phenomena" (Collins, 2015: 1). Thus, the theory does not seem to engage in a fight for equality in society but simply suggests that, even through the differences that exist in the society, everyone has a contribution to make towards the society in one's own capacity. The differences that exist among members of a society, therefore, should not be used as tools for domination but should partner with others towards making the society a better place for all. Collins, however, acknowledges that this definition results from a consensus among scholars even though there are still disagreements about what intersectionality really means. This theory has been used mostly by feminist thinkers to fight for equality in society. Nevertheless, its premises and its application surpass feminist ideology.

In line with Collins, Rachel A. Dudley defines intersectionality as "a tool for analysis, advocacy and policy development that addresses multiple discriminations and helps us understand how different sets of identities impact access to rights and opportunities" (Dudley, 2006: 37). In other words, Dudley looks at intersectionality as a tool that assesses how people relate in society in relation to the differences that exist among them. Leslie McCall's understanding, however, leans more towards Collins' than Dudley's. She conceives of intersectionality as a theory facilitating the relationships among multiple dimensions and modalities of social relations and subject formations (McCall, 2005: 1772). Dudley seems to differ from Collins and McCall on the fact that, while the former only sees intersectionality as a tool for analysis, the latter two view it as a means of constructing common phenomena among different people. Nevertheless, all of these give a valuable conception of intersectionality. So how can the Church in Africa harness intersectionality on the issue of abortion?

As it has been pointed out earlier on, the Church's problem in Africa is methodological, not doctrinal. Thus, the Christian moral teaching is still valid, but the method of imparting it does not suit the modern times. According to *Women's Rights and Economic Change*, intersectional analysis posits that we should not understand the combining of identities as additively increasing one's burden but instead as producing substantively distinct experiences (Women's Rights and Economic Change, 2004: 2). The Church should not view itself as possessing a monopoly on authority on moral matters. It has to engage in dialogue all those that are affected by its teaching. In other words, the Church should be aware that all sectors and members of society have distinct experiences and something unique to contribute towards the debate. The government authorities and the citizens should work hand in hand with the Church in dialoguing over matters of relevance. Kunhiyop argues that "the challenge of African morality lies in locating our true elements, so that we live our Christian life truly. A fruitful way forward is for the Church to recover and reaffirm what was good in her traditional culture" (Kunhiyop, 2017: 69). Kunhiyop's suggestion is in line with intersectionality. He suggests recovering what was good in traditional African culture as a solution. And, as we discussed earlier, Africans viewed life as a holistic entity with all its aspects interrelated. This is basically what intersectionality demands: that the different aspects in society should unite in constructing common phenomena.

Adding to Kunhiyop's suggestion, Bujo contends that, "to prevent the abortion mentality from taking over in Africa, we must remember that life, in its holistic sense, was the greatest concern for our ancestors" (Bujo, 2009: 151). Bujo too seems to be proposing a methodology that takes Africa back to its roots and restores the relationship between religion and social life, a relationship that respects all aspects of society in making decisions. But what is the role of the Church in this regard? For him, "the church in Africa must not content itself with writing pastoral letters. Catechesis must address the deepening of [. . .] the Gospel of Life, rooted in African tradition" (Bujo, 2009: 151). Thus, even if writing pastoral letters is important, so too is dialoguing with sectors and members of the society. In other words, the Gospel must dialogue with the local situation and, more so, the contemporary reality facing the African continent. Bujo, again, suggests that the Church of Africa needs dialogue with her sister churches in Europe and North America so that, in the proclamation of the Gospel life, their governments and economic powers become aware of the injustices and the mismanagement of the black continent (Bujo, 2009: 151). Here, Bujo suggests tackling the problem from its roots. There is no way, he seems to say, that the African church should hope for fruitful evangelization on abortion if she does not engage those influencing African culture. They too should have their voice heard in the debate.

Even *Gaudium et Spes*, the Vatican II document, posits:

> Let the layman not imagine that his pastors are always such experts, that to every problem which arises, however complicated, they can readily give him a concrete solution, or even that such is their mission. Rather, enlightened by Christian wisdom and giving close attention to the teaching authority of the Church, let the layman take on his own distinctive role.[8]

Thus, even though the clergy have an influential role in the Church, they should not exclude the laity in deciding on doctrinal matters that affect them.

Bujo also suggests that, to restore the concept of life in Africa in relation to abortion, "the position of women has to be improved" (Bujo, 2009: 149). Perhaps Bujo's argument originates from our previous discussion that sometimes women are neglected and ignored in the whole debate about abortion. That is why Nyakadoda and Singini, in the Malawian case study, bemoaned such exclusion of women. As those directly affected by abortion, women need to be engaged as well so that they can share their experiences. They too should be involved in the construction of common phenomena suggested by intersectionality.

However, *Women's Rights and Economic Change* offers some conditions required to fruitfully implement intersectionality. First and foremost, the organization argues, "using intersectionality in our work requires that we think differently about identity, equality and power. It requires that we focus on points of intersection, complexity, dynamic processes."[9] In other words, based on the fact that a number of differences exist among the people, the intersection point should be the focus. The dialogue is bound to fail if it is based on the differences. Second, "using intersectionality entails valuing a 'bottom-up' approach to research, analysis and planning. Information gathering should begin by asking questions about how women and men actually live their lives."[10] The Church has to study the situation at the grassroots and then put forward its teaching.

Conclusion

African morality is undergoing a lot of changes. This is a fact that cannot be denied anymore. Cultural relations with other nationalities are the main cause of this. That African traditional ethics was built on the concept of life and was communitarian is slowly fading and dying out. The Church too has faced resistance in imparting its moral doctrines because of the changing view of life among Africans. The chapter was a discussion on this new liberal phenomenon that is affecting African morality. It has attempted to suggest the source of this phenomenon, how it has been a big blow to African and Christian ethics, and how the Church can manage to live with it. In short, the chapter suggested that the Church has to engage other sectors and other members of society to be able to achieve its goal. In putting forward this suggestion, the chapter proposed and used the theory of intersectionality, which views the differences in society as unitary and interrelated. The Church should learn to embrace variety in society and engage people in meaningful dialogue. Just as Jesus Christ, through the incarnation, reconciled humanity and divinity, which were viewed as incompatible, and brought us salvation through it, through intersecting with others, the Church can also bring out something beautiful.

Notes

1 U.S Catholic Church *The Catechism of the Catholic Church*, Rev. ed. (Nairobi: Paulines Publications Africa, 1995), 2270–2271.
2 UNHCR and WFP, *Joint Assessment Mission Report*, 6.
3 UNHCR and WFP, *Joint Assessment Mission Report*, 6.
4 UNHCR and WFP, *Joint Assessment Mission Report*, 6.
5 UNHCR and WFP, *Joint Assessment Mission Report*, 30.
6 The Horn of Africa is an area covering Uganda, Kenya, Eritrea, Sudan, South Sudan, Ethiopia, Djibouti, and Somalia (UNHCR report 2015).
7 Vatican Council II. *The Conciliar and Post Conciliar Documents: Gaudium et Spes*, Gen. ed. Austin Flannery (New Delhi: St. Paul Publishing Company, 2001), #43.
8 Vatican II, *Gaudium et Spes*, #43.
9 *Women's Rights and Economic Change*, "Intersectionality: A Tool for Gender and Economic Justice." No. 9 (August, 2004), 5. Accessed March 10, 2017. https://lgbtq.unc.edu/sites/lgbtq.unc.edu/files/documents/intersectionality_en.pdf.
10 *Women's Rights and Economic Change*, "Intersectionality," 5.

References

Banda, Mezuwa Maxwell. 2016. "On Churches' Anti-Abortion March." *The Nation*, December 26. Accessed March 10, 2017, http://mwnation.com/on-churches-anti-abortion-march/

Bujo, Benezet. 2009. *Plea for Change of Models for Marriage*. Nairobi: Paulines Publications Africa.

U.S Catholic Church. 1995. *The Catechism of the Catholic Church* (Rev. ed.). Nairobi: Paulines Publications Africa.

Collins, Patricia Hill. 2015. "Intersectionality's Definitional Dilemmas." *Annual Review of Sociology*, 1–20. Accessed March 10, 2017, www.annualreviews.org/doi/abs/10.1146/annurev-soc-073014-112142

Dudley, Rachel A. 2006. "Confronting the Concept of Intersectionality: The Legacy of Audre Lorde and Contemporary Feminists Organisations." *McNairs Scholars Journal*, 10(1): 37–45. Accessed March 10, 2017, http://scholarworks.gvsu.edu/cgi/viewcontent.cgi?article=1063&context=mcnair

Haralambos, Mike and Martin Holborn. 2008. *Sociology: Themes and Perspectives* (7th ed.). London: HarperCollins Publishers Limited.

Kachulu, Pilirani. 2016. "On Recent Anti-Abortion March." *The Nation*, December 9, Accessed March 10, 2017, http://mwnation.com/on-recent-anti-abortion-march/

Kunhiyop, Samuel Waje. 2009. "The Challenge of African Christian Morality." *Conspectus: The Journal of the South African Theological Seminary: The Challenge of African Morality*, 7: 60–80, www.sats.edu.za/userfiles/Kunhiyop_AfricanChristianMorality.pdf

Magesa, Laurenti. 2010. "Moral and Ethical Issues in African Christianity." In Laurenti Magesa, ed. *African Theology Comes of Age: Revisiting the Twenty Years of the Theology of the Ecumenical Symposium of Eastern Africa Theologians (ESEAT)*. Nairobi: Pauline Publications Africa.

Mbiti, John S. 1975. *Introduction to African Religion* (2nd rev. ed.). Gaborone: Heinemann Educational Botswana (Publishing) (Pty) Limited.

Mbiti, John S. 1989. *African Religions and Philosophy* (2nd ed.). Gaborone: Heinemann Educational Botswana (Publishing) (Pty) Limited.

McCall, Leslie. 2005. "The Complexity of Intersectionality." *Signs*, Spring: 1771–1800. Accessed March 10, 2017, http://socialdifference.columbia.edu/files/social-diff/projects/Article_%20The%20Complexity%20of%20Intersectionality%20by%20Leslie%20McCall.pdf

Nankhonya, Jacob. 2016. "EAM, ECM to March against Abortion, Homosexuality." *The Nation*, November 17. Accessed March 10, 2017, http://mwnation.com/eam-ecm-to-march-against-abortion-homosexuality/

Nyakadoda, Winnie Botha. 2016. "Allow Women Voices on Abortion." *The Nation*, December 23, 2016. Accessed March 10, 2017, http://mwnation.com/allow-women-voices-on-abortion-laws/

Olowola, Cornelius. 1993. *African Traditional Religion and the Christian Faith*. Ibadan: African Christian Press.

Singini, Sellah. 2017. "It's My Womb, I'm in Charge of It." *The Nation*, January 29. Accessed March 10, 2017, http://mwnation.com/its-my-womb-im-in-charge-of-it-3/

Ssekyanzi, Robert. 2011. "The Ethical Problem of Abortion and the Intricacies of Its Penalty in the Catholic Church." *Chiedza Journal*, 14(1): 95–105.

Stevens, John. 2016. "10,000 Migrants Cross from North Africa to Italy in Just Four Days as It Is Revealed Less than 6% of Those Ordered to Return Home Last Year Actually Went back." *Mail Online*, June 27. Accessed March 10, 2017, www.dailymail.co.uk/news/article-3662601/10-000-migrants-cross-North-Africa-Italy-just-FOUR-DAYS-revealed-6-ordered-return-home-year-actually-went-back.html

Stinton, Diane B. 2008. "Amani ye Juu ('A Higher Peace'): African Refugee Women Living Out Reconciliation in Nairobi." *Religion and Politics in Africa: Theological Reflections for the 21st century*, Peter I. Gichure and Diane B. Stinton (eds). Nairobi: Pauline Publications Africa.

UNHCR. 2015. *Forced Displacement and Mixed Migration in the Horn of Africa*. Geneva: UNHCR. Accessed March 10, 2017, http://pubdocs.worldbank.org/en/892801436371029880/forced-displacement-horn-of-africa-Report.pdf

UNHCR and WFP. 2014. "Joint Assessment Mission Report: Dzaleka Refugee Camp, Malawi." *Lilongwe*, November. Accessed March 10, 2017, www.unhcr.org/5680f7d09.pdf

Vatican Council II. 2001. *The Conciliar and Post Conciliar Documents*, Austin Flannery (Gen. ed.). New Delhi: St. Paul Publishing Company.

Velasquez, Manuel., Claire Andre, Thomas S. J. Shanks and Michael J. Meyer. 1987. "What is Ethics?" *Issues in Ethics*, 1(1): Fall.

Women's Rights and Economic Change. 2004. "Intersectionality: A Tool for Gender and Economic Justice." No. 9 (August): 1–6. Accessed March 10, 2017, https://lgbtq.unc.edu/sites/lgbtq.unc.edu/files/documents/intersectionality_en.pdf

11 Polished violence

Changing notions about the spirituality of the todɔlɛ[1] (vagina) in popular Nzema[2] indigenous religious philosophy

Genevieve Nrenzah

Introduction

An earlier happenstance involving me and drawing my attention to the link between a woman's vagina and her healing abilities in Nzema raised questions that prompted this chapter.[3] After the encounter, my subsequent research revealed that the Nzema viewed the vagina as a spiritually charged part of a woman's body. It is the locus of the sacred process that creates human beings. Because a woman has a vagina, she is able to participate with God in the creation of another human. I wondered about the power of the female in traditional African societies; if African communities believe women have such spiritual powers, what has happened to this power through the times and the vagina's current so talked about deprecation. Tracing the trajectory of Nzema ideas about the vagina from pre-colonial days to the present, this chapter offers an account of the history of religious ideas about the *todɔlɛ* (vagina hereafter) from its celebrated past to the decline in the respect for it in the present times. I argue that Nzema beliefs about the vagina are social commentaries on the power of the female. The decline in the fortunes of the vagina and the subsequent violence implied in popular notions about the vagina therefore parallel women's loss of power in post-colonial Nzema society. I will illustrate my argument with empirical data and draw on an array of text and song genres.

The vagina in indigenous Nzema thinking

Nzema women have always occupied important positions in both the social–religious and political terrains. Religion in African societies

> provides people with a language that they use to express their realities. For the Nzema, society's appreciation of the crucial roles that the female plays in society finds expression in a variety of religious beliefs featuring and celebrating the power [of women].
>
> (Nrenzah, 2008: 37)

Pre-colonial Nzema communities linked women to "earth":

> The Nzemas describe the earth, without which human life is practically
> impossible, as a female spirit called Azele Yaba. Azale Yaba is sometimes
> referred to as abrewa or "old woman." Azele Yaba ranks next to God
> and is in a class of her own as she is not an oracular deity like the other
> lesser deities [awozonle, singular bozonle] whom people may consult
> in times of crisis. As humans are essentially created with clay in Nzema
> religious thinking, it is said that Azele Yaba is the one from whom
> humans emerge. Also, her bowels are the final resting place of humans.
> Thursday is a special day set aside for her and on these days there is no
> tilling of the land because she is resting. Severe punishment was meted
> in the past to whoever infringed this taboo. Azele Yaba is also the cus-
> todian of morality. She is a keen upholder of truth and whenever the
> veracity of a statement is in doubt the person who made the statement
> is challenged to touch the tip of his tongue with some earth to prove
> that he/ she is telling the truth. Azale Yaba abhors the spilling of human
> blood – wherever murder occurs she has to be appeased. When angered,
> Azele Yaba becomes a killer mother who unleashes untold calamities on
> a community.
>
> (Nrenzah, 2008: 38)

This view reflects the place of the mothers as the primary transmitters of
moral values in Nzema homes and society, who do not hesitate to unleash
the severest form of punishment such as spanking, denial of meat, or pep-
pering of the buttocks of recalcitrant children.

Again, there is a strong affinity between the woman and water in African
religious beliefs. For the Nzema, social commentaries on the indispensability
of the woman in relation to her role in society's origination are condensed in
analogies between the woman and water.

> Both women and water sources are the originators of human commu-
> nities. Just as women originate a person's life by giving birth, so are
> the beginnings of towns and villages determined by the presence of a
> water source. As nurturers of life, women are just like water upon which
> society depends for their sources of food to grow. Just as water cools
> and calms the body on a very hot day or is a softening agent, so do
> women contribute to the peaceful coexistence of members in homes and
> in larger Nzema society as the crucial mediators and negotiators during
> conflict among individuals or groups.
>
> (Nrenzah, 2008: 39)

The supreme God or *Nyamele*, though male, is sometimes cast in a female
role as *Obaatampa* in Nzema religious thinking. A libation prayer goes:
"*Eradane kpale, mame mo oma amaa aleye* [mother who gives food], *Mame*

mo abo ama awo bane [mother who protects], *Obaatampa*." This can be translated literally as "the ideal woman who knows what her children would eat and provides for them without their asking, the woman who clothes her children, takes care of them and protects them when they are ill." The providential aspect of God in this prayer is described in terms of a female, shedding light on Nzema ideas about women as providers.

As the core of this chapter rests on the woman's body, the vagina, I will now focus attention on it. The sense of power associated with women in traditional or pre-colonial Nzema is reflected in the awe, respect, and reverence accorded the vagina. The vagina has a special spiritual significance, according to Nzema beliefs. In the creation of a human, *Edenkema Nyamele* donates a soul that is the source of breath, a father donates a spirit that determines the person's personality, and a mother donates the blood[4] [or body] that encases all the other elements and without which a person cannot function. The "womb which is in Nzema thinking an extension of the vagina is the locus of this creative process and the passage through which the created being emerges while making an entry into the world."[5] The vagina then is a source of life – the place where all humans began. It is the part of the female's body that benefits from the direct experience with the hand of God in the creation of the human. For this reason, the vagina is considered to be sacred. This sense of sacredness was reflected in a number of different ways.

The vagina can only be mentioned in euphemisms and never directly during conversation. Indirect references such as "yourself," "the place," "woman hood," or "the woman" are used to preserve the sacredness of the vagina. Referring to it by its name in public profanes the woman and her vagina. It is also said that if *Edenkema* equipped the vagina with powers to create life, he also gave it powers to protect life, so the vagina is considered to be endowed with medicinal properties. The urine of a female, because of its contact with the vagina, has the power to heal and neutralize the effect of evil charms.

In pre-colonial times, the spiritual power of the vagina was pressed into service to ensure the security of the state during war. Obeng and Akyeampong describe the ritual of "*mmomomme*," a distinct type of spiritual warfare involving the use of female power among Akans, of which Nzemas are a part (Akyeampong and Obeng, 1995: 492). According to these two authors, in pre-colonial times, during warfare, while the men were on the battlefield, the women in the village would chant daily, marching in partial nudity (exposing their vaginas) from one end of the village to the other, until the soldiers, their children, returned. This ritual was meant to protect the soldiers at war mystically. Sometimes the rituals involved the partially nude women pounding empty mortars with pestles as a form of spiritual torture of the state's enemies (Akyeampong, and Obeng, 1995: 494). In fact, the belief in witchcraft – *ayene*[6] – is a reflection of the fear society has of the female's spiritual power. Sometimes it is said that a woman's witchcraft power is located in her vagina.

In the pre-colonial past, the vagina was always covered, even when the breast of a woman was exposed. Even in modern Ghana, a woman faced with the choice between covering the breast or the vagina from exposure to male eyes would choose to cover the vagina – to protect its sacredness. It is a repository of supernatural power as the source of life, and its exposure in public could unleash curses on those, especially male, eyes that saw it. Aben-lima, an elderly woman in Half Assini, told me of how an angry woman who wanted to curse a male that offended her could simple untie her loincloth, exposing the vagina to him. A chain of misfortunes may befall such a person if the appropriate remedies are not taken to revoke the effect of the curse. The idea here is that a power source that creates can also be deployed for destructive purposes.

The vagina was not seen as a part of the body to be toyed with and men were not encouraged to view it in the act of sex with women. The most ideal context for sex then was in the dark, in which condition it would be difficult for the eyes of a man to see the vagina of a woman.[7] It was said that only the eyes of a penis can see a vagina's opening. To taste the vagina in a sensual way was also considered a privilege of the male that proved himself worthy of it by waiting to reach the appropriate age. There is a proverb that spells out the concept: "Penis that does not die young will have the privilege of tasting bearded meat." Sex between children, then, was an abomination not only because it might lead to child pregnancy but also because it is insulting to the vagina for a boy – who has not reached the appropriate age – to taste of it. The language of sexual intercourse reflected the respect for the vagina. Thus, it was said of a man who slept with a woman that he lay with her – or "they met," pointing to the culture of negotiations between equals that often preceded coitus.

So sacred was the vagina considered to be that it could not be opened except the day after a woman rightfully married. Thus, a virginity test was performed on that day to ensure that a vagina had not been used or pro-faned before that day. The virgin and her new husband would proceed to a room specifically prepared for them. They would have sex on a bed laid with white sheets. If the hymen broke and blood from the vagina soiled the bed sheet, the young man would scream in joy. Happy observers would rush in and carry the woman shoulder high and parade her through the streets joyfully.[8]

There was no such thing as prostitution as it is described today based on a transaction involving the exchange of money for the purpose of sexually consuming a woman's vagina. It was too sacred for its benefits to be exchanged for any profane object. Through the performance of certain

> sacred rituals involving the vagina, certain women in a village were transformed into public wives. The community would build a home for them in the center of the village and provide adequately for them. Any

man who felt the need to satisfy a sexual urge could go and negotiate with any public wife.[9]

Sex would take place only when the public wife consented. Although consecrated and made a public wife, she had rights over the usage of her vagina and chose who she wished to share it with. Married men were not to enjoy such benefits – only widowers and men who had attained marriageable ages but not yet found a wife could enjoy those facilities.

Menstrual blood is said to have superior spiritual powers that can neutralize other supernatural power sources. Thus, a "ritual specialist must not come near a menstruating woman, neither should a menstruating woman visit the shrine of priests until their cycle of flow ends,"[10] lest the power of the indigenous priest/priestess be contaminated or ineffectual by the menstrual blood because of its higher potency. Komle Bomo stressed on this very issue saying that:

> Sometimes when a person is brought here with a swollen or burning leg, I divine to diagnose the cause of the problem if it is found out that he has stepped on juju or evil medicine, I make my assistant look for a woman in her period to urinate on the leg outside the shrine, she will keep urinating till the pain/burning subside before I add herbs to heal the wounds if there is any.[11]

The blood and the "urine from a female is infused with medicinal abilities because of its contact with the vagina."[12] It is believed that these attributes made women spiritual and often venerated. The Nzema hold the vagina in high esteem because of its special spiritual significance. According to Nzema beliefs, this is where all life begins and is also the "door" through which humans pass as they descend from heaven to earth to begin their lives as babies. For this reason, the vagina is sacred. Other cultures have similar views about the vagina. Raitt asserts that the vagina "dentata" or the vagina with teeth is an ancient, widely known, if not widely discussed, mythical theme; it is one of the most basic notions underlying men's fear of women (Raitt, 1980: 416) that the toothed vagina has the ability of consuming, injuring or castrating a man. This fear of what it entails made men press for the removal of the teeth as a form of control over the sexuality and spirituality of the woman. This act of removing the teeth or clitoris is also performed in the northern and some part of the Brong-Ahafo regions of Ghana, and though it is criminal and has been banned recently, it is believed that it is still being done secretly. However, what we seek to point out is that is, among the Nzema, the woman and for that matter the vagina were venerated and celebrated in pre-colonial times, partly because of the spirituality associated with woman but also because of the social roles they played at the time. The worth, ability, and sexuality of women would decline with the introduction of colonialism. I turn my attention to this development in the next section.

Colonialism and Nzema women's power

During the second half of the fifteenth century, the Portuguese came to West Africa and landed in what is now Ghana, which they christened the Gold Coast. The idea of trading brought different European nations, such as the "Danish, French, Dutch and the English" (Omenyo, 2006: 14). Trade in goods turned into trade in humans – the slave trade – and finally the establishment of direct rule by the British. With colonialism came Christianity and the introduction of Western gender ideologies into Nzema society. Everything from the socio-cultural, political, and religious lives of the people were changed, tampered with, or destroyed to suit the colonial administration. The

> structural changes that were introduced by the imposition of colonial rule resulted in women being dislocated from the socio-economic spaces they had occupied as traders, owners of lands and farms, to name only a few, and placed them in domestic roles where they lost the power they hitherto held in society.
>
> (Nrenzah, 2008: 47)

Again, the introduction of modern medical practices and facilities replaced the need for traditional healers and midwives, roles that women had been charged with filling in pre-colonial times. Male-controlled Western-originated medicine attempted to supplant the need for rituals and sacrifices the women had previously undertaken for the welfare of their communities. My point here is that colonialism resulted in the loss of women's influence in both the social and religious worlds of the Nzema. A typical instance is the new vocation (white-collar jobs) the British introduced. In the "synod and district councils, men occupied the seats. Positions of priest belonged only to men in colonial Christian Africa" (Nrenzah, 2008: 47). A patriarchal British society plus an androcentric Christian religion that recognized and celebrated the male and men within its ranks replaced the feminine principle in Nzema religion where the active and "prominent role women have traditionally played in political, economic and religious as well as the domestic spheres" (Oppong et al., 1975: 71) was not encouraged. Historically, we have had courageous "political women like Nana Dokua, queen mother of Akyem Abuakwa, Yaa Asantewaa queen mother of Edweso and Naa Dedei of the Ga State,"[13] but the worth, ability, and sexuality of women would decline with the introduction of colonialism. For example, Ghanaian women in pre-colonial period were independent. "This stems from our traditional concept of marriage. British culture and laws dictated that married couples became one person after the execution of the marriage contract";[14] what is more, when Ghanaians became "British" owing to colonialism, women's education rights were cut off as fathers now decided for their female children. Boys went to school and girls stayed home to help with chores to fulfill what became the "new tradition"; if they were privileged enough to be in school, the highest they could attain was to become a caterer, teacher, or nurse. Nzema women were removed from their socio-religious locations, where they exhibited power that they had previously held in the pre-colonial religious order. This is reiterated by Christine Oppong and others that the 1960s and 1970s Ghana census showed limited women in higher education (Oppong et al., 1975: 71). One thing we poignantly wish to point out is that Christianity is shaped by the cultures of wherever it finds itself; unfortunately, the Christianity that was brought to Ghana was wrapped in European culture. The missionaries did not leave room for local religious dialogue; for them, the Africans did not have a religion and there was no need to negotiate. Instead, their task was to "clean" the Africans of their barbarism and fill them with civilized religious culture and socio-political living. They were in a hurry to "rescue the perishing." The missionary-established churches introduced the idea of God as a male, which replaced the Nzema bisexual notion of "*Nyamenle Eradane kpale.*"[15] The male was at the helm of affairs on both the political and religious front, and Ghanaians who were under colonial domination had no choice but to learn and behave like their master. It is said that Christian theology was developed by men. They wrote theology; they were the heads and preachers in the churches and therefore put their stamp of authority on it and on the women, too. Men defined women, in what Fausto-Sterling calls a "legal interest in maintaining only two sex system" (Fausto-Sterling, 2000: 45), in an attempt to control the bodies of women and society as a whole. They defined the sexes to be male and female, leaving out for example the hermaphrodites who could have also formed a category of sex. Beauvoir argues that "one is not born a woman; one becomes one. Women became the other defined by men and patriarchy and consequently they are less than fully human" (Beauvoir, 1949/1972: 46). There is a sense in which Beauvoir assertion that men defined women fits the then and current states of women, for men were in control and dominantly so now and what they willed counted and not the women even if they are against it. This structure worked for other societies, but the variety and complexity of African cultures makes it tough to define who a woman is. Hafkin and Bay, for example, have said the decade that followed successful women suffrage in the West and Europe, they turned attention to Africa to liberate them as well, suggesting that "a greater number of indigenous societies (in Africa) reserve for women a place which is clearly inferior, approaching that of a domestic animal" (Hafkin and Bay, 1976: 2). Most often than not women are perceived as inferior to men and must as such occupy a subordinate place. Where they rise above their sexuality to occupy higher positions, they are alleged to have been thereby favors from men This is the thinking now, when in actual sense women had power in precolonial African societies. People think colonialism rather brought alleviation to women but Hafkin and Bay think otherwise, they have asserted that "recent scholarship suggested that the colonial impact, far from liberating African women actually diminished the prerogative and rights they formerly enjoyed" (Hafkin and Bay 1976: 4). Issue is, the plight of women in other societies cannot be the same. Who a woman is or how she got to the position she is occupying in a particular society is not same and must not be generalized. Roles of women are different in the diverse African communities – bearing in mind the roles of women in pre-colonial Africa societies and even to date. We can therefore suggest that the definition of a woman is more Western in orientation; that is why Haraway suggested that

> any effort to define the essence of any particular racial, gender, class, or ethnic group becomes problematic: it requires excluding some, and including others; it provokes accusations of political impurity and dubious genealogies; it leads to fights for the higher, more righteous ground of political truth . . . the proposition that we are all hybrids – offers a way to give up the effort to define the "real nature of women" or of any person, animal or thing,
>
> (Haraway, 1991: 152)

In this context, the definition of a woman could be more meaningful if we glean insight into the lives of some women by adopting a perspective that studies a particular group rather than lumping the experiences of women all over the world together. What we want to particularly stress here is that colonialism somehow took some of the roles of women and rendered woman "secondary," as the "new colonized" Ghanaian had to do what the colonial master did in order to be like them "somewhat," and that rendered women redundant and functioning sometimes only behind a man. These were vestiges of colonialism. The issue then is, did it change after colonialism? Next, we discuss post-colonial Nzema.

The vagina in post-colonial Nzema

We discussed the loss of Nzema women's power during the colonial and Christian era in Ghana. It must be noted that the woman in this discussion refers to everything about a woman, including her vagina. The earlier submission was that colonialism broke down the various functions of women, but that was not all. Presently, in modern Nzema society, it would seem that the vagina is losing its indigenous sense of power and respect. It has become one of the most disparaged parts of the female anatomy in popular Nzema imagination. Nowadays, there are numerous negative socio-cultural representations of the vagina and its functions in Ghana and among the Nzema, to be more specific. I have identified the following themes underlying the negative constructions of the vagina in popular Ghanaian culture: the vagina as an economic venture, the vagina as inferior to the penis, the vagina as absence, the vagina as a passive receptacle for the penis, the vagina as vulnerable and abused, the vagina as sexually inadequate, the vagina as disgusting, and the vagina as dangerous (Berer, 2001: 7–8).

During colonialism, the introduction of a modern exchange economy based on money spread to other facets of society. The woman and her vagina became a commodity that could be bought and consumed by anyone with the money to pay for it. Prostitution became a very lucrative business. This included males who in traditional society would be considered underage and therefore not worthy of enjoying the benefits of "bearded meat" [vagina]. The vagina became easily accessible. The commoditization of the vagina translated into a loss in the sense of sacredness that had been accorded it in the past. Nowhere is this loss of respect for the vagina more poignantly demonstrated than in the following song by the "vandal choir,"[16] a male hall of the University of Ghana called Commonwealth Hall, which depicts it as an economic venture.

(Twi) εtwe, εtwe, εtwe, εtwe,
εtwe so hwin, be gye wo bronya adie 2x
medo Nyame ɔwo soro se εma gyi won pe sika
εma, ema, ema gyi won twe pe sika

Vagina, vagina, vagina, vagina
Oh bearded vagina, come for your Christmas gift. 2 xs.
I swear to God, women are using their vagina to get rich.
Women, women are using their vagina for money.

In the next song below, the singers, who are mainly males, are threatening to inflict pain on a young woman. The mechanism is rape and the vagina is the channel through which this will be effected. The song expresses the tendency of some males in Ghanaian society to feel more masculine by the pain that they inflict on a woman during sexual intercourse. Young Ghanaian males would often boast "if you fuck a girl and she scream in pain then you are a man."[17] The vagina has become a part of the female body that renders her vulnerable to male violence.

In this second song, the vagina is cast as the passive party during sexual intercourse, expressing the commonplace Ghanaian notion that a woman's role during sex is to "lie there and receive a male's penis."

(Twi) Tukoro bi na εda hɔ te se elastic
Kote koshye mu a ema abae
Sεε na εyε εtwe

There is a hole like elastic
When the penis is inserted, it opens up
It is the vagina.

In the song, the vagina "receives" what seems like a large penis and is extended as a result. The encounter is described more as a violent intrusion of the female body than a play between a willing male and female. The vagina has become an item commonly violently used in insults – *wo mame twe*, meaning your mother's vagina; *wo mame twe apro* – your mother's rotten vagina; *wo mame twe ba* – your mother's clitoris – insults that in the past would have attracted downright banishment from the community.

Nowadays, the spirituality of the vagina is viewed in a negative light. It has become an object of fear as perceived in "vagina dentata (teeth in the vagina)" (International Dictionary of Psychoanalysis, 2017), something men are supposed to be wary of. Again, tales float around in Nzema villages of females washing their vaginas, especially during their menses, into soups as love potions to entrap unsuspecting men; so too are numerous versions of stories told of female traders with snakes in their vaginas that supposedly suck the seminal fluid of men and transform this into money. The vagina is still spiritual – but its powers are supposed to be deployed negatively, reflecting a loss of the status of females in the post-colony as compared to their status in pre-colonial Nzema. Even the images used in describing sex in post-colonial Ghana reflect a new sense of the vagina as a commodity that could be owned and consumed by males. Men use expression such as to "chop," to "dig," or to "finish." He finished her, he dug her, and he chopped her, reflecting the asymmetrical nature of the relationship between male and female in the post-colony and the tendency of males who occupied positions of power to exploit the sexuality of their female subordinates. Males began to prey upon females. The vagina and the penis ceased to be partners. The penis became the hunter and the vagina the hunted. The words in the above songs, for instance, reflect a male proclivity for inflicting violence on women using the vagina as a medium.

In conclusion, we have highlighted that the negative representations have implications for a woman's dignity and her place in society, and we have pointed that the dignity of the woman in the pre-colonial Nzema imagination has suffered a decline in the colonial and post-colonial periods. The female has lost power, and so too is the symbolic representation of her power, the vagina, losing respect. There are portrayals of violence against the woman's vagina in modern day Ghana in pictures of women in magazines, music videos shown on TV, and themes in movies, just to mention a few, though we see it now more as polished, it is imperative that we state that the Nzema society, and for that matter Ghanaian society, is an ever-changing one. New opportunities are emerging and providing spaces for women to regain their power bases in the various religious and secular cultures. The question we need to still probe in the progress so far is whether the image of the vagina is becoming more positive now that women are regaining power or whether it is deteriorating.

Notes

1 Todɔlɛ simply means vagina in Nzema language.
2 The Nzema are a part of the largest ethnic groups in Ghana called the Akan. They occupy the extreme southwestern part of Ghana, extending in some places beyond the border into Ivory Coast. Some Nzemas live along the Atlantic coast

and others in the forest belt bordering this coastline. Traditionally they were farmers and fishermen.

3 I was 20 years old and as a favorite of my grandmother – Nana Bene – when I would go to the village during school vacations, I would accompany her to her stall in the market to sell her items on Tuesdays and Saturdays, which were the main market days. It was during one such trip to the market that I was introduced to a local discourse and practice relating to women and their healing powers through an experience. I had stepped on an object and suddenly a burning sensation ran through my left foot. "It is evil medicine," my grandmother said. "It may have been placed there for someone else and you stepped on it accidentally. Let's get help," she said. We quickened our pace and dashed into the market . . . "Which of you is in her menses, please come and urinate on Mame Homa's foot for me, she just stepped on bad medicine," my grandmother screamed. I looked on, puzzled, not knowing what to do or think. Suddenly an elderly woman emerged from behind her wares in a stall, tied a cloth around her waist, and urinated on my foot. Encouraged by this act, other women took turns to urinate on my foot. Suddenly the burning sensation went away and I felt no pain in my foot any longer.

Genevieve Nrenzah, "Inventing indigenous religious belief and practice within the spaces of Ghanaian Pentecostalism: The Mame Wata healing churches of Half Assini" (MA Thesis presented to Florida International University, 2008), 1.
4 Komle Somia Nyamekeh, interview by Genevieve Nrenzah, August 15, 2008.
5 Nana Benee, interview by Genevieve Nrenzah, August 1, 2008.
6 Witch or wizard.
7 Mamaa, interview by Genevieve Nrenzah, August 1, 2008.
8 Komle Somia Nyamekeh, interview by Genevieve Nrenzah, April 24, 2012.
9 Efrisane, interview by Genevieve Nrenzah, April 20, 2012.
10 Nana Kwaku Bonsam, interview by Genevieve Nrenzah, February 10, 2013.
11 Komle Bomo, interview by Genevieve Nrenzah, July 15, 2008.
12 Komle Bomo, interview by Genevieve Nrenzah, July 15, 2008.
13 Women's Rights Recognized in Colonial Ghana? www.hracghana.org.
14 Women's Rights Recognized in Colonial Ghana? www.hracghana.org.
15 God, the good mother.
16 Vandal is the nickname for one of the male halls at University of Ghana. The real name of the hall is Commonwealth.
17 Yaw Barima, interview by Genevieve Nrenzah, April 15, 2015.

References

Akyeampong, Emmanuel and Pashington Obeng, 1995. "Spirituality, Gender and Power in Asante History" *The International Journal of African Historical Studies*, Vol. 28, No. 3: 492.

Berer, Marge. 2001. "Images, Reproductive Health and the Collateral Damage to Women of Fundamentalism and War in Images of Sexuality and Reproduction Services: Meeting Women's Needs." *Reproductive Health Matters*, Vol. 9, No. 18: 6–11.

Beauvoir, Simone de. 1972. *The Second Sex* (translated by H. M. Parshley). Harmondsworth: Penguin.

Fausto-Sterling, Anne. 2000. *Sexing the Body: Gender Politics and the Construction of Sexuality*. New York: Basic Books, 45.

Hafkin, Nancy J. and Bay, Edna G. 1976. Introduction. In *Women in Africa: Studies in Social and Economic Change*. (eds) Hafkin, Nancy J. and Bay, Edna G. Stanford, CA: Stanford University Press, 1–18.

Haraway, Donna J. Simians. 1991. "A Cyborg Manifesto Science, Technology, and Socialist-Feminism in the Late Twentieth Century." In Donna J. Harawa, ed. *Simians, Cyborgs And Women: The Reinvention of Nature.* New York: Routledge, 149–181.

Nrenzah, Genevieve. 2008. *Inventing indigenous religious belief and practice within the spaces of Ghanaian Pentecostalism: The Mame Wata healing churches of Half Assini.* A Thesis Submitted to Florida International University in partial fulfilment of a Masters in Religious Studies, https://digitalcommons.fiu.edu/etd/1564/

Omenyo, Cephas Narh, 2002. *Pentecost Outside Pentecostalism: A Study of the Development of Charismatic Renewal in Mainline Churches in Ghana.* Zoetermeer: Boekencentrum.

Oppong, Christine, Okali, Christine and Houghton, Beverley. 1975. "Woman Power: Retrograde Steps in Ghana." *African Studies Review*, Vol. 18, No. 3: 71–84.

Raitt, Jill. 1980. "The Vagina Dentata and the Imamaculatas Utterus Divini Fontis." *Journal of the American Academy of Religion*, Vol. 48, No. 3: 416.

12 A critical engagement of *botho/ubuntu* and Mt 25:35 in the debate on the provision of antiretroviral drugs to cross-border migrants in Botswana

Rosinah Mmannana Gabaitse and
Simangaliso Raymond Kumalo

Introduction

This chapter discusses the implications, claims, and relevance of practicing *botho/ubuntu* as well as applying Mt 25:35–36 in the context of global migration and HIV. We focus on Botswana, a country that calls itself a Christian country but also practices and embodies the values of *botho/ubuntu*. Botswana has made good progress in the fight against HIV/AIDS. Information and education about HIV and AIDS are made available in print and social and electronic media. There are free testing centers throughout the country in urban and rural areas, and most importantly, antiretroviral drugs (ARVs) are free and accessible for all citizens of Botswana. Because of the efforts of government and non-government organizations, rates of HIV infections and mortality rates have gone down significantly over the years. However, the country has failed in the global fight against HIV because Botswana's health policy denies cross-border migrants access to HIV services and treatment. Migrants affected by this policy are the undocumented ones who have already been exposed to different sorts of vulnerabilities because of their illegal status. Although there is no active hostility towards cross-border migrants in Botswana, and although Botswana has a good and progressive refugee policy, the health policy is repressive towards migrants because it is designed to exclude and discriminate against them. Hence, in this chapter we seek to discuss how *botho/ubuntu* and the ethic of care of the stranger alluded to in Mt 25:35–36 can be utilized as a resource for persuading and convincing the Botswanan and African governments to offer ARVs to cross-border migrants.[1] *Botho/ubuntu*, Matt 25:35–36, and their values are significant for engaging governments to make HIV treatment available to cross-border migrants. *Botho* is revered in Botswana as an indigenous text to the Batswana value system, and Matt 25:35–36 fits well in this debate because of the very simple reason that Botswana calls herself a Christian nation, and the Bible is the only sacred text used in policy formulation, presidential inaugurations, the swearing in of judges, and the passing of laws.

Further, engaging with these two reveals the irony of Batswana existence, a country known for its peace and good governance and a people known for their extreme kindness and compassion, who nevertheless fail to extend that compassion to migrants who need HIV treatment.

Botswana, migration, and denial of HIV treatment

Botswana is a landlocked Southern African country with a population of 2.2 million people. It is surrounded by Namibia, South Africa, and Zimbabwe.[2] It has been characterized by political stability since its independence from Britain in 1966 and good governance, with a thriving economy due to natural resources like diamonds and the best wilderness and wildlife resources on the African continent.[3] The Global Peace Index (GPI) 2015 ranks Botswana as one of the most peaceful countries in Africa, the second after Mauritius. Despite all its glory, Botswana has not been hospitable towards cross-border migrants, the majority of whom are Africans, especially Zimbabweans.[4] Because of the political instability in Zimbabwe, economic and health care systems, among others, collapsed (Chirongoma, 2006). As a result, Zimbabweans fled to neighboring countries such as South Africa and Botswana in search of economic opportunities and means of survival. As a result, Botswana is host to thousands of legal and illegal migrants from Zimbabwe as well as from other African countries such as Sudan and Congo, among others (Reitzes, 1997). Data from the International Organization for Migration indicate that the documented migrant population of Botswana made up 7.10% of Botswana's 2015 population of 2 million.[5] The volume had increased by 2017, in addition to the undocumented migrants who enter the country through un-gazetted border points.[6] We are not so much interested in the number of cross-border migrants in Botswana as in how they are treated by the host country/countries and how their health needs are met.

Cross-border migrants have numerous challenges and needs, including health needs, with the treatment for HIV and its opportunistic infections at the top. This is not at all surprising given the context of high rates of HIV infection in Southern Africa. This is not to suggest that HIV prevalence is higher among cross-border migrants; in fact, HIV prevalence is higher in Swaziland and Botswana. In Batswana, 21.1% are living with the HIV virus, and 84% of those infected are on ARVs.[7] However, the citizens of Batswana have access to HIV treatment and cross-border migrants do not. This is unfortunate because the negative effect of immigration on health indicates that migration generates possibilities for stress leading to ill health, exacerbated by unfriendly health policies, threats of violence, and poor integration. Therefore, HIV positive cross-border migrants may need more urgent medical attention than a citizen who is also HIV positive because the new environment might provoke a weakened immune system.[8]

Botswana's government has made all health services in public government clinics and hospitals free for all citizens, i.e. treatment of all ailments such as cancer and diabetes are free. However, health services are not free for migrants, whether legal or not. Accessing health care services for migrants is rigid for general ailments and impossible for HIV treatment. For all ailments, legal cross-border migrants pay a fee at public government hospitals, and they cannot be treated before the fee is paid.[9] After they are attended to by the doctors, they pay for medication at the pharmacy before it is dispersed. However, cross-border migrants can never buy ARVs from government pharmacies because it is illegal for ARVs to be sold to migrants. While citizens of Botswana access them for free, cross-border migrants cannot because, according to the ministry of health, ARVs are expensive and migrant populations are overwhelming to such a degree that making ARVs available to migrants is not economically sustainable.[10] As a result, cross-border migrants, especially illegal ones who live with HIV, who have opportunistic infections, some critical, and are in need of treatment cannot freely access treatment. As a result, there are numerous reports that suggest that ARVs are stolen from pharmacies to be sold on the black market. Legal middle- to high-class migrants who have employment within government and private sectors can buy medical insurance, which they can use to subsidize their supply of ARVs only at privately owned clinics and hospitals, but at extremely high prices.[11] The ability to purchase ARVs for legal migrants is complex because they must go through rigorous health background and tedious screening before they are admitted into the medical insurance to determine if they had HIV prior to migration. This denial of ARV is not only a denial of their right to health and life but also a demonstration of a lack of *botho/ubuntu* from the people of Botswana, who have failed to extend and exercise hospitality and generosity towards the stranger, and a failure to manifest the core principles and values espoused in Mt 25: 35–36.

Defining *botho/ubuntu*

Botho in Tswana, *ubuntu* in Zulu, and *unhu* or *hunhu* in Shona carry the same meaning.[12] *Botho* has its roots in the term *motho*, and *ubuntu* has its roots in *umuntu* (Zulu); in both languages, the term refers to a person, a human being. As a result of their deep roots, *botho* and *ubuntu* are not just words but also an indigenous concept revered even today, as they communicate an African philosophy, ethic, spirituality, moral compass, and culture that convey deep meanings translated into actions that are associated with good manners, solidarity, shared humanity, and generosity. *Botho/ubuntu* are indigenous texts embodied in the lived realities and ways of life of Africans and are performed daily through acts of mercy, love, justice, mutuality, interdependence, care, and the interconnectedness of human beings. In the specific context of Botswana, *botho* is all of the above in addition to being a principle that guides men, women, and children in their daily dealing with other people, situations, and the environment.[13]

Desmond Tutu admits that *ubuntu* is very difficult to render into Western language the closest equivalent of the word means that, "my humanity is caught up, is inextricably bound up, in what is yours" (Tutu, 1999:35). Tutu further says that

> a person with Ubuntu is open and available to others, affirming of others, does not feel threatened that others are able and good, based from a proper self-assurance that comes from knowing that he or she belongs in a greater whole and is diminished when others are humiliated or diminished, when others are tortured or oppressed.
>
> (Tutu, 1999: 35)

During his speech at the Ubuntu women Institute in 2008, Tutu offered yet another explanation of *botho/ubuntu* as

> the essence of being human. Ubuntu speaks particularly about the fact that you can't exist as a human being in isolation. It speaks about our interconnectedness. You can't be human all by yourself, and when you have this quality – Ubuntu – you are known for your generosity.[14]

Tutu's assertion of *ubuntu* is complimented by Nelson Mandela, who emphasized the interdependence of humanity for their success when he said that

> in Africa there is a concept known as "ubuntu" – the profound sense that we are human only through the humanity of others; that if we are to accomplish anything in this world it will in equal measure be due to the work and achievement of others.[15]

Mandela and Tutu attempt to capture the concept of *botho/ubuntu* in a way that demonstrates *botho/ubuntu* is not only a philosophy and ethic but also a recognition of the existence of other people other than an individual, in that to live a meaningful life is to recognize and be in solidarity with others in need through acts of care, kindness, compassion, mercy, justice, mutuality, and dependence. In the specific context of Botswana, we say *motho ke motho ka batho*, the Zulu equivalent of *umuntu ngumuntu ngabantu* – meaning, "I in you and you in me," "I am because we are," "I exist because you exist" and "your burdens are mine." *Botho/ubuntu* evokes communal and egalitarian existence; no individual and no community can exist without the other and outside the values of care, generosity, and hospitality.

In their famous book, *Hunhuism or Ubuntuism: A Zimbabwe Indigenous Political Philosophy* (1980), Stanlake Samkange and Tommie Samkange highlight three characteristics of a human being guided by the principles of *botho* or *ubuntu*, two of which we find helpful for discussions about the health of migrants globally and in Botswana. They write that "to be human is to affirm one's humanity by recognizing the humanity of others and, on that basis, establish respectful human relations with them" (Samkange & Samkange 1980: 6). The second characteristic of *botho/ubuntu* is that "when a person is forced to make a choice between wealth and the preservation of the life of another human being, then one should opt for the preservation of life" (Samkange & Samkange 1980): They confirm Mandela and Tutu's definition and description of *botho/ubuntu*: first, that *botho/ubuntu* is or should be a way of life for Africans. Second, it is enacted, performed, and lived in African day-to-day actions, feelings, and thinking such that in the *botho/ubuntu* framework, all human beings regardless of race and ethnicity are affirmed. Third, preservation of human life is more important than accumulation of wealth and riches. Lastly, the way human beings treat each other is a measure of whether one has *botho/ubuntu* or not. A person who is not open to others and is selfish, greedy, and stingy is said to be without *botho*.[16] A good Tswana description of that person would be *ga ana botho*, meaning he/she is without humanness. A person who opens their house to orphans, widows, and strangers in need has *botho*, i.e. he or she possesses the desirable, positive, and loving qualities of an ideal human being. A person like that is often praised and desired within the African *botho/ubuntu* worldview. Therefore, *botho/ubuntu* are deeply felt as they almost dictate and encourage acts of generosity among human beings.

Lovemore Mbigi (1997) demonstrates that *botho/ubuntu* in different African societies encouraged the ethic of care for strangers, widows, orphans, and the poor. Mbigi confirms that

> when you call at an African home, you are immediately made to feel welcome. There is instant hospitality. You are invited into the house and given food, drink or water as a token of the spirit of hospitality.
>
> (1997: 5)

According to Mbigi's submission, generosity, hospitality, and kindness and acceptance of other ethnic groups and races were central to the *botho/ubuntu* worldview, and these were extended with no expectation of payback. These were extended to persons not related by blood through recognizing the value and dignity of a person and making them feel at home in a foreign land. Hence, within the ideal *botho/ubuntu* worldview, vulnerable people would never go hungry or suffer because the community derived pleasure in taking the responsibility of caring for them. Taking care of these vulnerable ones was what defined the community members' humanity: their ability to be moved and respond adequately to need. Therefore, the presence of *botho/ubuntu* is characterized by acts of selflessness, deep compassion, generosity, hospitality, kindness, sharing, caring, good manners, connection, dignity, solidarity, and harmony, and these should be extended to persons near and far. In the *botho/ubuntu* worldview, no human being must be allowed to suffer from hunger and illness. In Zulu there is a saying, *umuntu akalahlwa*, meaning that you don't give up on any human being's life, regardless of who they are.

The darker side of *botho/ubuntu*

Impulses of *botho/ubuntu* are easily exhibited and upheld when people are at peace with no external threats, and so *botho/ubuntu* is ambivalent at times.[17] Because it is the foundation of ethics, morality, and law, *botho/ubuntu* has been blamed for the domination and marginalization of women, children, gays and lesbians. Several African scholars have unmasked *botho/ubuntu*'s not so positive side by exposing its ambivalence. For example, Dick Louw argues that *botho/ubuntu* detests difference. He writes that

> although it articulates such important values as respect, human dignity and compassion, *ubuntu* has a darker, negative side to it . . . it demands an oppressive conformity and loyalty to the group. And failure to conform will be met by harsh punitive measures.[18]

Although communal identity versus individual identity is one of the strengths of *botho/ubuntu*, it can also be its weakness, as individuals who do not conform to communal identity can be oppressed. Therefore, Louw is right in his observation because the *botho/ubuntu* worldview does not have tolerance for people whose sexual preferences fall outside the tenets of heterosexuality. They are often undermined, abhorred, and ostracized in most African societies as those lacking *botho*. Further, constitutions in Africa are drafted to exclude and marginalize such human beings, although those constitutions are drafted within communities defined by *botho/ubuntu*. In addition, *botho/ubuntu* co-exists with patriarchy in promoting hierarchical relations between men and women that lead to the marginalization and/or exclusion of women and girl children. Magadla and Chitando observe that *ubuntu*'s ambivalence allows it to be "owned by the perpetrators of gender violence as well as advocates of gender justice," because "there is a space in which to claim and use *ubuntu* in order to advocate for the reinvention of violent masculinity" (Magadla and Chitando, 2014: 190). Elsewhere, Chitando elaborates on how *botho/ubuntu* is implicated in supporting the marginalization of women. He writes that

> whereas *Ubuntu* expresses the notion that, "I am because we are, and we are because I am," in practice, the personhood in African cultures has been construed and constructed in a hierarchical manner, with men enjoying a full privileged status. The full membership of women in a community that places emphasis on the solidarity has not been taken as a given.
>
> (Chitando, 2015: 276)

Not only is *botho/ubuntu* implicated in marginalizing and detecting sexual and gender difference, the recent xenophobic attacks on migrants in South Africa are a demonstration of how *botho/ubuntu* is forgotten when Africans turn on each other and the care for the stranger, generosity, and hospitality are forgotten through acts of brutality and violence. In fact, the xenophobic attacks have been described as Afrophobic because they turn to focus on other Africans rather than other race groups that are not African. Further, the denial of ARVs to cross-border migrants by the government of Botswana and other governments in Africa is another example of the hostility of African communities towards each other even within the claims and existence of *botho/ubuntu*.

Failure to translate *botho/ubuntu* into action negates the glorification of *botho/ubuntu* by African elders such as Nelson Mandela and Desmond Tutu and African academics who believe that *botho/ubuntu* is a universal acceptance of outsiders "based on common human traits; it breaks down barriers derived from the construction of self and otherness" (Mzamane, 2009). Therefore, when migrants are denied HIV treatment in Botswana and physically attacked and killed in South Africa, otherness and marginal status are constructed as their very humanity is challenged: a demonstration of hostility towards *botho/ubuntu* by the very communities who are defined by it. The theory of liminality reminds us that the fact that some characteristics are not visible does not mean that they are not there or are totally obliterated. It may mean that they are just marginal, but they are still there. In the case of *botho/ubuntu*, when human beings are confronted by the desperation that comes with hunger, poverty, disease, and even war, their response is usually out of character. That does not mean they have completely lost the positive traits of *botho/ubuntu*, but rather that at the moment of desperation, their response turns situational, i.e. their response is determined by their needs at the time. However, all is not lost, as *botho/ubuntu* can still be reclaimed as a resource for community building and integration of migrants among the host community. *Botho/ubuntu* is still a resource that can be used in engaging governments and funders to assist cross-border migrants access HIV services.

Reclaiming *botho/ubuntu* and migrants' health in Africa

Migration is a reality in today's world with current economic and political challenges and instabilities globally. New forms of community across the world are emerging and being formed as countries in Africa and the West receive significant numbers of cross-border migrants daily. Host populations have to adapt and be open to new humanitarian ways of existence and community by promoting and protecting the health of cross-border migrants as they would with the host population. The guiding principle in doing this in Southern Africa could be the *botho/ubuntu* framework, which when embraced fully creates atmospheres for governance and health policies characterized by the preservation of life of the strangers and generosity towards migrants in need. The time to intentionally reclaim and forcefully apply *botho/ubuntu* to extend compassion and generosity towards migrants, "the stranger among us," is now. Three simple attributes/characteristics of *botho/ubuntu* – as dignity, as interconnectedness, and as preservation of life – are useful and can be engaged in the fight to achieve HIV treatment for cross-border migrants.

Botho/ubuntu is dignity, and all human beings regardless of race and ethnicity should be treated with dignity. Chirongoma, Manda and Myeni (2008: 194) write that "since *ubuntu* means being human or humanness, then the central ethical value and starting point is dignity, that is, the dignity of persons because they are persons." Treating a person with dignity requires respect for their human rights and right to health and life. Migrants too deserve to be treated with dignity, and providing them with HIV services dignifies them. *Botho/ubuntu* is also interconnectedness. All human beings are connected in their need to be recognized as fully human in tangible ways. Mangaliso (2001) rightfully submits that *botho/ubuntu* embodies "a pervasive spirit of caring and community, harmony and hospitality, respect and responsiveness that individuals and groups display for one another" (Mangaliso, 2001) and a demonstration that all human beings are interconnected. Since *botho/ubuntu* embraces interconnectedness and a "belief in a universal bond of sharing that connects all humanity,"[19] this interconnectedness should therefore be expressed through acts of compassion, empathy, and generosity towards migrants in offering them access to HIV treatment and services. Lastly, *botho/ubuntu* is preservation of life, as captured well by Samkange and Samkange, who say, "when a person is forced to make a choice between wealth and the preservation of the life of another human being, then one should opt for the preservation of life" (Samkange & Samkange, 1980: 7). *Botho* foregrounds preservation of life over wealth because all human beings, regardless of where they are geographically located, are worthy of life. The argument that ARVs are expensive should be secondary to the desire to preserve the life of migrants. Therefore, denying migrants access to ARV because they are expensive violates and diminishes *botho/ubuntu*, not only of the migrants but of the hosts as well.

The fight against HIV has been successful because of the generosity and compassion of donors who recognized that the fight against HIV infections requires global collaboration. For example, Global Fund recently gave the Botswana National AIDS Coordinating Agency (NACA) over 3 million pula towards work on HIV. Other organizations, such as Institute of Human Virology and Harvard Partnerships (IHVHP), among others, have given grants towards HIV work and services to Botswana over the years when the country was in need. In 2000, the then-president of Botswana, Dr. Festus Mogae, declared HIV an epidemic in Botswana. In order to fight deaths due to HIV complications, the organizations above contributed large sums of money. This is a typical example of the fact that *botho/ubuntu* is not limited to the African people. There are impulses and demonstrations of it even from other countries in the West. Therefore, it would seem just and fair for Botswana to extend this generosity embodied in the richness of *botho/ubuntu* to cross-border migrants. In concluding this section, if countries hold these three attributes of *botho/ubuntu* – dignity, interconnectedness, and preservation of life – together, then they cannot stand by and watch migrants being ravaged by HIV while withholding ARVs from them. Therefore, *botho/ubuntu* teaches the global community that human beings, regardless of race, age, ethnicity, and gender, have shared needs and require good health services and nutrition, for without these, loss of life is imminent.

Mat. 25:35, "the stranger among us"

Mat 25:35–36 describes a person who is hungry, thirsty, naked, homeless/displaced, and a prisoner. The person described here is in need of tangible care. He needs food, water, a home, and a visitor in prison. The person/s described here is faced with the need to have their basic needs met; food, water, clothes, and a home are basic needs of all human beings. Any person without these is not dignified. The person described here seems displaced – perhaps a refugee among the Jews? It describes a person who is different, in that she/he occupies a place in the margins where there is a lack of basic life necessities; the text is clear that they were invited in (vs. 35). What is not mentioned in the text, because it is not important, are the gender, race, legal status, and nationality of those in need. It is fair to conclude the people described here could be anyone: men, women, children, Jews, Samaritans, or Romans. The beauty with biblical texts is that they allow us, the readers, to imagine and fill in the gaps to make sense of them, and since Matt 25:35–36 does not give us specific descriptions of the needy, we are allowed to imagine what those could be. For all intents and purposes, these could easily be descriptions of the homeless, widows who might be dispossessed of their properties after the death of their husbands, and orphans who might be left homeless in our society today. More importantly, these texts accurately describe cross-border migrants. Often, illegal migrants especially go for days without food, water, and shelter. They are sometimes caught and put in prison awaiting deportation. What does not seem to adequately and accurately fit the situation of cross-border migrants is the part where they are taken in and cared for unreservedly by most host societies.

The text also presents a person who was able to give the needy persons food, water, and a home. The climax of the parable is that the person in need is a stranger who is not in a position to pay back the person taking care of them. The text does not say much about the status of those who were the givers, so we do not know much about their economic status and gender. What we know is that they extended genuine generosity and hospitality to others with no expectation of return, as indicated in their words: "Lord, when did we see you hungry and feed you, or thirsty and gave you water." This is a testament to their genuineness, because they were not conscious about the gravity of performing acts of mercy and generosity. These are the people who are true to Leviticus 19:34: "look after the foreigner amongst you remembering that you yourselves were once foreigners in Egypt."

According to this Matthean text, the people who meet the needs of needy person possess desirable Godly qualities and operate within God's love for people in need. Therefore, selflessness and care of strangers is at the heart of Mt 25:35–36, demonstrating that those who have these qualities will inherit God's kingdom. The text evokes the exercise of mercy, kindness, and compassion towards strangers: a call to take care of the sick, to feed those that are hungry, to clothe the naked, to visit those in prison, and to care for those in difficult situations. According to Jesus, the people who engage in these acts of mercy and compassion and generosity have a special place in God's kingdom. These are the people the world of migrants need today – people who can formulate policies of health guided by God's love and generosity. Based on this text, Botswana has not adequately taken care of cross-border migrants.

Botho/ubuntu and Mt 25:35

Botho/ubuntu embodies the same ideals and values espoused in Matt 25:35–36. *Botho/ubuntu* and Mt 25:35 seek to promote the ideals of hospitality, genuine compassion, and solidarity as desirable qualities of being human. They both seek to encourage caring for those in difficult situations, especially the stranger with no expectation of being paid back. At the core of both *botho/ubuntu* and Mt 25:35 is the desire to preserve the life of the "stranger." The care of the stranger has to be manifested in tangible ways that meet their physical needs in order for them to regain their dignity. Both recognize that the value of a person is not determined by their possessions or what they have or don't have. The presence and application of *botho/ubuntu* and Mt 25:35–36 is tangible in the way the "stranger among us" is treated, clothed, and given food and shelter; his basic needs are taken care of.

Conclusion

Although we singled out Botswana in its failure to extend generosity towards migrants in the area of HIV treatment, all African communities are implicated in failing to commit to migrants' access to HIV treatment. Africans who believe in *botho/ubuntu* have to interrogate how they practice *botho/ubuntu* towards migrants who are faced with a need for health services, especially HIV treatment. There is a need to interrogate and engage with health policies that do not allow migrants access to free health. This interrogation needs to go deeper so that even the sacred texts that call for better treatment of migrants are engaged with. In this chapter, we submit that by not giving ARVs to migrants, Botswana is violating not only its culture but also its Christian conviction. We have highlighted the advantages of *botho/ubuntu* in the building of a humane society, where people take care of each other. We also observed that the effectiveness of *botho/ubuntu* is limited or determined by the situations in which people find themselves. For instance, when communities like Botswana and South Africa are faced with struggling economies leading to high rates of unemployment, they resort to desperate measures that are devoid of *botho/ubuntu* towards migrants. Complex as it may seem, *botho/ubuntu* also goes with the responsibility of taking care of one's own people. It is contrary to *botho/ubuntu* to support the "stranger" and neglect one's own people. Therefore, in our critique of Botswana's repressive health policies, we also critique and place blame on the pharmaceutical companies for the high prices of ARVs s well as African and Western countries that have not committed to the health of migrants so that Botswana does not have to take on the responsibility of providing treatment to cross-border migrants alone, because that may completely cripple its economy. All these actors should be part of the solutions to providing ARVs to cross-border migrants within and outside of Botswana.

Lastly, *botho/ubuntu* remains a reminder to care for one another, especially in the context of need and struggle. The Bible and culture remind communities in Africa of their need to practice *botho/ubuntu* towards others. Sometimes they succeed and other times they may fail, but *botho/ubuntu* remains the ideal that African communities cannot give up on as they engage in finding dignified ways of affirming the right to health of cross-border migrants.

Notes

1 As we use Botswana as a case study, and as we hold Botswana health policies accountable, we are also holding other South African governments accountable in failing to protect the right to health of cross-border migrants. We are not naive in thinking that Botswana can easily provide all migrants with HIV treatment. This can be done through the help of other African countries as well as regional and global donors and organizations that take care of refugees and immigrants. We are suggesting that the medical access for all migrants should be the result of collaboration between the different African countries so that no one country carries the economic burden of caring for migrants' health alone. South Africans Development Agency (SADC), African Union (AU), should have a functioning department that focuses on providing for HIV treatments for migrants. SADC was awarded grants to work on and improve the region's response to HIV among mobile populations and migrants, including by the Global Fund in 2010. As of 2013, there was no initiative taken to set mobile sites for this initiative. This is a demonstration of lack of commitment and absence of functioning departments that focuses on cross-border migrants and HIV treatments.
2 www.nationonline.org/oneworld/botswana.htm. Accessed on 01-11-2017.
3 www.nationonline.org/oneworld/botswana.htm. Accessed on 01-11-2017.
4 Zimbabwean refugees suffer in Botswana and South Africa. www.sundaystan dard.info/zimbabwean-refugees-suffer-botswana-and-south-africa. Accessed on 01-11-2017.
5 www.iom.int/world-migration. See also "Campbell E Reflections on Illegal Immigration in Botswana and South Africa 2013," http://aps.journals.ac.za. Accessed on 25-10-2017.

6 International Organization for Migration, n.d. Glossary on Migration. Geneva. www.iom.int/world-migration. See also "Campbell E. 'Reflections on Illegal Immigration in Botswana and South Africa 2013'," http://aps.journals.ac.za. Accessed on October 25, 2017.

7 www.avert.org/professionals/hiv-around-world/sub-saharan-africa/botswana.

8 International Organization for Migration, *Glossary on migration*. Geneva: IOM 2004.

9 Citizens have to produce some form of identity before they are attended at hospitals, as do migrants. Illegal ones can hardly access treatment for any illness because before they are treated, they need to produce proof of residence or passport to show that that they are in the country legally. Even if this is not stringently enforced, it impedes accessibility to medical services because of the real risk of deportation migrants face daily. They are afraid that the police may be alerted to their presence at the hospital. According to the UN Integrated Regional Information Networks (IRIN), 8,394 Zimbabweans were deported between January and March of 2004. Although the data is over ten years old, it demonstrates that fear of deportation is a real risk for Zimbabweans on a daily basis.

10 This argument is valid; ARVs are extremely expensive as they are manufactured outside the continent and their prices are determined by the big pharmaceutical companies that manufacture and sell them. Hence, we noted earlier that making ARVs accessible for migrants should be a collective effort, not just between African nations but also Western nations because they have the resources and means to call pharmaceutical companies to reduce the prices of ARVs. It is also necessary that in the global fight against HIV African countries are included as both agents and beneficiaries of the initiatives aimed at combating HIV, as it is African countries that are consumers of ARV and yet they have no say in the pricing of these. In light of the high ARV prices, it is not realistic to expect for one African country to give ARVs to all migrants without assistance from outside. However, in the spirit of *botho/ubuntu*, Botswana should be seen to be trying; at the very least, it should make efforts to provide basic services such as HIV education and voluntary testing, as the country committed itself to doing at the 2006 United Nations General Assembly high-level meeting. There is neither concern nor effort to source funds or use the funds given by donors to erect mobile sites to enable access to HIV treatment for cross-border migrants. For example, the grants given towards this initiative by Global Fund in 2010 have not been used.

11 Medical insurance in Botswana can be bought and paid for by individuals. The medical insurance companies require proof of employment because employers contribute a certain percentage towards the insurance, as do individuals. The majority of people from Botswana do not have medical insurance, making it elitist. Health care is free for all citizens at government clinics and hospitals but not for migrants. If migrants have illnesses such as flu, headaches etc., they can be attended to at government hospitals for a fee. However, they can never buy ARVs at government hospitals; it is illegal to do so. However, cross-border migrants who are legal and have medical insurance can buy their ARVs at private clinics, and those clinics charge exorbitant amounts of money.

12 Although *botho* and *ubuntu* and all other related terms used in different parts of Africa are the same in meaning and application, *ubuntu* is well-known globally, partly because it was used by global icons Nelson Mandela and Desmond Tutu when they tried to reconcile different races in South Africa after apartheid. Therefore, we will refer to the same terms together throughout the chapter for the benefit of the global community, which is accustomed to the use of *ubuntu*. Tswana, Shona, and Zulu are languages spoken by different ethnic groups in the Southern African region.

13 *Botho* determines the daily lives of the people in Botswana, so much so that the choice of a spouse, for example, is determined to a large extent by the person's *botho* (good manners and dignity) and that of their family. Questions such as is the family dignified? are they known as bad people? among others are often asked by either the bride's family or the groom's family to determine the family's *botho*. If the answers to these questions are negative, it means the person and/or their family lacks *botho* and marrying into that family might not be acceptable.

14 Tutu, D. n.d. *Ubuntu Women Institute USA with SSIWEL at its First South Sudan Project.* www.azquotes.com. Accessed on 01–11–2017.

15 www.azquotes.com/quote/823165. Accessed on 01–11–2017.

16 When used in this instance, it literally means that the person is not human and by implication it means one is an animal. Witches, murderers, and rapists are among people who are without *botho* and are shunned.

17 Cross-border migrants are easily seen as threats to the host's jobs and resources.

18 Louw, D. "Ubuntu: An African Assessment of the Religious Other," www.bu.edu/wcp/Papers/Afri/AfriLouw.htm. Accessed on 26-10-2017.

19 "Ubuntu (Philosophy)," www.wikipedia.org/wiki/Ubuntu_philosophy.

References

Campbell, E. 2013. Reflections on Illegal Immigration in Botswana and South Africa 2013. http://aps.journals.ac.za.

Chitando, E. 2015. 'Do not tell a person carrying you the s/he stinks: Reflections on *ubuntu* and masculinities in the context of sexual and gender-based violence and HIV' in Elna, M. et. al. (eds.), *Living with Dignity: African Perspectives on Gender Equality*, 269–284, Stellenbosch: Sun Press.

Chirongoma, S. 2006. 'Women, poverty and HIV in Zimbabwe: An exploration of inequalities in health care' in Sabel P. and Nadar S. (eds.), *African Women, Religion and Health: Essays in Honor of Mercy Amba Ewudziwa Oduyoye*, Maryknoll: Orbis.

Chirongoma, S., Manda, D. S. & Myeni, Z. 2008. 'Ubuntu and women's health agency in contemporary South Africa' in De Gruchy, S., Koopman, N. and Strijbos, S. (eds.), *From Our Side: Emerging Perspectives on Development and Ethics*, Pretoria: UNISA Press.

International Organization for Migration, n.d. *Glossary on Migration*, 2011 Geneva: IOM.

Louw, D. Ubuntu *An African Assessment of the Religious Other* www.bu.edu/wcp/Papers/Afri/AfriLouw.htm. accessed October 26, 2017.

Magadla, S. & Chitando, E. 2014. 'The self become God: Ubuntu and the scandal of manhood' in Praeg, L. and Magadla, S. *Ubuntu: Curating the Archive.* Pietermaritzburg: University of KwaZulu-Natal Press.

Mangaliso, M. 2001. 'Building competitive advantage from ubuntu: Management lessons from South Africa.' *Academy of Management Executive* 15(3).

Manyonganise, M. 2015. Oppressive and liberative: A Zimbabwean woman's reflections on ubuntu. *Verbum Eccles.* [online]. 36(2), pp. 1–7. ISSN 2074–7705. http://dx.doi.org/10.4102/VE.V36I2.1438.

Mbigi, L. 1997. *Ubuntu: The African Dream in Management*. Randburg: Knowledge Resources.

Mzamane, M. 2009. 'Building a society using the building block of ubuntu/botho/vhuthu' in Brown, D. (ed.), *Religion and Spirituality in South Africa: New Perspectives*, Pietermaritzburg: UKZN Press.

Reitzes, M. 1997. *The Migrant Challenge to Realpolitik: Towards a Human Rights based Approach to Immigration Policy in South and Southern Africa.* Johannesburg: Foundation for Global Dialogue. Occasional paper 1997. Campbell E Reflections on Illegal Immigration in Botswana and South Africa 2013. http://aps.journals. ac.za.

Samkange, S. & Samkange, T. 1980. *Hunhuism or Ubuntuism: A Zimbabwe Indigenous Political Philosophy.* Salisbury: Graham Pub Ubuntu (Philosophy) www. wikipedia.org/wiki/Ubuntu_philosophy.

Tutu, D. 1999. *No Future without Forgiveness.* New York: Double Day.

Tutu, D. n.d. *Ubuntu Women Institute USA with SSIWEL at its first South Sudan Project.* www.ssiwel.org. accessed October 25, 2017.

Online sources

HIV AND AIDS in Botswana. www.avert.org/professionals/hiv-around-world/sub-saharan-africa/botswana.

www.azquotes.com. accessed November 1, 2017.

Migration. www.iom.int/world-migration.

Zimbabwean refugees suffer in Botswana and South Africa www.sundaystandard. info/zimbabwean-refugees-suffer-botswana-and-south-africa.

13 The question of healing and forgetting

Disturbing realities in short stories of Ritu Menon and Uravashi Butalia

Sonu Shiva

Introduction

The weaker sections of society are often subjected to violence, whether in terms of caste, race, religion, or gender. The experience of women often reveals histories of mass or gang rape. Violence tends to take on the shape of asserting power, especially where the situation is polarized into "our women," who are weak or scared, and "theirs," who are fit targets to attack. Violence against women ranges from abuse to severe oppression. The concept of violence against women becomes even more confusing when it is used as a legitimate means of resolving problems and when it is socially accepted. When on one side we believe that all forms of coercion of any individual or a group is violence, the pressure that women face due to the existence of that punishes non-compliance severe physical and mental punishment. The hierarchical structure of violence is so deeply interwoven in the social fabric that some women live in an atmosphere of terror, threat, as some forms of social expressions of what is considered right and wrong is embedded in the norms that legitimize aggression. Traditional societies have often divided men and women into their own spaces, where men are in control of the outer world while women in the household are governed by men. They relate to the outer world through male eyes. How have women coped with their subordinated positions? How have they internalized norms rooted in patriarchal ideology and expressed them in old forms and sometimes in new guise? Whether traditional or modern, women remain in oppressive realities. Such questions crowd the mind when one reads narratives on women.

Writing from the margins

When it comes to writings by women about their experiences, very few have turned to writing to express openly their harassment and the strategies they have used to cope up with it. They have always been made to assume and brainwashed to believe that they are the carriers of the family reputation and that they bear the burden of histories, memories, and their bodily experiences:

> when men and women narrate the same reality, even then the descriptions, the images and comparisons the perspective and perceptions may

differ. It is not merely a question of two different kinds of articulation or voices. More often it is the male gaze which frames the women even as a writer. So the first need becomes to shake off this hold, to find a voice which can free itself of this gaze to find a space or create one outside this spacing.

(Jasbir and Agarwal, 2002:8)

Whenever an experience is narrated, gender is an important aspect to look for because men and women experience it differently. Gender is not only expressed in terms of "contextualizing, analyzing and communicating," but it is also about different identities. Men and women have their own strengths and weaknesses, and they have witnessed history and culture differently. Political discourses and writing of history have conventionally been the domain of men, in which we surprisingly find hardly any women's voices. The realities that women have undergone have never been the expectation of a history reader or one interested in politics. The language in history has been consciously used to display mere factual details of incidences, and women's experiences of that time is missing, even in the background. Subsequently, there develops a need to explore in these historical narrations the suppressed voices of women, their inner being, and how they relate themselves to it.

Political facts and the oral history of loss

The Partition of India in August 1947 was one of the great human convulsions, where in a few months about 12 million people crossed borders, resulting in inexplicable savagery expressed in looting, rape, abduction – all that remains in human memory are migration, violence, and uproar. The main reason for partition of British India into the two dominion states of India and Pakistan was the policy of "divide and rule" by British rulers, to tide over the growing national demand for independence with the communal demands of Muslims. By failing to convert Congress into a "safety valve" in order to avert any 1857 revolution like an event, the government desperately tried to break the growing nationalist outlook of Indian leaders – liberals and extremists alike. It set up separate organizations based on religion, caste, and vested interests. The Muslim League demanded a separate electorate and reservation of seats for Muslims, which was readily accepted by a 1909 act. This was the first step that led most of the Muslims to believe that their solution lay in supporting British rule over the tyranny of the Hindu Raj if ever the national independence movement was to succeed in the future.

Muslim leaders like M.A. Jinnah and the Ali brothers soon shed their garb of nationalism and became staunch advocates for Muslim communalism. Jinnah proposed a 14-point program in response to Nehru's plan; his participation in the second roundtable conference in London, his opposition to Gandhi's demand, his criticism of Congress ministers, and ultimately his enunciation of the "two nation theory" led to the Lahore resolution of Pakistan. He ultimately won his cherished goal through tactical cooperation with the British in World War II, by sabotaging the "interim government" and withdrawing the approval of the cabinet mission plan.

Britain decided to withdraw and declared the intention of leaving India by June 15, 1948. Wavell was replaced – Mountbatten became viceroy. He could not reconcile the difference between Congress and the League. Finally, Mountbatten's plan of June 3, 1947 was approved both by Congress and the League, and the date of the British departure was agreed upon as August 15, 1947; on the same date, Pakistan came into existence and India gained independence. Politically, the borders were created based on head counts of Hindus versus Muslims but neither government ever anticipated that this would lead such a huge population to flee to what they considered safer places. Urvashi Butalia in *The Other Side of Silence* and Ritu Menon and Kamla Bhasin in *Borders and Boundaries* narrate the experiences of partition survivors, a form of oral history that expresses painful memories and moments of violence. Partition is not only a political fact:

> Partition was surely more than just a political divide, or a division of properties, of assets and liabilities. It was also, to use a phrase that survivors use repeatedly a "division of hearts". It brought untold suffering, tragedy, trauma, pain and violence to communities who had hither lived together in some kind of social contact. It separated families across an arbitrarily drawn border, sometimes overnight and made it practically impossible for people to know if the parents, sisters brothers or children were alive or dead.
>
> (Butalia, 1998:8)

People traveled across the borders several times in search of their family members, facing the danger of being arrested on the charge of espionage. Some met again after a span of 50 years, but for others it was an empty-handed "search."

Women suffered the most in the crisis days. If men suffered displacement, loss of material possessions, and physical suffering, these could be made up with the passage of time; women during partition suffered the loss of dignity that is closely aligned with "sexual purity." The writers Urvashi Butalia and Ritu Menon narrate these incidents through the characters within the text. They relate their experience from memory, and it requires a leap of imagination by the readers to understand what is represented in partition literature's multidirectional flow of time and space. According to the political facts, partition was one incident in the past, but the reality associated with it is scattered throughout the pages of time. Partition is seen everywhere in the form of communal riots and religious fundamentalism. Both communities keep on targeting each other. There is a lot of repressed rage and aggression of that one political happening where memories are used selectively by aggressors who argue that, because Muslims have killed Hindus and raped their women, so in turn they must be killed and their women must be raped as well. "There were no good people and no bad ones. Virtually every family had a history of being both victims and aggressors" (Butalia, 1998:11). *The Other Side of Silence* and *Borders and Boundaries* are written based on the interviews of partition survivors, where language becomes the controlling factor. Narrators move back and forth into personal and collective memories, trying to relate incidents from the mind's eye, negotiating their social locations and roles. Writers feel that while listening to the survivors, they could recognize that there is such a thing as "gender telling of partition." Most interviews took place in family situations and over an extended period of time, with no neat chronologies; it was a reliving of the past from the context of the present. It must have been challenging for writers to ask difficult and disturbing questions in order to bring out these oral histories, especially female memories and bodily experiences, and interpreting their pain about the violence they faced from strangers as well as their near and dear ones. As the narration unfolds, one finds complex psychological emotional space in their "lived experience," their compromises and silences. Both the works discussed are by women writers. They have a kind of sensibility in translating and sharing every act and movement, and give meaning to every pause and silence. Such invisible areas might remain unknowable to the patriarchal eye, but women, due to their cultural knowledge, can instinctively relate to it.

One immediately comes to recognize gendered positions of narration or readership. Those who have studied modern Indian history have never learned this side of reality, of women suffering and the intensity of their gendered experience. In history, one always finds politicians and kings fighting for power and supremacy. They change, but people never had to change. August 1947 witnessed a huge exchange of population. The phase of partition was a phase of mental frenzy that neither Hindus or Muslims had control over. Between August and November 1947, about 673 trains moved 2,800,000 refuges. The rich traveled in planes that flew six to seven every day between India and Pakistan, but the poor could not get any means of transport. They moved in foot columns called *kafilas* that took almost eight days to cross a given spot. These columns were initially 30,000–40,000; the largest consisted of about 400,000 people. Twenty-four *kafilas* of people are said to have moved from Layallpur and Montogomery to India, bringing 849,000 people from west to east. These *kafilas* made murderous attacks. As people fled, the weak or disabled children and women were left behind. A large number of women were picked from the edges of *kafilas* and raped.

The drawing of boundaries was a difficult task, as religious associations in the area did not match geographical patterns or political considerations. Therefore, the complex geographical boundaries ran through people's lives. "The Amrita Bazar Patrika labeled it the 'departing kick of British imperialism at both Hindus and Muslims' while Dawn called it 'territorial murder'"

(Butalia, 1998: 85). With this, everything was put at stake: "jobs, livelihoods, property and homeland." Urvashi Butalia and Ritu Menon in their
works do not consider the partition to be a "political negotiation" or people
as "numbers" of history or "informants"; they reflect the lives of survivors
as part of the history of partition. The disappearance of the women was
talked of in whispers. It was considered something to be ashamed of. In this
silence and whispering lies the history of the partition that forms the search
of both texts.

Violence against women: a gendered reality

The mass rape of women was used as a weapon. Thousands of women jumped
into the well or took poison to preserve their honor and chastity. Instead
of allowing themselves to be sexually defiled by men of other religions,
they chose to face death with courage. They allowed their own men to cut
their throats or jumped into the fire. In some instances, walls were closed
on women, leaving them with no choice except to face death, because once
abducted or raped, their restoration in the social system was impossible.
They would not be recognized by their own families if they had a stigmatized past. Women who survived faced the same insensitivity, and therefore
their rehabilitation became the most difficult and neglected task. If a woman
is seen as a property, an effective way of penalizing a man is to snatch her
away and violate his property. "This kind of large-scale violation of women
with rape was used as an instrument of revenge upon men and was widely
experienced in situations of ethnic violence" (Kosambi, 1998:25).

Ritu Menon and Kamla Bhasin, in the section "Honorably Dead," write
about the injury inflicted on women by men of both communities. They
write:

> We began to discern some specific features of communal crimes against
> women: their brutality, their extreme sexual violence and their collective
> nature. The range of sexual violation explicit in the above accounts strip-
> ping; parading naked; mutilating and disfiguring; tattooing or branding
> the breasts; knifing open the womb; raping, of course; killing fetuses is
> shocking not only for its savagery, but for what it tells us about women
> as objects in male constructions of their own honor. Women sexuality
> symbolizes "manhood"; its desecration is a matter of such shame and
> dishonor that it has to be avenged. . . . Tattooing and branding the body
> with "Pakistan Zindabad" or "Hindistan Zindabad" not only mark the
> woman for life, they never allow her (or her family or community) the
> possibility of forgetting her humiliation. . . . Marking the breasts and
> genitalia with symbols like crescent moon or trident makes permanent
> the sexual appropriation of the woman and symbolically extends this
> violation to future generations who are thus metaphorically stigmatized.
>
> (Menon and Bhasin, 2000:43–44)

Urvashi Butalia, in the section "A Tradition of Martyrdom," gives evidence that lots of women and children were killed or rather offered themselves for death in front of their families because they preferred death to rape or conversion. For all this killing by one's own people, the word "martyr" is used to emphasize the fact that the race of Sikhs is fearless. The only feared "dishonor" was if they allowed themselves to be caught by Muslims. They felt pride in giving up their lives. There is no record of women and children whose death is attributed to their families. The question of "abducted women" disappeared into a realm of silence, whereas women who were killed by their families or took their own lives entered the realm of "martyrdom."

Among many incidences of violence narrated and recorded in these volumes, one finds how women, in the moment of crisis, can be seen as caught in the web of authority and modestly constructed families.

> This created world has located itself in the power of man and the subordination to women. This intent has been camouflaged by other myths – myths of protection, of punishment for transgression, and of the power of women, their indispensability and the glory of motherhood.
>
> (Jain, 2011: 13)

> An example of it is the story of Dr. Versa Singh from Shekhupura. Versa Singh claimed he had shot 50 women personally. First, he shot his own wife because the Muslims came to get them. Once he had done this, all the women in the neighborhood gathered around, saying "Viran Pehle Mannu Maar, Pehle Mannu Maar" (Brother kill me first). Some would push their daughters forward saying, "Shoot her, put a bullet through her now." He says he just kept shooting and shooting. "They kept bringing them forward and I kept shooting. There was shooting all around. At least 50 women I shot my wife my mother, daughter." I used to talk to him about it, ask him how he had killed like this. He would say "How could I see my wife, my daughter fall into the hands of Muslims? I recalled Sikh history, the bravery of our people I wasn't a murderer, I was their savior." I said to him "This must be a terrible burden for you to bear." He said "Not at all, no burden." He subsequently remarried, had children and wrote a book about it, called Bhuler da Saka.
>
> (Menon and Bhasin, 2000: 49–50)

There are scores of incidents in which women took their own lives by swallowing poison, jumping off bridges, etc. The narrators of the incidents, like Iqbal, do not even acknowledge the role of men in women's deaths. Though he himself strangled his cousin, he repeatedly said that the decision was theirs – they had no choice, since the men who were supposed to protect them were going to be killed. Iqbal's wife meaningfully interrupted her husband, saying: "They must have encouraged them. After all what could ladies do in this situation? They must have persuaded them, what could the women do?" (Menon and Bhasin, 2000:51). According to social cognitive theory, "when collective efforts fail to produce quick results or meet forcible opposition, their vulnerability to discouragement, and the social changes they are able to realize" is significant (Sinha, 2011:120). Such incidents project more than this. One becomes aware of how caste plays an important part in gender roles. Sikhism has its own history based on boldness and military strength. Performing the role of protectors or offering oneself to martyrdom has been a common feature of this history. Such heavy qualities that were associated with men can be seen manifested in women. As "gendered reality" was defined based on priorities for a human being and their sexual role models. The individual self-respect, self-assertion and conscience vis-a-vie the code of respectability are important (Jain, 1997:102). Therefore, if a Hindu woman was abducted, she felt that she would become impure and not worthy of showing her face in public. Muslim women did not feel like this because this was not in their blood. Even with their men, there was no problem of their women's purity, and they felt no hesitation in taking them back.

Displacement, loss, and social boundaries

There were thousands of women taken away by the abductors, never to be found. During rehabilitation, some of the poor women were disillusioned with regard to going back to their original families because their abductors were providing them with a better lifestyle, materially. Moreover, they were unsure of whether they would be reaccepted to their families. Some were forced to give up children they had conceived with a man of another religion. Pregnant women were sent to be cleansed or secluded in ashrams until the birth of their children and then were forced to give up these children to orphanages for adoptions. To this day, there are many women in ashrams who have suffered double dislocation – whose histories are hidden and who are often referred to as "child[ren] of history with no history." Jasbir Jain raises a lot of questions with regard to the construction of women's sense of "self" and many other women-related issues. She writes:

> In this opposition between the self and the role, the body plays a significant role. The sexual act and the ensuing pregnancy emphasize the physicality of life, thus it is by negotiating these realities that women can find themselves. Negotiation does not mean rejection. It means a rearrangement. But the physical realities are worked out at another level, that of homelessness.
>
> (Jasbir and Agarwal, 2002: 192)

While these stories supplement each other at times, others raise counter-arguments, because in the recovery process, the woman as a person did not matter. All that mattered was national honor or the honor of the community. They were not expected to voice their opinion because they were in a state of "mental oppression." Even if this wasn't true, they had no freedom of choice but had to leave "other," not acceptable families to get relocated in real ones.

In a culture that gives a lot of importance to women's chastity, women are forced to give up their lives in order to avoid sexual violence and to preserve the honor of their community. The reasoning is that men can fight and use their strengths, but women can become impure by being impregnated with the seed of other religions, leading to the birth of impure children. As Jain explains, the "notion of respectability, the custodianship of culture, the purity of lineage has come to rest on the female body" (Jain, 2011:14). Through the narration of partition, the authors enable survivors to articulate women's experiences in a patriarchal society. It is not only about reading the past; the narratives also describe how patriarchal mechanisms regulate gendered conduct. They deal with how one is extremely guided and directed to gender-linked conduct in order that one's actions are regulated accordingly. In other words, the experiences of women are evidence of "socially guided control over gender-linked conduct" (Sinha, 2011:129).

In the rehabilitation process, the women that came from Pakistan looked mentally disturbed. They came with their emaciated children who were almost dead and looked like skeletons. Some were pregnant and had to stay in camp to have a child or opt for abortions. These women were reluctant to show their faces to their families. "They wanted to burn themselves alive or die rather than face their people. They said they would rather go to hell" (Menon and Bhasin, 2000:83). There are innumerable incidents where women refused to be relocated but were pushed by both governments to go back to their original families. These women were looked at not as individuals with their own will but as Hindu women or Muslim women. There are instances of Hindu girls kept by Muslim men who were happy and well-adjusted, following their own religion in a Muslim family, but who were soon identified and recaptured from their settled condition of being emotionally attached with Muslim husband and having three children. This was heartbreaking for the women who faced such situations in 1957–1958, ten years after partition. They protested, because they had almost achieved their individual adjustments to life and started living again. One recovered girl confronted Mridula Sarabhai thus:

> You say abduction is immoral and so you are trying to save us. Well, now it's too late. One marries only once – willingly or by force. We are now married – what are you going to do with us? Ask us to get married again? Is that not immoral? What happened to our relatives when we were abducted? Where were they? You may do your worst if you insist but remember, you can kill us, but we will not go.
>
> (Menon and Bhasin, 2000:97)

Conclusion

After 66 years of partition, much has changed in India and Pakistan but borders have not disappeared. Cultural and social borders between Hindus and Muslims continue to exist. Both works examined in this study highlight a discourse between personal and social worlds: the challenges women faced sexually and the control of their movements towards or away from their home. At one level, Urvashi Butalia's *The Other Side of Silence* and Ritu Menon and Kamla Bhasin's *Borders and Boundaries* are deeply interlaced with historical references to the construction of two nations and contextualized through actual happenings, but on the other hand, they deal with real problems faced by hundreds and thousands of women in this complex social system. The literary history interacts with political history, opening events for the reader through the two narrators, the author, and the character who is the narrator. These works create a realistic picture of the social, cultural, and mental boundaries that still exist and have filtered down through generations through the memory of survivors. Women's experience of partition is a painful truth that may worsen or improve in the course of time.

Bibliography

Beauvoir, Simone de. 1997. *The Second Sex*. London: Vintage.

Bharathi, Thummapudi. 2012. *Writing Resistance: Beads of Thought on Women*. Jaipur: Mark.

Butalia, Urvashi. 1998. *The Other Side of Silence: Voices from the Partition of India*. New Delhi: Penguin Books.

Cobley, Paul. 2001. *Narrative*. Oxon: Routledge.

Jain, Jasbir. 1997. *Feminizing Political Discourse: Women and the Novel in India 1857–1905*. Jaipur: Rawat.

Jain, Jasbir. 2011. *Women in Patriarchy: Cross-Cultural Readings*. Jaipur: Rawat.

Jain, Jasbir and Supriya Agarwal. eds. 2002. *Gender and Narrative*. Jaipur: Rawat.

Kaul, Suvir. 2001. *The Partitions of Memory: the afterlife of the division of India*, edited by S. Kaul (Bloomington: Indiana University Press).

Kosambi, Meera. 1998. "'Tradition' 'Modernity' and 'Violence' against Women" In Shirin Kudchedkar and Sabiha al-Issa ed. *Violence against Women, Women against Violence*. New Delhi: Pencraft.

Kupiainen, Jari, Erkki Sevanan and John A. Stolesbury. eds. 2004. *Cultural Identity in Transition: Contemporary Conditions, Practices and Politics of Global Phenomenon*. New Delhi: Atlantic.

Menon, Ritu and Kamla Bhasin. 2000. *Borders and Boundaries: Women in India's Partition*. New Delhi: Kali for Women.

Shaw, E. Marvin and Philip R. Costanzo. 1982. *Theories of Social Psychology*, second edition. New Delhi: McGraw Hill.

Sinha, Narendra Pratap. 2011. *Psychology of Gender and Sexuality*. New Delhi: DPS.

14 Immigration and gender-based violence in the West

Mary Nyangweso and Jacob K. Olupona

Introduction

In 1992, Miriam Medina, a 20-year-old from Guanajuato, Mexico, arrived in the United States after paying a smuggler to help her cross the San Ysidro mountains, in hopes of better opportunities for her life. When she arrived in San Diego, she met the man who would become the father of her two children. Little did she know that this man would abuse her physically and emotionally for over a decade. She was bruised, raped, and manipulated under his power such that he controlled her life, Miriam explained. The violence and manipulation left Medina mentally scarred. As Kate Morrisey, who narrates her experience, explains, Miriam still tears up when she talks about her experience, especially how fearful and helplessness she felt. She was separated from her sons when this man threatened as part of the abuse to get her deported. "Just because I was illegal, he had the power over me," she explained. Medina said she didn't know about her rights as an immigrant and the protection options she was entitled to. She explained, "I didn't want to make the situation worse than what it was. [. . .] I got used to the routine all those years. I figured it was normal" (Morrissey, 2017).

On New Year's Eve in 2009, when the violence intensified, Medina defended herself in a fight and left a scratch on his arm. The man called the police. Medina said he gouged his arm deeper himself to make it look like she'd really hurt him while he was waiting for police to arrive. In court filings, he accused Medina of being the abuser and of cheating on him with a female coworker. He denied hurting her and accused her of lying about bruises that she reported to police. Medina, who was arrested, spent four days in jail before being deported, leaving her two young sons with their father. Fearing for her young sons and worried about their safety with their father, she decided to cross into the US once again about a month after she was deported.

She moved back in with her abuser out of desperation. Shortly after, Child Protective Services showed up and interviewed her and her sons. The agency staff advised her to get out of this abusive situation. With their help, she filed a restraining order after an abusive incident and was granted protection in May 2010, even though domestic violence charges weren't brought against the man. The morning of August 2010, around 7 am as Medina was getting ready for work, she heard a knock on her door. It was Immigration and Customs Enforcement officers. Immediately she suspected that her ex-husband had reported her. She was taken to the immigration detention facility.

On the way, Medina decided to share about the abuse she and her sons had endured. Sorry for her situation, the officer helped her to get released from the detention facility with an ankle monitor as she awaited the decision on her case. Meanwhile, she got a lawyer who helped her apply for a U-visa and avoid deportation. She is no longer living in fear. "He thought he was going to harm me, but at the end, whatever happened to me happened for a reason," Medina said. "I just missed all my good years. I feel like my life is starting now. Everything else was taken by him." She now lives in Point Loma with her sons, 17 and 12, of whom she has full custody. She was promoted in April to general manager of a fast food restaurant in Clairemont. Medina hopes that her story will encourage other domestic violence victims to come forward, knowing they have options for protection. "It's hard to take action to do it," she said. "You have to have the courage" (Morrissey, 2017).

Fatima Mohammed, a 45-year-old immigrant living in Massachusetts, USA, is faced with a question most American parents never worry about: "Should my daughter be circumcised?" Mohammed explains how difficult the decision is for her since she went through this very painful experience herself as a child in Africa. She strongly opposes the idea of cutting her 11-year-old daughter, an American-born Somali girl. According to Mohammed, not every family in her African community in Massachusetts feels the same way. Most cannot swiftly make the decision not to cut their daughters because it is a cultural ritual. It is a practice that is integral to a woman's identity. According to Muhammad: "Some think I'm disrespecting my own culture. . . . Others say you act like an American now. You forgot about who you are" (Chen, 2010).

Aisha (pseudonym) is an 11-year-old immigrant girl in the United Kingdom who is desperate to avoid female genital cutting. She does not want to be exposed to this procedure, to which her unsuspecting sister was exposed against her will. With the help of her teacher, she wrote a letter to Equality Now, a charity organization in the country that advocates against this procedure. Her courageous letter, shown below, expresses her anxiety about this procedure.

Dear Madam,

My name is XXX and I am 11 years old. I and my mum, sisters, and brother came to England in 2005 when I had just turned 6 years old to join my dad who was at University. We come from the Gambia in West Africa.

Three weeks ago we were watching a TV programme on African culture and as they were showing girls having their private cut, my older sister who is 12 years old started crying. After 2 days she told my dad that she also had her private cut.

Mum and Dad never knew about it and she was told if she ever tells anyone the spirits will come and kill her immediately. She said it was done one weekend by my aunties at my Nan's house. Last Friday, mum took her to our GP to have her checked and the doctor said it was done to her. . . . I went to school I told one of my teachers about it and together we went on the computer and found your group. . . . I don't want my private cut by anyone.

My dad loves us very much and he did not like what they did to my sister and he is very confused. We should be going back to the Gambia any time after Eid and he is worried and upset that they would do the same to me. I don't what that too . . .

Please madam, help me, and my dad. . . . I really hope you can help me, not to have my private cut. I am really confused especially seeing my dad so unhappy and not knowing what to do.

Thank you very much.

(Maim, 2010)

Although Aisha was lucky to receive the help she needed to be protected from the procedure, not many migrant girls are as lucky. As migrants seek a better life in the West on the assumption that Western countries are more progressive and their values encourage autonomy and personal growth, this is not the reality of most immigrants. Gender and immigration rights are central to this chapter because gender is a significant factor in international immigration. Studies indicate that women constitute about half of the world's migrants (UNDP, 2009; UN DESA, 2017). In this chapter, we highlight how gender-based violence intersects with immigration and religion. Drawing on examples from experiences of intimate partner violence (IPV) and female genital cutting, the chapter highlights challenges that some immigrant women live with as they seek to negotiate legitimate cultural and religious values and practices with their claims to human rights in their new world. In highlighting the role of religion in an immigrant's life, the chapter argues for the significance of incorporating faith-based organization in addressing gender-based violence in immigrant communities.

Although the mention of gender-based violence often leads most to think of spousal abuse, gender-based violence is much more than just spousal abuse. In this chapter, we use gender-based violence to refer to family or household forms of discrimination and violence often perpetrated for cultural, religious, or other reasons that are directed at one because of their gender. According to the Co-ordination Action on Human Rights Violations (CAHRV), the most pervasive form of *gender-based violence* is an abuse of women by intimate male partners, with studies showing that 20 to more than 30% of women experience intimate partner violence in their lifetime

(CAHRV). It involves a spectrum of physical, sexual, and psychological acts of control, threats, aggression, abuse, and assault. It often takes many forms, such as female infanticide, girl child abuse, incest, rape, sexual harassment, intimate partner violence (IPV), and abuse and neglect of older women.

Although gender-based violence is a serious global problem, the risk is reported to be higher in immigrant women than their counterparts due to their status as both immigrants and women. A recent study in New York found that 51% of intimate partner homicide victims were foreign-born.[1] Married migrant women experience higher levels (60%) of physical and sexual abuse than unmarried immigrant women (Dutton, Orloff, and Hass, 2000). According to a separate study, violence against women is one of the most common victimizations experienced by immigrants (Raj and Silverman, 2002). Some immigrant women often suffer higher rates of battering than locals because they may come from cultures that accept domestic violence as the norm, or because they have insufficient or limited access to legal and social services compared to native citizens. In such cases, abusers often use their partner's immigration status as a tool of control. As Orloff explains, it is common for a barterer to exert control over his partner's immigration status in order to force her to remain in the relationship (Orloff, 1995, 313; Orloff and Kaguyutan, 2002: 95–183). Some immigrant women fail to report their situation for fear of deportation or abandonment by their spouses. Others have expressed concern regarding the perpetrator's possible withholding of important personal documents, such as passports, to prevent them from seeking or accessing necessary legal services and support services.

Female genital cutting, also known as female circumcision or female genital mutilation, is a practice that is embraced in some communities across the globe. It involves excision of the clitoris and/or the removal of part or all of the tissues around a woman's reproductive organ and sometimes infibulation: the stitching together of the vulva in order to narrow the vaginal opening. As discussed in chapter 7, female genital cutting is generally classified into four typologies to reflect its severity. Type 1, clitoridectomy, Type 2, excision, Type 3, infibulation, Type 4, unclassified procedures that involve inflicting pain on the female genitalia. It is commonly performed on girls between the ages of 4 and 16, among other reasons as an initiation rite into womanhood (Rahman, 2001: 8). The practice is a concern in immigrant communities because it is culturally and religiously sanctioned as tradition. As Africans continue to immigrate to the Americas, along with them comes their culture. For instance, in the US, it is estimated that 228,000 females live with the risk of genital cutting, a recorded statistical rise of 35% (AWHC, 2012). In the UK, it is estimated that 279,500 women have been exposed to female genital cutting, with about 33,000 others living with the risk and fear of having their genitalia excised (Leye, 2004: 23–24). In England and Wales alone, the organization Equality Now reports that 66,000 women have been subjected to female genital cutting, with an estimated 23,000 still at risk for genital mutilation (Equality Now, 2012).

As a form of gender-based violence, female genital cutting is in the category of cultural practices that are considered to be a violation of the human rights of children and women for two main reasons. First, health concerns, including severe pain; hemorrhage; urinary tract infection; fractures or dislocation; sexual dysfunction; complications in pregnancy and childbirth; and psychological damage often exhibited as fear, the suppression of feelings, anxiety, flashbacks, phobias, and depression are viewed as a violation of human rights of those exposed to the procedure. Although the degree of complications increased in relation to the severity of the procedure, Nahid Toubia, one of the few doctors in the US has cautioned against overlooking psychological consequences that undermine health of children and women who live with the scars from this procedure (Rahman and Toubia, 2001). Second, moral concerns associated with the procedure related to gender discrimination. Genital cutting is described by feminists as a form of sexual control of the woman's sexual pleasure in an effort to promote or enforce chastity, virginity, and subordination of females. It is viewed as an expression of patriarchy, sexism, and sexual control of female sexuality (Gruenbaum, 2001: 133). It is considered in the category of other cultural practices designed to control women's sexuality based on the patriarchal ideology that asserts male dominance and female subjugation. The ideology that promotes the notion that women are incapable of restraining their sexual needs is critiqued in the Hite Report, which explains how female sexuality is compromised through genital cutting (Hite, 1976: 99). To deny women sexual pleasure for any reason, including cultural reasons, is to participate in patriarchal power dynamics that are oppressive to women. It should be noted here that some cultural feminists, such as Fuambai Ahmadu (2000) and Amede Obiora (1997), have refuted the claim of sexual fulfillment based on cultural norms (Ahmadu, 2000: 284). Despite these concerns, some parents who want to stay true to their tradition ask doctors to perform the procedure on their daughters. Where it is performed without informed consent, it is considered by the United Nations and the World Health Organization as a violation of the human rights of children and women. Although most Western countries have outlawed the practice, some parents hope to evade legal consequences by arranging for their unsuspecting toddlers and babies to be cut illegally in homes or hospitals. Although the prevalence of female genital cutting in Western countries is not fully recognized because of the secret nature of the practice, available statistics point to a serious concern for immigrant communities in these countries.

In a survey of immigrant women and experts on this issue, specific themes emerged with regard to opinions and challenges about the persistence of female genital cutting. First, female genital cutting is performed among immigrant communities. Second, the procedure has taken place both within the United States and abroad during vacation trips. Third, most immigrants were aware that the practice is illegal in the United States. Fourth, most of the immigrants cited culture or religion as the reason for the persistence.

Fifth, although a majority of my respondents – 80% – believe the practice is unnecessary, most were of the opinion that cultural diversity should be respected. It is important to note that reasons for the practice vary from group to group. Religion was often cited. While most believe female genital cutting is sanctioned by God or its messengers, others reiterated myths that are often used to justify genital cutting. For instance, it is often believed in some of these communities that a child of an uncircumcised woman will die during childbirth. Another myth relates to the husband of the uncircumcised woman dying during sexual intercourse if her clitoris touches him. Yet another myth states how the genitals of a woman who is not excised will grow and hang down between her legs. Others have claimed that food cooked by an uncircumcised woman smells bad (Spencer, 2002: 3).

Social pressure ranks high in reasons for female genital cutting. In most communities, it is advised that women who marry in genital cutting communities have their genitals cut. Social pressure techniques include advice to men to not marry uncircumcised women. This technique often leads to isolation, and a dilemma for many women to find social acceptability. Social pressure is mostly effective in an illiterate community. Statistics indicate that women with more education are less likely to practice female genital cutting (PRB, 2001). Unfortunately, women often undergo the procedure too early for education to make any difference in their decision-making process. The categorization of female genital cutting as a cultural right appears to resonate with calls for its practice. The most surprising reason was the claim that a western/modern "promiscuous" lifestyle demands the maintenance of the practice. Female genital cutting is encouraged as a defense against the corrupting influences of Europeanization and modernization.[2]

An immigrant is any person who lives temporarily or permanently in a country where he or she was not born.[3] Migration is an ancient and natural human response to survival. It is a natural response to hunger, deprivation, persecution, war, or natural disaster. Migrants often leave their countries in search of a decent living for various reasons. Often, they move in search of jobs, opportunities, education, and quality of life. This move is often precipitated by conflict, poverty, social inequality, and a lack of sustainable livelihood, circumstances that compel them to leave their homes and sometimes their families. In modern society, the increasingly interconnected world has made international migration easy as transport has become cheaper and faster, and it is easier to move around the globe. With international migrants reaching 258 million in 2017, immigration is an irreversible fact of life. Because some Western countries abide by the International Convention on the Protection of the Rights of All Migrants Workers and Members of Their Families, which was held in 1990, these countries have vowed to protect basic human rights norms and ensure that the vulnerable and unprotected, such as migrant workers and members of their family, legal or illegal, are protected. This convention was adopted by the General Assembly of the United Nations that same year, making it a universal document to be respected by all member states in the United Nation. Unfortunately, not all migrants in Western countries are fortunate enough to experience the dream of being protected. Immigration by nature consequently consigns immigrants to growing minority communities, and within Western countries, these communities face significant challenges related to social inequality, such as discrimination, racism, sexism, and economic disadvantage. Immigrant women are the most vulnerable of these groups. While in some instances, migration has enhanced individual autonomy, power, and personal growth by providing access to new norms and opportunities, personal growth is inhibited for most, especially where these norms and opportunities are suppressed and undermined. The most affected of the immigrant population are women. While it must be noted that some immigrant women have fared well, most find themselves vulnerable due to social and personal barriers such as legal status, illiteracy, language, deprivation, discrimination, hardship, culture, or religion. As immigrants and women, most face discrimination because they find themselves in relationships where they are dependent upon an on a citizen or a "primary migrant." Consequently, their agency is often undefined. Some have limited access to education and therefore lack the same opportunities for employment as their male counterparts. Others find themselves in situations where abuse is justified by culture, identity, or religion, a reality that undermines their situation and ability to claim rights. Immigrants are often vulnerable to gender-based violence because they have to negotiate their cultural values and the human rights values they find in Western countries. Understanding that some of the values normally accepted in their home countries are prohibited in their new countries is a challenge that they have to negotiate as they adjust themselves to a new life.

Religion is a significant factor in promoting and undermining gender-based violence. This is because the intersection of culture and religion is complex, as religious texts and traditions both perpetuate and destabilize social behavior. Studies have suggested that religious people may be less likely to perpetrate gender-based violence (Fergusson et al., 1986). A 1999 study of US couples found that both men and women who attend religious services regularly are less likely to commit acts of domestic violence than those who attend rarely or not at all (Ellison et al., 1999). A follow-up study identified three pathways through which religious involvement may operate – namely, increasing levels of social integration and social support, reducing the likelihood of alcohol or substance abuse, and decreasing the risk of psychological problems (Ellison and Anderson, 2001). Other studies indicate that regular religious involvement promotes the perpetration of domestic violence by both men and women (Ellison and Anderson, 2001). Why might religious involvement have this protective effect vis-à-vis domestic violence? Both female genital cutting and intimate partner violence find legitimacy in religion directly or indirectly. Religious mythologies have legitimized female genital cutting in indigenous, Judeo-Christian, and Islamic writings (Wangila, 2007). As indicated in chapter seven, notions behind female genital cutting are rooted in indigenous/ancient notions of natural androgeneity, bisexuality, and hermaphroditism. While claims that extraordinary characteristics of the gods that are part of the human souls express themselves in the bisexual nature of all humans at birth may seem illogical to outsiders of cultures that believe in this practice, they are real for those who embrace them. While female genital cutting is not mentioned in the Bible, studies indicate that around 1,000 tribes of Eastern Jewish communities practiced female genital cutting to reduce sexual sensitivity. Although Islam is widely associated with this practice, the word does not even appear in the Qur'an. Important to note is that fact that sometimes, cultural practice that have nothing to do with religions sometimes find legitimacy in religious values, and over time, they become sanctioned by such religions.

For instance, behavior related to intimate partner's violence or domestic violence has also found legitimacy in religious values even as religions tend to teach about love of all unconditionally. Over the years, for instance, studies have shown that people who identify themselves as religious, either through self-reported attendance or devotion, have higher indicators of marital quality, including happiness and satisfaction, adjustment, and duration (Dudley and Kosinski, 1990; Filsinger and Wilson, 1984; Hansen, 1987). And yet, some have cited religious verses to justify gender-based violence. The controversial role of religion in sanctioning conflicting behavior is the dilemma of all believers. Believing men and women draw from sacred texts to provide friendship and mutual protection for one another as they collectively reflect the ideals of gender relations. Many scholars have reflected on the ambiguity of several religious traditions (including Christianity, Islam, Hinduism, Confucianism, Taoism, Buddhism, and Judaism) with regard to gender-based violence and gender roles. The complexity of religious traditions lies in the fact that they have both perpetuated violence against women and offered resources for healing. Recognizing that all religions, such as Judaism, Christianity, Islam, Hinduism, Buddhism, Confucianism, Daoism, and indigenous religions, incorporate values and beliefs that greatly impact women who live with gender-based violence is central to addressing the root cause and persistence of gender-based violence in various immigrant communities.

Human rights concerns

Should governments extend basic human rights to migrant women and their families regardless of legal status? This is the fundamental question at the heart of discourse on gender-based violence among immigrants. While violence against women and girls has been recognized as a human rights issue, a public concern, and a barrier to development, it has not received enough attention in Western countries (UNIFEM, 2010). International human rights apply to all human beings regardless of social status. Everyone enjoys basic human rights, such as the rights to life, liberty, and security of person; freedom from torture; equal protection of the law; and freedom from discrimination. International treaties include the Universal Declaration of Human Rights (UDHR); the International Covenant on the Civil and Political Rights (ICCPR); and the International Covenant on Economic, Social, and Cultural Rights (ICESCR). Other treaties that address human rights of migrants include the Convention on the Status of Refugees and the Convention on the Protection of the Rights of All Migrant Workers and Members of Their Families. These treaties outline rights of importance to migrants as well.

The historical movement of civil and human rights is an attraction for most immigrants who migrate to the West. As pioneers of human rights efforts, the Western countries, specifically the United States, are perceived as endowed with the responsibility of protecting the human rights of all human beings. It is based on this understanding that the United Nations declared that governments should extend basic human rights to humans regardless of cultural, racial, religious, or legal status. International human rights were adopted by the United Nations General Assembly; according to the Convention on the Elimination of Discrimination Against Women (CEDAW) General Recommendations No. 19, domestic violence against immigrant women is a violation of human rights. All country members of the UN are obligated to ensure protection and support of all women, including immigrant women. In the United States, the constitution guarantees rights for all people, whether citizens or not. These include equal protection under the law, the rights to due process, freedom from unlawful search and seizure, and the right to fair criminal proceedings. The United States is also bound by international treaties such as the ICCPR, the Refugee Convention, and the International Convention on the Elimination of All Forms of Racial Discrimination (ICERD), all of which grant basic human rights to all people, including migrants. Some governments find themselves conflicted regarding the need to protect immigrant women and fulfilling their goal of controlling illegal immigration. Even countries that have constitutional guarantees for migrants sometimes fail to protect the rights of migrants. It is therefore common to find existence of certain domestic laws that discriminate between citizens and migrants, especially in the provision of services. For this reason, migrants encounter prejudices and intimidation in the workplace and in society at large. Some countries have unequal access to basic services such as health care, housing, and education and arbitrary infringement of their civil liberties. This especially affects undocumented immigrant women.

In the UK, for instance, people with insecure immigration status are subject to the No Recourse to Public Funding (NRPF) rule as stipulated in Section 115(9) of the Immigration and Asylum Act 1999. This rule denies them access to public funds such as income support and housing benefit (UKBA, 2011b). The assumption behind NRPF is that "migrants coming to the U.K. should be able to provide for themselves financially without relying on benefits from the state" (Home Office, 2011). For immigrant women in domestic violence relationships, NRPF means they cannot access shelters or financial support to enable them to leave violent situations. Some of these women, who may live in a country on a visa based upon marital status (spouse is a citizen); employment; student status; visitor or temporary stay/exchange; or sometimes illegally without a visa, are often subject to a five-year probationary period of residency. This probationary period is contingent upon being a lawfully abiding resident, and if their visa expires or marriages are illegitimately terminated, they instantly become illegal residents and therefore are subject to deportation. Although the "Sojourner Project" and the "Destitution Domestic Violence" (DDV) Concession were launched to correct flaws in the NRPF, as effectively explained by Voolma, they are also flawed due to their restrictive eligibility requirements (Voolma, 2012: 8–9). Requiring that only immigrants with a visa be assisted is discrimination against undocumented immigrants and therefore condones domestic abuse in these communities.

As previously mentioned, most Western countries have pledged to fight domestic violence by enacting policies in this regard or by ratifying CEDAW. In the United States, for instance, domestic law protects migrants against violence and intimidation. According to the FBI, 11% of hate crimes in 2008 were based on the national origin of the victims. And yet, the US cannot guarantee the safety of migrants. For instance, when migrant women are more vulnerable to domestic violence and sexual assault due to language barriers, social isolation, lack of financial resources, and fear of deportation, the violence often goes unreported, and where it is reported, migrant women do not receive the critical services they need. Migrants are constantly denied rights to necessary services such as medical care and the right to effective representation. However, when a country does not follow through with its rhetoric, policy enactment is inhibited, meaning that when a country subscribes to an approach that specifically excludes defined individuals from certain social services, its ability to respond effectively to the issue of domestic violence is undermined. The tension between the conflicting priorities of immigration and the goal of protecting women from violence needs to be addressed and reconciled if an adequate response is to be realized. Some have argued that allowing immigrants access to social services encourages "pull factors" and will draw more immigrants to break the law. Often forgotten is the fact that no one chooses to suffer violence just so she can access support services. Domestic violence is an emergency situation for those affected and is sometimes life-threatening. It is important that human rights are recognized values that are independent of race, religion, or citizenship.

Intervention strategies

Statistics indicate that female genital cutting intervention programs that have relied on outside authorities or financial incentives have been unsuccessful when compared to those that have focused on community-based behavior change (PRB, 2001: 17). Unless intervention programs are broad enough and community-based, the diverse and often influential audience – men, opinion leaders, religious leaders, and traditional midwives – cannot be captured. Broad-based community intervention programs that have been said to be successful are characterized by an empowerment initiative. These programs are based on the individual and social change or empowerment model. According to this theory, social change is effected through cultural appraisal of the existing social reality (Parker, 1996). This means that if a community is empowered about its social reality, problem-solving becomes a participatory endeavor. This is because as participants, community members are not only informed about their personal, social, economic, and political situations but also become able to initiate action to improve their situations (Israel, Checkoway, and Schulz, 1994). An empowered community is enabled to take control of factors that determine their health and lives (Werner et al., 1997). An empowerment-based education enables community members to own their situation and to seek solutions that they deem fit. Thus, all community leaders and survivors of female genital cutting are enabled to transform cultural practices that undermine their rights.

An empowerment intervention initiative offers alternative rituals to community members. Discussing female genital cutting in communities is encouraged as leaders are advised to publicly decry the practice. It seeks the celebration of coming of age rituals even as it enables community leaders to publicly decry actual genital cutting of girls. By celebrating coming of age through alternative rituals, a community publicly declares that female genital cutting is not necessary to coming of age. This program was first employed in Kenya through Program for Appropriate Technology in Health (PATH) (Geneva, 1998). It is believed to have succeeded because it involved family and community members. Girls in the program have reported how training helped build the self-esteem and confidence that was necessary to resist community pressure to engage in female genital cutting. Also, initiates are helped to form support groups that strengthen their new role in the community culture. This community-based skill training program is necessary for countering the social pressure that sustains female genital cutting everywhere.

Immigration is a social reality in the globalization process, and domestic abuse is a global and local issue. Since domestic violence is not unique to immigrant residents in these countries, it should not be viewed as an exclusively immigrant issue. Industrialized countries should acknowledge it as a national concern since it affects a significant population of their communities. Due to the fact that immigrant women are half of the world's migrant population, their significance as a social group in these countries should not be underestimated. While immigration and the diversity it brings to these countries should be appreciated, the cultural difference should not be a reason to undermine the rights of migrants or native citizens. Industrialized countries attending to the struggles of civil and human rights, as leaders among nations, must set the example in protecting the rights of all social groups in order to demonstrate that their goals transcend local concerns.

To effectively address gender-based violence among immigrants, it is important that the response to this issue is intersectional and grounded in human rights. It is important that domestic abuse of immigrants is examined within the framework of multidimensional and intersectional social inequalities in order to understand how these matrices of social relations undermine progress in this area. As described earlier, responses to domestic abuse cannot be isolated from other policy areas such as immigration. It is important to ensure that social agendas such as immigration control do not undercut the national goal of preventing domestic violence. Western countries should find ways of reconciling both. It is important that established policies and programs empower citizens, immigrants, and refugee women to enable their active participation in decisions that affect them. Their voice should be integrated into these matters through voluntary organizations. For instance, in the UK, the government should review the criminal requirements of the Domestic Violence Rule to ensure nondiscrimination against other cases of domestic violence. Reducing the probationary period for spousal visa holders to relieve them of the possibility of abuse is a significant step.

Although most industrialized countries have worked in conjunction with the World Health Organization and the United Nations to establish and expand policies to discourage or prohibit domestic violence, these policies are far from being effective. Studies indicate that there are serious flaws in existing intervention programs, necessitating a review of existing mechanisms. Legal instruments must be effective in order to protect migrant and refugee women from domestic abuse. Further, nonbinding resolutions are difficult to enforce unless they become law. The efficacy of any law lies in its enforcement. Industrialized countries should ensure that laws prohibiting domestic violence are enforceable by removing all obstructive elements. While criminalization is crucial in discouraging abusive behavior, the prosecution is essential for attitude change. As Sophie Poldermans observes, each prosecuted case is a warning signal to others that the behavior is not condoned (2005).

Criminalization should be supplemented by localized and broad-based intervention strategies in order to involve the community at large in the process. Community-based initiatives have been described as effective because they address cultural values that promote certain behavior. Successful community-based initiatives have often relied on the human rights approach in order to empower the abused to reclaim their rights (Dugger, 2011). This approach recognizes that educating the individual and the community about unacceptable behavior is likely to influence behavior change. Consequently, including the subject of domestic abuse in public education and national campaign programs is fundamental to cultivating social change. Training teachers so they can empower children and women on matters of abuse is yet another significant step. Ensuring that immigrant communities have access educational programs is crucial to combating domestic abuse in their communities. For the effectiveness of such programs, this education should be made available in the local and native languages.

Since social norms are sometimes invoked to justify gender-based violence, faith-based initiatives should be part of the community-based intervention programs. It is particularly important to recognize that many of the problems women immigrants face are directly related to the differences in cultural/religious norms. Religion is therefore a useful response to issues related to gender-based violence. In African immigrant communities, for instance, women actually make up the vast majority of their congregations, and as such mosques and churches have been dealing directly with issues facing these women. The opportunities these communities can offer immigrant women of all legal statuses should not be overlooked, as this is a natural way for them to build a community that can respond to their needs. Religious groups are in a position to serve as the first point of entry towards addressing the problem. This is because religion is hugely important for African immigrant women, as in the US they are gaining more and more institutional power in how social behavior is to be handled in their new world.

As community-based initiatives, faith-based initiatives work at challenging religious narratives that justify domestic abuse (Wangila, 2007). Important to recognize, though, are some efforts that have been made in the United States for educating immigrants. There are instances where Muslim leaders have been invited to explain to refugee African communities that female genital cutting is not required in the Qur'an. While we recognize this important step on the part of the United States, we recommend serious integrated faith-based intervention programs in female genital cutting immigrant communities. The discussion about the role of religion in the transformation of social behavior is embedded in the diffusion of innovation and empowerment theories (Roger, 1983). According to this theory, when people are exposed to new ideas, they are likely to adopt the idea that has received favorable evaluations, especially from respected members of the community (Kegele, 1996). Because community leaders are authoritative and respected members in female genital cutting communities, their opinion is likely to influence attitudes toward female genital cutting (Wangila, 2007). In using the pulpit, religious leaders have an opportunity to express their opinions on matters that are likely to influence attitudes and behavioral change. Because their opinions are often accepted as sacrosanct, they are often not challenged. It is within this framework that the role of religion in social transformation is acknowledged.

Sociologist Christian Smith has described religious authority as embedded in the "transcendent motivation": an inherent ability associated with religion that grants it sacred authority to sanction social behavior (Smith, 1996: 9). Because female genital cutting is a cultural practice that finds justification in religious norms, it makes sense that religious values are used to demystify such legitimation. The notion that female genital cutting is required by a God or other divine beings elevates the practice beyond the rational discourse. Knowing that most religions teach the need to sacrifice oneself for God, religious values associated with genital cutting have been accepted by some as a way to demonstrate their commitment to God or their ancestors (Wangila, 2007). Where faith is concerned, scientific evidence of the harm associated with genital cutting may not matter.

As agents of social change, religious leaders therefore have the responsibility of promoting the social welfare of their congregants. This responsibility includes the need to demystify long-held, religiously sanctioned myths that inhibit the rights of women. Recognition of this role is a significant step towards strategizing against female genital cutting. When religious institutions serve as activist agents of their communities, they become moral articulators of social justice. When they acknowledge how religion can be used to undermine the rights of women, they become participants in the critical appraisal of their culture, a necessary step in undermining harmful cultural practices such as female genital cutting.

Religious leaders have the task of initiating social justice within their communities. It is important, however, that these leaders are trained through seminars and workshops to impart skills of demystifying harmful cultural practices to them. These forums not only can serve as training sessions for conscious raising process but will also provide them with an opportunity to conceptualize effective religious-based intervention programs. For instance, they will learn to disentangle more transcendent human values of social justice from culturally defined behavior that undermines the humanity of others. Most importantly, these leaders will learn how to promote individual and social involvement at all levels. It should be remembered, however, that although religious social institutions can be instrumental to social transformation, the success of any intervention program hinges on the cooperation of all individuals involved. It is therefore important that the reality of female genital cutting in the United States is acknowledged in the entire community.

Since health is a significant component of concern for immigrant women, industrialized countries should ensure that all have access to these services without discrimination. Regardless of immigration status, survivors of domestic violence should have the opportunity to access emergency support services like any other law-abiding citizen/resident. As Voolma explains, the UK should extend the Domestic Violence Rule to include survivors of domestic violence with insecure immigration status (Voolma, 2012: 16). For instance, survivors of female genital cutting should not have to worry about receiving medical attention or encountering health care workers who do not understand their condition. More health care workers should be trained and equipped with the necessary tools to address the medical concerns of survivors. Publicizing existing support services should be followed by the preparation of an appropriate support package highlighting domestic abuse as a concern and how to seek support. Access to social support is a significant step in addressing gender-based violence. Also, women can be supported through training in professions that they feel able to access, such as nursing and hairdressing. This can provide them with more power in family relationships as well as help in interventions towards freeing them from violent situations.

To effectively protect everyone from domestic violence, it is important that such behavior is tracked at a central research center where important data is collected from national and international migration centers. Tracking demographic data is crucial for identification of areas and reasons for such behavior and thus the necessitation for modification of strategy where necessary. This is an area where the government and non-governmental organizations can collaborate towards alleviating gender-based violence. Because non-governmental organizations (NGOs) are often small and rely heavily on volunteers and donations, policy making, financial support, and technical assistance from governments can go a long way to assist with intervention programs. It would help if the support included providing adequate resources to help fund organizations, such as South Hall Black Sisters, National Center on Domestic and Sexual Violence, Immigration Legal Resource Centers, and others that work towards ensuring that the rights of immigrants are protected.

Conclusion

In this chapter, we have discussed the challenges that immigrants face with regard to gender-based violence in the West. We have acknowledged that gender-based violence comes in various forms. We have focused on domestic violence and female genital cutting as examples of gender-based violence that immigrants confront in the West. We have argued that some of the behaviors that promote gender-based violence among immigrants are socially and culturally legitimate in their home countries. For this reason, most immigrants find it difficult to report these aspects of gender-based violence as they assume they are normal. Quite often, they are ignorant of their rights to protection in their new countries. We have also argued that often, even where responsibility for protection of human rights of all humans exists, immigrants, especially women, are often ignorant of the protections and services they are entitled to. Illegal immigrants are often the most vulnerable, as in the case of Medina discussed above.

It is worth concluding that immigration as a social reality experienced all over the world. Coming to grip with this reality is central to confronting challenges of immigrant communities elsewhere. The challenge for immigrants lies in immigration vulnerabilities. It is important that unique situations that inform or complicate situations for immigrant women are explored and addressed. As leading nations in the world, industrialized countries should prioritize their goals to fight abuse without allowing policies on immigration to inhibit the achievement of this goal. While efforts to acknowledge the existence of domestic violence and pledging to end it is crucial, the rhetoric should be followed with policies that are effective and attainable. Countries that allow themselves to succumb to or be inhibited by immigration as a factor to ensuring that everyone has access to social services are continuing to condone the violation of human rights of immigrant women. Industrialized countries should ensure that the basic human right to have life, health, and freedom from torture takes precedence over any other concern.

In addition to efforts by various governments in the West, it is important that immigrant communities take on the responsibility of addressing gender-based violence. Leaders in the Diaspora have a responsibility of ensuring that immigrant girls and their mothers live fulfilled lives without the fear of gender-based violence. Most importantly, the role of faith-based communities and religious leaders in transforming attitudes toward gender-based violence is crucial. The importance of integrating religion in intervention programs is a significant step toward the efficacy of addressing gender-based violence. It is important that human rights of girls and women from female genital cutting communities are upheld, especially in countries that claim to embrace these rights. It is the moral responsibility of the United States government and the community at large to protect the rights of immigrant girls and women.

Notes

1 Femicide in New York City: 1995–2002. New York City Department of Health and Mental Hygiene, October 2004.
2 Family Law Council, "Female Genital Mutilation, Cranberra, Family Law Council," June 1994, accessed at law.gov.au.
3 United Nations Educational Scientific and Cultural Organization, "Migrant," accessed at August 2010, www.unesco.org/new/en/social-and-human-sciences/ themes/social-transformations/international-migration/glossary/migrant/C. The Advocate for Human Rights.

References

African Women's Health Center (AWHC). 2012. "Brigham and Women's Hospital: A Teaching Affiliate of Harvard Medical School," accessed at www.brighamand womens.org on February 26, 2012.

Ahmadu, Fuambai. 2000. "Rites and Wrongs: An Insider/Outsider Reflects on Power and Excision," *Female "Circumcision" in Africa: Culture, Controversy and Change*, edited by Bettina Shell-Duncan and Ylva Herlund (London: Lynne Reinne Publishers). 283–312.

Al-Krenawi, Alean and Rachel Wiesel-Lev. 1999. "Attitudes toward and Perceived Psychosocial Impact of Female Circumcision as Practiced among the Bedouin-Arabs of the Negev," *Fam Process*, 38: 431–443.

CAHRV (Co-Ordination Action on Human Rights Violations). 2006. "State of European Research on the Prevalence of Interpersonal Violence and Its Impact on Health and Human Rights," accessed at www.carve.uniosnabrueck.de/reddot/CAHRVre portPrevalence(1).pdf on April 2014.

CEDAW (Convention on the Elimination of All Forms of Discrimination against Women). 1992. "General Recommendation No. 19," accessed at www.un.org/ womenwatch/daw/cedaw/recommewndations/recom.htm on April 16, 2014.

Chen, Stephanie. 2010/2012. "Pressure for Female Genital Cutting Lingers in the U.S.," http://edition.cnn.com/2010/health.

Dudley, Margaret G. and Kosinski, Frederick A. 1990. "Religiosity and Marital Satisfaction: A Research Note," *Review of Religious Research* 32(1), September: 78.

Dugger, Celia. 2011. "Senegal Curbs a Bloody Rite for Girls and Women," *New York Times*, October 15, accessed at www.nytimes.com.

Dutton, Mary, Leslye Orloff and Giselle Aguilar Hass. 2000. "Characteristics of Help-Seeking Behaviors, Resources, and Services Needs of Battered Immigrant Latinas: Legal and Policy Implications," *Georgetown Journal on Poverty Law and Policy* 7(2).

Ellison, Christopher G. and Kristin L. Anderson. 2001. "Religious Involvement and Domestic Violence among U.S. Couples," *Journal for the Scientific Study of Religion* 40(2): 269–286.

Ellison, Christopher G., John P. Bartkowski and Kristin L. Anderson. 1999. "Are There Religious Variations in Domestic Violence?" *Journal of Family Issues* 20(87–113).

Equality Now. 2012. "Celebrating Twenty Years of Advocacy and Action," accessed at www.equalitynow.org on May 10, 2014.

Femicide in New York City: 1995–2002. 2004. "New York City Department of Health and Mental Hygiene," October, www.ci.nyc.ny.us/html/doh/html/public/press04/pr145-1022.html.

Fergusson, David M., L. John Horwood, Kathryn L. Kershaw and Frederick T. Shannon. 1986. "Factors Associated with Reports of Wife Assault in New Zealand," *Journal of Marriage and the Family* 48(2): 407–412.

Filsinger, Erik E. and Margaret R. Wilson. 1984. "Religiosity Socioeconomic Rewards and Family Development: Predictors of Marital Adjustment," *Journal of Marriage and the Family* 46: 663–670.

Gruenbaum, Ellen. 2001. *The Female Circumcision Controversy: An Anthropological Perspective* (Philadelphia: University of Pennsylvania Press).

Hansen, Gary L. 1987. "The Effects of Religiosity on Factors Predicting Marital Adjustment," *Social Psychology Quarterly* 50: 264–269.

Hite, Shere. 1976. *The Hite Report: A Nationwide Study of Female Sexuality* (New York: Macmillan Publishing Co., Inc).

Home Office. 2011. "Victims of Domestic Violence without Indefinite Leave to Remain," London: Home office, accessed at www.homooffice.gov.uk/crime/violence-against-women-girls/domestic-violence-rule on April 14, 2014.

Israel, Barbara, Barry Checkoway, and Amy Schulz. 1994. "Health Education and Community Empowerment: Conceptualizing and Measuring Perceptions of Individual, Organizational and Community Control," *Health Educational Quarterly* 21(2): 149–170.

Kegeles, Susan M. Robert B. Hays, Lance M. Pollack, and Thomas Coates. 1999. "Community Mobilization Reduces HIV Risk among Gay Men: A Two Community Study," AIDS, 13. 1753–1762.

Leye, Els and Jessika Deblonde. 2004. "Comparative Analysis of the Different Legal Approaches toward Female Genital Mutilation in the 15th EU Member States, and the Respective Judicial Outcomes in Belgium, France, Spain, Sweden, and the United Kingdom," *International Centre for Reproductive Health (ICRH)*, Publications No. 8, Ghent, *The Consolatory*, April 23–24.

Maim, Sara. 2010. "Please Help Me: I don't Want to Be Cut Like My Sister . . .," accessed at www.dailymail.co.uk.

Morrissey, Kate. 2017. "Immigration Status Can Make Matters Worse for Domestic Violence Victims," accessed at www.sandiegouniontribune.com/news/immigration/sd-me-domestic-violence-20170107-story.html.

Obiora, Amede L. 1997. "Bridges and Barricades: Rethinking Polemics and Intransigence in the Campaign against Female Circumcision," *Case Western Reserve Law Review* 47(2): 275–378.

Orloff, Leslye and Janice V. Kaguyutan. 2002. "Offering a Helping Hand: Legal Protections for Battered Immigrant Women: A History of Legislative Responses," *Journal of Gender, Social Policy and the Law* 10(1): 95–183.

Orloff, Leslye, et al., 1995. "With No Place to Turn: Improving Advocacy for Battered Immigrant Women." *Family Law Quarterly* 29(2): 313.

Parker, Richard G. 1996. "Empowerment, Community Mobilization and Social Change in the Face of HIV/AIDS," *AIDS* 10(suppl. 3): S27–S31.

Poldermans, Sophie. 2005. "Combating Female Genital Mutilation in Europe: A Comparative Analysis of Legislative and Preventative Tools in the Netherlands, France the United Kingdom and Austria," a Masters' Thesis, University of Vienna, Vienna.

Rahman, Anika and Nahid Toubia (eds.). 2001. *Female genital mutilation: A guide to worldwide laws and policies*. New York: Zed Books.

Raj, Anita and Jay Silverman. 2002. "Violence against Immigrant Women: The Roles of Culture, Context, and Legal Immigrant Status on Intimate Partner Violence," *Violence against Women* 8(3): 367–398.

Rogers, Everette M. 1983. *Diffusion of Innovations* (3rd ed., New York: The Free Press).

Science News. 2006. "Female Genital Mutilations Affects Births: Study," *Science Daily*, June 2, accessed at www.sciencedaily.com.

Smith, Dorothy. 1999. *Writing the Social Critique: Theory and Investigations* (London: University of Toronto Press).

Spencer, Zara. 2002. "The Criminalization of Female Genital Mutilation in Queensland," *Murdoch University Electronic Journal of Law* 9(3), September.

Voolma, Haliki. 2012. "The Private Is International: Domestic Violence against Immigrant Women," Center for Gender Studies, University of Cambridge, UK, accessed at www.worldwewant2015.org.

UKBA. 2011b. "Public Funds," accessed at www.ukba.homeoffice.gov.uk/while-inUK/rightsandresponsibilities/publicfunds/ on April 16, 2014.

UN DESAS. 2017. *The International Migration Report 2017* (Highlights), accessed at https://www.un.org/development/desa/publications/international-migration-report-2017.html

UNDP (United Nations Development Programme). 2009. "Measuring Key Disparities in Human Development: The Gender Inequality Index." Human Development Research Paper 2010/46, New York UNDP, accessed at http://hdr.undp.org/en/reports/global/hdr2010/papers/HDRP201046.pdf on April 27, 2014.

UNIFEM. 2010. "The Facts: Violence against Women and the Millennium Development Goals," accessed at www.unifem.org/attachments/products/EVAWkit02VA WandMDGsen.pdf, April 2, 2014.

Wangila, Mary Nyangweso. 2007. *Female Circumcision: The Interplay between Religion, Gender and Culture* (New York: Orbis Books).

Werner, D., D. Sanders, J. Weston, S. Babb and B. Rodriguez. 1997. "Questioning the Solution: The Politics of Primary Health Care and Child Survival with an In-Depth Critique of Oral Rehydration Therapy," *Healthwrights* 967.

15 From Africa to America

Religio-cultural influence on Nigerian immigrants in a foreign land

Enoch Olujide Gbadegesin and Tolu Adegbola Adefi

Introduction

From time immemorial, human beings, together with other living organisms, have moved around and relocated from place to place for many reasons. Reasons for human migration in particular include prospects for better living conditions, such as assurance of food security, safety, and economic opportunities; political and religious asylum; and the pursuance of dreams and ambitions, among others (Parker, 2007). However, the movement of citizens of developing countries to more developed nations over the past centuries, especially during the period of the slave trade, was informed by a need for labor on farmlands and plantations and the desire to keep domestic servants and other unskilled manpower across the Atlantic. With time, prospects for the acquisition of Western education and specialized skills in various human endeavors, better living conditions, international trade, and other engagements have continued to characterize the movement of Africans and especially Nigerians to America.

A lot of scholarly work has been carried out on immigrants, migrations, and immigration; some have focused on the immigrants and how they have continued to use religion to transform their host American society (Levitt, 2007; Corten and Marshall-Fratani, 2001; Olupona, 2007; Biney 2011; Ogungbile, 2010); some have looked at the economic and political injustice and marginalization suffered by immigrants because of their religions (Nussbaum, 2012); some have looked at how the figure of the migrant has come to be seen as a potential terrorist in the West (Nail, 2016); some have looked at how to respond to domestic violence in general (CPCSP, 2009); and some have also considered intimate violence among West African immigrants (Akinsulure-Smith et al., 2013), yet there has not been enough research focusing on the influence of culture on Nigerian immigrants and its negative impact on the family in foreign lands as leading to domestic violence, juvenile delinquency, broken homes, and imprisonment. This vacuum will be our scholarly engagement in this chapter.

Based on an eye-witness account of one of the authors of this paper, our argument is that Nigerian immigrants are themselves negatively affected by some of their exported African cultural values, which thus lead to family violence and alarming rates of divorces in the United States. In this chapter, we shall look at Nigerian cultures, especially those that have direct connections to marriage and family life; then we shall look at how these cultures have continued to condition the behaviors of many Nigerian immigrants in America, to the point of negatively affecting the ways they behave and act; we shall next consider how some have gotten relief or solutions from the religions or religious communities of which they are a part; and, finally, we shall conclude with some suggestions.

Nigerian culture and family life

Before we look at Nigerian culture and family life, we shall first look at what culture is and what religion is. Culture is a complex whole according to anthropologists. In fact, Clifford Geertz, an American anthropologist, defines culture as "an historically transmitted pattern of meanings embodied in symbols, a system of inherited conceptions expressed in symbolic forms by means of which men communicate, perpetuate, and develop their knowledge about and their attitudes toward life" (Geertz, 1973:89). Geertz once stated that

> believing, with Max Weber, that man is an animal suspended in webs of significance he himself has spun, I take culture to be those webs, and the analysis of it to be therefore not an experimental science in search of law but an interpretative in search of meaning.
>
> (Geertz, 1973:5)

For Geertz, culture is not a force or causal agent in the world, but rather a context in which people live out their lives (Geertz, 1973:14). He does not only look at culture in isolation but argues that religion is actually part and parcel of any given culture.

He defines religion as "a system of symbols that acts to establish powerful, pervasive, and long-lasting moods and motivations in men by formulating conceptions of a general order of existence and clothing these conceptions with such an aura of factuality that the moods and motivations seem uniquely realistic" (Geertz, 1973:90). He breaks down this definition into different components that make sense to his readers. What we can draw from Geertz's definitions of both culture and religion is that any given people lives in a cultural world of which religion is an important part. For example, Geertz himself claims that a man may not be religious, but when a man needs to find meaning at its deepest level, religion will be the system of symbols he uses. In spite of the criticisms leveled against Geertz in his theory about religion and culture (Bourdieu, 1977; Asad, 1993), we still believe that Geertz is closer in his theoretical imagination of how culture helps people to make meaning and how majority of people order their lives than many other anthropologists of his time. As a result of this reality, we shall use the Geertzian connection of religion to culture as our launching pad in our discussion in this paper.

Given the reality of the intricate connection of religion to culture, we shall proceed to claim that family life is part and parcel of any given culture that religious rituals and practices have greatly impacted. No doubt, Nigeria has very rich and diverse cultural practices, yet such cultural practices as hospitality, care, and respect for the elderly; helping those in needs; hard work; marriage and child welfare; and so on could be said to be common to all these various Nigerian cultures. There may, however, be some variations in how people in those diverse Nigerian cultures practice these values. Religion definitely plays a part in how these cultural values are perceived and lived out. Yet still, certain aspects of these diverse Nigerian cultures have already outlived their values and usefulness, and there is need to either do away with or revise them. The cultural practices of female genital mutilation (FGM), the polygamous marital system, wife beating, child abuse and child and teen (ladies) trafficking, patriarchy, and so on that have occupied the front burner of the feminist fight for women's rights should be completely done away with.

Family life, which many Nigerians hold very dear, has continued to suffer serious setbacks in recent times due to various ways by which it is being handled. This is not to say that family has not been badly hit in the long-gone years; it certainly has. Notwithstanding, in recent times the family has continued to witness serious disintegration. This is due not only to cross-cultural influences, as some people will argue (Fadipe, 1970), but also, and most importantly, to some of the religious–cultural practices people have been socialized into (or inherited), which have continued to negatively influence the way many Nigerians think and behave. Some negative Nigerian cultural practices have affected marriage and family to such a degree that many families and marriages continue to break down. Needless to say, globalization also has had its fair share of redefining family and marriage as we enter the twentieth century (Bellah, 2005:21).

A closer look at the many Nigerian families and their marital systems could make anyone simplistically conclude that they are all steeped in a patriarchal structure. There is no doubt that there are many families in Nigeria's diverse cultures that are run on a patriarchal model, yet there are others that are actually matriarchal. In a patriarchal family setting, however, male and female roles are highly differentiated. Female members of the family are expected to play certain roles that often diminish and/or dehumanize them. Unfortunately, many religious leaders and followers in the three major religious traditions in Nigeria – namely African Indigenous Religions (AIRs), Christianity, and Islam – have this kind of theology that puts women and/or female counterparts at a disadvantage. It seems this theology of dehumanizing women is backed up by social forces that are assumed to be unchangeable. In his book *Sociology of the Yorùbá*, in particular, Fadipe (1970) seems to be swept off his academic feet by (maybe) unconsciously reinventing patriarchal structures while treating marriage and marital systems in Yorùbá society. He unfortunately fails to raise serious critiques against some of the negative aspects of marriage and family life. Here, we shall critically look at and raise some issues with many of these negative practices.

Marriage is regarded as a nomos building institution and a protection against anomic situations (Berger and Kellner, 1974) and as something desirable among all tribes in Nigeria, especially the Yorùbá (Fadipe, 1970). Yet, the prevailing patriarchal, social, and religious values of the Nigerian nation in which the family exists is under the garb of cultural practices and norms are also common in Ghana as noted by Adasi (2015). Perhaps both Idowu (1962) and Mbiti (1969) are right in saying that "in all things, Africans are religious." The inherited religious and cultural values affect the way the majority of Nigerians perceive, think, act, and in fact construct their social reality, which of course is common to many nations of the world. Unfortunately, Nigerian people often misuse and abuse this religious and cultural value, to the extent that they use these values as weapons of oppression, alienation, subjugation, and marginalization against the vulnerable people in society, especially women.

One quick example that readily comes to mind is the practice of making the house chores the exclusive duty of women, especially by traditional[1] people and those educated elites that continue to support such a practice. Another example is that of depriving women of making concrete life decisions that affect their lives directly.[2] The worst of these is when some men blame women for fertility problems and/or inability to give birth to male children. Some women are even accused of witchcraft. Unfortunately, and ironically too, some women's religious leaders also teach their women's counterparts to unduly submit to these unwarranted cultural beliefs and practices with the support of some scriptural verses.[3] We observe that people carry their religious and cultural heritage or values with them everywhere they go, and the majority finds it difficult to detach themselves from those inherited traits, even if they continue to have a negative impact on their lives.

Nigerian immigrants' families in America

This no doubt affects the way they live their lives in a place other than their own; we might say that because there is difficulty in detaching the self from inherited cultural practices, adjustment to a culture other than one's own become very difficult.[4] There are tons of reasons why many Nigerian families might not fare well in a foreign land. Certain cultural role reversals are inherent, for example, in American culture, such as the equality of sexes in a majority of states. In America, women cannot be treated abusively or one risks being jailed; women can talk about sex freely, which is often treated with secrecy in most African countries, including Nigeria: a woman who talks about sex openly in Nigeria risks being named a prostitute. More importantly, many Nigerian women are exercising their newfound, unfettered rights just like their American counterparts, which may eventually jeopardize their marriages. An example could be dressing the way one likes without fearing or pleasing anybody or making decisions without giving any consideration to the husband. This is possible because American culture is so inherently individualistic (Bellah, 2005:21–23) that nobody tells anybody what to do or what not to do, how to do a thing or how not to. Many of these freedoms that are inherent in American culture provide room for women to exercise their rights as and when they want to. We observe that lack of proper adjustment to other cultures has also led to many broken families, juvenile delinquency, divorce, and even life imprisonment in the United States of America.

Incidences of domestic violence among Nigerians in the United States can be said to be promoted and sustained by values and practices held by the people over a long period of time back in their homeland. Traditionally, more of the violence and discrimination was perpetrated by the men, but not exclusively; certain women have been found to be more violent than their menfolk, especially among those migrant Nigerians in America.[5] Violence against women manifests in several forms. These include physical, sexual, economic, mental, emotional, and psychological (Nworah, 2010). Violence against women has been conceptualized to mean patterns of abusive behaviors in any relationship that is used by one partner to gain control over another intimate partner. It also includes threats of actions that influence another person. In addition, it includes any behaviors that intimidate, manipulate, humiliate, isolate, frighten, terrorize, coerce, threaten, blame, hurt, injure, or wound someone (Nworah, 2010).

Many times, women keep their sad experiences to themselves, away from public knowledge due to fears of what the outcome might be, and this continues to terrify them in secret. For example, information obtained from the NHRC document shows that the Nigerian police are "insensitive to women . . . [and] sometimes even go out of their way to intimidate or harass women" (UK May 25, 2007, 96).[6] Many other reasons have been given for the continuous silence of women in spite of their suffering and marginalization.[7] These include respect for tradition; lack of knowledge of their fundamental human rights; pressure from family members to not disrupt the family peace; fear of reprisals from the abuser; the belief that their complaints will not be taken seriously by the police and justice system; and fear of financial insecurity. As a result, many women probably have concluded that physical, sexual, or psychological violence in the home is "normal" and only needs to be endured. In Nigeria, many assaulted and battered married women often claim that it is not that they are helpless to take revenge against the unjust and inhuman treatments they have suffered at the hands of their husbands, but that they often reasoned that they have held back because of their children (Fadipe, 1970).

The case is not as straightforward as it is in Nigeria, as immigrant women in American could easily damn and in fact have damned the consequences and walked away from their marriages when their suffering became unbearable. It is even becoming easy nowadays for Nigerian women either at home or in diasporas to initiate divorce when they are no longer pleased with men they have married.[8] This is due, as already highlighted above, to cross-cultural influences, especially the Western influence of living a life of self-sufficiency, respect for personal space, and individualism (Bellah et al., 2007). The culture of silence that characterizes marriage and family in Nigeria is usually challenged in America, where every person is given the liberty to sue and be sued for any kind of offence, especially the issue of domestic or family violence.[9] The Nigerian culture of women deferring to men in all matters pertaining to family and childrearing may not be all that permissible in the United States, where there is a constant campaign by women for equality of the sexes. We need to state clearly that this chapter is not primarily about family or marital violence as it is about how Nigerian culture has continued to have negative effects on Nigerian immigrants' marriages and families. Yet, a few examples of domestic violence will be mentioned.

During a relatively short time spent in the United States, one of the authors witnessed many examples of failed marriages, dislocated families, juvenile delinquencies, and in fact divorces.[10] Incidentally, many of these examples are found among the so-called religious people, especially the Nigerian Pentecostal/Charismatic Christian churches in America as well.[11] Many of the incidences also occurred among those Nigerians who married either African American men/women or white or other women or men from other countries.[12] It has rightly been shown that

> like all women, immigrant women are at high risk for domestic violence, but due to their immigration status, they may face a more difficult time escaping abuse. Immigrant women often feel trapped in abusive relationships because of immigration laws, language barriers, social isolation, and lack of financial resources.
>
> (Orloff and Little, 1999)

What we intend here is to show concrete examples of families or marriages in America that have suffered serious setbacks. In that endeavor, we will restrain ourselves from mentioning the names of those individuals who are concerned except in a few cases that we feel are very obvious, and perhaps those who have told their own stories openly elsewhere. We shall use anonymizing initials throughout so as to respect the privacy of those concerned.

A couple (Mr. and Mrs. A.A.) who, when in Nigeria, people thought were doing well, won the American Diversity Visa Lottery or Diversity Immigrant Visa (DV) in 1999. On arriving in the US, they tried their best to incorporate themselves into the American economic system, i.e. they tried as much as possible to get fairly well-paid jobs that could cater to their needs after the initial job problems faced by virtually all newly arrived immigrants in America. In time, they made progress and in fact helped to start a branch of the church they had been attending before they left for America. They already had a daughter before they migrated to America. However, while the couple was doing relatively well economically, they were unfortunately not doing well in their marriage. There were many occasions when friends and church members settled quarrels for them. The marriage eventually crumbled in 2004. According to the husband, with whom one of the authors of this chapter interacted in September 2006,[13] his wife's extended family contributed remotely to their marriage crumbling. He said that his wife's parents had been controlling his marriage since the day of their wedding.[14] When he was asked why he had kept quiet until the problem reached an unmanageable state, he said he thought they (himself and his wife) could fix it with the passage of time.

The problem, however, got out of hand, according to him, when his wife began to "misbehave." This showed initially in verbal abuse and then later in physical attacks so violent that on many occasions the police intervened, until he finally had to take the drastic step of putting an end to their barely ten-year marriage. The story from the husband was confirmed by three other people; one was a university professor at the University of New Hampshire, and two women who had at one time or another intervened. Unfortunately, one of the authors of this chapter was only able to interact with Mrs. A.A. on Facebook twice; the social media site was not suitable for such a sensitive discussion as this. The university professor who shared his experience of his intervention with the couple blamed the failure of this couple's marriage on the wife's parents. He claimed that undue interventions or incursions, on the one hand, and the adverse effect of American cultural influence on the marriage, on the other, were responsible for the couple's marriage to crumble. Of course, Mr. A.A. later confessed to having had an extra-marital affair with another woman when his wife continued to refuse his sexual gestures. One might conclude hastily that this was the reason for the wife's misbehavior. This is one of the not-too-straight forward examples of how African culture has continued to have an untoward effect on marriage. Fadipe has observed that many parents, especially fathers of the bride, often take undue advantage of their sons-in-law to either work for them on their farms or help them settle their many debts (1970:74–78).

This other story seems rather unfortunate. A man (O.M.) who is a professor at a university in Massachusetts, USA, pretended to be looking for a wife some 20 years ago and came back to Nigeria for a search. He was lucky enough to find one woman (Ms. F.A.),[15] who was not that lucky herself to have said yes to the man. After the woman consented, an elaborate wedding program was made in Nigeria. Arrangements were later made for Ms. F.A. to emigrate to the US to be with her newfound "lover." No sooner had she arrived the States than O.M. began to ill-treat her; he not only refused to come to the apartment he had rented for them to settle down but also lied to her about various "busy engagements" at universities across the States. When the woman began to complain, the professor asked if she had already tired of the marriage, and that she had his permission to sue for divorce. According to Ms. F.A., she continued to weep endlessly, regretting letting herself be deceived into a "marriage of lies" as she called it.

The day the truth was discovered, she said, she almost lost her mind. The professor's wife, who had already had four (grown) children for him, came to threaten[16] Ms. F.A. and tell her that she would make sure she was deported back to Nigeria. The woman became afraid and lived in continuous terror and fear until she met some of the members of the Redeemed Christian Church of God (RCCG) in Melrose, MA, who eventually came to her rescue. This woman was forced to sue for divorce and has remained single since then (18 years now). She ended up being a single mother to the daughter she had had with the professor, whom she has continued to take care since her divorce according to the law of the States. She said that even though she was awarded alimony and custody of her daughter, she continued to have fears and anxieties, and this culminated in a morbid hatred for men until what she called "deliverance for trauma healing" was performed on her.

The above is one example of violence perpetrated by men against women. The irony of the whole story is that until this author left America for Nigeria in 2009, the woman continued to wear her wedding rings. When she was asked why she was still wearing the rings, she answered that they served as a "bad" memory. Obviously, this woman has still not been totally healed of the trauma she suffered from the violence directed against her. One could be justified in believing the evolutionary theorists, who concluded that "human beings, rather than initially created in a well-ordered manner and then fallen by a perverse act of pride, have always been conflicted, manipulative, selfish, and prone to deceit and violence, though capable of derivative forms of altruism" (Pope, 2005:61).

One of the few Nigerian cultures that seems inimical to marriage and family life is the practice of an arranged marriage between a man and a woman. This has negatively affected a couple (Mr. and Mrs. O.A.) that was married for more than 14 years before each went their own way. Perhaps out of sheer emotional concern, some close friends of the woman had arranged a man for her because, in their own opinion, she was already "outgrowing the time of marriage." Indeed, the woman in question was already 34 years old,[17] which in most Nigerian cultures in those days was a big issue that could even need "spiritual intervention."[18] After her marriage in 1993, the wife got a very lucrative job in the United States because she had trained as a physical therapist in one of the foremost Nigerian universities (University of Lagos). As time went on, after the man was well situated in the US and had landed a good job, he began not only to harass his wife physically but also to have extra-marital affairs with "strange women" in America.[19] The wife claimed that she could have continued to endure the physical assaults she was getting from her husband, believing that it would stop one day, but for the strange women that were continuously being brought to her matrimonial home; she had to opt for ending her marriage of 14 years through divorce. According to her: "I am afraid of contracting HIV when I am supposed to be enjoying the fruits of my labor in the USA."

Incidentally, this woman, who happened to be one of the "vibrant" Christians when she was in Nigeria, almost lost her faith, and might have if not for the faith community she belonged to. Her faith community provided her with support, which has continued to help her cope with her divorced experience. The couple had three children together, all boys. Custody of the children had to be alternated between the parents every two weeks. One of the children, according to Mrs. O.A., has developed a morbid hatred of her for divorcing his father. Of course, one of the many consequences of dislocated families or broken marriages is children turning violent themselves or resorting to playing truancy or becoming delinquents. As carefully noted in their research, Fischer and Hout say that "children have easier lives and do somewhat better when they live with two parents instead of one" (2005:130). Waite and Doherty, while agreeing with Andrew Cherlin and his colleagues, actually push the argument further by claiming that "children whose parents would later divorce already showed evidence of more emotional problems even before the divorce, which suggests that marriage dissolution tends to occur in families that are troubled to begin with" (Waite and Doherty, 2005:154).

A few more examples before we move on to how divorced couples or dislocated families have turned to religion or faith communities for refuge, comfort, and consolation. One of the examples has to do with a cross-cultural marriage, which ended on a sad note. It is a story of a Yorùbá woman (Mrs. D.M.) who migrated to America in the late seventies in her late teens.[20] In America, when she was ready for marriage, she could not get any Nigerian man to marry her.[21] She eventually married a white American man, who initially proved very responsible and decent. But the marriage did not last for more than ten years before the man started to misbehave; he not only turned alcoholic but also became abusive and violent. He soon started to abscond and playing truant from home. The woman said that she resolved to go to a psychotherapist, because she was already going into depression. Her psychotherapist advised her to find a means of bringing her husband, which she eventually succeeded in doing. The therapy worked after they both attended a few sessions of psychotherapy, but this therapy only worked temporarily albeit temporarily.

The man (Mr. J.M.), according to the woman, soon relapsed into his alcoholism and actually became a drug addict and then more violent. The marriage eventually broke down and the woman had to file for divorce. This woman blamed her broken marriage on the Nigerian culture she had wrongly inherited, namely hoarding information from her husband, going to Nigerian social parties with no due consideration for her husband, and, of course, her untamed acquisition of materials, which eventually led to losing their home to foreclosure. Perhaps the husband may have had many reasons to blame himself, but the truth of the matter is that many poorly managed cross-cultural marriages break down. Lack of proper knowledge of another person's culture or inability to properly adjust to another person's cultural practices and values could be one of the factors that lead to family disloca-tion or maladjustment. While it is true that some men or women who marry from their villages, cities, or cultural backgrounds always have had family problems, there is likelihood that such problems may aggravate and even worsen when people like that marry from other cultures.

Another important area in which many Nigerian immigrants have been having problems is that of single-parent families, which is equally common among African Americans and white Americans, too (Wilson, 2002:107). In America today, Nigerian children with single parents are on the rise. Churches are not spared from this problem, especially Pentecostal churches.[22] In many of the Nigerian churches are found children whose parents have either divorced or whose fathers have died or are already in jail as a result of one crime or another. The story is the same across the states, in Massa-chusetts, California, Texas, Maryland, Maine, Rhode Island, New York, and Florida. Ironically, pastors are not spared in this respect. There are pastors in Nigerian churches in America who have divorced and remarried, while their wives continue to bear the burden of catering to the needs of the children. As hard as many Nigerian women are trying to keep their children in check, many of them still go wild. In fact, many of these children have complained bitterly that their parents want to use African methods of raising children – spanking, shouting, and abuse – to control them; they said this would never work in America! While many Nigerian immigrant children are not living up to expectations in the United States, a few of them, however, are doing well. For example, three children (a male and two females) of Nigerian immigrant families in a Redeemed Christian Church of God in Houston won scholar-ships to study in three different Ivy-league schools in 2014 before one of the authors left for Nigeria. A child of a pastor led his 2013 graduating class at the University of Houston, Texas.

And in order not to risk generalizing, there are quite a number of young Nigerian women in America who have never married,[23] yet have children, which is a phenomenon that is also common among young African American and white American women (Wilson, 2002:115; Tipton and Witte, 2005:14). There are different reasons given for the incidence of single, young, unmar-ried women having children. For example, Wilson blames the problem of unmarried single parents on poverty, especially among African Americans who live in rural areas, whereas Tipton and Witte Jr. blame the effect of marital delay among sexually active singles to be responsible for the increase in the risk of unwed parenthood, which sharply reduces the chance of ever marrying, especially for women (see Wilson, 2002:115; Tipton and Witte, 2005:14). Brilliant as these two observations may look, they do not touch on another very important reason. The sexual freedom that characterizes the West,[24] common especially among American young girls eager to lose their virginity as soon as they reach the age of puberty. Fiona Bowie observes that

> while in other cultures such as Arab and African societies,[25] to lose one's virginity before marriage (to talk less of getting pregnant) is a shame to the family . . ., on the other hand, being a girl at an American high school, virginity may be seen as a sign of failure – of not being sufficiently attractive to members of opposite sex (or of being a lesbian).
>
> (Bowie, 2000:104)

Our observations show that some Nigerian immigrant marriages and families are not faring too well due to the already highlighted reasons and many others that we are not able to touch on here. But while some married people continue to find it difficult to adjust in America, many have been greatly helped by their active engagements in their respective faith communities. It has been rightly shown that

> religious faith and religious organizations remain vital to many, if not most, persons in the modern world. It is only through religion, or other spiritual beliefs, that many people are able to find solace for the inevitable human experiences of death, suffering, and loss.
>
> (Burk, 2005)[26]

And

> churches, and other religious organizations, also play an important role in the creation of community and as a major source of social and economic assistance for those in need. . . . The idea of community of shared values and enduring association are often sufficient to motivate persons to trust and help one another even in the absence of long personal relationships.
>
> (Burk, 2005)[27]

What we intend to do in the next section is to show how some people with failed marriages, single parents (mothers), dislocated families, and others have been finding solace with religion and the religious communities with which they have identified.

Faith communities and support

Perhaps due to the distance from their home countries, faith communities have continued to provide families with spiritual, economic, and psychological supports. This could have otherwise been provided by the extended family members in Nigeria in times of crisis and distress, especially for those individuals whose marriages have fallen apart. It could also be as a result of a few people who have found it difficult to cope, especially with mortgages, rent, and even jobs. For example, in the Redeemed Christian Church of God (RCCG) in America with which we are more familiar, pastors and church leaders are in the habit of providing counseling and teachings to help people to readjust and resettle their lives after their marriages have crumbled. In Boston, Massachusetts, for example, many single mothers are constantly helped by the church in the form of provision of food and groceries, which has continued to help them augment the pittance they get from their jobs. Many of them, unfortunately, have not gotten an American green card, which makes it more difficult to get jobs they would love. Many women, because of the shame of a broken marriage, left for another church; some even stopped going to church altogether. At least, in 2008 alone, in one RCCG in Boston, five women left the church because their marriages broke down.

One of the duties of the pastors apart from preaching to and teaching their flock is to oversee them. They do this in by making sure those members that are having problems and hurting are supported with prayers, constant phone calls, counseling, and at times visits at home.[28] To make them happy and feel fulfilled, churches often organize special memorial services on behalf of their members' dead relations back in Nigeria. Most importantly, birthday ceremonies are usually well celebrated in the Nigerian churches in the US, especially in the RCCG. A woman (Mrs. K.A.), who turned 50 in 2015, has been taking care of her youngest child (a boy, now 13) since her marriage fell apart.[29] She confessed that the consolation she has had is the support and encouragement of her pastor and his wife as well as of the entirety of the RCCG she attends, who have not allowed her to feel too much of the impact of her marriage falling apart.[30] There is a sense in believing that this woman is consoled by the support and the encouragement she has been receiving from the community of faith she belongs during her joyous moment. American society is highly individualized and characterized by social isolation, so much so that one could be a loner and not be able to gather enough people together as one would have loved on one's day of celebration.

There is no doubt that pastors and members of the faith communities where the victims of violence and assault of the Nigerian immigrants are attending are doing this much, the pastors may have to do more of sensitizing and teaching their members of the need to drop those Nigerian cultural norms and values that are no longer acceptable and could lead to marriage breakdown. This will be possible, though, if the pastors themselves are not in the habit of abusing their wives and children or have not been infested with negative Nigerian cultural practices. It could be other way round, too; the wives of the pastors should also cultivate habits that will promote healthy relationships in their families before they teach others. In this way, the pastors should get well educated or be well informed about marriage and family life so as to be able to help victims of abuse, whether women, men, or children, in their religious organizations. Pastors and leaders in the immigrants' faith communities should be careful enough not to perpetuate the problems of the victims of abuse and violence, by not taking sides and by not using those scriptures that further diminish the value of the most vulnerable (women and children) in their midst. Pastors and leaders should even know their own limits in counseling. In essence, there is need for prompt referrals to marriage counselors and family psychologists when needed instead of making the matter worse or letting it get out of hand.

Perhaps it would be helpful for Nigerian immigrants' faith community to have "Welcome to America" brochures that contain teachings about adapting and integrating into a new culture to be taught and distributed to newly arrived immigrants. This could be taught in such a way that will not look as if their acceptable inherited cultural values from Africa are no longer useful. It has been discovered, for example, that when some men and women who are married get to America and eventually get jobs, there may be role reversal in terms of women landing better jobs than their male counterparts. In the process, the women may bring in more money to the homestead than their husbands. What the men should do in this case is encourage their wives instead of feeling envious or trying to exercise the role of the head of the house through control and subjugation.

Based on information received with regard to Ghanaian immigrants in the US, Moses Biney says ". . . women seek greater autonomy and independence from patriarchal and hierarchical home culture as a result of their changed economic circumstances. . . ." He then adds, "what is not often factored into the debate are the legal and social protections America offers women" (Biney, 2011:129). And, just like Biney, one of the authors here had heard from women when he was in America that African men in general and Nigerian men in particular are not romantic; they do not even buy flowers to show how much they love their wives (cf. Biney, 2011:129). A couple (Mr. and Mrs. O.K.) has separated but is yet to be legally divorced as a result of this singular act of lack of affection by the husband for his wife.[31] Perhaps, due to the cross-cultural influence – that of American culture of openly showing affection for their partners in form of kissing, necking, petting in public spaces, etc., which is obviously lacking among the majority of families in Africa at large and Nigeria in particular – Nigerian immigrant women could have felt they were being devalued by their husbands. Perhaps in order to bring happiness into their marriages and families, Nigerian immigrants in the US need to explore different positive methods that make for good homes.

Conclusion

In this chapter, we have been able to show with a few concrete examples of living persons and their locations in the US that many Nigerian immigrant families are facing a lot of challenges, some of which stem from their inherited cultural backgrounds and some of which are wrongly absorbed from the host culture. We looked at those Nigerian cultural values and habits that have always contributed to family breakdowns, dislocation, and even violence. What we first looked at were the different reasons people migrate to other countries. We also critically reexamined some of the Nigerian cultural practices that are considered anachronistic and suggested that those cultural practices should be done away with. While we were able to notice that the faith community has always provided spiritual and community support, we were still able to offer some suggestions as to how religion or faith communities could be a great resource in helping hurting and troubled Nigerian immigrant families in their midst. We were able to suggest that the faith community might need to consider giving some sort of orientation to newly arrived immigrants to America so as to help them to be well adjusted and adapted to their new cultural settings. We suggest in closing that it is also high time Nigerian people in Nigeria and America do away with those cultural habits that have continued to negatively impact on marriage and family.

Notes

1 The way traditional is used in this sense has to do with the way things have always been, that is, anachronistic modes of thinking and behaving, such as seeing women to be inferior to men in all dimensions of life.

2 In many Yorùbá families, women have little or no say in what concerns the way the house is run or how certain decisions that affect the members of family are made.

3 A very senior pastor's wife (herself a pastor) in Houston, Texas, once counseled women from the church's pulpit that women should see husbands as heads and follow their decisions. Drawing some inferences from the Bible, she said there is nothing they (women) could do about it. Doing or acting contrarily leads to disobedience against God and his words, which could lead to grave consequences. One of the authors attended one of the fastest growing Redeemed Christian Church of God's chapels while studying for his doctoral program between 2009 and 2014 at Rice University in Houston, Texas.

4 This is usually not true in all cases, though, to avoid hasty generalization; at least, there are many women in the United States who have borrowed American cultural values and absorbed them to such a degree that they seem not to have any interest in inherited cultural values from where they were born. They seem to have gone to the extreme, too, and this singular trait has affected the way they relate to other people from their home country.

5 Even in Nigeria, a few women have been reported on the daily news for killing their husbands, bathing their husbands with acid, maiming their husbands, and in fact, rendering their husbands invalid for life due to injuries inflicted on them.

6 Canada: Immigration and Refugee Board of Canada, *Nigeria: Domestic violence; recourse and protection available to victims of domestic violence (2005–2007)*, August 10, 2007, NGA102510.E, available at: www.refworld.org/docid/46fa 536f17.html (accessed March 4, 2017). NHRC means Nigerian Human Rights Commission.

7 Canada: Immigration and Refugee Board of Canada, *Nigeria: Domestic violence; recourse and protection available to victims of domestic violence (2005–2007)*.

8 Many women have initiated divorce, even in Ile-Ife and especially at Obafemi Awolowo University, Ile-Ife, to speak less of Nigeria as a whole. Quite a number of educated women have divorced their husbands, basing their actions on the unfair and unjust treatment they have suffered from their husbands.

9 In certain quarters in America, it has been reported that many women suffer in silence because of the fear of reprisal or of being killed by their husbands on knowing that they might be put in jail. See An Interfaith Resource Guide, *Family Violence and Religion* (Volcano, CA: Volcano Press, 1995); see pages 5–9.

10 Our documentation of examples shall be solely based on Christian communities because of the intimate connection we have with the "victims" or persons concerned. This does not mean that marriage and family problems are exclusive to the Christian faith. There are a few Muslims marriages that have problems as well.

11 Many others occurred among other people who have chosen to attend American churches, too, in order not to risk generalization.

12 One of the author's cousin's marriage broke down and led to divorce due to cross-cultural misunderstandings. The cousin still lives in Baltimore, Maryland.

13 This is when the author had resumed for his graduate program in Harvard in 2006.

14 The said author was once one of the couple's pastors in Ile-Ife between 1994 and 1999, before the couple left for the United States. The husband was actually a deacon in this same church before he emigrated to the US.

15 This story was shared by the woman, who we anonymize as F.A., with one of the authors in November 2006, when the author in question was given the opportunity to preach in the Redeemed Christian Church of God he was attending in Melrose, MA, USA from 2006 to 2009. The author preached on many adverse effects of some inherited African culture and how it could affect human life negatively. This was what prompted the woman to open up about her divorce. The woman turned 60 in October 2017. The professor in question moved to the US during the brain-drain syndrome that was an aftereffect of Nigeria's failed economy in the 1980s.

16 Perhaps the Professor in question and his first wife might have been separated without any legal divorce; otherwise, it would not have been possible for the professor to go to Nigeria and marry to another woman legally. Or it could be that Mrs. F.A. was not married legally as she claimed.

17 This woman is personally known to one of the authors, and he was able to hear the woman more than five times narrate the ugly experience of her marriage. She turned 56 years old in November 2017, while her husband turned 53. One might simplistically conclude that it was the age differential that was responsible for the marriage foundering. The question to ask, though, is: how are those couples who have age differentials – such as wives older than their husbands by five, six, or even ten years –and yet have stable and pleasant marriages managing their homes?

18 Even in most Nigerian churches today, a woman who is not married by age 30 becomes a target for deliverance from personal, family, and lineage demonic attacks. Many women in this category are themselves becoming anxious and apprehensive if they have not married or at least have potential men to marry.

19 The said couple is still living in Minnesota, USA, but separately as of the time of writing.

20 The woman told her story to one of the authors in November 2007, when he was invited to come and preach at the church the woman was attending in Manchester, New Hampshire. As said earlier, one of the authors is an ordained pastor in one of the Pentecostal churches in Ile-Ife, Osun State, Nigeria.

21 One of the evil sides of taking children, especially female children, to America is difficulty in finding men to marry. There are many examples to prove this.

22 Emphasis is placed on Pentecostal churches here due to the fact that their teachings seem to pay more attention to marriage and family life; one would expect that a phenomenon like marriage crisis would not be found in the midst of these churches at all.

23 In one Redeemed Church in Boston, Massachusetts, there are more than ten single mothers present and yet never married. One of the authors of this paper interacted with some of them when he was in the US studying for his graduate program between 2006 and 2008.

24 Sexual freedom has pervaded almost every society of the world with the exception of the Islamic countries. As said earlier, one of the effects of globalization and developments it brings is the influence of social media on the world at large. Social media serves as means of imaging and absorbing other cultures, either consciously or unconsciously (Appadurai, 1996: 1–4). Appadurai believes that "whatever else the project of the Enlightenment may have created, it aspired to create persons who would, after the fact, have wished to have become modern." According to him, he long wished for American life when he was in Bombay as a young secondary school boy through the power of media and the interest he had already shown for American Hollywood.

25 The additional example of Africans is ours and not in the original.

26 See Robin Burk, "Immigrants, Religion and Conflicts: The US Experience," available at: www.windsofchange.net/archives/immigrants_religion_and_conflict . . . posted on March 6, 2005; downloaded on March 25, 2017.

27 Burk, ibid.

28 One of the authors was privileged on many occasions to accompany the lead pastor of one of the RCCG Zonal Headquarters in Boston to members' homes for prayers, counseling, or identifying with them, in either their times of sorrow for the loss of their parents and loved ones back in Nigeria or their own moments of joy such as birthdays, naming ceremonies, etc.

29 One of the authors got this information from the woman when he went to an academic conference in March, 2016.

30 This woman's case is very sad in that the husband invited her to come to America and promised that when they were settled, they would bring the three children they had had together before the husband left for America. By the time the woman got to America, the man had reneged and in fact had gone away with another woman at time of writing.

31 This couple – the wife is an ordained pastor, while the husband is an ordained deacon – migrated to America in 1998. The husband (Deacon O.K.) told one of the authors of this chapter that his wife had denied him sex for more than two years as of 2014, when he was giving the information. He said his wife was fond of nagging at him about showing affection to outside ladies more than to her, and hence that he should go look for those "better" ladies outside to have sex with. Information date was February 22, 2014, Beechnut, Texas.

References

Adasi, Grace Sintim. 2015. "Couples and Roles: Issues of African Women" *Canadian Social Science*, 11(9): 104–108. www.cscanada.net/index.php/css/article/view/7553. doi:http://dx.doi.org/10.3968/7553.

Akinsulure-Smith, Adeyinka M., Tracy Chu, Eva Keatley and Andrew Rasmussen. 2013. "Intimate Partner Violence among West African Immigrants" *Journal of Aggression Maltreatment & Trauma*, 22(1): 109–129. doi:10.1080/10926771.2013.719592.

Appadurai, Arjun. 1996. *Modernity at Large: Cultural Dimensions of Globalization*. Minnesota: University of Minnesota Press.

Asad, Talad. 1993. *Genealogies of Religion: Discipline and Reasons of Power in Christianity and Islam*. Baltimore, MD: Johns Hopkins University Press.

Bellah, Robert N. 2005. "Marriage in the Matrix of Habit and History" in Tipton, Steven M. and John Witte, Jr. (eds.), *Family Transformed: Religion, Values, and Society in American Life*. Washington, DC. George Town University Press, 21–33.

Bellah, Robert N., Richard Madsen, William M. Sullivan, Ann Swindler and Steven M. Tipton. 2007. *Habits of the Heart: Individualism and Commitment in American Life*. Berkeley, CA: University of California Press.

Berger, Peter L. and Hansfried Kellner. 1974. "Marriage and the Construction of Reality" in Coser, Rose Laub (ed.), *The Family: Its Structures and Functions*. New York: St. Martin's Press, 157–174.

Biney, Moses O. 2011. *From Africa to America: Religion and Adaptation among Ghanaian Immigrants in New York*. New York: University of New York Press.

Bourdieu, Pierre. 1977. *Outline of Theory of Practice*. Cambridge, London, New York, Melbourne: Cambridge University Press.

Bowie, Fiona. 2000. *The Anthropology of Religion*. Malden, MA: Blackwell Publishers.

Burk, Robin. 2005. "Immigrants, Religion and Conflicts: The US Experience" www.windsofchange.net/archives/immigrants_religion_and_conflict, posted on March 6, 2005 downloaded on March 25, 2017.

Corten, Andre and Ruth Marshall-Fratani (eds.). 2001. *Between Babel and Pentecost: Transnational Pentecostalism in Africa and Latin America*. Indianapolis: Indiana University Press.

Crime Prevention and Community Safety Project. 2009. *Responding to Domestic Violence with New and Emerging Communities Reported by Sophie Diamandi and Patricia Muncey, 2009* www.migrantwomensservices.com.au/media/files/1034.pdf.

Fadipe, Nathaniel A. 1970. *The Sociology of the Yorùbá*. Ibadan: Ibadan University Press.

Fischer, Claude S. and Michael Hout. 2005. "The Family in Trouble: Since When? For Whom?" in Tipton, Steven M. and John Witte, Jr. (eds.), *Family Transformed: Religion, Values, and Society in American Life*. Washington, DC: George Town University Press.

Geertz, Clifford. 1973. *The Interpretation of Cultures: Selected Essays*. New York: Basic.

Idowu, Bolaji E. 1962. *Olodumare: God in Yorùbá Belief*. London: Longman Press.

Interfaith Resource Guide (IRG). 1995. *Family Violence and Religion*. Volcano, CA: Volcano Press.

Levitt, Peggy. 2007. *God Needs No Passport: Immigrants and the Changing American Religious Landscape*. New York: New Press.

Mbiti, John S. 1969. *African Religions and Philosophy*. London: Heinemann.

Nail, Thomas. 2016. "A Tale of Two Crises: Migration and Terrorism after the Paris Attacks" *Journal of the Studies in Ethnicity and Nationalism*, 16, No. 1, 158–167.

Nussbaum, Martha C. 2012. *The New Religious Intolerance: Overcoming the Politics of Fear in an Anxious Age*. Cambridge, MA: Belknap Press of Harvard University Press.

Nworah, Uchenna. 2010. "Violence against Women in the Nigerian Community: Issues of Power and Control" *USAfricaonline.com*, accessed at www./usafrica online.com/2010/08/06/violence-against-nigerian-women-by-uche-nworah/ on March 13, 2017.

Ogungbile, David O. 2010. "Faith without Borders: Culture, Identity, and Nigerian Immigrant Churches in Multicultural American Community" in Ogungbile, David

O. and Akinade, Akíntúndé E. (eds.), *Creativity and Change in Nigerian Christianity*. Lagos: Malthouse Press Limited, 311–331.

Olupona, Jacob K. 2007. *African Immigrant Religions in America*. New York: New York University Press.

Orloff, Leslye and Rachael Little. 1999. "Overview of Domestic Violence and Battered Immigrant Issues" in Leslye Orloff and Rachael Little (eds.), *Somewhere to Turn: Making Domestic Violence Services Accessible to Battered Immigrant Women. A 'How to' Manual for Battered Women's Advocates and Service Providers*. Harrisburg, PA: Ayuda Inc., 1–21.

Parker, Lynette M. 2007. "The Ethics of Migration and Immigration" *Markkula Center for Applied Ethics Sourced*, accessed at www.scu.edu/ethics/focus-areas/more/resources/the-ethics-of-migration-and-immigration/ on March 12, 2017.

Pope, Steven J. 2005. "Sex, Marriage, and Family Life: The Teachings of Nature" in Tipton, Steven M. and John Witte, Jr. (eds.), *Family Transformed: Religion, Values, and Society in American Life*. Washington, DC: George Town University Press, 52–70.

Tipton, Steven M. and John Witte Jr. 2005. "Introduction: No Church Like Home" in Steven M. Tipton and John Witte, Jr. (eds.), *Family Transformed: Religion, Values, and Society in American Life*. Washington, DC. George Town University Press, 1–20.

Waite, Linda J. and William J. Doherty. 2005. "Marriage and Responsible Fatherhood: The Social Science Case and Thoughts about a Theological Case" in Tipton, Steven M. and John Witte, Jr. (eds.), *Family Transformed: Religion, Values, and Society in American Life*. Washington, DC: George Town University Press, 143–167.

Wilson, James Q. 2002. *The Marriage Problem: How Our Culture Has Weakened Families*. New York: HarperCollins Publishers.

16 Clerics and community-based organizations as agents of social change

Mary Nyangweso

Introduction

Socialization is a process of acquiring values, some of which impact the way we view the world and ourselves. Because attitudes we acquire shape social behavior, it is important that social norms should promote social welfare. Religious socialization is central to social processes. Whether implicit in scriptural writings or not, social behavior that is legitimized by religion or religious leaders can gain significant support. To address concerns associated with a religious behavior, therefore, it is important not only that faith-based initiatives are interrogated but also that religious leaders be part of the process. As respected social agents, religious leaders also possess unique authority that if well utilized can effect positive change. In this chapter, I examine the role of social agents in the social constructions of attitudes and general behavior. In particular, I examine the role of clerics – imams, rabbis, and pastors – in the social transformation of attitudes towards female genital cutting.

Religion and social behavior

Despite claims that religion is declining, persistent social behavior maintains its legitimacy in religious beliefs. The role of religion in the social construction process is clearly articulated by the sociologist Peter Berger, who describes the relationship between religion and culture as dynamic such that while religion constructs the world, the world in turn constructs religion. This process of legitimation lies in the grounding of social realities in the "sacred *realissimum* which is beyond the contingencies of human meanings and human activity" (Berger, 1969: 27–28, 32). By referencing something beyond the human realm – supernatural being; God, divinities, or ancestors – religion infuses reality with fear, awe, and reverence. The result is an unwavering authority from adherents, since sanctioned practices are viewed as unchangeable. Once socialized, such behavior is difficult to change. The power of religion in sanctioning social behavior lies in what sociologist Christian Smith calls the "transcendent motivation": an inherent ability of religion to grant social behavior sacred authority (Smith, 1996: 9).

Studies of female genital cutting have recognized the role of religion in attitude formation and behavior related to this practice (Wangila, 2007). This practice, otherwise known as female genital mutilation (FGM) or female circumcision (FC), is controversial partly because it is often associated with religious values even where scriptures do not deal with the subject. This practice, which involves non-therapeutic surgery and modification of the woman's reproductive organ and in some cases infibulation, is a worldwide practice; it is particularly prevalent in Africa and in the Middle Eastern countries, where it is performed on girls and young women as a rite of passage (Rahman and Toubia, 2001: 8; Dorkenoo, 1994: 14ff). As an example of socialized behavior, female genital cutting finds justification in religious norms.

In a survey of 113 women to investigate the role of religion in the persistence and eradication of female genital cutting in the West, of specific concern was an examination of the role of religious leaders in deconstructing values and the attitudes that surround the practice. The central questions in the survey were: (1) whether female genital cutting was practiced in the West; (2) the reason for the persistence of female genital cutting; (3) whether religious values were a factor in the persistence of the practice; (4) the perceived flaws in existing intervention programs; (5) whether a religious component ought to be incorporated in intervention programs for effectiveness; and (6) whether religious leaders such as clerics, imams, and rabbis should be involved in intervention programs. This investigation was part of an exploration of S. Roger's theory of the diffusion of innovation and empowerment theories, in which he states that when people are exposed to new ideas they are likely to adopt them if the ideas receive favorable evaluations from authoritative and respected members of the community (Rogers, 1983; Kegele, Hays, Pollack, and Coates, 1996). The sample was randomly selected through a respondent-driven snowball sampling technique derived from an existing contact. Most respondents were from communities in the United States. The objective was to find out why the practice persisted, ways to address this concern, and most importantly, whether religious leaders had a role in intervention programs.

According to findings of the study, over 60% connected the persistence of female genital cutting in immigrant communities with tradition or culture (Nyangweso, 2014), but 25% considered religion to be a significant factor. Some of these respondents believed that the practice was a religious injunction. Of the surveyed, 89% believed that religious leaders should be involved in intervention programs. Eleven percent, who did not see the need to involve leaders, argued that these leaders are unlikely to have any impact. They argued that these leaders are unlikely to oppose accepted norms in their communities. Drawing on the findings, I argue that attempts to eradicate female genital cutting are futile unless the religious "transcendent motivation" is evoked, as argued by Christian Smith, since this is necessary to demystify values that make it sacrosanct. The notion that female genital cutting is required by a God or other divine beings is to elevate the practice beyond the rational discourse. Knowing that most religions teach the need to sacrifice oneself for God, religious values associated with genital cutting have been accepted by some to demonstrate their commitment to God or their ancestors (Wangila, 2007). Where faith is concerned, scientific knowledge may not matter. When religious institutions serve as activist agents of their communities, they become moral articulators of social justice. When they acknowledge how religion can be used to undermine the rights of women, they become participants in the critical appraisal of their culture, a necessary step in undermining harmful cultural practices such as female genital cutting.

As discussed in chapter fourteen, female genital cutting is rooted in indigenous/ancient notions of natural androgeneity, bisexuality, and hermaphroditism, extraordinary characteristics of the gods, which express themselves in the bisexual nature of all humans at birth. In some indigenous communities of Africa, for instance, this theme is clear in mythology. The Dogon and Bambara of Mali, West Africa, for example, believe that female genital cutting is used to distinguish the sex of a child. They argue that when a child is born, it has two souls, which are inhabited by an evil power – *wanzo*. This evil spirit *wanzo* prevents fertility. To destroy the power of *wanzo*, the prepuce and the clitoris must be cut off (Griaule, 1970: 21). The myth clearly narrated by Marcel Griaule is part of the creation narrative, which describes how the Supreme Being – *Amma* – created the earth from clay. It says:

> After creation, the myth states, the earth lay down flat in the form of a female body facing upwards in a line from north to south. The earth, which is often viewed as the feminine aspect in the universe, is described in feminine terms. Its sexual organ, the vulva, is represented by an anthill, which symbolizes its clitoris; a termite hill. Amma, feeling lonely and desiring sexual intercourse with this beautiful creature he had created, approached the earth. This act, often described in this Dogon myth as the first breach of the order of the universe, is considered as the origin of troubles in the world. To the Dogon, god is the origin of human troubles. As the myth explains further, at the approach of Amma, the termite hill rose up, thus preventing intercourse. The ant hill – the earth's clitoris – obstructed the union, "barring the passage and display of Amma's masculinity. . . . The termite hill was as strong as the organ of the stranger" (Griaule, 1970: 17). According to this myth, the clitoris obstructed any sexual union because it "housed" the jealous male aspect of the female earth which resisted the Supreme Being's sexual advances (Griaule, 1970: 17). But because the Supreme Being was all powerful, he used his power to cut down the termite hill – the earth's clitoris, and proceeded to have intercourse with the excised earth. . . . According to this myth, all human beings are created as androgynous beings with both male and female souls, a status similar to that of the gods. Every individual's soul is revealed in and through reproductive organs. The

female soul of a man is believed to be in his prepuce or foreskin, while the male soul of a woman is in her clitoris. Realizing that each human being was endowed with two souls of different sex, or two principles corresponding to two distinct persons, it was revealed to the spirits that humans are not capable of supporting both beings. To ensure the balance, each person would have to merge himself or herself into the sex for which s/he appeared to be best fitted. The Nummo therefore circumcised the man, to remove the femininity from his prepuce. . . . The removal of the woman's masculinity was to detach her clitoris which is symbolized by a scorpion. Possessing a dual soul is dangerous and the only remedy is circumcision.

(Griaule, 1970: 16–29)

Both male and female genital cutting are therefore rituals intended for boys to shed their feminine and for girls to shed their masculine "souls." The idea is to perfect the femininity and masculinity of the initiates. It is believed that a woman whose genitals are not cut is likely to encounter misfortunes arising from curses and the wrath of her ancestors and gods. Perceived misfortunes include infertility, still births, the death of siblings or a spouse, incurable diseases, insanity, and even death.

The practice of female genital cutting is traced to the 1,000 tribes of Eastern Jews who are said to have embraced the practice a one way of reducing sexual sensitivity. Strabo, a Greek philosopher of the first century BCE, mentions female genital cutting as a practice of Creophagi Jews. He describes the males as having "their sexual glands are mutilated, and the women are excised in the Jewish fashion" (*United Nations High Commissioner for Refugees Newsletter*, 3–4). The Jews that Strabo was referencing were the Falasha Jews of Ethiopia, who are said to have practiced female genital cutting in Jerusalem during King Solomon's time (Abu-Sahlieh, 2001: 19). Some Christians have used the Old Testament and New Testament narratives to make a case for female genital cutting. For instance, Abraham's circumcision in the Old Testament has often been used to argue that both male and female genital cutting existed at the same time and if God approved of one, he implicitly approved of both. The narrative of the Virgin Mary narrated in Matthew 1:23ff and Luke 1:27 has been used to argue for female genital cutting. As Abu-Sahlieh explains, the argument that is made is that there is no way Mary's virginity would have been ascertained unless circumcision ritual which often associates this exam was also performed. As Abu-Sahlieh explains, the term "Virgin Mary" means "an unmarried woman who is initiated, and therefore circumcised" (2001: 219). Christian women who believe in genital cutting consider the emulation of Mary as the model of chastity and true submission of God. Virginity and genital cutting are viewed as ways to demonstrate chastity and faith in their God as Mary did.

Although Islam is widely associated with female genital cutting, the word does not even appear in the Qur'an. Yet, during research, while some respondents attributed female genital cutting to Islam, others did not see any connection between the two. Important to note is the fact that female genital cutting was a common practice in some Middle Eastern countries such as Egypt, Sudan, Yemen, and even in Arabia prior to Islam (Abu-Sahlieh, 2001: 176–177). Today, female genital cutting persists in countries such as Oman, South Yemen, Libya, Algeria, Lebanon, Iraq, and Palestine. In these cultures, female genital cutting is referred to as *tathir* or *tahara*, an Arabic word for purification. Genital cutting is said to rid the woman of the "dirty surpluses that if left would hide the demon" (Abu-Sahlieh, 2001: 143).

In spite of the fact that the practice is pre-Islamic, advocates of female genital cutting continue to cite religious teachings related to purity. They often considered it *khitan al-sunna* or *al-sunna*, which means "compliant with the tradition of Muhammad" (Abu-Sahlieh, 2001: 11). Most advocates of female genital cutting often base their claims on the sacred narratives in the *Hadith*, a record of sayings and actions of the Prophet Muhammad. The *Hadith* is one factual report of the prevalence of female genital cutting during the time of Prophet Muhammad. The *Hadith* records numerous instances where the prophet discussed the issue of genital cutting. In one of the narratives frequently cited, the prophet is said to have given some advice to Um-Habibah/Um-Atiyyah on the subject. In this conversation, he is said to have asked her whether she continued her profession of circumcising *jawari*. In response to the prophet, Um-Habiba asked whether she should abandon the practice. He replied, "Yes, it is allowed. Come close so I can teach you. If you cut, do not overdo it, because it brings radiance to the face and it is more pleasant for the husband" (Abu-Sahlieh, 2001: 112–113). Advocates of female genital cutting believe that the prophet sanctioned the practice in this conversation; otherwise he would have disapproved of it then.

Narratives in the *Hadith* also record the circumcision of Hagar, the Egyptian slave girl to Abraham and Sarah. According to the story, Sarah, who was unable to give Abraham a child for fertility reasons, offered him their slave girl Hagar as a wife so he could beget an heir who would inherit his property, a common tradition at the time. Hagar conceived a child and gave birth to Ishmail, Abraham's first-born son through whom Muslims claim descent from Abraham. Out of jealousy, Sarah vowed to cut three of Hagar's body parts. Fearing that she would cut her nose and two ears, Abraham ordered Sarah to pierce Hagar's ears and to circumcise her (Gen. 16:1–16). In African communities, this narrative is used by some to sanction female genital cutting. Awa Thiam narrates:

> Long before the time of Mahout, there was a prophet named Ibrahima [Abraham] who was married to his cousin Sarata [Sara]. He went up to the land of Gerar, where reigned King Abimelech, who delighted in taking to himself all men's wives who are remarkable for their beauty. Now it happened that Sarata was unusually fair. And the king did not hesitate to try to take her from her husband. A supernatural power prevented

him from taking advantage of her, which so astonished him that he set her free. And he restored her back to her husband and made her the gift of a handmaid named Hadiara [Hagar].

Sarata and her husband lived together for a long time but Sarata bore Ibrahima no child. And eventually, Ibrahim took Hadiara to wife; some say it was Sarata who said to her husband that he should take her handmaid to wife since she herself could not bear any children. And so Sarata and Hadiara became co-wives to Ibrahima and Hadiara bore him a son and his name was Ismaila [Ishmael] and Sarata also bore a son to Ibrahima and he was called Ishaga [Isaac]. In the course of time, the relationship between the two women deteriorated. And so, it came to pass that one-day Sarata excised Hadiara. Some say that she only pierced her ears while others maintain she did indeed excise her.

(Thiam, 1986: 59)

Fatwa (opinion of Muslim religious leaders) is a component of Islam that speaks to the authority of Muslim leaders to decree a practice or behavior. A *fatwa* that is often cited by Shiite Muslims is that of Ali the fourth caliph (successor) of Prophet Muhammad. Ali is said to have sanctioned female genital cutting by declaring it a "meritorious act." Although he is said to have maintained that "a man's circumcision is indispensable," he is said to have added that, "What thing is better than a meritorious act?" (Abu-Sahlieh, 2001). By this statement, advocates of female genital cutting believe that Ali left no choice for women. An honorable woman is expected to get cut. Another popular *fatwa* on this issue was issued in 1981 by Sheikh Mahmoud Shaltout, a former Sheikh of Al Azhar in Cairo – a famous university of Islam. Sheikh Shaltout urged Muslims not to give up female genital cutting because the prophet favored it. He argued that lessons of the prophet should not be abandoned in favor of the teachings of infallible beings such as doctors. Shaltout believes that parents have the responsibility of ensuring that their daughters are circumcised and that those who avoid it are violating their duty.

While advocates of female genital cutting have turned to religious teachings to sanction the practice even where such a link is missing, it is important to note that opponents of the practice have also objected to any such link. For instance, as early as 1943 a Muslim scholar, Abu-Sahlieh Usamah dismisses arguments about cleanliness, chastity, and aesthetics associated with this practice in a magazine – *Al-Risalah*. He describes female genital cutting as a "crime against a girl's body that no one has the right to commit" (Abu-Sahlieh, 2001: 262). To most critics, female genital cutting is a violation of basic women's rights to good health, sexuality, and choice.

As a cultural practice that finds justification in religious norms, it makes sense that religious values are used to demystify such legitimation. The persistence of the practice in the world today probably speaks to questions of meaning and social identity. As a practice that is embedded in social norms and advocated by some religious individuals, female genital cutting should be addressed as a religious practice whether or not it is scripturally sanctioned. Religious claims that female genital cutting is required by a God or some other divine beings are intended to elevate the practice beyond a rational discourse. Knowing that most religions promote self-sacrifice on behalf of the higher being, sacred values associated with a practice such as female genital cutting are likely to be accepted by some as a way to demonstrate their commitment to God or their ancestors.

Social critique and behavior change

Change is a social fact. Therefore, all social behavior is bound to change at some point as part of the social process. Social change is a fundamental factor in cultural variety because it is responsible for variation in cultural values. It determines what values and behavior ought to remain relevant and therefore be preserved or retained and which ones ought to be discarded by subsequent generations. The acceptance, maintenance, rejection, or abandonment of values and subsequent behavior often depends on prevailing normative and/or other rational grounds. Reasons for social change vary from community to community and may be triggered by certain events or needs in the society. For instance, some fundamental changes emerge out of an encounter with foreign agents or values such as through cultural borrowing. Individuals as rational beings are capable of initiating change. They may find some aspects of their cultures irrelevant and undignified, thus the need to question and reevaluate. This process is called cultural criticism.

Cultural criticism, which is a catalyst for change, is a healthy social exercise. It is often undertaken if: (1) a cultural value considered a drag on the progress of a given society is often rendered dysfunctional and therefore irrelevant; (2) a cultural practice is in contradiction with the ethos of a new set of cultural values and/or a new generation; (3) a cultural practice is morally unacceptable due to various reasons; (4) a value is often rendered irrelevant or contradicts other parts of the tradition; and (5) a cultural practice becomes irrelevant because the metaphysical foundation on which it is based is found implausible, unconvincing, and therefore unnecessary. Cultural practices that are often discarded as a result are what the philosopher Alasdair MacIntyre calls "dead" tradition, while those that are retained are known as the "living" tradition since they maintain their relevance in contemporary society (MacIntyre, 2007: 222). MacIntyre argues that any moral society should seek to situate its virtues in relation to the good life of the individual and not for the sake of tradition (220).

The process of social transformation depends on the individual as the agent of social construction. As agents of social construction, humans are responsible for evaluating cultures and religions in order to adapt them to current situations. As sociologist Margaret Archer observes, the response of an individual to his or her own culture depends on its effects on him/her

(1988: 143). Human needs and actions can reinforce a cultural system or resist its influence when it is perceived to be inhibitive to the common good. Even though culture acts on humans, it is important to remember that it is also a product of human agency (Archer, 1988: 77–78; Berger, 1969: 32–33).

Calls for the eradication of female genital cutting, for instance, base their claims on health and human rights consequences of the practice, as discussed in earlier chapters. Studies indicate that female genital cutting has immediate and long-term health problems, including severe pain, urine retention, shock, hemorrhage and infection, cysts, abscesses, keloid, scarring, damage to the urethra, dyspareunia, difficulties with childbirth and sexual dysfunction, sterility. This includes the frequent need for episiotomies during childbirth (Coquery-Vidrovitch, 1997: 208). Statistics indicate that infertility rates among women who have had female genital cutting are as high as 25 to 30% (PRB, 2001; Women's Health.gov, 2009). As a result, female genital cutting is rendered a violation of human rights of girls and women to health by those who embrace moral values such as human rights, including the World Health Organization and the United Nations. Those concerned with gender equity view it as an expression of patriarchy, sexism, and sexual control of female sexuality (Gruenbaum, 2001: 133). Calls for the eradication of the practice are based on claims that the practice is no longer relevant given the health and moral harm to the individual. Reasons for the practice are implausible, unconvincing, and unnecessary.

Community-based organization and intervention

Intervening against a cultural practice such as female genital cutting should be strategic and contextual. As indicated earlier, intervention programs that have relied on outside authorities or financial incentives have been unsuccessful when compared to those that have focused on community-based behavior change (PRB, 2001: 17). It is for this reason that broad-based approaches to female genital cutting are said to be effective. The advantage of broad and community-based intervention programs lies in their diversity and influence on the target audience – men, opinion leaders, religious leaders, and traditional midwives. Broad-based community intervention programs that are successful are often characterized by an empowerment initiative, an initiative that is based on the individual and social change or empowerment model. According to Parker, social change is affected through cultural appraisal of the social–cultural reality (Parker, 1996). In other words, a community that is empowered about its social reality is not only invited to participate in the problem-solving enterprise but is also enabled to take control of factors that determine their health and lives (Werner et al., 1997). As participants, community members are not only informed about their personal, social, economic, and political situations but also become initiators of action to improve their situations (Israel, 1994). By asking community members to pledge not to engage in female genital cutting activities and their sons not to insist on marrying cut women, such a program counters social coercion that is central to the sustenance of this practice. It is for this reason that approaches that have ignored certain target audiences such as men are bound to fail. Studies indicate that men play a significant role in the persistence of female genital cutting. In Burkina Faso, studies indicate how important a father's decision is to the practice female genital cutting (PRB, 2001: 23).

Significant to the process and close units to the community are faith-based organizations. Integrating faith-based communities in efforts toward protecting girls and women who live with the risk of female genital cutting is fundamental since religion is a crucial element to the persistence of female genital cutting. As indicated earlier, religious institutions as agents of activism are moral articulators of social justice. When they acknowledge how religion has been used to undermine the rights of women, they become participants in the critical appraisal of their culture, a necessary step in undermining harmful cultural practices such as female genital cutting.

Community leaders as empowering agents are central to the effectiveness of this intervention model. As agents of social transformation, their role lies in propelling community participation. Enabling community leaders to discuss female genital cutting encourages public decrying of the practice. It is important, therefore, that religious leaders, as agents of social transformation, should be part of the intervening process because of their roles as socializing agents. As social agents of social transformation, these leaders can socialize communities against embracing this practice by dispelling the widespread, erroneous belief about the practice.

Imams, pastors, ministers, and social deconstruction

Religious leaders are significant in the process of social reconstruction because they claim authority from a beyond – the divine command; an authority described by Smith as rooted in its inherent sacred ability to sanction social behavior (1991: 9). Most Jews, Christians, and Muslims are familiar with the story of Moses as narrated in Exodus 3:1–22. Moses' ability to accomplish the very difficult task of freeing slaves from the Pharaohs can be attributed to the power of divine command. Just like any ordinary human being, Moses was resistant about going to Egypt because, as a mere mortal, he did not see how he would accomplish the task before him. However, reassurance from God set him in motion. The authority of religion to "move mountains" is well explained in this narrative. Many religious leaders – Abraham, Old Testament prophets, Jesus, Muhammad, the Buddha in Buddhism – were able to make a difference because they claimed some extraordinary experience.

As agents of social transformation, religious leaders draw on liberative values of the religions they embrace to mobilize collective action against social injustice (Smith, 1991: 53). The idea of liberation is informed by the notion that human beings can be motivated by reason, community, human nature, and religious values to reject social injustice. Most liberative social movements are driven by the recognition of their agency in social construction. Religious movements are particularly aware of the potent force they possess in relating the social to the extraordinary (Berger, 1969: 27–32). Religious leaders who recognize this fact can be significant agents in social transformation.

Charismatic leaders are particularly effective in social construction because they possess a spiritual gift that makes them extraordinary communicators (Conger and Kanungo, 1988; Weber, 1964). Through charisma, they sanction and justify or condemn and discourage moral claims. Because their opinions are often accepted as sacrosanct, they are often not challenged. If properly utilized, charisma and sacred authority can propel social transformation of attitudes towards female genital cutting. As agents of social change, therefore, religious leaders have the responsibility of promoting the social welfare of their congregants. Religious leaders have the task of demystifying long held, religiously sanctioned myths that undermine the rights of women. In using the pulpit, religious leaders have an opportunity to express their opinions on matters that are likely to influence attitudes and behavioral change.

A good illustration of the effectiveness of religious leaders in curbing persistent cultural practice is found in the experience of Isnino Shuriye, an elderly mother of eight from a small village of Ijara, Garissa in Northeastern Kenya. As a trained exciser of girls in her community, Shuriye believed in her practice as a "good thing mandated by her God." This was a practice her mother had performed before. She remembers holding girls down for circumcision when her mother performed the practice. In an interview by Mark Lacey of the *New York Times*, Isnino Shuriye recounts the pride she felt as an exciser. She recalls how, many years ago, when she leaned over each of her three daughters, knife in hand, and sliced their genitals. Each time, as the blood started to flow, she quickly dropped the knife and picked up a needle and thread. Quickly, expertly, she sewed her daughters' vaginas almost shut. "I was full of pride," she recalled. "I felt like I was doing the right thing in the eyes of God. I was preparing them for marriage by sealing their vaginas." Shuriye would cut off the clitoris and all the labia of 7-year-old girls and sew them up, leaving a small, pencil eraser-sized opening for menses and urine. Ms. Shuriye did not use any form of anesthesia and would bind the girl's legs together for weeks so scar tissue would form.

One day, a grassroots activist group that works with the Somali community, known as members of Womankind Kenya, visited her home. The group, which was founded by Sophia Abdi Noor, tried to convince her to abandon the practice. She sent them away from her property, claiming that she had no use for people who came to denounce her way of life. She believed they were there to plant Western ideologies in her mind. Persistence by members of Womankind paid off. Sophia Abdi explains: "It was difficult to change her mind. . . . We knew she was respected, and we wanted her on our side."

It was this group's hope that converting Shuriye would influence other excisers like her and in fact, other women, to abandon the practice. They hoped to convince her that cutting girls' genitals was not only a violation of their rights but also that Islam does not condone the practice. When the women's activist group realized that they could not convince her to abandon the practice on their own, they invited liberal Muslim clerics to accompany them. As a Muslim, Shuriye could not turn an imam away. She was soon convinced that genital cutting was not only harmful but also was not dictated by or consistent with the teachings of the Qur'an. The clerics also told her to apologize to her victims and offer them camels as compensation. Although Ms. Shuriye had no camels to give to her victims, she begged for forgiveness from the women she had cut. "I now feel like I've committed a sin against God," she said. It is worth noting that when Shuriye was informed about genital cutting not being an Islamic practice, she was shocked beyond words. She expressed her shock by abandoning the practice she once valued. Her reaction is indicative of the authority of religion in social behavior. Due to conscientization, Shuriye turned from being an exciser to an active opponent of female genital cutting. She made house calls on other girls to convince them to abandon the practice. With her help, she has persuaded 12 other excisers to denounce the practice. After her transformation, she recounted with remorse the brutal acts that she believed were divinely sanctioned (Lacey, *New York Times*, June 8, 2004).

To be effective, however, it is important that these leaders undergo awareness training sessions to acquire skills about their specific roles and how to demystify harmful cultural practices. Through these sessions, they will learn how to disentangle more transcendent human values of social justice from culturally defined behavior that undermines the humanity of others. Most importantly, these leaders will learn how to promote individual and social welfare at all levels. It should be remembered, however, that although religious social institutions can be instrumental to social transformation, the success of any intervention program hinges on the cooperation of all individuals involved. It is therefore important that the reality of female genital cutting in the West is not only acknowledged but also that community involvement to end it is promoted.

Religious reform is usually based in hermeneutics. Hermeneutics of scriptural interpretation helps one to transform religion through reconstruction of the past to make it relevant to present experience. Feminist hermeneutics as articulated by the prominent feminist theologian Elisabeth Shussler Fiorenza is understood among feminists as necessary in reforming religion to promote women's rights. Fiorenza begins by acknowledging that all scriptures are "historical prototype rather than a mythic archetype" (Fiorenza, 1984: 10). This means scriptures should be viewed as models of continuous revelation that adapts to social experience. This means that a scriptural message that ignores social norms that promote social justice should be reconstructed and retold to affirm the rights of women (Fiorenza, 1984, 1998; Gross, 1996).

While it is difficult to transform attitudes that are rooted in faith, it is not impossible to transform them through faith-based conscientization process. However, attempts toward conscientization of communities that practice female genital cutting must be undertaken with caution to avoid confrontation. Any form of social reform that is perceived as an affront to religion or culture will be resisted. It ought to be remembered that religions, like all social phenomena, are dynamic and susceptible to social change. As they transform, they represent an adaptation to new norms that are often reflective of a contemporary state of the community. In Islam, for instance, it is particularly crucial that the egalitarian message of the Prophet Muhammad is highlighted to promote the welfare of the Muslim woman. In recognition of this fact, the Muslim scholar Muhammad Mashuq ibn Ally advocates that Muslims must continue to grapple with the task of rediscovering the relevance of Islam to present day problems. As they formulate answers to challenges of the modern age, renewal of religious thought is necessary to meet the modern ideational challenge (Ally, 1992: 59–60).

Conclusion

In this chapter, I have argued that cultural and religious reasons remain significant factors in the persistence of female genital cutting in the West. While religious values are cited by some as the reason for the persistence, cultural and identity values are not exempt. It is therefore important for social values that influence behavior to be identified and addressed if behavioral change is to be affected. Indigenous values often thought to be extinct remain significant in reinforcing identity and the persistence of female genital cutting in modern industrialized societies. Since female genital cutting is grounded in the social norms of a community, it is important that cultural appraisal of these norms is examined to promote the relevant and affirming values. It is important that religious values that sanction female genital cutting are examined and demystified as health and moral consequences associated with the practice are highlighted.

Central to the prevention argument is the fact that real change must emanate from within the communities themselves. To promote real change, therefore, challenges related to the procedure must be addressed within the community's framework. The need to improve community-based initiatives is fundamental to be effective. The content of community-based initiatives must be clearly defined and stated. Since the purpose of prevention programs is to protect the vulnerable in society – children and women – it is only logical that community-based initiatives encompass the element of awareness and the provision of information to communities regarding female genital cutting. Governments should set up awareness programs in communities that live with the risk and consequences of the practice. The rest of the community needs to be informed as well about the practice. To promote effective awareness, the subject of female genital cutting should be addressed in all public education and national campaign programs. It is also important that awareness programs are transmitted in English and in local languages to reach a wider audience. Families must be brought to understand that norms and values associated with female genital cutting are untrue. Changing norms is a significant step in delinking female genital cutting and marriageability. It is important that community members are informed that female genital cutting is not a mark of a good woman and that women who have not been cut have made good wives as well. With these, men will not seek cut wives, a gesture that will demotivate cutting. Achieved at the community level, the deconstruction process can have a significant impact. The often cited Tostan program in Senegal worked not only because it was a collective effort, but because its programs also targeted norms that support the practice.

Community-based initiatives must seek to integrate *faith-based initiatives*. Integrating faith-based initiatives in intervention programs will help to broaden attitude changes towards the practice. Since prevention of female genital cutting is often embedded in the human rights framework, it is important that faith-based organizations invoke human worth values to justify and sanction human rights values as the basis for discouraging female genital cutting. Thus, religious communities are in the best position to address issues that find justification in religious values. Since leadership is central to intervention programs, it is important that imams, rabbis, pastors, and other relevant religious leaders are included in the intervention programs against female genital cutting. As Abdi Gele et al. (2013) observe, leaders are opinion shapers. Whenever they are sympathetic to a cause such as female genital cutting, it can be very difficult to eradicate it. It is therefore important that they understand what is at stake in the practice and how girls and women are affected if they are to work towards changing the practice.

References

Abu-Sahlieh, Sami Awad Aldeeb. 2001. *Male and Female Circumcision: Among Jews, Christians and Muslims: Religious, Medical, Social and Legal Debate*. Warren Center, PA: Shangri-La Publications.

Archer, Margaret S. 1988. *Culture and Agency: The Place of Culture in Social Theory*. Cambridge: Cambridge University Press.

Berger, Peter. 1969. *The Sacred Canopy*. New York: Anchor Books.

Conger and Kanungo. 1988. "The Empowerment Process: Integrating Theory and Practice." *The Academic of Management Reviews*, accessed at www.jstor.org on June 24, 2013.

Coquery-Vidrovitch, Catharine. 1997. *African Women: A Modern History*. Boulder, CO: West View Press.

Dorkenoo, Efua. 1994. *Cutting the Rose: Female Genital Mutilation, the Practice, and Its Prevention*. London: Minority Rights Publication.

Fiorenza, Elisabeth Shussler. 1984. *Bread Not Stone: The Challenge of Feminist Biblical Interpretation*. Boston: Beacon Press.

———. 1998. *In Memory of Her*. New York: Crossroad.

Gele, Abdi, et al. 2013. "Attitudes towards Female Circumcision among Men and Women in Two Districts in Somalia: Is It Time to Rethink Our Eradication Strategy in Somalia?" *Obstetrics and Gynecology International*, Vol. 2013, accessed at www.hindawi.com.

Griaule, Marcel. 1970. *Conversations with Ogotemmeli: An Introduction to Dogon Religious Ideas*. Oxford: Oxford University Press.

Gross, Rita. 1996. *Feminism and Religion: An Introduction*. Boston: Beacon Press.

Gruenbaum, Ellen. 2001. *The Female Circumcision Controversy: An Anthropological Perspective*. Philadelphia: University of Pennsylvania Press.

Israel, Barbara, Barry, Checkoway, Amy, Schulz and Zimmerman, Marc. 1994. "Health Education and Community Empowerment: Conceptualizing and Measuring Perceptions of Individual, Organizational and Community Control." *Health Educational Quarterly*, 21(2): 149–170.

Kegele, Susan, Robert Hays, Lance Pollack and Thomas Coates. 1996. "Community Mobilizations Reduces HIV Risk among Gay Men: A Two Community Study," AIDS, 13(13): 1753–1762.

Lacey, Mark. 2004. "Genital Cutting Shows Signs of Losing Favor in Africa." *The New York Times*, accessed at http://query.nytimes.com on June 22, 2013.

MacIntyre, Alasdair C. 1984/2007. *After Virtue*, 3rd edition. Notre Dame: University of Notre Dame Press.

Mashuq Ibn Ally, Muhammad. 1992. *Theology of Islamic Liberation*. Maryknoll, NY: Orbis Books.

Parker, R. 1996. "Empowerment, Community Mobilization and Social Change in the Face of HIV/AIDS." *AIDS*, 10(suppl. 3): S27–S31.

Population Reference Bureau. 2001. *Abandoning Female Genital Cutting: Prevalence, Attitudes and Efforts to End the Practice*. Accessed at https://assets.prb.org/pdf/AbandoningFGC_Eng.pdf, January, 2017.

Rahman, Anika and Nahid Toubia (Eds.). 2001. *Female Genital Mutilation: A Guide to Worldwide Laws and Policies*. New York: Zed Books.

Rogers, Everette M. 1983. *Diffusion of Innovations*, 3rd edition. New York: The Free Press.

Smith, Christian. 1991. *The Emergence of Liberation Theology: Radical Religion and Social Movement Activism*. Chicago: University of Chicago Press.

———. 1996. "Correcting a Curious Neglect or Bridging Religion Back." *Disruptive Religion: The Force of Faith in Social Movement Activism*, Christian Smith, ed. New York: Routledge.

Thiam, Awa. 1986. *Black Sisters Speak Out: Feminism and Oppression in Africa*. London: Pluto Press.

Wangila, Mary Nyangweso. 2007. *Female Circumcision: The Interplay between Religion, Gender and Culture*. Orbis Books.

Weber, Max. 1964. *Sociology of Religion by Max Weber. Maryknoll, New York*: Beacon Press.

Werner, David, David Sanders, Jason, Weston, Steve, Babb and Bill, Rodriguez. 1997. "Questioning the Solution: The Politics of Primary Health Care and Child Survival with an In-Depth Critique of Oral Rehydration Therapy." *Healthwrights*, 967.

Women's Health.gov. 2009. "Female Genital Cutting Fact Sheet," accessed at www.womenshealth.gov, June 23, 2013.

17 Conclusion

Mary Nyangweso and Jacob K. Olupona

In this volume, we have examined the relationship between religion, gender-based violence, immigration, and human rights. The discussion, which was framed within intersecting social categories, has demonstrated that gender-based violence is local, regional, and international and that its origins are both cultural and religious. Drawing on diverse experiences of gender-based violence, the book highlights how complex and varied forms of gender-based violence are. It shows how various communities identify the problem in their local communities and that violence is not only a perennial problem but is a universal challenge the world over. By highlighting local battles of gender-based violence, the experiences of immigrant communities are placed in a context that informs their situations in the new world. A key point that emerges in all chapters is that gender-based violence is a socially constructed behavior, a process that begins in childhood. It is a phenomenon that is intrinsically social, and it deserves local and international redress. Recognizing this fact is fundamental to acknowledging how serious and deeply rooted the problem is. This is a significant step in strategizing efforts toward combating such behavior.

To address gender-based violence, the roots of the problem must be located in the socialization processes. The origins of gender-based violence are rooted in the tendencies for humans to desire to exert power over one another. This volume highlights how the viciousness of gender-based violence in our society is enabled by the inadequate approach to this problem and the legitimization of the violence by cultural and especially religious values. This makes it difficult to challenge, as value-based attitudes and behavior are often difficult to change. To grasp gender-based violence fully, the complex and interrelated social factors that design violent attitudes and behavior must be interrogated. It is important that one understands the complex intersection between violence, immigration, religious values, and human rights. It is especially important that the social matrices that inform socialization processes and the structures of power are examined. One of the recommendations in the book is that attitude formation in the globalizing world must account for the reality of pluralism and be cognizant of human rights values.

In order to understand the experience of gender-based violence among immigrant communities across the globe, it is important to examine local experiences, especially how social construct of behavior occurs and how this process informs immigrant behavior. While unique forms of gender-based violence are highlighted and similarities acknowledged where necessary, all forms of gender-based violence must be interrogated within their social contexts. It is important to acknowledge how social structures such as patriarchy and systemic sexism influence attitude formation that leads to gender-based violence. Further, the book highlights the role of religion in enabling gender-based violence and how, as a social institution, it can help prevent this problem.

Drawing on this understanding, the volume draws on the interdisciplinary approach and intersectionality as a framework of analysis to highlight how various approaches and perspectives must intersect in efforts to combat gender-based violence. It is argued that the intersectional approach is critical to deconstructing the thought process that defines identity, power, and opportunities that influence social behavior and that this approach can help in finding an effective resolution to the problem. As feminists like Peggy Miller and Nancy Biele have argued, a challenge to sexual violence must contextualize the problem of violence within general assumptions about gender and gender expectations. It is agreed that the best way to respond to gender-based violence requires changing social assumptions about gender. It is argued that the analytical framework that ignores the diversity present within women such as color, disability, gender, poverty, and religious affiliation is insufficient for addressing social problems such as domestic violence. Utilizing human rights theories such as moral universalism and cultural relativism, questions of agency and the respect of diverse cultures have been explored. Specifically, the challenges that immigrant communities face, which range from citizenship, unfamiliarity with national language, laws, practice, and even claims of basic human rights, have been explored. Challenges of discrimination and subjection to unequal treatment and unequal opportunities at work and in their daily lives have been placed in focus. Effects of marginalization and exclusion influence various forms of violence. It has been noted in this volume that gender-based violence is a serious problem among immigrant communities. Immigrant women are at a higher risk of suffering domestic violence than their counterparts due to their status as both women and migrants.

It has been established that gender-based violence can lead to health concerns, including long-term physical, mental, and emotional health problems. Reproductive health concerns have been associated with common practices such as child marriage and female genital cutting, including hemorrhage, infertility, complications during childbirth, the risk of sexually transmitted infections like HIV, and even death in extreme cases. Efforts to change gender-based violence must begin with a change in the attitudes and behavior of everyone in the community.

The role of religion in gender-based violence is highlighted in the various chapters in this volume. The influence of religion is both overt and covert as it is evident in public, history, modern politics, immigration, gender violence, and human rights. The significant role of religion in perpetuating or challenging social behavior affirms the intersection paradigm that is necessary for understanding social behavior. Thus, the presence or absence of religion as a dimension in discourses about immigration, violence, and human rights is likely to redirect the conversation away from fundamental issues and decisions. Understanding the role of religious ideologies helps to determine when and how different religious traditions are made culpable. As long as some in our society continue to pursue "purity culture," religious assumptions about immigration, gendered violence, and social behavior will continue to influence perceptions and general behavior (Valenti, 2009).

Religious diversity is often a consequence of immigration. Religious values are closely linked to immigration and social behavior. Illustrations from various chapters point to the power of religion in policing behavior. It is established that the majority of women find religious beliefs and teachings a resource or a roadblock. Religion is a significant factor in gender-based violence and immigration as it is significant in general behavior regardless of religious affiliation. The intersection of culture and religion presents a complex scenario for locals and immigrants. Assumptions that religion is something personal and private fail to appreciate this complex relationship and the efforts necessary to address this issue by integrating religious ideas into secular experiences. As Moslener observes, this makes it difficult to talk explicitly about religion outside of the most intimate contexts (2015). As illustrated in various chapters, many scholars have reflected on the ambiguity of several religious traditions – including Christianity, Islam, Hinduism, Confucianism, Taoism, Buddhism, and Judaism – with regard to gender-based violence and gender roles. For this reason, religious ideologies have been invoked to justify certain forms of violence.

Religion provides texts, traditions, teachings, and doctrines that religious communities and institutions draw from to convey values and a belief system to their members. Religious texts and teachings also serve as resources to assist those who have experienced violence. The fact that religious texts and traditions have been cited to perpetuate and destabilize social behavior poses significant obstacles in addressing gender-based violence. Community members often seek direct support or counseling, the guidance of instruction from religious leaders, since these are the closest models of support and protection in their communities (Fortune and Enger, 2005). The fact that religious survivors turn to religious leaders for recourse is a significant factor in considering the role of religion in understanding gender-based violence.

As a personal and institutional reality, religion is significant in addressing many dimensions of social experience. Recognizing that all religions incorporate values and beliefs that greatly impact women who live with gender-based violence is central to addressing the root cause and persistence of gender-based violence in various immigrant communities. While there are scriptural texts and ideologies that perpetuate violence, scriptural texts and ideologies that condemn violence tend to affirm human rights and social justice in general. It is also argued that religion as an agent of virtues of social justice can provide solutions to gender-based violence. By drawing on scriptural verses that emphasize love, compassion, and treatment of one's neighbor as one would hope they would be treated if they were in their neighbor's shoes, the golden rule that is embraced by all religions is emphasized. The challenge lies in how these scriptures and ideologies are utilized by enablers and social activists to perpetuate or inhibit gender-based violence in their societies. In order to respond appropriately to religious teachings that condone gender-based violence, there is a need for an articulation of the faith that will provide women with resources for strength rather than for endurance. Empowering victims and survivors of gender-based violence should be the goal of religious communities. The religion that serves as a challenge to dominant patriarchal norms goes a long way to promoting social justice.

Although the role of religion in social behavior is particularly emphasized, the special role of religious leaders as agents of social change is especially highlighted. Religious agents as authorities in religious morality are noted in the various chapters in the volume. Their view of religion will promote the persistence or change of attitude toward gender-based violence. As mentioned in chapter 16, charismatic leaders can be very particularly effective in the social construction of behavior. This is because their extraordinary communication skill is often compelling, and it sets them apart as persuaders and transformers of opinion (Conger and Kanungo, 1988; Weber, 1964). Through their charisma, they have the ability to sanction, justify or condemn, and discourage moral claims. When their opinion is accepted as sacrosanct and unchallengeable, they are likely to sway opinion. If religious leaders can tap in this charisma and the sacred authority they possess, they can propel social transformation of attitudes toward empowering behavior against gender-based violence. They can demystify long held, religiously sanctioned myths that undermine the rights of women. The pulpit is the right place to express this because of the influence this is likely to have a larger community. A deconstruction of social values in light of human rights would effectively promotes social transformation and general welfare of those affected. Community leaders as empowering agents are central to the effectiveness of this intervention model. The responsibility to change behavior, however, belongs to the entire community. All should be part of the process and the leaders should find ways of ensuring that all segments in the community are engaging gender-based values that uphold the basic human rights of all.

General recommendations

Quite often, underestimation of the problem or its complex origins and expressions can lead to narrow, unfocused, and unrealistic strategies and efficacy of the solutions presented. Drawing on specific contexts, each chapter provides its conclusions for strategic options toward preventing gender-based violence. While there are solutions specific to local and national experiences, they offer a glimpse into the broad gender-based solution to the problem. Specific highlights suffice here. Even though practices such as homosexuality are considered criminal in countries such as Nigeria, efforts to address violence-related behavior must acknowledge the reality of this lifestyle among young men in modern society, argues Oguntola-Laguda. He argues further that changes in modern society need to be reviewed alongside indigenous values through cultural appraisal as a social process that is necessary for social adjustment to the reality societies are confronting. There is a need to transcend cultural or religious values that inform the persecution of those whose lifestyle deviates from the norm by striking a balance between the respect of basic human rights and cultural values that promote human flourishing. The government should protect all human life regardless of lifestyle. Oguntola-Laguda's solution is in line with Margaret Archer's argument that perceives social change as a dynamic process that involves cultural reflection, a process that leads to abandoning values that are no longer desired while embracing those that are relevant.

In examining the experience of Latina immigrant population in the United States, Burke and Early argue that violence, coupled with the cultural issue of being a Latina immigrant, makes gender-based violence even more complex and challenging. As they argue, most women in their findings were courageous to leave their abusive situation because they realized they did not have more to give. Early intervention in abusive behavior is particularly important in the rescue of women facing gender-based violence. As Burke and Early argue, community outreach is a tremendous potential for helping women confront their abuse. Outreach provides such women with a safety and social services to guide them through confidential counselling in addition to seeking general assistance. Community outreachs can be efficient in the prevention strategies that include the recognition of early warning signs of control and power abuse. They can also be cites for education in egalitarian concepts necessary to promote gender equality. When children are instructed that women should be treated as equals of boys and that they have just as much decision-making power as men and that they are as important in their family as men, is critical. Burke and Early highlight the important role of the mass media in increasing awareness of intimate partner violence.

In her discussion of gender-based violence toward sexual and gender minorities in the country of Georgia, Pearce argues that the experience of the minorities in Georgia is not unique as the neighboring Caucasus countries of Armenia and Azerbaijan share a similar experience. Her examination of Georgia is significant since it exemplifies the tensions that exist in various communities in a country with regard to the issues of values and gender equality. The dynamic interplay between individual, group, and institutional actors, often involving transnational parties, she argues, indicates the difficulty of resolving and settling issues of gender-based violence. As such it often a challenge to make claims on polity based on their membership in the political body.

In discussing the implications, claims, and relevance of practicing *botho/ubuntu* as well as applying Mt 25:35–36 in the context of global migration and HIV, Gabaitse and Kumalo argue that the health policy is Botswana is repressive toward immigrants. Although as they point out there is no hostility toward migrants, the fact that a health policy is designed to discriminate migrants is injustice. Gabaitse and Kumalo aptly argue that, their findings implicate other African communities policies that discriminate against migrants in the same way. Their suggestion that Africans should invoke *botho/ubuntu* toward embracing migrants is significant in efforts to care for all on the continent who seek health services, especially HIV treatment. It is important that health policies that be reviewed to promote inclusive norms to cater to all including migrants' access to free health.

Nyangweso and Mansi argue for the need to recognize and respect perspectives and rationale that inform ideals. While it is important to acknowledge the different perspectives and the rationale given in support for gender-based violence as dictated by various cultural contexts and social experience, they argue, the rights of women should not be compromised in the process. It is important to transcend cultural and religious values that promote gender-based violence to affirm basic women's rights. The general welfare of all should be the driving force of any discourse on culture and religion in order to respect basic rights that are central to the humanity of all. Religious literacy must be taken into account while considering attitude formation and civic education, and in effective preparation of any individuals toward countering negative values, the school curriculum must incorporate critical cultural reflection as a skill and the values of human rights. Recognizing how intersectionality defines gender relations is key to the development of sound policy toward protecting the rights of women. In exploring child marriage and female genital cutting, they argue that while moral actions are often difficult to comprehend since what counts as moral differs throughout the world, and while differences in our moral systems ought to be respected, those differences that undermine basic human rights ought to be challenged, reconstructed, and adapted to the contemporary values of any given community. Since the cultural system is dynamic and adaptive, efforts toward the transformation of communities for social good should receive support as natural occurrences necessary in progressive societies. As modern society embraces human rights values that transcend cultural differences, a reflection of cultural norms that undermine these rights is necessary in order to promote human flourishing. Njibwakale argues for strategies that seek to reform social structures that promote social inequality and power in gender relations.

With regard to the influence of religion on reproductive health, Nihorowa argues that Christian ethics on reproductive health has not outlived its usefulness but that what is needed is a new approach that suits the current times.

The failure of the Church to engage other sectors and other members of the society, including immigrants, leads to a failure to achieve its goal. Using intersectionality as a framework, the church can address the differences that exist in society for unitary coexistence and interrelation. The values of the church should evolve to adapt to social changes, she argues.

In examining traditional views of reproductive parts – the todɔlɛ – Nrenzah proposes a return to indigenous concepts that promote sexuality as a spiritual component of a healthy lifestyle. In spite of the shifts that have taken place in Africa that have led to a decline in the respect for ideas about women's spirituality and the sense of sacredness the Akan Nzema societies embraced, it is important that a return to traditional values central to restoring the humanity of women be restored. Examining the immigrant's situation in Germany, Petra Klug argues for the need to criticize harmful cultural or religious practices without stigmatizing all adherents. Drawing on the human rights and integrated approach, she argues for human-based guidelines toward developing future policies respect that rights of immigrant women and all others who do not conform to the gender norms of their communities. To ignore social constructions that reproduce racist and (post-)colonial divisions of humanity into those who deserve an emancipated life and those who do not is discriminatory and a violation of human rights. She is critical of the cultural relativistic approach in her proposition of integration policies that are based upon the human rights of all: minors, women, and nonconformists, regardless of origin and cultural background.

In examining the intersectionality of gender, religion, and immigration among the Ghanaian migrants in churches in Amsterdam, Kyei argues that the oppressive socialization process that is inherent in the Ghanaian culture transfers in most churches, and this makes it difficult to disentangle the unequal power relations. To confront oppressive religious practices that impede access to full religious citizenship, he argues, second-generation female Ghanaian migrants must exercise their agency to redefine and reinterpret the existing gendered religious citizenship. In her investigation of gender-based violence at the time of partition in Indian society, Shiva decries the failure of history to address the issue of dislocation and especially the relationship between community, caste, and gender violence that undermined the process of healing and forgetting that is necessary to move forward. It is her argument that this attitude should be reconsidered in efforts to promote healing in India. In their discussion of gender-based violence among immigrants in the West, Nyangweso and Olupona argue for the need to recognize cultural values that influence gender-based violence in local and immigrant communities in an effort to develop strategies to combat the practice. They specifically argue for the need to integrate religion in efforts to transform mindsets about gender-based violence among immigrants. They note the fact that while some African immigrants in the West want to embrace Western lifestyles not all need to abandon their lifestyle. Despite this, there should be no dilemma for immigrants in negotiating their cultural values and human rights as long as women's rights are protected, they argue.

Recognizing the role of religion as a significant agent of socialization, Gbadegesin and Adejolu argue for the need for a reexamination of religious values that are a burden toward embracing those that are more liberating. While acknowledging that African immigrants export their values to the new world, they recommend that immigrants should find a recourse to downplay or ignore cultural values that serve as sources of family problems and disintegration. In her discussion of the role of faith-based initiatives, Nyangweso argues for community initiatives that ensure that religion is a significant role in transforming social attitudes and general behavior. She argues for the need to integrate faith-based initiatives in efforts toward changing attitudes toward harmful practices. She specifically highlights the role of religious authority in combating gender-based violence. She argues that religious leaders have a responsibility to call out misinterpretation of sacred texts to justify harmful practices. It is the responsibility of religious leaders to demystify these scriptural misreadings since their word is often viewed as sacrosanct. This, she argues, is a special role in the deconstruction process of attitudes and general behavior.

As a phenomenon constructed to serve human beings, religions must promote positive ideals that empower human flourishing. In deeply patriarchal societies where gender-based violence is engrained in social values of male dominance and female subjugation, the legislature is important in combating entrenched attitudes and behavior. However, as Shiva argues, legislature alone can be ineffective if measures to punish, prosecute, and prevent honor-based violence are not tough and enacted accordingly.

It is the general argument of the book that the interdisciplinary as an approach is significant in identifying and understanding origins and possible solutions to gender-based violence. Using intersectionality as a framework, it is easier to discern the holistic view of reality and to account for complex social dynamics that shape religion, gender-based violence, immigration, and human rights. To understand or to address issues plaguing any immigrant community, it is important that values that inform their social formation are understood. Recognizing how intersected social relations are is fundamental to developing effective strategies for combating the problem. The book concludes by recognizing the interconnectedness of social issues and that gender-based violence is embedded within social matrices that contribute to the existing problem. It is argued that intersectionality as an approach recognizes this interconnectedness of social behavior and that a holistic view of reality is important in the way social behavior ought to be viewed. Therefore, to understand or to address issues plaguing any immigrant community, cultural and religious values ought to be reflected upon in a natural way of cultural appraisal in order to negotiate cultural and moral values that promote general welfare for all. It is the book's recommendations that attitude formation in the local and globalizing world must embrace the common good as described in modern values of human rights and the reality of pluralism even as the difference is respected. Leaders, including religious leaders, should lead this process.

References

Conger, Jay A. and Rabindra N. Kanungo. 1988. "The Empowerment Process: Integrating Theory and Practice." *The Academic of Management Reviews*, accessed at www.jstor.org on June 24, 2013.

Fortune, Marie and Rabbi Cindy G. Enger. 2005. *Violence Against Women and the Role of Religion*. VAWNET: Applied Research Forum, 1–7.

Moslener, Sarah. 2015. *Virgin Nation: Sexual Purity and American Adolescence*, New York, NY: Oxford University Press.

Valenti, Jessica. 2009. *The Purity Myth: How America's Obsession with Virginity is Hurting Young Women*, Berkeley, CA: Seal Press.

Weber, Max. 1963. / 1993. *The Sociology of Religion*, Boston: Beacon Press.

Index